Foreword

This is the 9th edition of the *Hidden Places of East Anglia*. The guide has been been fully updated and in this respect we would like to thank the Tourist Information Centres in East Anglia for helping us update the editorial content. The guide is packed with information on the many interesting places to visit in the area. In addition, you will find details of places of interest and advertisers of places to stay, eat and drink included under each village, town or city, which are cross referenced to more detailed information contained in a separate, easy-to-use section to the rear of the book. This section is also available as a free supplement from the local Tourist Information Offices.

East Anglia offers plenty for the visitor to explore in real *Hidden Places* country. **Norfolk** is rightly famous for the Norfolk Broads, but also possesses gentle rolling hills, delightful pastoral scenes and a beautiful coastline rich in wildlife. **Suffolk** is blessed with incomparable rural beauty. Meandering tidal rivers and numerous streams, brooks and gullies intersect a land blended with low hills and vast open spaces. Suffolk was made famous by the brush of John Constable and his paintings reflect the sheer beauty and tranquility of this attractive county. **Essex** with its large estuaries and fishing communities, has a rich maritime tradition going back as far as Roman times. The county is equally well endowed with pretty stone-built villlages and contains the oldest recorded town in England, namely Colchester. **Cambridgeshire** is most famous for its ancient university as well as being the birthplace of Oliver Cromwell and Samuel Pepys. The county offers a wealth of peaceful and attractive countryside with many towns and villages steeped in history and tradition.

The Hidden Places of East Anglia contains a wealth of interesting information on the history, the countryside, the towns and villages and the more established places of interest. But it also promotes the more secluded and little known visitor attractions and places to stay, eat and drink many of which are easy to miss unless you know exactly where you are going.

We include hotels, bed & breakfasts, restaurants, pubs, bars, teashops and cafes as well as historic houses, museums, gardens and many other attractions throughout East Anglia, all of which are comprehensively indexed. Many places are accompanied by an attractive photograph and are easily located by using the map at the beginning of e
merit marks or rankings but concentrate on describing the
features of each place with the aim of making the reader's st
and stimulating experience.

Whether you are travelling around East Anglia on business or
enjoy reading and using this book. We are always interested

D1497785

covered (or not covered) in our guides so please do not hesitate to use the reader reaction form provided to give us your considered comments. We also welcome any general comments which will help us improve the guides themselves. Finally if you are planning to visit any other corner of the British Isles we would like to refer you to the list of other *Hidden Places* titles to be found to the rear of the book and to the Travel Publishing website.

Travel Publishing

Did you know that you can also search our website for details of thousands of places to see, stay, eat or drink throughout Britain and Ireland? Our site has become increasingly popular and now receives over **500,000** visits annually. Try it!

website: **www.travelpublishing.co.uk**

Location Map

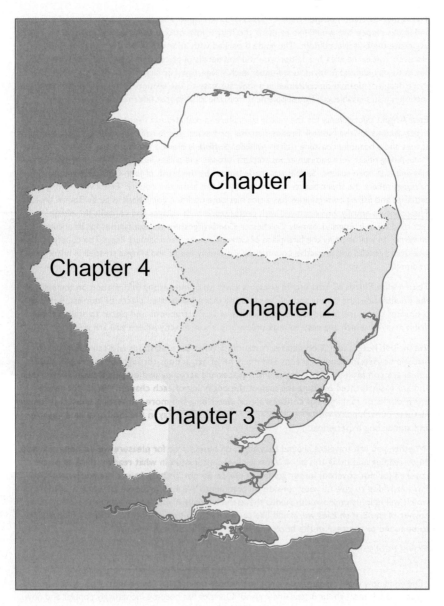

Contents

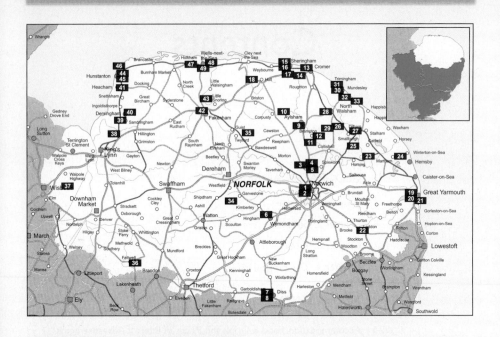

Norfolk

The area that lies between the county capital of Norwich and the border with Suffolk is mainly flat farmland, with quiet villages, handsome old farmhouses and the charming spires and towers of churches. The valleys of the Rivers Nar and Wensum boast some of the most enchanting scenery in the county, and the area can claim one of the finest Gothic parish churches in England, at Cawston.

The major centres of population include Diss, an old market town with a mix of Tudor, Georgian and Victorian houses, and Wymondham with its timber-framed buildings, picturesque market place and an Abbey church that can compare even with the majestic Norwich Cathedral. Norwich, once an important centre of the worsted trade, retains many

medieval buildings, some of which now serve as museums relating the fascinating history of the region.

The area to the east of this fine city contains the unique Norfolk Broads, beautiful stretches of shallow water, most of then linked by navigable rivers and canals. This is Britain's finest wetland

Cromer Pier and Beach

area, a National Park in all but
name. Broadland covers some 220
square miles in a rough oval to the
northwest of Great Yarmouth.
Three main rivers – the Ant, the
Thurne and the Bure – thread their
way through the marshes, providing
some 120 miles of navigable
waterways. The Broads, long
popular for restful, relaxing
holidays, remain also a refuge for
many species of endangered birds
and plants, and during the spring
and autumn they area a favourite
stopping-off place for migrating
birds.

On the coast due east of
Norwich is the old port and
modern holiday resort of Great
Yarmouth, where the visitor will
find miles of sandy beaches, a
breezy promenade, two grand old
traditional piers and all the fun of
the fair, as well as a rich marine
heritage that lives on to this day.

Norfolk Broads

Miles of quiet sandy beaches,
spectacular sea views and bracing sea air are the
rewards awaiting visitors to the Norfolk coast,
which stretches from Great Yarmouth in the east
up to Cromer and west to Sheringham,
Hunstanton and beyond. The northeast coast
includes what are sometimes known as 'the
Highlands of Norfolk' – the Cromer Ridge,
which rises to the not-so-dizzy heights of 330
feet above sea level. The most important town
on the northwest coast is the busy seaside resort
of Hunstanton, which has cliffs comprising red,
white and brown geological layers. Another
curious thing about Hunstanton: it is the only
east-coast resort that actually faces west!

King's Lynn, on the Great Ouse three miles
inland from The Wash, was one of England's
most important ports in medieval times, sitting at
the southern end of an underwater maze of

sandbanks. To the northeast of King's Lynn is
the prosperous market town of Fakenham,
around which lie a remarkable variety of places
of interest. To the north, in the valley of the
River Stiffkey, the shrine of Our Lady of
Walsingham was in medieval times second only
to that of St Thomas à Becket at Canterbury as a
pilgrim destination.

Breckland, which extends for more than 360
square miles in southwest Norfolk and northwest
Suffolk, is underlain by chalk with only a light
covering of soil. The name 'Breckland' comes
from the dialect word breck, meaning an area of
land cultivated for a while and then allowed to
revert to heath after the soil has become
exhausted. This quiet corner of the county is
bounded by the Rivers Little Ouse and
Waverney, which separate Norfolk from Suffolk.

NORWICH

Back in prehistoric times, there were several settlements around the confluence of the Rivers Wensum and Yare. By the late fourth century, one of them was important enough to have its own mint. This was Northwic. By the time of the *Domesday Book* 700 years later, Northwic/Norwich, had become the third-most populous city in England, only outnumbered by London and York. To the Norman conquerors, such a major centre of population (about 5,500 residents) needed a Castle to ensure that its Saxon inhabitants could be kept in order.

The first castle structure, in wood, was replaced in the late 1100s by a mighty fortress in stone which, unlike most blank-walled castles of the period, is decorated with a rich façade of blind arcades and ornamental pilasters. This great fort never saw any military action, and as early as the 13th century was being used as the county gaol, a role it continued to fill until 1889. From its walls, in December 1549, the leader of the rebellion against land enclosures, Robert Kett, was hung in chains and left to starve to death.

The Castle is home to the **Norwich Castle Museum and Art Gallery**, which contains some of the most outstanding regional collections of fine art, archaeological exhibits and natural history displays. The former dungeons are home to a forbidding display of instruments of torture, along with the death masks of some of the prisoners who were executed here. Among the countless other fascinating exhibits are those devoted to Queen Boudica (Boadicea), which features the life of the Iceni tribe with an interactive chariot ride, the Egyptian gallery with its mummy Ankh Hor, and interactive displays in the Castle keep and keep basement, recently made accessible to the public.

The Art Gallery has an incomparable collection of paintings by the celebrated Norwich artist, John Sell Cotman (1782-1842), and others in the group known as the Norwich School. Their subjects were mostly landscape scenes, such as John Crome's The Poringland Oak. Quite apart from the artistic quality of their works, they have left a fascinating pictorial record of early 19th century Norfolk.

The **Bulwer and Miller** collection of more than 2,600 English china teapots makes its home in the Twinings Gallery, while the museum's Langton collection of around 100 cats fashioned in porcelain, ivory, bronze, glass and wood, originating from anywhere between Derbyshire and China, and Margaret Elizabeth Fountaine's mind-boggling accumulation of 22,000 butterflies which she had personally netted during her travels around the world, are available to view by appointment at the Shirehall Study Centre, next door to the Royal Norfolk Regimental Museum on Market Avenue.

•

There are a large number of beautiful and well-maintained parks in the city, some of which offer chess, lawn tennis and hard tennis courts, bowls, pitch and putt, rowing and more, together with a programme of entertainments ranging from theatre to concerts. One worth particular mention is The Plantation Garden in Earlham Road, three acres of Victorian plantings restored after having fallen into disrepair, and thought to be the only one in the nation with a Grade II listing.

•

NORWICH CATHEDRAL

Norwich

The splendour and tranquillity of Norwich Cathedral have attracted visitors and pilgrims for over 900 years.

 see page 226

5

On the western edge of the city stands the University of East Anglia. It's well worth making your way here to visit the Sainsbury Centre for Visual Arts. Housed in a huge hall of aluminium and glass designed by Norman Foster, the Centre contains the eclectic collection of a 'passionate acquirer' of art, Sir Robert Sainsbury. For more than 50 years, Sir Robert purchased whatever works of art took his fancy, ignoring fashionable trends. Thus the visitor finds sculptures and pictures by Henry Moore, Bacon and Giacometti, along with African and pre-Columbian artefacts, Egyptian, Etruscan and Roman bronzes, works by Native Americans and Inuit Eskimos, and sculptures from the Cyclades, the South Seas, the Orient and medieval Europe. This extraordinary collection was donated to the University by Sir Robert and Lady Lisa Sainsbury in 1973; their son David complemented his parents' generosity by paying for the building in which it is housed.

The great open space of the Market Square, where every weekday a colourful jumble of traders' stalls can be found, offers just about every conceivable item for sale. Dominating the western side of the Market Square is **City Hall**, modelled on Stockholm City Hall and opened by King George VI in 1938. Opinions differ about its architectural merits, but there are no such doubts about the nearby Guildhall, a fine example of 15th century flintwork that now houses a tea room.

Around the corner from London Street, in Bridewell Alley, is the **Bridewell Museum**, a late 14th century merchant's house now dedicated to Norfolk's crafts and industries.

An interesting museum/shop, located in the Royal Arcade, a tiled riot of Art Nouveau fantasy, celebrates the county's great contribution to world cuisine: mustard. Back in the early 1800s, Jeremiah Colman perfected his blend of mustard flours and spice to produce a condiment that was smooth in texture and tart in flavour. Together with his nephew James he founded J & J Colman in 1823; 150 years later **The Mustard Shop** was established to commemorate the company's history. Other notable sons of Norwich include Matthew Parker, first Anglican Archbishop of Canterbury, nicknamed Nosey by Queen Elizabeth because he had a big nose and was prying by nature; Luke Hansard (1752-1828), Printer to the House of Commons, who

gave his name to the official report of parliamentary proceedings; and the actor Rupert Everett. The **Assembly House** in Theatre Street is one of the city's finest historical houses and also a leading venue for the arts. With two concert halls, three galleries featuring changing exhibitions and a restaurant and tea rooms, this magnificent Georgian home must be included in any visit to the city.

Millennium Plain just off Theatre Street is where visitors will find **The Forum**, an architecturally stunning modern building designed by Sir Michael Hopkins. Combining a unique horseshoe shape with an all-glass façade, this spectacular structure has, at its heart, the Atrium and Bridge, meeting places where you can enjoy a meal or drink anytime through to midnight, seven days a week. At the **Origins Visitor Centre**, an attractive multi-media display on three floors affords the opportunity to experience the life and times of Norwich and the wider Norfolk region. Here can also be found the Tourist Information Centre. The **Norfolk & Norwich Millennium Library** houses 120,000 books and offers the best in information and communication technology.

While the Castle has been used for many purposes over the years, the Cathedral remains what it has always been: the focus of ecclesiastical life in the county. It's even older than the castle, its service of consecration taking place over 900 years ago, in 1101. This peerless building, its flint walls clad in creamy-white stone from Caen is, after Durham, the most completely Norman cathedral in England, its appeal enhanced by later Gothic features such as the flying buttresses. The Norman cloisters are the largest in the country and notable for the 400 coloured and gilded bosses depicting scenes from medieval life. Another 1,200 of these wondrous carvings decorate the glorious vaulted roof of the nave.

It's impossible to list all the Cathedral's treasures here, but do seek out the Saxon **Bishop's Throne** in the Presbytery, the lovely 14th century altar painting in St Luke's Chapel, and the richly carved canopies in the Choir.

Outside, beneath the slender 315-feet spire soaring heavenwards, the **Cathedral Close** is timeless in its sense of peace. There are some 80 houses inside the Close, some medieval, many Georgian, their residents enjoying an idyllic refuge free from cars. At peace here lie the remains of Nurse Edith Cavell. A daughter of the rector of Swardeston, a few miles south of Norwich, Nurse Cavell worked at a Red Cross hospital in occupied Brussels during the First World War. She helped some 200 Allied soldiers to escape to neutral Holland before being detected and court-martialled by the Germans. As she faced execution by firing squad on 12 October 1915, she spoke her own resonant epitaph: 'Standing as I do, in the view of God and eternity, I realise that patriotism is not enough. I must have no hatred or bitterness towards anyone.'

A stroll around the Close will take you to **Pull's Ferry** with its picturesque flint gateway fronting the River Wensum. In medieval times a canal ran inland from here so that provisions, goods and, in the earliest days, building materials, could be moved direct to the Cathedral. Along the riverside walk is Cow Tower, built around 1378 and the most massive of the old city towers.

At the western end of the Cathedral Close is the magnificent

It was Dutch weavers who introduced the canary to Norwich, which perhaps explains why Norwich football Club is called the Canaries (and wears a yellow strip).

Pull's Ferry, Norwich

Elm Hill, Norwich

2 DRAGON HALL

Norwich

Dragon Hall is a Grade 1
listed medieval trading hall
and one of Norwich's most
important historic buildings.

 see page 226

Erpingham Gate, presented to the
city in 1420 by a hero of the Battle
of Agincourt, Sir Thomas
Erpingham.

Beyond this gate, in Tombland
(originally Toom or wasteland), is
Samson and Hercules House, its
entrance flanked by two 1674
carvings of these giants. Diagonally
opposite stands the 15th century
Maid's Head Hotel.

Norwich is home to some 32
medieval churches in all, every one
of them worth attention, although
many are now used for purposes
other than worship. Outstanding
among them are **St Peter
Mancroft**, a masterpiece of Gothic
architecture built between 1430-55
(and the largest church in
Norwich), and **St Peter Hungate**,
a handsome 15th century church
standing at the top of **Elm Hill**, a
narrow, unbelievably picturesque
lane where in medieval times the
city's wool merchants built their
homes, close to their warehouses

beside the River Wensum.
St Gregory's Church
in Pottergate is another
Norwich church to have
been deconsecrated, and its
fate might well have been a
sad one.

When the basic
structure of the present St
Gregory's was built in the
late 14th century, the
general rule seems to have
been that any parish of
around 1,000 people would
have its own place of
worship. St Gregory's was
founded on the site of a
Saxon church in 1210 and rebuilt in
its present form in 1394. The
church takes it name from Gregory
the Great, the 6th century Pope
best known for his campaign to
convert the heathen Anglo-Saxons
of 'Angle-land' to Christianity,
despatching a party of 40 monks to
Angle-land in AD 596, led by
Augustine, whom the Pope
consecrated as the first Archbishop
of Canterbury.

The **Inspire Discovery
Centre**, housed in the medieval
church of St Michael in Coslany
Street, just across the Wensum,
northeast of the city centre, is full
of exciting hands-on displays and
activities that make scientific
enquiry come to life.

To the south of Norwich in the
village of Caistor St Edmund are
the remains of **Venta Icenorum**,
the Roman town established here
after Boudica's rebellion in AD 61.
Unusually, this extensive site has
not been disturbed by later

developments, so archaeologists have been able to identify the full scale of the original settlement. Most of the finds discovered during excavations in the 1920s and 1930s are now in Norwich Castle Museum, but the riverside site still merits a visit.

AROUND NORWICH

HORSHAM ST FAITHS

1 mile N of Norwich on the A140

Brown tourist signs from the A140 lead to the **City of Norwich Aviation Museum**, dedicated to keeping Norfolk's aviation heritage alive. The most impressive craft on display is a massive Avro Vulcan bomber that saw service in the 1982 Falklands conflict, but there are several other aircraft as well as displays showing the development of flying in Norfolk. The major roles played by Norfolk-based aircraft during the Second World War are remembered by exhibitions on the RAF and USAAF.

WYMONDHAM

9 miles SW of Norwich off the A11

The exterior of **Wymondham Abbey** presents one of the oddest ecclesiastical buildings in the county; the interior reveals one of the most glorious. The Abbey was founded in 1107 by the Benedictines - or Black Monks, as they were known because of the colour of their habits. The richest and most aristocratic of the monastic orders, the Black Monks apparently experienced some difficulty in respecting their solemn

vows of poverty and humility. Especially the latter. Constantly in dispute with the people of Wymondham, the dissension between them grew so bitter that in 1249 Pope Innocent IV himself attempted to reconcile their differences. When his efforts failed, a wall was built across the interior of the Abbey, dividing it into an area for the monks and another for the parishioners. Even this drastic measure failed to bring peace, however. Both parties wanted to ring their own bells, so each built a tower. The villagers erected a stately rectangular tower at the west end; the monks an octagonal one over the crossing, thus creating the Abbey's curious exterior appearance.

Step inside and you find a magnificent Norman nave, 112 feet long (it was originally twice as long, but the eastern end, along with most of the Abbey buildings, was demolished after the Dissolution of the Monasteries). The superb hammerbeam roof is supported by 76 beautifully carved angels. There's also an interesting 16th century tomb, of the last Abbot, in delicate terracotta work, and a striking modern memorial: a gilded and coloured reredos and tester commemorating the local men who lost their lives in the First World War.

The rectangular western tower of the Abbey was the setting for one of the last acts in the ill-fated Kett's Rebellion of 1549. From its walls, William Kett was hung in chains and left to die: his brother

3 BECKLANDS GUEST HOUSE

Horsford, nr Norwich

A friendly owner, good personal service, space, comfort and a pleasant village setting bring back guests year after year to Becklands Guest House.

see page 227

4 THE KINGS HEAD

Horsham St Faith, nr Norwich

A delightful pub, very popular with the locals for its cheerful ambience and good home cooking

see page 228

5 CITY OF NORWICH AVIATION MUSEUM

Horsham St Faiths

The City of Norwich Aviation Museum is a museum dedicated to keeping Norfolk's aviation heritage alive.

see page 229

9

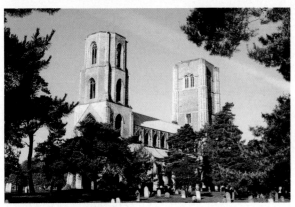

Wymondham Abbey, Wymondham

6   THE WYMONDHAM CONSORT HOTEL

Wymondham

A centrally located, superbly run hotel with every comfort and convenience for both leisure and business guests.

 see page 230

Robert, the leading figure in the uprising, suffered the same fate at Norwich Castle.

Although many of Wymondham's oldest houses were lost in the fire of 1615, when some 300 dwellings were destroyed, there are still some attractive Elizabethan buildings in the heart of the town. The Market Place (Friday is market day, and on the first Friday of every month there's an antiques and collectors' fair held in Central Hall) is given dignity by the picturesque octagonal **Market Cross**, rebuilt two years after the fire. Crowned by a pyramid roof, this appealing timber-framed building is open on all sides on the ground floor, and its upper floor is reached by an outside stairway. Also of interest is **Becket's Chapel**, founded in 1174 and restored in 1559. In its long history it has served as a pilgrim's chapel, grammar school, and coal store. Currently, it houses the town library. The **Bridewell**, or House of Correction, in

Bridewell Street was built as a model prison in 1785 along lines recommended by the prison reformer, John Howard, who had condemned the earlier gaol on the site as 'one of the vilest in the country'. Wymondham's Bridewell is said to have served as a model for the penitentiaries established in the United States. Now owned by the town's Heritage Society, Bridewell is home to several community projects, including the **Wymondham Heritage Museum**. Railway buffs will want to visit the historic **Railway Station** at Wymondham, built in 1845 on the Great Eastern's Norwich-Ely line. At its peak, the station and its section employed over 100 people. Still providing a rail link to Norwich, London and the Midlands, the station has been restored, and its buildings house a railway museum, restaurant and tearoom, and a piano showroom.

ATTLEBOROUGH

14 miles SW of Norwich off the A11

The greatest glory of this pleasant market town is to be found in its **Church of St Mary**. Here, a remarkable 15th century chancel screen stretches the width of the church and is beautifully embellished with the arms of the 24 bishoprics into which England was divided at that time. The screen is generally reckoned to be one of the most outstanding in the country, a remarkable survivor of the Reformation purging of such beautiful creations from churches across the land.

BANHAM

18 miles SW of Norwich on the B1114

Banham Zoo provides the opportunity to come face to face with some of the world's rarest wildlife - many of the animals who find a home here otherwise face extinction. The Zoo is particularly concerned with monkeys and apes, but in the 25 acres of landscaped gardens you'll also come across tigers, cheetahs, lemurs, penguins and many other species. There are educational talks and displays, a children's play area, Shire Horse dray rides, and a restaurant.

BRESSINGHAM

22 miles SW of Norwich off the A1066

Bressingham Steam and Gardens has plenty to interest the visitor. The Museum boasts one of the world's finest collections of British and Continental locomotives, housed under cover in the museum's extensive locomotive sheds; they also contain many steam-driven industrial engines, traction engines, a Victorian steam roundabout, and The Fire Museum, whose collection of fire engines and fire-fighting equipment could form a complete museum in its own right. Visitors can view the interior of the Royal Coach, ride on a narrow-gauge railway and walk through the delightful dell and Foggy Bottom Gardens. Bressingham is renowned for its special 'Steam Days' when the engines can be seen in full steam on the three narrow-gauge lines, and talks and

footplate rides are given on the standard-gauge locomotives. It is also home to the **National Dads Army Collection**.

DISS

20 miles S of Norwich on the A1066/A140

The popular Poet Laureate, John Betjeman, voted Diss his favourite Norfolk town, and it's easy to understand his enthusiasm. The River Waveney running alongside forms the boundary between Norfolk and Suffolk, but this attractive old market town – winner of Best Kept Market Town in Norfolk, whose town centre is now a designated conservation area - keeps itself firmly on the northern bank of the river. The town is a pleasing mixture of Tudor, Georgian and Victorian houses grouped around **The Mere**. The old town grew up on the hill above The Mere, perhaps because, as an 18th century resident observed, 'all the filth of the town centring in the Mere, beside the many conveniences that are placed over it, make the water very bad and altogether useless ... it stinks exceedingly, and sometimes the fish rise in great numbers, so thick that they are easily taken; they are chiefly roach and eels.' A proper sewerage system was finally installed in 1851.

There's a public park beside the six-acre Mere, and from it a narrow street leads to the small Market Place. This former poultry market is dominated by **St Mary's Church**. The oldest parts date back some 700 years, and the St Nicholas Chapel is

Collectors of curiosities will be interested in a strange memorial in the churchyard of St Mary's, Attleborough. It takes the form of a pyramid, about 6 feet high, and was erected in 1929 to mark the grave of a local solicitor with the rather splendid name of Melancthon William Henry Brooke, or 'Lawyer' Brooke as he was more familiarly known. Melancthon was an amateur Egyptologist who became convinced by his studies of the Pharaohs' tombs that the only way to ensure an agreeable after-life was to be buried beneath a pyramid, precisely placed and of the correct physical dimensions. Several years before his death, he gave the most punctilious instructions as to how this assurance of his immortal existence should be constructed and located.

7 THE WATERFRONT INN

Diss

A pleasant Greene King pub with an outside decked area overlooking The Mere.

see page 229

8   THE PARK HOTEL

Diss

Perfect position within attractive market town of Diss with 19 bedrooms, bar and fine dining

  see page 231

particularly enjoyable with its wonderful corbels, angels in the roof, and gargoyles. In the early 1500s, the Rector here was John Skelton, Court poet and tutor to Prince Henry, later Henry VIII. A bitter, quarrelsome man, Skelton was appointed Poet Laureate through the patronage of Cardinal Wolsey, despite the fact that most of Skelton's output has been described as 'breathless doggerel'. Appointed Rector of Diss in 1502, he appears to have been suspended nine years later for having a concubine. Not far from his church is the delightful Victorian **Shambles** with a cast-iron veranda and a small museum inside. This award-winning museum is packed with memorabilia and information about 'the town's past, its trade, famous people and 'orrible murders'.

SCOLE

2 miles E of Diss on the A140

Scole's history goes back to Roman times, since it grew up alongside the Imperial highway from Ipswich to Norwich at the point where it bridged the River Waveney. Traffic on this road (the A140) became unbearable in the 1980s, but a bypass has now mercifully restored some peace to the village. There are two hostelries of note: a coaching inn of 1655, built in an extravagant style of Dutch gables, giant pilasters and towering chimney stacks, and the Crossways Inn, which must have a good claim to being the prettiest pub in the county.

LANGMERE

6 miles NE of Diss on minor road off the A140 (through Dickleburgh)

Veterans of the Second World War and their families and friends will be interested in the **100th Bomb Group Memorial Museum**, a small museum on the edge of Dickleburgh Airfield (now disused). The Museum is the 'Bloody Hundredths' tribute to the US 8th Air Force, which was stationed here during the war, and includes displays of USAAF decorations and uniforms, equipment, combat records and other memorabilia and photographs. Facilities include refreshments, a museum shop, visitor centre and a picnic area. The Museum is open Saturdays, Sundays and Bank Holidays, also on Wednesdays between May and September. Closed November, January and February. Tel: 01379 740708

HARLESTON

7 miles NE of Diss off the A143

This pretty market town with some notable half-timbered and Georgian houses, and a splendid 12th century coaching inn, was a favourite of the renowned architectural authority, Nikolaus Pevsner, who particularly admired the early Georgian Candlers House at the northern end of the town. Another writer has described the area around the marketplace as 'the finest street scene in East Anglia'. The town of Harleston lies in the heart of the Waveney Valley, a lovely area which inspired many paintings by the locally-born artist, Sir Alfred Munnings.

PORINGLAND

6 miles S of Norwich on the B1332

The name of this sizable village will be familiar to those who love the paintings of the Norwich artist John Crome (1794-1842) whose Arcadian painting of The Poringland Oak hangs in the Tate Gallery.

GREAT WITCHINGHAM

11 miles NW of Norwich off the A1067

The Animal Ark & Country Park is home to an interesting collection of rare, or ancient, breeds of farm livestock such as Highland cattle, white-faced woodland and Shetland sheep, pygmy goats and Exmoor ponies. Set in 40 acres of peaceful parkland, the Centre also has reindeer, llamas, wallwbies, polecats, parakeets, otters and badgers, pools teeming with wildfowl and a huge colony of wild herons nesting in the trees. There are also 'Commando' and Adventure Play Areas, one of the finest collection of trees and flowering shrubs in the county, a café and gift shop. Open Easter to the end of October. For more details and special events call 01603 872274.

Anyone who has ever read Parson Woodforde's enchanting Diary of a Country Parson will want to make a short diversion to the tiny village of **Weston Longville**, a mile or so south of the Dinosaur Park. The Revd James Woodforde was vicar of this remote parish from 1774 until his death in 1803, and throughout that time he conscientiously maintained a daily diary detailing a wonderful mixture of the momentous and the trivial. 'Very great Rebellion in France' he notes when, ten days after the fall of the Bastille, the dramatic news eventually arrived at Weston Longville. More often he records his copious meals ('We had for dinner a calf's head, boiled fowl and tongue, a saddle of mutton roasted on the side table, and a fine swan roasted with currant jelly sauce for the first course. The second course a couple of wild fowl, larks, blamange, tarts etc. etc.'), the weather (during the winter of 1785, for example, the frost was so severe that it froze the chamberpots under the beds), and his frequent dealings with the smuggler Andrews, who kept the good parson well-supplied with contraband tea, gin and cognac. Inside the simple village church there's a portrait of Parson Woodforde, painted by his nephew, and across the road the inn has been named after this beguiling character.

SWANNINGTON

11 miles NW of Norwich off the A1067/B1149

The gardens of **Swannington Manor** are famous for the 300-year-old yew and box topiary hedge. Other features of this small town are the 13th century St Margaret's church, Swannington Hall – where can be seen the remains of the former moat – and the charming thatched village water pump.

To the southwest of Poringland is The Playbarn, an indoor and outdoor adventure centre specially designed for the under-sevens. All the play equipment is based on a farmyard theme, with a miniature farm, bouncy tractors, soft play sheep pens, and donkey rides among the attractions. Refreshments and light lunches are available, or you can bring along your own picnic.

Swannington's Ketts Lane was named after Robert Kett, leader of the peasants' revolt, who reputedly was captured in a barn nearby.

REEPHAM

12 miles NW of Norwich on the B1145

Reepham is an attractive spot set in the rich countryside between the Wensum and Bure Valleys. Lovely 18th century houses border the Market Place, and there is delightful walking along the Marriott's Way

St Agnes Church, Cawston

cycle path. Market day is Wednesday, and regular antiques fairs are held at the Old Reepham Brewery.

CAWSTON

12 miles NW of Norwich on the B1145

'Lovers of the Norfolk churches can never agree which is the best,' wrote Sir John Betjeman. 'I have heard it said that you are either a Salle man or a Cawston man.' In this county so rich in exceptionally beautiful churches, Salle and Cawston are indeed in a class of their own. **St Agnes Church** in Cawston, among many other treasures, boasts a magnificent double hammerbeam roof, where angels with protective wings 8 feet across float serenely from the roof, and a gorgeous 15th century rood screen embellished with lovely painted panels of saints and Fathers of the Church. The two churches are just a couple of miles apart, so you can easily decide for yourself whether you are 'a Salle man or a Cawston man'. Surprisingly for such a genial character, Sir John seems to have overlooked the possibility that other visitors to these two remarkable churches might define themselves as either 'a Salle woman or a Cawston woman'.

AYLSHAM

14 miles N of Norwich on the A140

The attractive market town of Aylsham is set beside the River Bure, the northern terminus of the Bure Valley Railway. This 15" gauge railway was built in 1990 and is operated mainly by steam locomotives. It runs for nine miles between Aylsham and Wroxham, with intermediate stations at Brampton, Buxton and Coltishall. There are several Days Out with Thomas the Tank Engine during the year, and one- and two-day steam driving courses available during off-peak periods are aimed at everyone from the absolute beginner upwards. The 15th anniversary of this charming little railway was celebrated in grand style on the 8th and 9th of October 2007. Tel: 01263 733858.

Aylsham's unspoilt Market Place is surrounded by late 17th and early 18th century houses, reflecting the prosperity the town enjoyed in those years from the cloth trade, and a 14th/15th century church, St Michael's, said to have been built by John O'Gaunt. In the churchyard is the tomb of one of the greatest of the 18th century landscape gardeners, Humphry Repton, the creator of some 200 parks and gardens around the country.

One of Repton's many commissions was to landscape the grounds of **Blickling Hall** (National Trust), a 'dream of architectural beauty' which stands a mile or so outside Aylsham. Many visitors have marvelled at their first sight of the great Hall built for Sir Henry Hobart in the 1620s. 'No-one is prepared on coming downhill past the church into the village, to find the main front of this finest of Jacobean mansions, actually looking upon the road, unobstructed, from behind its velvet lawns' enthused Charles Harper in 1904. 'No theatrical

manager cunning in all the artful accessories of the stage could devise anything more dramatic.'

From the outside, Sir Henry's house fully satisfied the contemporary architectural vogue for perfect symmetry. Four towers topped with lead-covered turret-caps rise at each corner, there are lines of matching Dutch gables and mullioned windows, and even the chimneys were placed in corresponding groups of twos, threes or fours.

Inside, the most spectacular feature is the Long Gallery, which extends for 135 feet and originally provided space for indoor exercise in bad weather. Its glory is the plaster ceiling, an intricately patterned expanse of heraldic panels bearing the Hobart arms, along with others displaying bizarre and inscrutable emblems such as a naked lady riding a two-legged dragon.

Other treasures at Blickling include a dramatic double-flight carved oak staircase, the Chinese Bedroom lined with 18th century hand-painted wallpaper, a library of over 12,000 books, an exhibition on the RAF at Blickling and the dazzling Peter the Great Room. A descendant of Sir Henry Hobart, the 2nd Earl of Buckinghamshire, was appointed Ambassador to Russia in 1746, and he returned from that posting with a magnificent tapestry, the gift of Empress Catherine the Great. This room was redesigned so as to display the Earl's sumptuous souvenir to its full effect, and portraits of himself and his

•

On the B1149, just before the junction with the B1145, stands a large stone on a plinth that commemorates a duel that took place in 1698 between Sir Henry Hobart and Oliver Le Neve. The former was killed in this duel, and his son John, 1st Earl of Buckinghamshire, erected the 'Duelling Stone' in his father's memory. Sir Henry, 4th Baronet of Blickling, had been knighted at the age of 13 when Charles II visited Blickling Hall and was the MP for King's Lynn in Charles' last parliament. Le Neve was a Tory and JP who inherited a small fortune from his rich uncle, a notable stationer.

•

9   THE OLD PUMP HOUSE

Aylsham

The **Old Pump House** is an elegant, civilised retreat for those who appreciate quality.

see page 232

15

10 THE WALPOLE ARMS

Itteringham, nr Norwich

The skills of the kitchen team have made the **Walpole Arms** the leading pub restaurant in the region.

see page 233

11 THE OLD CROWN

Buxton, nr Aylsham

Well-kept ales and fine home cooking in a very friendly, popular village pub.

see page 234

Countess by Gainsborough were added later.

The Earl was a martyr to gout, and his death in 1793 at the age of 50 occurred when, finding the pain unbearable, he thrust his bloated foot into a bucket of icy water, and suffered a heart attack. He was buried beneath the idiosyncratic Egyptian Pyramid in the grounds, a 45-feet high structure designed by Ignatius Bonomi that combines Egyptian and classical elements to create a mausoleum which, if nothing else, is certainly distinctive.

Blickling also offers its visitors miles of footpaths through extensive parkland, a formal woodland wilderness garden, a Victorian parterre and a dry moat with scented plants, a plant centre, a picnic area, a superb restaurant, a shop and cycle hire.

Within a few miles of Blickling Hall are two other stately homes, both the properties of Lord and Lady Walpole. **Mannington** is a 15th century moated manor house whose grounds feature a wide variety of plants, trees and shrubs, including thousands of roses, and particularly classic varieties. The Heritage Rose Garden and Twentieth century Rose Garden are set in small gardens reflecting their period of origin; the gardens contain more than 1,500 varieties of roses. In 2003 a sensory garden was created, with plants chosen for scent, touch, sight, taste and hearing. There are also garden shops, with plants, souvenirs and crafts, and tea rooms. The grounds are open Sundays May to September and also Wednesday to Friday June to August.

Wolterton Park is a stately 18th century Hall built for Horatio Walpole, brother of Sir Robert, England's first Prime Minister. The grounds, landscaped by Humphry Repton, contain walks and trails,

Mannington Hall, nr Aylsham

16

orienteering and an adventure playground, and various special events are held throughout the year here and at Mannington. The Hall is open for tours every Friday from April to late October.

Over 20 miles of waymarked public footpaths and permissive paths around Mannington and Wolterton link into the Weavers Way long-distance footpath and Holt circular walk.

Just north of Mannington Hall stands the village of **Little Barningham**, where St Mary's Church is a magnet for collectors of ecclesiastical curiosities. Inside, perched on the corner of an ancient box pew, stands a remarkable wood-carved skeletal figure of the Grim Reaper. Its fleshless skull stares hollow-eyed at visitors with a defiant, mirthless grin: a scythe gripped in one clutch of bones, and an hour-glass in the other, symbolise the inescapable fate that awaits us all. This gruesomely powerful memento mori was donated to the church in 1640 by one Stephen Crosbie who, for good measure, added the inscription: *'As you are now, even so was I, Remember death for ye must dye.'* Those words were a conventional enough adjuration at that time, but what is one supposed to make of Stephen's postscript inscribed on the back of the pew: *'For couples joined in wedlock this seat I did intend'?*

THE NORTHEAST COAST

CROMER

As you enter a seaside town, what more reassuring sight could there be than to see the pier still standing? **Cromer Pier** is the genuine article, complete with Lifeboat Station and the Pavilion Theatre, which still stages traditional end-of-the-pier shows. The Pier's survival is all the more impressive since it was badly damaged in 1953 and 1989, and in 1993 it was sliced in two by a drilling rig which had broken adrift in a storm.

Cromer has been a significant resort since the late 1700s and in its early days even received an unsolicited testimonial from Jane

12   THE GOAT INN

Skeyton, nr Aylsham

No kidding – the **Goat** is one of the friendliest pubs in the region, a great place for a drink and a meal.

 see page 235

13   BON VISTA GUEST HOUSE

Cromer

Comfortable guest house close to the seafront at the West Cliff end of Cromer.

See page 236

Cromer Pier and Beach

17

Cromer Museum, housed in a row of restored fishermen's cottages near the church, invites visitors to follow the story of Cromer from the days of the dinosaurs, some of whose bones were found nearby, up to the present, and access the computer for thousands of pictures and facts about this attractive town. The new Geology Gallery houses an amazing collection of fossils.

14 THE ROMAN CAMP INN

Aylmerton, nr Cromer

All the attributes of a fine country inn, including real ales, home cooking and comfortable B&B rooms.

 *see page 236

Austen. In her novel *Emma* (1816), a character declares that 'Perry was a week at Cromer once, and he holds it to be the best of all the sea-bathing places.' A succession of celebrities, ranging from Lord Tennyson and Oscar Wilde to Winston Churchill and the German Kaiser, all came to see for themselves.

The inviting sandy beach remains much as they saw it (horse-drawn bathing machines aside), as does the **Church of St Peter & St Paul**, which boasts the tallest tower in Norfolk, 160 feet high. And then as now, Cromer Crabs were reckoned to be the most succulent in England. During the season, between April and September, crab-boats are launched from the shore (there's no harbour here), sail out to the crab banks about 3 miles offshore, and there the two-man teams on each boat deal with some 200 pots.

Housed in the former Lifeboat Station, the **RNLI Henry Blogg Museum** tells the dramatic story of the courageous men who manned the town's rescue service. Pre-eminent among them was Henry Blogg, who was coxswain of the lifeboat for 37 years, from 1910 to 1947. During those years his boat, the *H F Bailey*, was called out 128 times and saved 518 lives. In 1991, the *H F Bailey* was purchased by Peter Cadbury of the chocolate manufacturing family and presented to the Museum as its prime exhibit.

AROUND CROMER

AYLMERTON

3 miles W of Cromer on minor road off the A148

Aylmerton is home to one of Norfolk's grandest houses, **Felbrigg Hall** (National Trust). Thomas Windham began rebuilding the old manor house at Felbrigg in the 1620s, erecting in its place a grand Jacobean mansion with huge mullioned windows, pillared porch, and at roof-level a dedication in openwork stone: *Gloria Deo in Excelsis*, 'Glory to God in the Highest'. Later that century, Thomas' grandson William Windham I married a wealthy heiress and added the beautifully proportioned Carolean West Wing, where visitors can see portraits of the happily married couple painted by Sir Peter Lely. Their son, William Windham II, returning from his four-year-long Grand Tour, filled the house with treasures he had collected - so many of them that he had to extend the Hall yet again. The Windham family's ownership of Felbrigg Hall came to a tragi-comic end in the 1860s when William Frederick Windham inherited the estate. William was one of the great English eccentrics. He loved uniforms. Dressed in the Felbrigg blue and red livery, he would insist on serving at table; in guard's uniform he caused chaos on the local railway with his arbitrary whistle-blasts; dressed as a policeman, he sternly rounded up the ladies of easy virtue patrolling London's Haymarket. Inevitably,

'Mad' Windham fell prey to a pretty fortune-hunter and Felbrigg was only saved from complete bankruptcy by his death at the age of 26.

The Hall was acquired by the National Trust in 1969, complete with its 18th century furnishings, collection of paintings by artists such as Kneller and van der Velde, and a wonderful Gothic library. The 1,750-acre estate includes a traditional working walled garden containing an elegant octagonal dovecote, an orangery of 1707, a 500-acre Great Wood and a restaurant, tea room, gift shop and plant shop.

WEST RUNTON
3 miles W of Cromer on the A149

The parish of West Runton can boast that within its boundaries lies the highest point in Norfolk - **Beacon Hill**. This eminence is 330 feet high, so you won't be needing any oxygen equipment to reach the summit, but there are some excellent views. Nearby is the Roman Camp (National Trust), a misleading name since there's no evidence that the Romans ever occupied this 70-acre stretch of heathland. Excavations have shown, however, that in Saxon and medieval times this was an iron-working settlement.

West Runton's major tourist attraction is undoubtedly the **Norfolk Shire Horse Centre** where twice a day, during the season, these noble beasts are harnessed up and give a half-hour demonstration of the important

role they played in agricultural life right up until the 1930s. They are the largest (19 hands/6 feet 4 inches high) and heaviest horses in the world, weighing more than a ton, and for generations were highly valued both as war-horses and draught animals. Several other heavy breeds, such as the Suffolk Punch, Clydesdale and Percheron, also have their home here, along with no fewer than nine different breeds of pony. The Centre also has a video room showing a 30-minute film, a small animals' enclosure and an adventure playground for children, a café and gift shop. A horse-drawn cart will transport you around the village and at the West Runton Riding School (on site) you can hire riding horses by the hour.

SHERINGHAM
5 miles W of Cromer on the A149

Sheringham has made the transition from fishing village to popular seaside resort with grace and style. There are plenty of activities on

Sheringham

19

offer, yet Sheringham has managed to avoid the brasher excesses of many English seaside towns. The beach here is among the cleanest in England, and markedly different from the shingle beaches elsewhere on this part of the coast. Consisting mainly of gently sloping sand, it is excellent for bathing and the team of lifeguards makes it ideal for families with children. Rainfall at Sheringham is one of the lowest in the county, and the bracing air has also recommended the town to sufferers from rheumatism and respiratory problems.

A small fleet of fishing boats still operates from the beach at Sheringham, mostly concentrating on crabs and lobsters, but also bringing in catches of cod, skate, plaice, mackerel and herring. Several original fishermen's cottages remain, some with lofts where the nets were mended. Sheringham has never had a harbour, so boats are launched from the shore where stacks of creels stand as they have for generations. A 'golden lobster' in the town's coat of arms celebrates this traditional industry.

Like so many other former fishing villages in England, Sheringham owes its transformation into a resort to the arrival of the railway. During the Edwardian peak years of rail travel, some 64 trains a day steamed into the station but the line became yet another victim of the Beeching closures of the 1960s. Devotees of steam trains joined together and, by dint of great effort and enthusiasm, managed to re-open the line in 1975 as the **North Norfolk Railway**, better known as The Poppy Line.

The name refers to 'Poppyland', a term given to the area by the Victorian journalist Clement Scott who visited in pre-herbicide days when the summer fields were ablaze with poppies. In 1883, Scott travelled to Cromer on the newly-opened Great Eastern Railway's extension from Norwich. Walking out of the town, he was entranced by the tranquillity of the countryside. In his dispatch to the Daily Telegraph he wrote: 'It is difficult to convey an idea of the silence of the fields through which I passed, or the beauty of the prospect that surrounded me - a blue sky without a cloud across it, a sea sparkling under a haze of heat, wild flowers in profusion around me, poppies predominating everywhere ...' Spurred by Scott's enthusiasm, a succession of notable Victorians made their way here - painters, writers, actors, even a youthful Winston Churchill. Later, during the Second World War, Churchill returned to the area, staying at Pear Tree Cottage in Mundesley.

Although greatly diminished in number, plenty of brilliant poppies can still be seen as you travel the scenic five-mile journey, steam or diesel operated, from Sheringham to Holt via Weybourne. Sheringham Station, just across the road from the Network Rail station on the Bittern Line, was built in 1887 and retains all the charm of steam railway days, complete with luggage piled on the platform and smartly uniformed staff. Tel: 01263 820800 for timetable details

Sheringham Museum on Station Road recently closed and will relocate to a new site on the seafront. Just to the west of the town, at Upper Sheringham, footpaths lead to the lovely grounds of Sheringham Park (National Trust). The Park was landscaped by Humphry Repton, who declared it to be his 'favourite and darling child in Norfolk'. There are grand views along the coast (one viewing tower is on the site of a Napoleonic lookout), many species of trees and shrubs, and banks of rhododendrons which are at their most dazzling from May to early June. There is also an exhibition barn, café-style catering and a small shop.

WEYBOURNE

9 miles W of Cromer on the A149

Here, the shingle beach known as **Weybourne Hope** (or Hoop) slopes so steeply that an invading fleet could bring its ships right up to the shore. Which is exactly what the Danes did many times during the 9th and 10th centuries. A local adage states that 'He who would Old England win, Must at Weybourne Hoop begin,' and over the centuries care has been taken to protect this stretch of the coast. A map dated 1st May 1588 clearly shows 'Waborne Fort', and Holt's Parish Register for that year of the Armada notes that 'in this yeare was the town of Waborne fortified with a continuall garrison of men bothe of horse and foote with sconces

(earthworks) ordinaunce and all manner of appoyntment to defend the Spannyards landing theare.'

As it turned out, the 'Spannyards' never got close, but during both World Wars the same concern was shown for defending this vulnerable beach. The garrison then became the Anti-Aircraft Permanent Range and Radar Training Wing, providing instruction for National Servicemen until the camp finally closed in 1959. It was reckoned that by then some 1,500,000 shells had been fired out to sea. The site has since been returned to agricultural use, but the original NAAFI building remains and now houses the **Muckleburgh Collection**, a fascinating museum of military vehicles, weapons and equipment, most of which have seen action in battlefields all over the world. All the tanks, armoured cars and amphibious vehicles on display at the Muckleburgh Collection can be inspected at close quarters, and there are regular tank demonstrations. Meals and snacks are available - served in a NAAFI-style canteen.

Weybourne is the middle station on the Poppy Line (see under Sheringham) and alongside the station are the line's locomotive and carriage & wagon workshops.

HOLT

10 miles W of Cromer on the A148

A perennial finalist in the 'Anglia in Bloom' competition, Holt's town centre always looks a picture, with hanging baskets and flowers everywhere. Back in 1892, a guide-

Despite Weybourne's exposed position, it has in fact only been attacked once, by the Luftwaffe on 11th July 1940. A stick of bombs landed in the main street and badly damaged two cottages.

18   LETHERINGSETT WATERMILL

Letheringsett, Holt

In the attractive village of Letheringsett is a fully functional water powered Flour Mill generally accepted to be the only producing one in Norfolk

 see page 238

Look out for one of Holt's most unusual buildings, Home Place. Designed and built in 1905 by E S Prior, an architect follower of the Arts & Crafts movement, the exterior of the house is completely covered with an ingeniously contrived cladding of local pebbles. The station at Holt, on the Poppy Line, is really Stalham Station, lovingly re-erected complete with many of its original furnishings.

book to the county described Holt as 'A clean and very prettily situated market town, being planted in a well undulating and very woody neighbourhood.' More than a century later, one can't quarrel with that characterisation. The worst day in Holt's history was May 1st, 1708, when a raging fire consumed most of the town's ancient houses. The consequent rebuilding replaced them with some elegant Georgian houses, gracious buildings which played a large part in earning the town its designation as a Conservation Area.

The town's most famous building, **Gresham's School**, somehow escaped the disastrous conflagration. Founded in 1555 by Sir John Gresham, the school began as an altruistic educational establishment, its pupils accepted solely on the basis of their academic promise. Since then, the school has abandoned both its town centre location and its founder's

commitment to educating, free, those bright children who could not otherwise afford it. Among the school's many distinguished alumni are Lord Reith, the poets W H Auden and Stephen Spender, and the composer Benjamin Britten.

CLEY-NEXT-THE-SEA

12 miles W of Cromer on the A149

Cley's name is no longer appropriate. Cley-a-mile-away-from-the-Sea would be more truthful. But in early medieval times, Cley (pronounced Cly, and meaning clay) was a more important port than King's Lynn, with a busy trade exporting wool to the Netherlands. In return, Cley imported a predilection for houses with curved gables, Flemish bricks and pantiles. The windmill overlooking the harbour adds to the sense that a little piece of Holland has strayed across the North Sea. This is the famous **Cley Mill**, the subject of thousands of paintings. Built in 1713 and in use until 1921, the Mill is open to visitors during the season (afternoons only), and also offers bed and breakfast.

The village's prosperity in the past is reflected in the enormous scale of its 14th/15th century parish church, **St Mary's**, whose south porch is particularly notable for its fine stonework and 16 armorial crests. The gorgeous fan-vaulted roof is decorated with bosses carved with angels, flowers, and a lively

Cley Mill

scene of an old woman throwing her distaff at a fox running away with her chickens.

Half a mile east of Cley on the A149 coast road, the Norfolk Wildlife Trust's **Cley Marshes** have a well-earned reputation as one of the UK's premier birdwatching sites. The pools and scrapes attract water birds in their thousands, so there is something interesting to see whatever the season. From Cley it's possible to walk westward along the shoreline to Blakeney Point, the most northerly extremity of East Anglia. This spit of land that stretches three miles out into the sea is another twitcher's paradise. Over 250 species of birds have been spotted here, and the variety of flora is scarcely less impressive.

GLANDFORD

12 miles W of Cromer off the B1156

Near this delightful village, the **Natural Surroundings Wild Flower Centre** is dedicated to gardening with a strong ecological emphasis. There are wild flower meadows and gardens, organic vegetable and herb gardens, nurseries, a nature trail alongside the unspoilt River Glaven, and the Centre also organises a wide range of events with a conservation theme. A short walk down the valley from the Centre is the **Glandford Shell Museum**, a lovely Dutch-style building which houses the private collection of Sir Alfred Jodrell, a unique accumulation of sea shells gathered

from beaches all around the world, together with a fascinating variety of artefacts made from them.

MORSTON

13 miles W of Cromer on the A149

Great stretches of salt marshes and mud flats lie between this pleasant village and the sea, which is reached by way of a tidal creek that almost disappears at low tide. Morston is a particularly pleasing village with quiet lanes and clusters of cottages built from local flint cobbles. If the church tower looks rather patched-up, that's because it was struck by lightning in 1743. It's said that local people took this as a sign that the Second Coming of Christ was imminent, and that repairing their church was therefore pointless. It was many years before restoration work was finally undertaken, by which time the fabric of the tower had deteriorated even further.

LANGHAM

14 miles W of Cromer off the A149/A148

The minor road leading south from Morston will bring visitors, after a mile or so, to **Langham Glass & Rural Crafts** where, in a wonderful collection of restored 18th century barn workshops, a variety of craftspeople can be seen practising their traditional skills. In the churchyard of St Andrew and St Mary is the grave of the novelist Captain Marryat, who wrote Mr Midshipman Easy and devised a signalling code for the Merchant Navy.

A couple of miles south of Glandford you'll find a building of 1802 which, year after year, has been voted one of the top tourist attractions in North Norfolk. Letheringsett Watermill stands on the site of an earlier mill recorded in the Domesday Book, and was rescued from near-dereliction in the 1980s. This fully functional, water-powered mill produces 100% wholewheat flour from locally grown wheat; there are regular demonstrations of the milling process, with a running commentary from the miller; and the end product can be purchased in the gift shop.

To the north of the village are the Stiffkey Salt Marshes, a National Trust nature reserve which turns a delicate shade of purple in July when the sea lavender is in bloom. Here on the sandflats can be found the famous 'Stewkey blues' - cockles which are highly regarded as a delicacy by connoisseurs of succulent bivalve molluscs.

Seals at Blakeney Point

BLAKENEY

14 miles W of Cromer on the A149

One of the most enchanting of the North Norfolk coastal villages, Blakeney was a commercial port until the beginning of the 20th century, when silting up of the estuary prevented all but pleasure craft from gaining access. The silting has left a fascinating landscape of serpentine creeks and channels twisting their way through mud banks and sand hills. In a side street off the quay is the 14th century **Guildhall** (English Heritage), which was probably a private house and contains an interesting undercroft, or cellar, which is notable as an early example of a brick-built vaulted ceiling.

The beautifully restored **Church of St Nicholas**, set on a hill overlooking Blakeney village and marshland, has a lovely Early English chancel, built in 1220, and a magnificent west tower, 100 feet high, a landmark for miles around. In a small turret on the northeast corner of the chancel a light would once burn as a beacon to guide ships safely into Blakeney Harbour.

STIFFKEY

16 miles W of Cromer on the A149

Regarded as one of the prettiest villages in the county, Stiffkey lies beside the little river of the same name. Pronounced 'Stewkey', the name means 'island of tree stumps' and is most likely derived from the marshy river valley of reed beds and fallen trees, which indeed gives the village the appearance of an island. At the east end of the village is the church of St John the Baptist; from the churchyard there are fine views of the river and of **Stiffkey Hall** to the south. All that now remains of this once-impressive building, built by the Bacon family in 1578, are the

Stiffkey Hall

towers, one wing of the house, and the 17th century gatehouse. The stately ruins of the great hall have been transformed into a rose terrace and sunken garden and are open to the public.

The former Rectory is a grand Georgian building, famous as the residence of the Revd Harold Davidson, Rector of Stiffkey during the 1920s and 1930s. This gentleman launched a personal crusade to save the fallen women of London, and caused much gossip and scandal by doing so. Despite the fact that his notoriety regularly filled the church to capacity, he constantly fell foul of the ecclesiastical authorities and eventually lost his living. There is a rather bizarre ending to his story. After handing over the keys of Stiffkey Rectory, Harold joined a travelling show and was later killed by a lion whose cage he was sharing. A couple of miles south of Stiffkey stand the picturesque ruins of **Binham Priory** (English Heritage), its magnificent nave still serving as the parish church. This represents only about one-sixth of the original Priory, founded in 1091 by a nephew of William the Conqueror. The church is well worth a visit to see its unusually lofty interior with a Monk's Walk at roof level, its Seven Sacraments font, and noble west front.

GREAT YARMOUTH

The topography of Great Yarmouth is rather curious. Back in Saxon times, it was actually an island, a large sandbank dotted with fishermen's cottages. Later, the narrow estuary of the River Bure at the northern end was blocked off, causing it to flow down the western side of the town. It runs parallel to the sea for two miles before joining the larger River Yare, and then their united waters curve around the southern edge of the town for another three miles before finally entering the sea.

So Yarmouth is now a promontory, its eastern and western sides displaying markedly different characters. The seaward side is a 5-mile stretch of sandy beaches, tourist attractions and countless amusements, with a breezy promenade from which one can watch the constant traffic of ships in Yarmouth Roads. There are two fine old traditional piers, the Britannia (810 feet long) and the Wellington (600 feet long), as well as The Jetty, first built in the 16th century for landing goods and passengers. A host of activities are on offer for families: the **Sealife Centre** with many kinds of marine life including octopus and seahorses, and an underwater viewing channel passing through shark-infested 'oceans'; **Amazonia**, an indoor tropical paradise featuring the largest collection of reptiles in Britain; **Merrivale Model Village** which offers an acre of attractive landscaped gardens with over 200 realistic models of town and country in miniature, which are illuminated at dusk, and the **Pleasure Beach**,

At South Denes in Great Yarmouth stands the 144-feet high Nelson's Monument crowned by a statue, not of Norfolk's most famous son, but of Britannia. The fluted Doric column was based on the Monument to the Great Fire of London; its base is inscribed with the names of Nelson's great victories of Aboukir, St Vincent, Copenhagen and Trafalgar.

25

21 GREAT YARMOUTH ROW HOUSES

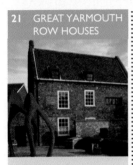

Great Yarmouth

Experience the sights and sounds of yesterday's Great Yarmouth. Visit these unique and vividly-presented houses

🏛 *see page 238*

featuring over 70 rides and attractions combining all the thrills of modern high-tech amusement park rides with the fun of traditional fairground attractions.

For heritage enthusiasts, Great Yarmouth has a rich and proud maritime history. The **Norfolk Nelson Museum** on South Quay features displays, paintings and contemporary memorabilia relating to the life and times of Horatio Lord Nelson. Also on South Quay is the **Elizabethan House Museum**, built by a wealthy merchant and now a museum of domestic life, with 16th century panelled rooms and a functional Victorian kitchen. In Row 117, South Quay, the Old Merchant's House is an excellent example of a 17th century dwelling and a showplace for local wood and metalwork. Nearby is **The Tollhouse**, originally built in 1262 as a gaol and later used as a courthouse. It is now a museum with original dungeons. Nearby is

the exciting **Time and Tide, Museum of Great Yarmouth Life**, where visitors can find out all about the town's fishing and maritime heritage.

Most of Yarmouth's older buildings are concentrated in the western, or riverside, part of the town. Here you will find **The Quay**, which moved Daniel Defoe, in 1724, to describe it as 'the finest quay in England, if not Europe'. It is more than a mile long and in places 150 yards wide. The **Town Hall** is well known for its grand staircase, Court Room and Assembly Room; the building itself is in use by the Local Authority. **The Rows**, a medieval network of tiny courtyards and narrow alleys, are a mere 2 feet wide in places. Badly damaged during a bombing raid in 1942, enough remains to show their unique character. There were originally 145 of these rows, about 7 miles in total, all of them built at right angles to the sea and therefore freely ventilated by onshore breezes which, given the urban sanitary conditions of those times, must have been extremely welcome.

The bombing raid of 1942 also completely destroyed the interior of **St Nicholas' Church**, but left its walls standing. Between 1957 and 1960 this huge building - the largest parish church in England - was completely restored and furnished in traditional style largely by using pieces garnered from redundant churches and other sources. The partly Norman font, for example, came from Highway

The Tollhouse, Great Yarmouth

church in Wiltshire, the organ from St Mary-the-Boltons in Kensington.

Just south of the church, off the Market Place, is the half-timbered **Anna Sewell House**, built in 1641, in which the author of *Black Beauty* lived. Sewell was born in the town in 1820, but it was only when she was in her late fifties that she transmuted her concern for the more humane treatment of horses into a classic and seemingly timeless novel. Anna was paid just £20 for the rights to a book which, in the five months that elapsed between its publication and her death in 1878, had already sold an incredible 100,000 copies. (Anna Sewell, who died in 1878, is buried in the Quaker burial ground in Lamas, a village between Coltishall and Aylsham.)

In Victorian times the whole town was pervaded with the aroma of smoked herring, the silvery fish that were the basis of Yarmouth's prosperity. Around the time of Dickens' stay here, the author of the town's directory tried to pre-empt any discouraging effect this might have on visitors by claiming that 'The wholesome exhalations arising from the fish during the operation of curing are said to have a tendency to dissipate contagious disorders, and to be generally beneficial to the human constitution which is here sometimes preserved to extreme longevity.'

Across the town, some 60 curing houses were busy gutting, salting and spicing herrings to produce Yarmouth's great contribution to the English

breakfast, the kipper. The process had been invented by a Yarmouth man, John Woodger: a rival of his, a Mr Bishop, developed a different method which left the fish wonderfully moist and flavoursome, and so created the famous Yarmouth bloater.

For centuries, incredible quantities of herring were landed, nearly a billion in 1913 alone. In earlier years the trade had involved so many fishermen that there were more boats (1,123) registered at Yarmouth than at London. The scale of over-fishing produced the inevitable result: within the space of two decades Yarmouth's herring industry foundered, and by the late 1960s found itself dead in the water. Luckily, the end of that historic trade coincided with the beginning of North Sea oil and gas exploitation, a business which has kept the town in reasonably good economic health up to the present day.

AROUND GREAT YARMOUTH

FRITTON

6 miles SW of Great Yarmouth off the A143

At **Fritton Lake Countryworld**, visitors will find a large undercover falconry centre with birds-of-prey flying displays twice daily. There are also heavy horse stables and a children's farm, 9-hole golf and 18-hole putting courses, lakeside gardens, boating and a large adventure playground. Open end-March to end-September every day, and weekends and half-term in October.

•

Charles Dickens stayed at the Royal Hotel on Marine Parade in 1847 and 1848 while writing David Copperfield. Dickens had visited the town as a child and had actually seen an upturned boat on the beach being used as a dwelling, complete with a chimney emerging from its keel. In his novel, this becomes Peggotty's house to which young Copperfield is brought following the death of his mother. 'One thing I particularly noticed in this delightful house,' he writes, 'was the smell of fish; which was so searching, that when I took out my pocket-handkerchief to wipe my nose, I found it smelt exactly as if it had wrapped up a lobster.'

•

BURGH CASTLE

4 miles W of Great Yarmouth off the A12 or A143

When the Romans established their fortress of Garionnonum, now known as **Burgh Castle**, the surrounding marshes were still under water. The fort then stood on one bank of a vast estuary, commanding a strategic position at the head of an important waterway running into the heart of East Anglia. The ruins are impressive, with walls of alternating flint and brick layers rising 15 feet high in places, and spreading more than 11 feet wide at their base. The Romans abandoned Garionnonum around AD 408 and some two centuries later the Irish missionary St Fursey (or Fursa) founded a monastery within its walls. Later generations cannibalised both his building, and much of the crumbling Roman castle, as materials for their own churches and houses.

CAISTER-ON-SEA

3 miles N of Great Yarmouth off the A149

In Boudica's time, this modern holiday resort with its stretch of fine sands was an important fishing port for her people, the Iceni. After the Romans had vanquished her unruly tribe, they settled here sometime in the 2nd century and built a castra, or castle, or Caister, of which only a few foundations and remains have yet been found. **Caister Castle**, which stands in a picturesque setting about a mile to the west of the town, is a much later construction, built between 1432 and 1435 by Sir John Fastolf with his spoils from the French wars in which he had served, very profitably, as Governor of Normandy and also distinguished himself leading the English bowmen at the Battle of Agincourt. Academics have enjoyed themselves for centuries disputing whether this Sir John was the model for Shakespeare's immortal rogue, Falstaff. Certainly

Caister Castle, Caister-on-Sea

the real Sir John was a larger-than-life character, but there's no evidence that he shared Falstaff's other characteristics of cowardliness, boastfulness or general over-indulgence.

Caister Castle was the first in England to be built of brick, and is in fact one of the earliest brick buildings in the county. The 90-feet tower remains, together with much of the moated wall and gatehouse, now lapped by still waters and with ivy relentlessly encroaching. The castle is open daily from May to September and, as an additional attraction, there is an impressive collection of veteran and vintage cars. About three miles west of Caister Castle, the pleasantly landscaped grounds surrounding an 1876 Victorian mansion have been transformed into the **Thrigby Hall Wildlife Gardens**, home for a renowned collection of Asian mammals, birds and reptiles. There are snow leopards and rare tigers; gibbons and crocodiles; deer and otters; and other attractions include a tropical house, aviaries, waterfowl lake, willow pattern garden, gift shop and café. The Gardens are open every day, all year round.

THE NORFOLK BROADS

REEDHAM

8 miles SW of Great Yarmouth off the B1140

Here in Reedham is the single remaining car and passenger ferry

Norfolk Broads

in the Broads. There's also an interesting craft showroom at the Old Brewery, and a great pub in The Reedham Ferry Inn.

ACLE

10 miles W of Great Yarmouth off the A47

A thousand years ago, this small market town, now 10 miles inland, was a small fishing port on the coast. Gradually, land has been reclaimed from the estuaries of the Rivers Bure, Waveney and Yare, so that today large expanses of flat land stretch away from Acle towards the sea. The town's importance as a boating centre began in the 19th century with

22   THE GARDEN HOUSE

Hales

A smartly refurbished village pub with a large menu of traditional dishes.

see page 239

29

boat-building yards springing up beside the bridge. When Acle's first Regatta was held in 1890, some 150 yachts took part. The town became known as the 'Gateway to the Broads' and also as the gateway to 'Windmill Land', a picturesque stretch of the River Bure dotted with windmills. The medieval bridge that formerly crossed the Bure at Acle has less agreeable associations, since it was used for numerous executions with the unfortunate victims left to dangle over the river.

Acle was granted permission for a market in 1272, and it's still held every Thursday, attracting visitors from miles around. Others come to see the unusual **Church of St Edmund** with its Saxon round tower, built some time around AD 900, crowned with a

Church of St Edmund, Acle

15th century belfry from which eight carved figures look down on the beautifully thatched roof of the nave. The treasures inside include a superbly carved font, 6 feet high, and inscribed with the date 1410, and a fine 15th century screen.

SOUTH WALSHAM

9 miles E of Norwich on the B1140

This small village is notable for having two parish churches built within yards of each other. Just to the north of the village is the **Fairhaven Woodland and Water Garden**, an expanse of delightful water gardens lying beside the private South Walsham Inner Broad. Its centrepiece is the 900-year-old King Oak, lording it over the surrounding displays of rare shrubs and plants, native wildflowers, rhododendrons and giant lilies. There are tree-lined walks, a bird sanctuary, plants for sale, and a restaurant. A vintage-

St Benet's Abbey Ruins, South Walsham

style riverboat runs trips every half-hour around the Broad.

The best way to see the remains of **St Benet's Abbey** is from a boat along the River Bure (indeed, it's quite difficult to reach it any other way). Rebuilt in 1020 by King Canute, after the Vikings had destroyed an earlier Saxon building, St Benet's became one of the richest abbeys in East Anglia. When Henry VIII closed it down in 1536 he made an unusual deal with its last Abbot. In return for creating the Abbot Bishop of Norwich, the Cathedral estates were to be handed over to the King, but St Benet's properties could remain in the Abbot/Bishop's possession. Even today, the Bishop of Norwich retains the additional title of Abbot of St Benet's, and on the first Sunday in August each year travels the last part of the journey by boat to hold an open-air service near the stately ruins of the Abbey gatehouse.

RANWORTH

14 miles NW of Great Yarmouth off the B1140

This beautiful Broadland village is famous for its church and its position on Ranworth Broad. From the tower of St Helen's church it is possible to see five Norfolk Broads, Horsey Mill, the sea at Great Yarmouth and, on a clear day, the spire of Norwich Cathedral. Inside, the church houses one of Norfolk's greatest ecclesiastical treasures, a breathtaking early 15th century Gothic choir screen, the most beautiful and the best preserved in the county. In glowing reds, greens

and golds, gifted medieval artists painted a gallery of more than 30 saints and martyrs, inserting tiny cameos of such everyday scenes as falcons seizing hares, dogs chasing ducks and, oddly for Norfolk, lions. Cromwell's men, offended by such idolatrous images, smothered them with brown paint - an ideal preservative for these wonderful paintings, as became apparent when they were once again revealed during the course of a 19th century restoration of the church. The Norfolk Wildlife Trust's **Ranworth Broad** is a popular family destination where interpreted boardwalks promote an understanding of Broads ecology. A thatched building with an information centre floats on pontoons on the edge of the Broad.

HORNING

12 miles NW of Great Yarmouth off the A1062

The travel writer Arthur Mee described Horning as 'Venice in Broadland', where 'waterways wandering from the river into the gardens are crossed by tiny bridges.' With its pretty reed-thatched cottages lining the bank of the River Bure and its position in the heart of the Broads, there are few more attractive places from which to explore this magical area.

POTTER HEIGHAM

13 miles NW of Great Yarmouth off the A149

Modern Potter Heigham has sprung up around the medieval bridge over the River Thurne, a

23 THE KINGS ARMS

Ludham

A convivial Broads pub serving a splendid variety of cooked-to-order dishes.

 see page 240

24 THE LION

West Somerton, nr Great Yarmouth

A friendly local that does a roaring trade serving drinks and food to the local community and holidaymakers.

 see page 240

A mile or so east of Wroxham Barns, Hoveton Hall Gardens offer visitors a splendid combination of plants, shrubs and trees, with rare rhododendrons, azaleas, water plants and dazzling herbaceous borders within a walled garden. There are woodland and lakeside walks, streams and bridges, plant sales, gardening books and a tea room.

---

25   THE WHITE HORSE

Neatishead, nr Wroxham

A real pub-lovers pub on the edge of the Broads, with real ales and home-cooked food.

see page 240

---

low-arched structure with a clearance of only 7 feet at its highest, a notorious test for novice sailors. The Thurne is a major artery through the Broads, linking them in a continuous waterway from Horsey Mere in the east to Wroxham Broad in the west. A pleasant excursion from Potter Heigham is a visit to **Horsey Mere**, about six miles to the east, and **Horsey Windpump** (both National Trust). From this early 20th century drainage mill, now restored and fully working, there are lovely views across the Mere. A circular walk follows the north side of Horsey Mere, passes another windmill, and returns through the village. There's a small shop at the Windpump, and light refreshments are available.

STALHAM

18 miles NW of Great Yarmouth on the A149 (or 13 miles NE of Norwich)

At the Staithe, Stalham, on the opposite side of the A149 from Stalham centre, lies the **Museum of the Broads**. Open from 10.30 to 4.30 (last entry) Monday to Friday and also during the local school summer holidays, the Museum has boats, displays, exhibits and videos telling the story of life in the Broads. **Stalham Fire Museum**, next to the church on the main street, houses the town's original fire engine. Four miles southeast of Stalham, the Norfolk Wildlife Trust's **Hickling Broad** is the largest Norfolk Broad and is home to a spectacular variety of wildlife that includes swallowtail

butterflies, bitterns, marsh harriers and other rare Broadland species. The Water Trail takes visitors by boat through the quiet backwaters to the tree Tower, with its breathtaking views of the Broads.

WROXHAM

8 miles NE of Norwich on the A1151

This riverside village, linked to its twin, Hoveton, by a hump-backed bridge over the River Bure, is the self-styled 'capital' of the Norfolk Broads and as such gets extremely busy during the season. The banks of the river are chock-a-block with boatyards full of cruisers of all shapes and sizes; there's a constant traffic of boats making their way to the open spaces of Wroxham Broad, and in July the scene becomes even more hectic when the annual Regatta is under way.

Wroxham is also the southern terminus of the **Bure Valley Railway**, a nine-mile long, narrow-gauge (15-inch) steam train service that closely follows the course of the River Bure through lovely countryside to the market town of Aylsham. A couple of miles north of Wroxham is **Wroxham Barns**, a delightful collection of beautifully restored 18th century barns set in 10 acres of countryside, and housing a community of craftspeople. There are 13 workshops, producing between them a wide range of crafts, from stained glass to woodturning, stitchcraft to handmade children's clothes, pottery to floral artistry, and much more. The complex also includes a cider-pressing centre, a junior farm with lots of hands-on activities, a traditional Family Fair (with individually priced rides), a gift and craft shop, and a tearoom.

Anyone interested in dried flower arrangements should make their way to the tiny hamlet of **Cangate**, another couple of miles to the east, where **Willow Farm Flowers** provides an opportunity of seeing the whole process, from the flowers in the field to the final colourful displays. The farm shop has an abundance of dried, silk, parchment and wooden flowers, beautifully arranged, and more than 50 varieties of dried flowers are available in bunches or made into arrangements of all shapes and sizes, or to special order. Willow Farm also has a picnic and play area, a guided farm walk, lays

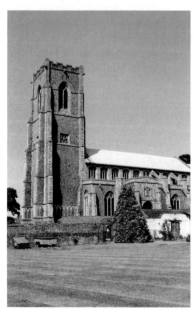

Church of St Mary, Worstead

on flower arranging demonstrations and also runs one-day classes.

COLTISHALL

8 miles N of Norwich on the B1150/B1354

This charming village beside the River Bure captivates visitors with its riverside setting, leafy lanes, elegant Dutch-gabled houses, village green and thatched church. Coltishall has a good claim to its title of 'Gateway to Broadland', since for most cruisers this is the beginning of the navigable portion of the Bure. Anyone interested in Norfolk's industrial heritage will want to seek out the **Ancient Lime Kiln**, next door to the Railway Tavern in Station Road. Lime, formerly an important part of Norfolk's rural economy, is obtained by heating chalk to a very high temperature in a kiln. Most of the county sits on a bed of chalk, but in the area around Coltishall and Horstead it is of a particularly high quality.

WORSTEAD

12 miles NE of Norwich off the A149 or B1150

Hard to imagine now, but Worstead was a busy little industrial centre in the Middle Ages. The village lent its name to the hard-wearing cloth produced in the region, and many of the original weavers' cottages can still be seen in the narrow side-streets. Worsted cloth, woven from tightly-twisted yarn, was

•

The kiln at Coltishall, one of the few surviving in the country, is a listed building of finely finished brickwork, built in a style unique to Norfolk. The top of the tapered kiln pot is level with the ground, and down below a vaulted walkway allowed access to the grills through which the lime was raked out. This was uncomfortable and even dangerous work since fresh lime, when it comes into contact with a moist surface, such as a human body, becomes burning hot. The lime had to be slaked with water before it could be used as a fertiliser, for mortar or as whitewash. Access to the kiln is by way of the Railway Tavern, but during the months from October to March you may find that the building has been taken over by a colony of hibernating bats which, by law, may not be disturbed.

•

26 THE NEW INN

Worstead

The **New Inn** is a convivial village local with well-kept ales and familiar pub fare.

see page 241

27 THE CROSS KEYS

Dilham

The **Cross Keys** is a popular village pub open every lunchtime and evening for food and drink.

‖ see page 242

28 THE COCKEREL TEA ROOM

North Walsham

The **Cockerel** is a lovely little tea room/café serving a good variety of food and drink.

‖ see page 243

29 THE JOLLY FARMERS

Swanton Abbot, nr North Walsham

A friendly, cheerful village pub with simple pub grub, real ales and a summer beer festival.

‖ see page 245

introduced by Flemish immigrants and became popular throughout England from the 13th century onwards. The Flemish weavers settled happily into the East Anglian way of life and seem to have influenced its architecture almost as strongly as its weaving industry.

The lovely 14th century **Church of St Mary** provides ample evidence of Worstead's former prosperity. Its many treasures include a fine hammerbeam roof, a chancel screen with a remarkable painted dado, and a magnificent traceried font complete with cover. The village stages an annual weekend of events in July to raise money for the restoration of the church. The festival started up some 35 years ago, attracting more than 35,000 visitors in 1999. The memory of Worstead's days of glory is kept alive by a still-functioning Guild of Weavers. The Guild has placed looms in the north aisle of St Mary's, and from time to time there are demonstrations of the ancient skill of weaving.

NORTH WALSHAM

This busy country town with its attractive Market Cross of 1600 has some interesting historical associations. Back in 1381, despite its remoteness from London, North Walsham became the focus of an uprising in support of Wat Tyler's Peasants' Rebellion. These North Norfolk rebels were led by John Litester, a local dyer, and their object was the abolition of serfdom. Their actions were mainly symbolic: invading manor houses, monasteries and town halls and burning the documents that recorded their subservient status. In a mass demonstration they gathered on Mousehold Heath outside Norwich, presented a petition to the King, and then retreated to North Walsham to await his answer. It came in the form of the sanguinary Bishop of Norwich, Henry Despenser, who, as his admiring biographer recorded, led an assault on the rebels, 'grinding his teeth like a wild boar, and sparing neither himself nor his enemies ... stabbing some, unhorsing others, hacking and hewing'. John Litester was captured, summarily executed and, on the orders of the Bishop, 'divided into four parts, and sent throughout the country to Norwich, Yarmouth, Lynn and to the site of his own house.'

A more glorious fate awaited the town's most famous resident, Horatio Nelson, who came to the **Paston School** here in 1768 as a boy of ten. Horatio was already dreaming of a naval career and, three years later when he read in the county newspaper that his Uncle Maurice had been appointed commander of a warship, he prevailed on his father to let him join the *Raisonnable*.

The Paston School had been founded in 1606 by Sir William Paston. His ancestors were the writers of the extraordinary collection of more than a thousand letters, written between 1422 and 1509, which present an astonishingly vivid picture of East Anglian life at the end of the turbulent Middle Ages. Sir William himself is buried in the parish church where he personally supervised (and paid for) the construction of the impressive marble and alabaster monument he desired to be erected in his memory.

About four miles east of North Walsham, near the village of Erpingham on the A140, Alby Crafts & Gardens has a Crafts Gallery promoting the excellence of mainly East Anglian and British craftsmanship - lacework, woodturning, jewellery, canework and much more. The 'Plantsman's Garden' displays a fine collection of unusual shrubs, plants and bulbs in a 4-acre site; there are also workshops where you can watch craftsmen at work, a Bottle Museum and a tearoom.

AROUND NORTH WALSHAM

MUNDESLEY

5 miles NE of North Walsham on the B1159

'The finest air in the kingdom has been wasted for centuries,' said a speaker celebrating the arrival of the railway at Mundesley in 1898, 'because nobody had the courage to bring the people to the district.' The railway has been and gone, but the fresh breezes off the North Sea remain as invigorating as ever.

After the hazards of the coastline immediately to the north where cliffs, fields and houses have all been eroded by the relentless sea, it's a pleasure to arrive at this unassuming holiday resort with its superb sandy beach, considered by many the very best in Norfolk. Mundesley village is quite small (appropriately, its Maritime Museum is believed to be the smallest museum in the country), but it provides all the facilities conducive to a relaxing family holiday. Best of all, there is safe swimming in the sea, and when the tide is out children can spend many a happy hour exploring the 'lowes', or shallow lagoons, left behind.

PASTON

5 miles NE of North Walsham on the B1159

It was in this small village that the Paston family entered historical record. The vivid collection of letters they wrote to each other during the years that England was being racked by the Wars of the Roses has already been mentioned, and the village boasts another

30 THE SHIP

Mundesley, nr Cromer

A convivial seafront pub open long hours for an excellent choice of food and drink.

‖ *see page 244*

31 WHINCLIFF

Mundesley

Whincliff offers a pleasant home from home by the sea for Bed & Breakfast guests

⊨ *see page 245*

32 CAFE LILIA

Mundesley

A pleasant family-run café serving snacks, meals and daily specials.

‖ *see page 245*

Tithe Barn, Paston

33 CASTAWAYS HOLIDAY PARK

Bacton-on-Sea

Lodges, flats and caravans provide a choice of self-catering accommodation close to the sea.

 see page 245

magnificent legacy from this remarkable family.

In 1581, Sir William Paston built a cavernous **Tithe Barn** here with flint walls and a thatched roof. It still stands, its roof still thatched: 160 feet long, almost 60 feet high - the longest, most imposing barn in Norfolk. In the nearby church, the most striking of the family memorials is the one dedicated to Katherine Paston. Sculpted in alabaster by Nicholas Stone in 1628, Katherine lies dressed to kill in her Jacobean finery of starched ruff, embroidered bodice, puffed sleeves and pearl necklaces. The monument cost £340, a staggering sum of money at that time.

HAPPISBURGH

6 miles E of North Walsham on the B1159

The coastal waters off Happisburgh (or 'Hazeborough', to give the village its correct pronunciation), have seen many a shipwreck over the centuries, and the victims lie buried in the graveyard of **St Mary's Church**. The large grassy mound on the north side of the church contains the bodies of the ill-fated crew of HMS *Invincible*, wrecked on the treacherous sandbanks here in 1801. The ship was on its way to join up with Nelson's fleet at Copenhagen when the tragedy occurred, resulting in the death of 119 sailors. Happisburgh's distinctive Lighthouse, built in 1791 and striped like a barber's pole, certainly proved ineffectual on that occasion, as did the soaring 110-feet tower of

the church itself, which could normally be relied on as a 'back-up' warning to mariners.

Inside the Church is a splendid 15th century octagonal font carved with the figures of lions, satyrs and 'wild men'; embedded in the pillars along the aisle are the marks left by shrapnel from German bombs dropped on the village in 1940.

LESSINGHAM

7 miles SE of North Walsham off the B1159

From this small village a lane winds down through spectacular dunes to the sands at Eccles Beach and, a little further north, to Cart Gap with its gently sloping beach and colourful lines of beach huts. About four miles south of Lessingham stands a windmill that is not just the tallest in Norfolk, but in the whole of England. Eighty feet high and covering nine storeys, **Sutton Windmill** was built in the year of the French Revolution, 1789, and its millstones only finally ground to a halt in 1940.

Owner Chris Nunn and his family have also built up a fascinating private collection of artefacts which reflect the social history of Norfolk over the past 150 years or so. These are on display in the family's privately-owned Broadlands Museum, a magpie's nest in which you'll find anything from vintage kitchen and veterinary tools to a reconstructed Pharmacy Shop of the 1880s, complete with a fine collection of patent medicines, ointments and pills.

KINGS LYNN & WEST NORFOLK

THETFORD

Some 2,000 years ago, Thetford may well have been the site of **Boudica's Palace**. In the 1980s, excavations for building development at Gallows Hill, north of the town, revealed an Iron Age enclosure. It is so extensive it may well have been the capital of the Iceni tribe which gave the Romans so much trouble. Certainly, the town's strategic location at the meeting of the Rivers Thet and Little Ouse made it an important settlement for centuries. At the

time of the *Domesday Book*, 1086, Thetford was the sixth-largest town in the country and the seat of the Bishop of East Anglia, with its own castle, mint and pottery.

Of **Thetford Castle**, only the 80-feet motte remains, but it's worth climbing to the top of this mighty mound for the views across the town. An early Victorian traveller described Thetford as 'An ancient and princely little town ... one of the most charming country towns in England.' Despite major development all around, the heart of the town still fits that description, with a goodly number of medieval and Georgian houses presenting an attractive medley of flint and half-timbered buildings. Perhaps the most striking is the

•

In King Street, the Thomas Paine Statue commemorates the town's most famous son, born here in 1737. The revolutionary philosopher and author of **The Rights of Man** *emigrated to America in 1774, where he helped formulate the American Bill of Rights. Paine's democratic views were so detested in England that even ten years after his death in New York, the authorities refused permission for his admirer, William Cobbett, to have the remains buried in his home country. And it wasn't until the 1950s that Thetford finally got around to erecting a statue in his honour. Ironically for such a robust democrat, his statue stands in King Street and opposite The King's House, named after James I, who was a frequent visitor here between 1608 and 1618. At the Thomas Paine Hotel in White Hart Street, the room in which it is believed that Paine was born is now the Honeymoon Suite, complete with four-poster bed.*

•

Winter Sunset over Thetford Forest

Ancient House, Thetford

Even older than the Ancient House is the 12th century **Cluniac Priory** (English Heritage), now mostly in ruins but with an impressive 14th century gatehouse still standing. During the Middle Ages, Thetford could boast 24 churches; today, only three remain.

Thetford's industrial heritage is vividly displayed in the **Burrell Steam Museum**, in Minstergate, which has full-size steam engines regularly 'in steam', re-created workshops and many examples of vintage agricultural machinery. The Museum tells the story of the Burrell Steam Company, which formed the backbone of the town's industry from the late 18th to the early 20th centuries, their sturdy machines famous around the world.

To the west of Thetford stretches the 90 square miles of **Thetford Forest**, the most extensive lowland forest in Britain. The Forestry Commission began planting in 1922, and although the woodland is largely given over to conifers, with Scots and Corsican Pine and Douglas Fir predominating, oak, sycamore and beech can also be seen throughout. There is a particularly varied trail leading from the Forestry Commission Information Centre which has detailed information about this and other walks through the area. On the edge of the forest, about two miles west of Thetford, are the ruins of **Thetford Warren Lodge**, built around 1400. At that time a huge area here was preserved for farming rabbits, a major element of the medieval diet.

Ancient House Museum of Thetford Life in White Hart Street, a magnificent 15th century timber-framed house with superb carved oak ceilings. Some of the most interesting exhibits are replicas of the Thetford Treasure, a 4th century hoard of gold and silver jewellery discovered as recently as 1979 by an amateur archaeologist with a metal detector. The originals of these sumptuous artefacts are housed in the British Museum in London.

The vast warren was owned by the Abbot of Thetford Priory, and it was he who built the Lodge for his gamekeeper.

Still in the forest, reached by a footpath from the village of Santon Downham, are Grimes Graves (English Heritage), the earliest major industrial site to be discovered in Europe. At these unique Neolithic flint mines, Stone Age labourers extracted the materials for their sharp-edged axes and knives. It's a strange experience entering these 4,000 year old shafts which descend some 30 feet to an underground chamber. The experience is even better if you bring your own high-powered torch. Opening times are Thursday to Monday in March and October, daily from April to September. Tel: 01842 810656

AROUND THETFORD

MUNDFORD

8 miles NW of Thetford on the A1065/A134

Mundford is a large Breckland village of flint-built cottages, set on the northern edge of Thetford Forest and with the River Wissey running by. If you ever watch television, you've almost certainly seen Lynford Hall, a mile or so northwest of Mundford. It has provided an impressive location for scenes in *Dad's Army*; *Allo, Allo*; *You Rang My Lord?* and *Love on a Branch Line*, as well as featuring in numerous television commercials. The Hall is a superb Grade II listed mansion, built for the Lyne-Stevens family in 1885 (as a hunting-lodge,

incredibly) and designed in the Jacobean Renaissance style by William Burn.

THOMPSON

10 miles NE of Thetford on a minor road off the A1075

This is a quiet village with a marshy man-made lake, Thompson Water, and a wild common. **The Peddars Way** long-distance footpath passes about a mile to the west and, about the same distance to the northeast, the Church is a splendid early 14th century building notable for its fine carved screen and choice 17th century fittings.

WATTON

14 miles NE of Thetford on the A1075

Watton's striking town sign depicts the 'Babes in the Wood' of the famous nursery story. The story, which was already current hereabouts in the 1500s, relates that as Arthur Truelove lay dying he decided that the only hope for his two children was to leave them in the care of their uncle. Unfortunately, the uncle decided to help himself to their inheritance and paid two men to take the children into nearby **Wayland Wood** and kill them. In a moment of unexpected compassion, one of the men decided that he could not commit the dastardly act. He disposed of his accomplice instead, and abandoned the children in the wood to suffer whatever fate might befall them. Sadly, unlike the nursery tale in which the children find their way back home and live happily ever after, this unfortunate

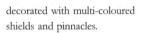

brother and sister perished. Their ghosts are said to wander hand in hand through the woods to this day.

Watton boasts an unusual Clock Tower, dated 1679, standing at the centre of its long main street.

EAST HARLING

8 miles E of Thetford on the B1111

This attractive little town boasts a beautiful 15th century church in a pastoral location beside the River Thet. Inside, a magnificent hammerbeam roof crowns the lofty nave, there's some outstanding 15th century glass and, in the Harling Chapel, the fine marble **Tomb of Robert Harling**. Harling was one of Henry V's knights, who met his death at the siege of Paris in 1435. Since this was long before the days of refrigeration, the knight's body was instead stewed, then stuffed into a barrel and brought back to East Harling for a ceremonious burial.

Harling's church houses another equally sumptuous memorial, the **Tomb of Sir Thomas Lovell**. Sculpted in alabaster, Sir Thomas is an imposing figure, clad in armour with a long sword, his head resting on a helmet, his feet on a spray of peacock's feathers. He and his wife lie beneath a wondrously ornamented canopy,

St Withburga's Well, Dereham

decorated with multi-coloured shields and pinnacles.

DEREHAM

One of the most ancient towns in the county, Dereham has a recorded history stretching back to AD 654 when St Withburga founded a Nunnery here. Her name lives on at **St Withburga's Well**, just to the west of the church. This is where she was laid to rest but, some 300 years later, the Abbot and monks of Ely robbed her grave and ensconced the precious, fundraising relic in their own Cathedral. In the saint's desecrated grave a spring suddenly bubbled forth, its waters possessed of miraculous healing properties, and St Withburga's shrine attracted even more pilgrims than before. Some still come.

In the church of St Nicholas, the second largest in Norfolk, there are features from every century from the 12th to the 16th: a magnificent lantern tower, a lofty Bell Tower, painted roofs, and a Seven Sacrament Font. This is the largest of these notable fonts, of which only 30 have survived - 28 of them in Norfolk and Suffolk.

In the northeast transept is buried a poet, some of whose lines have become embedded in the language:

"Variety's the very spice of life, that gives it all its flavour"

"I am the monarch of all I survey"

"God made the country and man made the town"

They all came from the pen of

William Cowper who, despite being the author of such cheery poems as John Gilpin ("A citizen of credit and renown"), suffered grievously from depression, a condition not improved by his association with John Newton, a former slave-trader who had repented and become 'a man of gloomy piety'. The two men collaborated on a book of hymns that included such perennial favourites as *"Oh! for a Closer Walk with God", "Hark, my soul, it is the Lord"* and *"God moves in a mysterious way"*. Cowper spent the last four years of his life at Dereham, veering in and out of madness. In a late-flowering romance he had married the widow Mary Unwin, but the strain of caring for the deranged poet drove her in turn to insanity and death. She, too, is buried in the church.

William Cowper died four years after Mary, in 1800. Three years later, another celebrated writer was born at the quaintly named hamlet of **Dumpling Green** on the edge of the town. George Borrow was to become one of the great English travel writers, producing books full of character and colour such as Wild Wales and The Bible in Spain. In his autobiographical novel Lavengro he begins with a warm recollection of the town where he was born:

"I love to think on thee, pretty, quiet D[ereham], thou pattern of an English market town, with thy clean but narrow streets branching out from thy modest market place, with thine old-fashioned houses, with here and there a roof of venerable thatch."

The house in which George Borrow was born, Borrow's Hall, still stands in Dumpling Green.

A character much less attractive than George Borrow connected with Dereham is Bishop Bonner, the enthusiastic arsonist of Protestant 'heretics' during the unhappy reign of Mary Tudor. He was rector of the town before being appointed Bishop of London, and he lived in the exquisite thatched terrace now called **Bishop Bonner's Cottage Museum**. The exterior is ornamented with delightful pargeting, a frieze of flower and fruit designs below the eaves, a form of decoration which is very unusual in Norfolk. The museum contains displays of local archaeology and the history of the town.

AROUND DEREHAM

GRESSENHALL

3 miles NW of Dereham off the B1146

The **Norfolk Rural Life Museum** is housed in an impressive late 18th century former workhouse built in rose-red brick. Gressenhall Workhouse was designed to accommodate some 700 unfortunates, so it was built on a very grand scale indeed. Now one of the UK's leading rural life museums and among Norfolk's top family attractions, there's ample room for the many exhibits illuminating the working and domestic life of Norfolk people over the last 150 years. Farming the old-fashioned way is there to be discovered on Union Farm, where heavy animals still work the fields. A stroll along the 1930s village high

The Mid-Norfolk Railway runs through 11 miles of attractive rural Norfolk linking the ancient market towns of Dereham and Wymondham, passing through river valleys and pretty villages and hamlets. The line running beyond Dereham to North Elmham and County School is under restoration. Most of the services are operated by heritage diesel railcars (DMUs) and heritage diesel locomotives, and the Railway offers the chance for visitors to fulfil childhood dreams by driving one of these diesels under supervision. 2005 saw the first running of steam locomotives 50 years after the withdrawal of steam from passenger services; a summer guest was the GWR pannier tank 9466 designed by Hawksworth and part of a class introduced in 1947. Tel: 01362 851723 for timetables, 01362 690633 for general enquiries.

35   THE QUEENS HEAD

Foulsham, nr Dereham

An attractive country pub serving well-kept ales and home-cooked favourites.

see page 246

street takes in the grocer's, post office and schoolroom. The surrounding 50 acres of unspoilt countryside are perfect for walking. The site hosts numerous special events during the season, ranging from Steam Days to an international folk dance festival with more than 200 dancers taking part.

A mile or so south of Gressenhall, the tiny community of **Dillington** is worth seeking out for **Norfolk Herbs** at Blackberry Farm, a specialist herb farm located in a beautiful wooded valley. Visitors are invited to browse through a vast collection of aromatic, culinary and medicinal herb plants, and to learn all about growing and using herbs.

NORTH ELMHAM

6 miles N of Dereham off the B1110

Near the village of North Elmham stand the sparse remains of a Saxon Cathedral. North Elmham was the seat of the Bishops of East Anglia until 1071, when they moved to Thetford (and then, 20 years later, to Norwich). Although there had been a cathedral here since the late 7th century, what has survived is mostly from the 11th century. Despite its grand title, the T-shaped ground plan reveals that the cathedral was no larger than a small parish church.

BRISLEY

7 miles N of Dereham on the B1145

Brisley village is well known to local historians and naturalists for its huge expanse of heathland, some 170 acres of it. It's reckoned to be the best example of unspoilt

common in Norfolk, and at its centre are scores of pits that were dug out in medieval times to provide clay for the wattle-and-daub houses of the period. Another feature of interest in the village is Gately Manor (private), an Elizabethan manor house standing within the remains of a medieval moat, and yet another moated house at Old Hall Farm in the southwest corner of the green.

SWAFFHAM

Swaffham's one-time claim to be the 'Montpellier of England' was justified by the abundance of handsome Georgian houses that used to surround the large, wedge-shaped market place. A good number still survive, along with the **Assembly Room** of 1817 where the quality would foregather for concerts, balls and soirees. The central focus of the market square is the elegant **Butter Cross**, presented to the town by the Earl of Orford in 1783. It's not a cross at all, but a classical lead-covered dome standing on eight columns and surmounted by a life-size statue of Ceres, the Roman goddess of agriculture - an appropriate symbol for this busy market town, from which ten roads radiate out across the county.

From the market place an avenue of limes leads to the quite outstanding **Church of St Peter & St Paul**, a 15th century masterpiece with one of the very best double hammerbeam roofs in the county, strikingly embellished with a host of angels, their wings widespread. The

Swaffham Butter Cross

unknown mason who devised the church's harmonious proportions made it 51 feet wide, 51 feet high and 102 feet long. Carved on a bench-end here is a man in medieval dress accompanied by a dog on a chain. The same two figures are incorporated in the town's coat of arms, and also appear in the elegantly designed town sign just beyond the market place.

Howard Carter, the man who discovered the tomb of Tutankhamen, was born at Swaffham in 1874; his death in 1939 was attributed by the popular press to 'the Curse of Tutankhamen'. If so, it must have been an extremely slow-acting curse. Some 17 years had elapsed since Carter had knelt by a dark, underground opening,

swivelled his torch and found himself the first human being in centuries to gaze upon the astonishing treasures buried in the tomb of the teenage Pharaoh.

Swaffham Museum in the Town Hall, recently fully refurbished, is the setting for the story of the town's past. Visitors can follow Howard Carter's road to the Valley of the Kings, see the Symonds Collection of handmade figurines, and admire the Sporle collection of locally-found artefacts.

Move on some 1,400 years from the death of Tutankhamen to Norfolk in the 1st century AD. Before a battle, members of the Iceni tribe, led by Boudica, would squeeze the blue sap of the woad plant onto their faces in the hope of frightening the Roman invaders (or any other of their many enemies). At **Cockley Cley Iceni Village and Museums**, three miles southwest of Swaffham off the A1065, archaeologists have reconstructed a village of Boudica's time, complete with wooden huts, moat, drawbridge and palisades. Reconstruction though it is, the village is remarkably effective in evoking a sense of what daily life entailed more than 1,900 years ago. The exhibits cover many centuries, up to the Second World War.

•

The figure on the town sign is 'The Pedlar of Swaffham', a certain John Chapman who, according to legend, dreamed that if he made his way to London Bridge he would meet a stranger who would make him rich. The pedlar and his dog set off for London, and on the bridge he was eventually accosted by a stranger who asked him what he was doing there. John recounted his dream. Scoffingly, the stranger said 'If I were a dreamer, I should go to Swaffham. Recently I dreamt that in Swaffham lived a man named Chapman, and in his garden, buried under a tree, lay a treasure.' John hastily returned home, uprooted the only tree in his garden, and unearthed two jugs full of gold coins. There was indeed a John Chapman who contributed generously to the building of the parish church in the late 1400s. Cynics claim that he was a wealthy merchant, and that similar tales occur in the folklore of most European countries. Whatever the truth, there's no doubt that the people of Swaffham took the story to their hearts.

•

A more recent addition to Swaffham's attractions is the EcoTech Discovery Centre, opened in 1998. Through intriguing interactive displays and hands-on demonstrations, visitors can discover what startling innovations current, and possible, technology may have in store for us during the next millennium.

AROUND SWAFFHAM

CASTLE ACRE

4 miles N of Swaffham off the A1065

Set on a hill surrounded by water meadows, Castle Acre seems still to linger in the Middle Ages. William de Warenne, William the Conqueror's son-in-law, came here very soon after the Conquest and built a Castle that was one of the first, and largest, in the country to be built by the Normans. Of that vast fortress, little remains apart from the gargantuan earthworks and a squat 13th century gateway.

Castle Acre Priory

Much more has survived of **Castle Acre Priory**, founded in 1090 and set in fields beside the River Nar. Its glorious West Front gives a powerful indication of how majestic a triumph of late Norman architecture the complete Priory must have been. With five apses and twin towers, the ground plan was modelled on the Cluniac mother church in Burgundy, where William de Warenne had stayed while making a pilgrimage to Rome. Despite the Priory's great size, it appears that perhaps as few as 25 monks lived here during the Middle Ages - and in some comfort, judging by the well-preserved Prior's House, which has its own bath and built-in wash-basin.

Castle Acre Priory lay on the main route to the famous Shrine at Walsingham, with which it tried to compete by offering pilgrims a rival attraction in the form of an arm of St Philip.

Today the noble ruins of the Priory are powerfully atmospheric, a brooding scene skilfully exploited by Roger Corman when he filmed here for his screen version of Edgar Allan Poe's ghostly story, *The Tomb of Ligeia*. The walled herb garden is divided into four sections containing medicinal, decorative, culinary and strewing herbs.

Castle Acre village is extremely picturesque, the first place in Norfolk to be designated a Conservation Area, in 1971. Most of the village, including the 15th century parish church, is built in traditional flint, with a few later houses of brick blending in remarkably happily.

LITCHAM

11 miles NE of Swaffham on the B1145

Small though it is, this village strung alongside the infant River Nar can boast an intriguing **Village Museum**, with displays of local artefacts from Roman times to the present, an extensive collection of photographs, some of which date back to 1865, and an underground lime kiln.

KING'S LYNN

In the opinion of James Lee-Milne, the National Trust's architectural authority, 'The finest old streets anywhere in England' are to be found at King's Lynn. Tudor, Jacobean and Flemish houses mingle harmoniously with grand medieval churches and stately civic buildings. It's not surprising that the BBC chose the town to represent early 19th century London in their production of Martin Chuzzlewit. It seems, though, that word of this ancient sea-port's many treasures has not yet been widely broadcast, so most visitors to the area tend to stay on the King's Lynn bypass while making their way to the better-known attractions of the north Norfolk coast. They are missing a lot.

The best place to start an exploration of the town is at the beautiful **Church of St Margaret**, founded in 1101 and with a remarkable leaning arch of that

original building still intact. The architecture is impressive, but the church is especially famous for its two outstanding 14th century brasses, generally reckoned to be the two largest and most monumental in the kingdom. Richly engraved, one shows workers in a vineyard, the other, commemorating Robert Braunche, represents the great feast which Robert hosted at King's Lynn for Edward III in 1364.

Marks on the tower doorway indicate the church's, and the town's, vulnerability to the waters of the Wash and the River Great Ouse. They show the high-water levels reached during the great floods of 11 March 1883 (the lowest), 31 January 1953 and 11 January, 1978.

Alongside the north wall of St Margaret's is the Saturday Market Place, one of the town's two market places, where visitors can explore the **Old Gaol House**, an experience complete with the sights and sounds of the ancient cells.

●

The organist at St Margaret's in the mid 18th century was the celebrated writer on music, Dr Charles Burney, but his daughter Fanny was perhaps even more interesting. She wrote a best-selling novel, Evelina, at the age of 25, became a leading light of London society, a close friend of Dr Johnson and Sir Joshua Reynolds, and at the age of 59 underwent an operation for breast cancer without anaesthetic. She only fainted once during the 20-minute operation, and went on to continue her active social life until her death at the ripe old age of 87.

●

Guildhall of the Holy Trinity, King's Lynn

45

At Walpole St Peter, between the A17 and A47, the church known as the 'Queen of the Marshland' is a graceful Perpendicular church with many treasures, including a font with an exotic Jacobean cover, a cobbled covered passageway and two aisle chapels in the nave; St Peter's has a rare example of a hudd, a portable cubicle to protect the priest from rain during burial.

You can also admire the municipal regalia. The greatest treasure in this collection is King John's Cup, a dazzling piece of medieval workmanship with coloured enamel scenes set in gold. The Cup was supposed to be part of King John's treasure which had been lost in 1215 when his overburdened baggage train was crossing the Nene Estuary and sank into the treacherous quicksands. This venerable legend is sadly undermined by the fact that the Cup was not made until 1340, more than a century after John's death.

A few steps further is one of the most striking sights in the town, the **Guildhall of the Holy Trinity** with its distinctive chequerboard design of black flint and white stone. The Guildhall was built in 1421, extended in Elizabethan times, and its Great Hall is still used today for wedding ceremonies and various civic events. It is also home to the King's Lynn Arts Centre, active all year round with events and exhibitions and since 1951 the force behind an annual Arts Festival in July with concerts, theatre and a composer in residence. Some of the concerts are held in St Nicholas' Chapel, a medieval building whose acoustics outmatch those of many a modern concert hall.

Next door to the Guildhall is the Town Hall of 1895, which in a good-neighbourly way is constructed in the same flint-and-stone pattern. The Town Hall also houses the **Museum of Lynn Life** telling the story of the town's 900 years.

A short distance from the Town Hall, standing proudly by itself on the banks of the River Purfleet, is the handsome **Custom House** of 1683, designed by the celebrated local architect Henry Bell. Among other important buildings are the Hanseatic Warehouse (1428), the South Gate (1440), the Greenland Fishery Building (1605), and the Guildhall of St George, built around 1406 and reputedly the largest civic hall in England. The Hall was from time to time also used as a theatre; it's known that Shakespeare's travelling company played here, and it is considered highly likely that the Bard himself trod the boards.

At Caithness Crystal Visitor Centre, you can watch craftsmen at close quarters as they shape and manipulate glass into beautiful objets d'art.

AROUND KING'S LYNN

TERRINGTON ST CLEMENT

5 miles W of King's Lynn off the A17

Terrington St Clement is a sizable village notable for its superb church, a 14th century Gothic masterwork more properly known as St Clement's Church, and for the **African Violet and Garden Centre**, where some quarter of a million violets are grown each year, in a wide range of colour and species. This unique working nursery, an all-seasons attraction, has earned many awards since opening in 1987, including Gold Medals at the Chelsea Flower Show.

STOW BARDOLPH

8 miles S of King's Lynn off the A10

Holy Trinity Church at Stow Bardolph houses one of the oddest memorials in the country. Before her death in 1744, Sarah Hare, youngest daughter of the Lord of the Manor, Sir Thomas Hare, arranged for a life-sized effigy of herself to be made in wax. It was said to be an exceptionally good likeness: if so, Sarah appears to have been a rather uncomely maiden, and afflicted with boils to boot. Her death was attributed to blood poisoning after she had pricked her finger with a needle, an act of Divine retribution, apparently, for her sin of sewing on a Sunday. Sarah was then attired in a dress she had chosen herself, placed in a windowed mahogany cabinet, and the monument set up in the Hare family's chapel, a grandiose structure which is larger than the chancel of the church itself.

DOWNHAM MARKET

10 miles S of King's Lynn off the A10/A1122

Once the site for a major horse fair, this compact little market town stands at the very edge of the Fens, with the River Great Ouse and the New Bedford Drain running side by side at its western edge. Many of its houses are built in the distinctive brick and carrstone style of the area. One of the finest examples of this traditional use of local materials can be seen at Dial House in Railway Road, built in the late 1600s.

The parish church has managed to find a small hill on which to perch. It's an unassuming building with a rather incongruously splendid glass chandelier from the 1730s. The town square has recently been regenerated and in it stands the elegant, riotously decorated cast-iron Clock. This was erected in 1878 at a cost of £450 and now chimes on the hour. The tower's backdrop of attractive cottages provides a charming setting for a holiday snap.

Near Downham Bridge on the A1122 you will find **Collectors World** and the **Magical Dickens World**. The first boasts a plethora of farming and household memorabilia, carts, carriages, radios, cameras, antique and collectable dolls, Armstrong Siddeley cars and much more, with rooms dedicated to Barbara Cartland, Horatio Nelson, the 1960s and more. Dickens World offers visitors a chance to step back in time into a maze of late 19th century streets, shops, sights and sounds.

DENVER

2 miles S of Downham Market off the A10/A1122

Denver Sluice was originally built in 1651 by the Dutch engineer, Cornelius Vermuyden, as part of a scheme to drain 20,000 acres of land owned by the Duke of Bedford. Various modifications were made to the system over the years, but the principle remains the same, and the oldest surviving sluice, built in 1834, is still in use today. Running parallel with it is the

36 THE MARSHLAND ARMS

Marshland St James, nr Wisbech

Traditional pub fare cooked by the host brings an appreciative band of regulars to this attractive old village inn.

see page 247

Poppy Field, Denver

37   THE WINE LODGE

Feltwell

Loyal locals and first-timers enjoy exceptional hospitality at the 17th century Wine Lodge. Also rooms for B&B.

🍴 🛏 *see page 248*

modern Great Denver Sluice, opened in 1964; together these two sluices control the flow of a large complex of rivers and drainage channels, and are able to divert floodwaters into the Flood Relief Channel that runs alongside the Great Ouse.

The two great drainage cuts constructed by Vermuyden are known as the Old and New Bedford rivers, and the strip of land between them, never more than 1,000 yards wide, is called the Ouse Washes. This is deliberately allowed to flood during the winter months so that the fields on either side remain dry. The drains run side by side for more than 13 miles, to Earith in Cambridgeshire, and this has become a favourite route for walkers, with a rich variety of bird, animal and insect life to be seen along the way.

Denver Windmill, built in 1835 but put out of commission in

1941, when the sails were struck by lightning, re-opened in 2000. This wonderful working mill set on the edge of the Fens has been carefully restored. On-site attractions include a visitor centre, craft workshops, bakery and tea shop. Holiday accommodation is also available.

HILGAY

3 miles S of Downham Market off the A10

When the *Domesday Book* was written, Hilgay was recorded as one of only two settlements in the Norfolk fens. It was then an island, its few houses planted on a low hill rising from the surrounding marshland. The village is scarcely any larger today, and collectors of unusual gravestones make their way to its churchyard seeking the last resting place of George William Manby. During the Napoleonic wars, Manby invented a rocket-powered life-line that could be fired to ships in distress. His gravestone is carved with a ship, an anchor, a depiction of his rocket device and an inscription that ends with the reproachful words, 'The public should have paid this tribute.'

OXBOROUGH

10 miles SE of Downham Market off the A134

How many hamlets in the country, one wonders, can boast two such different buildings of note as those to be seen at Oxborough? First there's the **Church of St John the Evangelist**, remarkable for its rare brass eagle lectern of 1498 and its glorious Bedingfeld Chapel of 1525, sheltering twin monuments to Sir Edmund Bedingfeld and his wife fashioned in the then newly popular material of terracotta.

It was Sir Edmund who built **Oxburgh Hall** (National Trust), a stunning moated house built of pale-rose brick and white stone. Sir Edmund's descendants still live in what a later architect, Pugin, described as 'one of the noblest specimens of domestic architecture of the 15th century.' Henry VII and his Queen, Elizabeth of York, visited in 1497 and lodged in the splendid State Apartments which form a bridge between the glorious gatehouse towers, and which ever since have been known as the King's Room and the Queen's Room. On display here is the original Charter of 1482, affixed with Edward IV's Great Seal of England, granting Sir Edmund permission to build with 'stone, lime and sand', and to fortify the building with battlements. These rooms also house some magnificent period furniture, a collection of royal letters to the Bedingfelds, and the huge Sheldon Tapestry Map of 1647 showing Oxfordshire and Berkshire. Another more poignant tapestry, known as the Marian Needlework, was the joint handiwork of Bess of Hardwick and Mary, Queen of Scots, during the latter's captivity here in 1570.

The Bedingfelds seemed always to draw the short straw when the Tudors needed someone to discharge an unpleasant or difficult task. It was an earlier Sir Edmund who was charged with the care of Henry VIII's discarded wife, Catherine of Aragon; Edmund's

Oxburgh Hall, Oxborough

son, Sir Henry, was given the even more onerous task of looking after the King's official bastard, the Princess Elizabeth. After Elizabeth's accession as Queen, Sir Henry presented himself at Court, no doubt with some misgivings. Elizabeth received him civilly but, as he was leaving, tartly observed that 'if we have any prisoner whom we would have hardlie and strictly kept, we will send him to you.'

As staunch Catholics, the Bedingfelds were, for the next two and a half centuries, consigned to the margins of English political life. Their estates dwindled as portions were sold to meet the punitive taxes imposed on adherents of the Old Faith. By the middle of the 20th century, the Bedingfelds' long tenure of Oxburgh was drawing to a close. In 1951 the 9th Baronet, another Sir Edmund, sold Oxburgh to a builder, who promptly announced his intention of demolishing the house. Sir Edmund's mother, the Dowager Lady Sybil, was shocked by such

The grounds at Oxburgh Hall provide the perfect foil for the mellow old building, reflected in its broad moat. There's a wonderfully formal and colourful French garden, a walled kitchen garden, and woodland walks.

38 CASTLE RISING CASTLE

Castle Rising

Explore the imposing keep and vast earthworks of this Norman castle.

 see page 248

vandalism and used her considerable powers of persuasion to raise sufficient funds to buy back the house. She then conveyed it into the safe keeping of the National Trust.

CASTLE RISING

5 miles NE of King's Lynn
off the A148/A149

As the bells ring for Sunday morning service at Castle Rising, a group of elderly ladies leave the mellow redbrick Bede House and walk in procession to the church. They are all dressed in long scarlet cloaks, emblazoned on the left breast with a badge of the Howard family arms. Once a year, on Founder's Day, they add to their regular Sunday costume a tall-crowned hat typical of the Jacobean period, just like those worn in stereotypical pictures of broomstick-flying witches.

These ladies are the residents of the almshouses founded by Henry Howard, Earl of Northampton in 1614, and their

regular Sunday attendance at church was one of the conditions he imposed on the original 11 needy spinsters who were to enjoy his beneficence. Howard also required that each inmate of his 'Hospital of the Holy and Undivided Trinity' must be 'be able to read, if such a one may be had, single, 56 at least, no common beggar, harlot, scold, drunkard, haunter of taverns, inns or alehouses'.

The weekly *tableau vivant* of this procession to the church seems completely in keeping with this picturesque village, which rates high on any 'not to be missed' list of places to visit in Norfolk. The church to which the women make their way, St Lawrence's, is an outstanding example of Norman and Early English work, even though much of it has been reconstructed. But overshadowing everything else in this pretty village is the massive **Castle Keep**, its well-preserved walls rising 50 feet high, and pierced by a single entrance. The Keep's towering presence is made even more formidable by the huge earthworks on which it stands. The Castle was built in 1150, guarding what was then the sea approach to the River Ouse. (The marshy shore is now some three miles distant and still retreating.)

Despite its fortress-like appearance, Castle Rising was much more of a residential building than a defensive one. In 1331, when Edward III found it necessary to banish his ferocious

Castle Keep, Castle Rising

French-born mother, Isabella, to some reasonably comfortable place of safety, he chose this far-from-London castle. She was to spend some 27 years here before her death in 1358. How could Edward treat his own mother in such a way? Her crime, in his view, was that the 'She-Wolf of France', as all her enemies and many of her friends called Isabella, had joined forces with her lover Mortimer against her homosexual husband Edward II (young Edward's father) and later colluded in the king's grisly murder at Berkeley Castle. For three years after that loathsome assassination, Isabella and Mortimer ruled England as Regents. The moment Edward III achieved his majority, he had Mortimer hung, drawn and quartered. His mother he despatched to a lonely retirement at Castle Rising.

The spacious grounds around the castle provide an appropriate backdrop for an annual display by members of the White Society. Caparisoned in colourful medieval garments and armed with more-or-less authentic replicas of swords and halberds, these modern White Knights stage a battle for control of the castle.

SANDRINGHAM

8 miles NE of King's Lynn off the A149/B1140

A couple of miles north of Castle Rising is the entrance to **Sandringham**, the Royal Family's charming country retreat. Unlike the State Rooms at Windsor Castle and Buckingham Palace, where visitors marvel at the awesome trappings of majesty, at Sandringham they can savour the atmosphere of a family home. The rooms the visitor sees at Sandringham are those used by the royal family when in residence, complete with family portraits and photographs, and comfy armchairs. Successive royal owners have furnished the house with an intriguing medley of the grand, the domestic and the unusual. Entering the principal reception room, The Saloon, for example, you pass a weighing-machine with a leather-covered seat, apparently a common amenity in great houses of the 19th century. In the same room, with its attractively carved Minstrels' Gallery, hangs a fine family portrait by one of Queen Victoria's favourite artists, Heinrich von Angeli. It shows the Prince of Wales (later Edward VII), his wife Alexandra and two of their children, with Sandringham in the background. New and exclusive for 2007 is a collection of landscapes by Their Royal Highnesses the Duke of Edinburgh and the Prince of Wales.

The Prince first saw Sandringham on 4th February 1862. At Victoria's instigation, the 20-year-old heir to the throne had been searching for some time for a country property, a refuge of the kind his parents already enjoyed at Balmoral and Osborne. A courtier accompanying the Prince reported back that although the outside of

Just across from Sandringham House, the old coach-houses and stables have been converted into a fascinating museum. There are some truly splendid royal vehicles here, including a 1900 Daimler, the first car owned by a member of the royal family, and a splendid Merrywaether fire engine once used by the estate's own fire brigade, the old estate game cart, several children's cars, game trophies, stunning Arts & Crafts ceramic tiles and plaques designed for the now-vanished Dairy, commemorative china and an evocative series of old photographs depicting the life of the royal family at Sandringham from 1862 until Christmas 1951. Other attractions at Sandringham include a visitor centre, adventure playground, nature walks, souvenir shop, plant centre, restaurant and tearoom.

Sandringham

Sandringham House is the charming country retreat of Her Majesty The Queen hidden in the heart of sixty acres of beautiful wooded gardens.

 see *page 249*

Dersingham

The **Feathers** offers a pleasant, relaxing stay with good food and prompt, personal service.

see *page 248*

house was ugly, it was pleasant and convenient within, and set in pretty grounds. The surrounding countryside was plain, he went on, but the property was in excellent order and the opportunity of securing it should not be missed. Within days, the purchase was completed.

Most of the 'ugly' house disappeared a few years later when the Prince rebuilt the main residence; the 'pretty grounds' have matured into one of the most beautiful landscaped areas in the country. And the 'plain' countryside around - open heath and grassland overrun by rabbits - has been transformed into a wooded country park, part of the coastal Area of Outstanding Natural Beauty.

One of the additions the Prince made to the house in 1883 was a Ballroom, much to the relief of Princess Alexandra. 'It is beautiful I think & a great success.' she wrote, '& avoids pulling the hall to pieces each time there is a ball or anything'. This attractive room is now used for cinema shows and the estate workers' Christmas party. Displayed on the walls is a remarkable collection of Indian weapons, presented to the Prince during his state visit in 1875-6; hidden away in a recess are the two flags planted at the South Pole by the Shackleton expedition.

DERSINGHAM

9 miles NE of King's Lynn off the A149

This large village just north of Sandringham was actually the source of the latter's name: in the *Domesday Book*, the manor was inscribed as 'Sant-Dersingham'. Norfolk tongues found 'Sandringham' much easier to get around. Dersingham village has expanded greatly in recent years and modern housing has claimed much of Dersingham Common, although there are still many pleasant walks here through Dersingham Wood and the adjoining Sandringham Country Park.

SNETTISHAM

11 miles N of King's Lynn off the A149

Snettisham is best known nowadays for its spacious, sandy beaches and the **RSPB Bird Sanctuary**, both about two miles west of the village itself. But for centuries Snettisham was much more famous as a prime quarry for carrstone, an attractive soft-red building-block that provided the 'light relief' for the walls of thousands of Georgian houses around the country, and for nearby Sandringham House. The carrstone quarry is still working, its product now destined mainly for 'goldfish ponds and the entrance-banks of the more pretentious types of bungalow'. Unfortunately, one has to go to the British Museum in London to see Snettisham's greatest gift to the national heritage: an opulent collection of gold and silver ornaments from the 1st century AD, the largest hoard of treasure trove ever found in Britain, discovered here in 1991.

HEACHAM

13 miles N of King's Lynn off the A149

Heacham Park Fishery on Pocahontas Lake is set within the original boundary of Heacham Hall. This three-and-a-half acre freshwater lake was re-established in 1996. Spring 1997 saw the introduction to the lake of specimen carp, to be followed in 1998 by rudd, bream, perch and roach. The lake takes its name from the renowned Native American princess, who married into the Rolfe family, owners of Heacham Hall, and lived here in the 1600s.

Just outside the charming village of Heacham is the famous Norfolk Lavender, the largest lavender-growing and distilling operation in the country. Established in 1932, it is also the oldest. The information point at the western entrance is sited in an attractive listed building, a Victorian watermill that has become something of a Norfolk landmark. On entering the site, visitors instinctively breathe in, savouring the unmistakable aroma that fills the air. The centre is open all year round, and guided tours of the grounds run throughout the day in the summer; and during the lavender harvest, visitors can tour the distillery and see how the wonderful fragrance is made. Among other attractions at Norfolk Lavender are a Fragrant Meadow Garden, Fragrant Plant Centre, Herb Garden, a gift shop selling a wide variety of products, and a tearoom serving cream teas and even lavender-and-lemon scones!

FAKENHAM

Fakenham is a busy and prosperous-looking market town, famous for its National Hunt Racecourse, antique & bric-a-brac markets and auctions, and as a major agricultural centre for the region. Straddling the River Wensum, this attractive country town has a number of fine late-18th and early-19th century brick buildings in and around the Market Place. And it must surely be one of the few towns in England where the former gasworks (still intact) have been turned into the **Museum of Gas & Local History**, housing an impressive historical display of domestic gas appliances of every kind. Fakenham Church also has an unusual feature, a powder room - a room over the large porch, built in 1497, used for storing gunpowder. Even older than the church is the 700-year-old hunting lodge, built for the Duchy of Lancaster, which is now part of the Crown Hotel. As an antidote to the idea that Norfolk is unremittingly flat, reinforced by Noel Coward in his Private Lives, take the B1105 north out of Fakenham and after about half a mile take the first minor road to the left. This quiet road loops over and around the rolling hills, a 10-mile drive of wonderfully soothing countryside that ends at Wells-next-the-Sea.

41 CHENEY HOLLOW COTTAGES

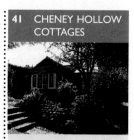

Heacham
Two well-equipped cottages provide a friendly, relaxed base for a self-catering holiday.

see page 249

42 SCULTHORPE MILL

Sculthorpe, nr Fakenham
An atmospheric converted mill with real ales, bar and restaurant menus and six rooms for B&B guests.

see page 250

AROUND FAKENHAM

Ten miles southeast of Fakenham, signposted from the A1067 Norwich to Fakenham road, the Norfolk Wildlife Trust's Foxley Wood is Norfolk's largest ancient woodland and is thought to be 6,000 years old. Visitors can see many varieties of wild flowers, butterflies and birds, including sparrowhawks, tawny owls and – with luck – great spotted and green woodpeckers. Open daily (except Thursdays) 10am to 5pm.

A mile southeast of Fakenham, on the A1067, lies **Penthorpe, the Natural Centre of Norfolk**. The aim of its owners is to combine world-class wildlife conservation, fabulous gardens, sustainable farming and fantastic food in a truly memorable visitor experience. The multi-award-winning attraction really does provide a wonderful day out at any time of the year. More than 70 species of birds breed here in the spring and summer, while autumn and winter see hundreds of migratory birds. The Conservation centre has the largest collection of cranes in the UK and works with other organisations on the 'great crane project', which aims to accelerate the re-establishment of the European crane into the British countryide. The site includes wonderful gardens, beautiful lakes, tranquil woodland, nature trails, water meadows, wild flowers, birds, bees, butterflies and dragonflies, a café and a gift shop. The centre is open from 10 to 5 (till 4 between January and March).

EAST RAYNHAM

3 miles SW of Fakenham, on the A1065

Raynham Hall is another superb Palladian mansion, designed by Inigo Jones and with magnificent rooms created a century later by William Kent. The house is only open to the public by appointment since it is the private residence of the 7th Marquess of Townshend. It was his 18th century ancestor, the 2nd Viscount (better known as 'Turnip' Townshend), who revolutionised English agriculture by promoting the humble turnip as an effective means of reclaiming untended land for feeding cattle in winter, and along with wheat, barley and clover, as part of the four-year rotation of crops that provided a cycle of essential nutrients for the soil. The Townshend family have owned extensive estates in this area for centuries, and in St Mary's Church there are some fine monuments to their ancestors, the oldest and most sumptuous of which commemorates Sir Roger, who died in 1493.

TATTERFORD

5 miles SW of Fakenham off the A148 or A1065

This tiny village is well known to botanists for **Tatterford Common**, an unspoilt tract of rough heathland with tiny ponds, some wild apple trees and the River Tat running through it to join the River Wensum about a mile away.

About four miles west of Tatterford stands **Houghton Hall**, home of the Marquess of Cholmondely and one of the country's most magnificent buildings. This glorious demi-palace was built in the Palladian style during the 1720s by Sir Robert Walpole, England's first Prime Minister. The Walpoles had been gentlemen of substance here since the 14th century. With his family revenues augmented by the considerable profits Sir Robert extracted from his political office, he was in a position to spend lavishly and ostentatiously on his new house. The first step was to destroy completely the village of Houghton (it spoilt the view), and re-house the villagers a mile away at New Houghton.

Although Sir Robert deliberately cultivated the manner of a bluff, down-to-earth Norfolk squire, the personal decisions he made regarding the design and furnishings of the house reveal a man of deep culture and refined tastes. It was he who insisted that the Hall could not be built in homely Norfolk brick, and took the expensive decision to use the exceptionally durable stone quarried at Aislaby in North Yorkshire and transport it by sea from Whitby to King's Lynn. More than two and a half centuries later, the Aislaby stone is still flawless, the only sign of its age a slight weathering that has softened its colour to a creamy gold.

To decorate the interior and design the furniture, Sir Robert commissioned the versatile William Kent. Kent was at the peak of his powers - just look at the decoration in the Stone Hall, the exquisite canopied bed in the Green Velvet Bedchamber, and the finely-carved woodwork throughout which made impressive use of the newly-discovered hardwood called mahogany. And then there were the paintings, an incomparable collection of Old Masters personally selected by Sir Robert. Sadly, many of them are now in the

Hermitage Museum in St Petersburg, sold by his wastrel grandson to the Empress Catherine of Russia.

This grandson, George, 3rd Earl of Orford, succeeded to the title at the age of 21 and spent the next 40 years dissipating his enormous inheritance. When his uncle Horace (the 4th Earl, better known as Horace Walpole, novelist, MP and inveterate gossip) succeeded to the title he found 'Houghton half a ruin ... the two great staircases exposed to all weathers; every room in the wings rotting with wet; the park half-covered with nettles and weeds; mortgages swallowing the estate, and a debt of above £40,000.'

Houghton's decline was arrested when the Hall passed by marriage to the Marquess of Cholmondely, Lord Great Chamberlain, in 1797. But it wasn't until 1913, when George, later the 5th Marquess, moved into the house with his new wife, Sybil Sassoon, that Houghton was fully restored to its former state of grace. The depleted collection of paintings was augmented with fine works by Sir Joshua Reynolds and others from Cholmondely Castle in Cheshire, and the Marchioness introduced new collections of exquisite French furniture and porcelain.

LITTLE WALSINGHAM

5 miles N of Fakenham on the B1105

Every year, some half a million pilgrims make their way to this little village of just over 500 souls, noted

One of the interests of the 6th Marquess was military history, and in 1928 he began the astonishing Model Soldiers Collection now on display at Houghton. More than 20,000 perfectly preserved models are deployed in meticulous reconstructions of battles such as Culloden and Waterloo, and in one exhibit, re-creating the Grand Review of the British Army in 1895, no fewer than 3,000 figures are on parade. St Martin's Church at the Hall contains the Walpole family vault, where Sir Robert and his youngest son Horace are buried.

43 THE WHITE HORSE INN

East Barsham, nr Fakenham

The **White Horse Inn** sets high standards in food, drink and accommodation in a quiet, attractive setting.

see page 251

In 1511, the same year that Erasmus visited, Henry VIII also made the pilgrimage that all his royal predecessors since Richard I had undertaken. He stayed overnight at the enchanting early-Tudor mansion, East Barsham Hall, a glorious medley of mullioned windows, towers, turrets, and a group of 10 chimneys, each one individually carved with an amazing variety of styles. After his overnight stay at East Barsham Hall, Henry VIII, like most other pilgrims, went first to the Slipper Chapel, a beautiful 14th century building about a mile away in Houghton St Giles. Here he removed his shoes and completed the last stretch on foot. Despite this show of piety, some 25 years later Henry had no hesitation in closing the Priory along with all the other monastic institutions in his realm, seizing its treasures and endowments, and having its image of the Virgin publicly burnt at Chelsea.

for its impressive timber-framed buildings and fine Georgian façades, to worship at the **Shrine of Our Lady of Walsingham**. In 1061 the Lady of the Manor of Walsingham, Lady Richeldis de Faverches, had a vision of the Holy Virgin in which she was instructed to build a replica of the Holy House in Nazareth, the house in which the Archangel Gabriel had told Mary that she would be the mother of Christ. Archaeologists have located the original house erected by Lady Richeldis. It was just 13 feet by 23 feet and made of wood, later to be enclosed in stone.

These were the years of the Crusades, and the **Holy House** at Walsingham soon became a major centre of pilgrimage, because it was regarded by the pious as an authentic piece of the Holy Land. Around 1153, an **Augustinian Priory** was established to protect the shrine, now encrusted with jewels, gold and silver, and to provide accommodation for the pilgrims. The Priory is in ruins now but the largest surviving part, a stately Gatehouse on the east side of the High Street, is very impressive.

For almost 500 years, Walsingham prospered. Erasmus of Rotterdam visited in 1511 and was critical of the rampant commercialisation of the Shrine with its plethora of bogus relics and religious souvenirs for sale. He was shown a gigantic bone, 'the finger-joint of St Peter' no less, and in return for a small piece of

translation was presented with a highly aromatic fragment of wood - a sliver of a bench on which the Virgin had once seated herself.

Little Walsingham itself is an exceptionally attractive village, set in the midst of parks and woodlands, with the interesting 16th century octagonal **Clink in Common Place**, used in medieval times as a lock-up for petty offenders, and the scant ruins of Walsingham's **Franciscan Friary** of 1347. In the 1770s the friary was converted into the shire hall for the quarter sessions, a role it filled until 1861; the petty sessions continued until 1971. The early-16th century building that now houses the **Walsingham Shirehall Museum** was once used as a hostel for visitors to the Priory Church. In the 1770s it was converted in to the shirehall for the quarter and petty sessions; the courtroom has survived unaltered and is now part of the museum that includes a display of Walsingham as a place of pilgrimage since 1061. It is also the entrance to the Abbey grounds.

GREAT WALSINGHAM

5 miles N of Fakenham on the B1388

English place names observe a logic of their own, so Great Walsingham is of course smaller than Little Walsingham. The two villages are very different in atmosphere and appearance, Great Walsingham displaying the typical layout of a rural Norfolk settlement, with attractive cottages set around a green watered by the River Stiffkey, and dominated by the fine 14th century **Church of St Peter**, noted for its superb window tracery, wondrously carved Norman font, and perfectly preserved 15th century carved benches.

WIGHTON

7 miles N of Fakenham, on the B1105

Just outside the village, the Wells to Walsingham Light Railway trundles its way between Little Walsingham and Wells-next-the-Sea. The longest 10¼-inch narrow-gauge steam railway in the world, it runs throughout the summer along a 20-minute scenic journey through the North Norfolk countryside.

THURSFORD GREEN

4 miles NE of Fakenham off the A148

About two minutes' walk from Thursford Green stands what is perhaps the most unusual museum in Norfolk, the **Thursford Collection Sight and Sound Spectacular**. George Cushing began this extraordinary collection of steam-powered traction engines, fairground organs and carousels back in 1946 when 'one ton of tractor cost £1'. Perhaps the most astonishing exhibit is a 1931 Wurlitzer organ whose 1,339 pipes can produce an amazing repertoire of sounds - horses' hooves, fire engine sirens, claps of thunder, waves crashing on sand, and the toot-toot of an old railway engine are just some of the Wurlitzer's marvellous effects. There are regular live music shows when the Wurlitzer displays its virtuosity.

Other attractions include a steam-powered Venetian Gondola ride, shops selling a wide variety of goods, many of them locally made, and a tearoom. The Collection is open from 12 to 5 every day except Saturday.

GREAT SNORING

5 miles NE of Fakenham off the A148

The names of the twin villages, Great and Little Snoring, are such a perennial source of amusement to visitors it seems almost churlish to explain that they are derived from a Saxon family called Snear. At Great Snoring the main street rises from a bridge over the River Stiffkey and climbs up to St Mary's Church.

THE NORTHWEST COAST

Although the whole of Norfolk lies on a foundation of chalk, 1,000 feet deep in places, it is only in this northwest corner that it lies close enough to the surface to have been used as a building material. Once exposed to the air, the chalk, or 'clunch' as it's known, becomes a surprisingly durable material. It was widely used in medieval buildings and can still be found in many barns, farmhouses and cottages in the area. Chalk was also quarried and then burnt to produce lime, prodigious quantities of which were used in building the sublime churches of the Middle Ages.

•

A mile or so north of the Thursford museum, in the village of Hindringham, Mill Farm Rare Breeds is home to dozens of cattle, sheep, pigs, goats, ponies, poultry and waterfowl which were once commonplace but are now very rare. These intriguing creatures have some 30 acres of lovely countryside to roam around. Children are encouraged to feed the animals and there's also an adventure playground, crazy golf course, craft & gift shop, picnic area and tearoom.

•

**44   FISHERS OF
HUNSTANTON**

Hunstanton

Fish and chips cooked the traditional way keep the crowds happy at **Fishers of Huntingdon** in the centre of town.

see page 252

**45   THE WASH & TOPE
HOTEL**

Hunstanton

A main street location for a fine hostelry that's a great place for a d rink, a meal or a B&B stay.

see page 254

**46   THE WHITE
COTTAGE**

Old Hunstanton

Guests return again and again to enjoy the friendly ambience and home-from-home comfort of the **White Cottage** guest house.

 see page 253

HUNSTANTON

The busy seaside resort of Hunstanton can boast two unique features: one, it has the only cliffs in England made up of colourful levels of red, white and brown strata, and two, it is the only east coast resort that faces west, looking across The Wash to the Lincolnshire coast and the unmistakeable tower of the 272-feet high Boston Stump (more properly described as the Church of St Botolph).

Hunstanton town is a comparative newcomer, developed in the 1860s by Mr Hamon L'Estrange of nearby Hunstanton Hall to take advantage of the arrival of the railway here, and to exploit the natural appeal of its broad, sandy beaches. The centre is well-planned with mock-Tudor houses grouped around a green that falls away to the shore.

Hunstanton's social standing was assured after the Prince of Wales, later Edward VII, came here to recover from typhoid fever. He stayed at the Sandringham Hotel which, sadly, has since been demolished, along with the grand Victorian pier and the railway. But Hunston, as locals call the town, still has a distinct 19th century charm about it and plenty to entertain visitors.

The huge stretches of sandy beach, framed by those multi-coloured cliffs, are just heaven for children who will also be fascinated by the **Sea Life Sanctuary**, on Southern Promenade, where an underwater glass tunnel provides a fascinating opportunity to watch the varied and often weird forms of marine life that inhabit Britain's waters. A popular excursion from Hunstanton is the boat trip to Seal Island, a sandbank in The Wash where seals can indeed often be seen sunbathing at low tide.

AROUND HUNSTANTON

HOLME NEXT THE SEA

3 miles NE of Hunstanton, off the A149

This village is at the northern end of the **Peddars Way**, the 50-mile pedestrian trail that starts at the Suffolk border near Thetford and, almost arrow-straight for much of its length, slices across northwest Norfolk to Holme, with only an occasional deviation to negotiate a necessary ford or bridge. This determinedly straight route was already long-trodden for centuries before the Romans arrived, but they incorporated long stretches of it into their own network of roads. It was from the Latin word pedester that the route takes its name. With few gradients of any consequence to negotiate, the Peddars Way is ideal for the casual walker.

At Holme, the **Peddars Way** meets with the **Norfolk Coastal Footpath**, a much more recent creation. Starting at Hunstanton, it closely follows the coastline all the way to Cromer. Holme next the Sea is famous in part as the site of '**Sea Henge**', a 4,500-year-old Bronze Age tree circle discovered on Holme Beach. This early religious monument was removed by English Heritage for study and preservation to Flag Fen, Peterborough, though after its restoration it is hoped that it will be returned to Holme.

RINGSTEAD

3 miles E of Hunstanton off the A149

Another appealing village, with pink and whitewashed cottages built in wonderfully decorative Norfolk carrstone. A rare Norman round tower, all that survives of St Peter's church, stands in the grounds of the former Rectory and adds to the visual charm. In a region well provided with excellent nature reserves, the one on Ringstead Downs is particularly attractive, and popular with picnickers. The chalky soil of the valley provides a perfect habitat for the plants that thrive here and for the exquisitely marked butterflies they attract.

DOCKING

9 miles SE of Hunstanton, on the B1454 & B1153

One of the larger inland villages, Docking was at one time called Dry Docking because, perched on a hilltop 300 feet above sea level, it had no water supply of its own. The nearest permanent stream was at Fring, almost three miles away, so in 1760 the villagers began boring for a well. They had to dig some 230 feet down before they finally struck water, which was then sold at a farthing (0.1p) per bucket. A pump was installed in 1928, but a mains supply didn't reach Docking until the 1930s.

GREAT BIRCHAM

7 miles SE of Hunstanton off the B1153

A couple of miles south of Docking stands the five-storey **Great Bircham Windmill**, one of the few in Norfolk to have found a hill to perch on, and it's still working. If you arrive on a day when there's a stiff breeze blowing, the windmill's great arms will be groaning around; on calm days, content yourself with tea and home-made cakes in the tearoom, and take home some bread baked at the Mill's own bakery.

TITCHWELL

7 miles E of Hunstanton, on the A149

Perhaps in keeping with the village's name, the church of St Mary at Titchwell is quite tiny - and very pretty indeed. Its circular, probably Norman tower is topped by a little 'whisker' of a spire, and inside is some fine late 19th century glass.

Just to the west of Titchwell is a path leading to **Titchwell Marsh**, a nationally important RSPB reserve comprising some 420 acres of shingle beach, reed beds, freshwater and salt-marsh. These different habitats encourage a wide variety of birds to visit the

Church of St Mary, Titchwell

area throughout the year, and many of them breed on or around the reserve. Brent geese, ringed plovers, marsh harriers, terns, waders and shore larks may all be seen, and two of the three hides available are accessible to wheelchairs.

BRANCASTER STAITHE

9 miles NE of Hunstanton, on the A149

In Roman times a castle was built near Brancaster to try and control the Iceni, Boudica's turbulent tribe. Nothing of it remains, although a Romano-British cemetery was discovered nearby in 1960. In the 18th century, this delightful village was a port of some standing, hence the 'Staithe', or quay, in its name. The waterborne traffic in the harbour is now almost exclusively pleasure craft, although whelks are still dredged from the sea bed, 15 miles out, and mussels are farmed in the harbour itself.

From the harbour a short boat trip will take you to **Scolt Head Island** (National Trust), a three-and-a-half mile sand and shingle bar separated from the mainland by a narrow tidal creek. It was originally much smaller, but over the centuries deposits of silt and sand have steadily increased its size, and continue to do so. Scolt Head is home to England's largest colony of Sandwich terns, which flock here to breed during May, June and July.

BURNHAM MARKET

9 miles E of Hunstanton, on the B1155

There are seven Burnhams in all, strung along the valley of the little River Burn. Burnham Market is the largest of them, its past importance reflected in the wealth of Georgian buildings surrounding the green and the two churches that lie at each end of its broad main street, just 600 yards apart. In the opinion of many, Burnham Market has the best collection of small Georgian houses in Norfolk, and it's a delight to wander through the yards and alleys that link the town's three east-west streets.

Burnham Market also boasts two

Mussel Fisherman, Brancaster Bay

excellent bookshops and probably the best hat shop in the county. Auctions are held on the village green every other Monday in summer.

BURNHAM THORPE

11 miles E of Hunstanton off the B1355

From the tower of All Saints' Church, the White Ensign flaps in the breeze, and the only pub in the village is the *Lord Nelson*, and the shop next door is called the Trafalgar Stores. No prizes for deducing that Burnham Thorpe was the birthplace of Horatio Nelson. His father the Revd Edmund Nelson was the rector here for 46 years; Horatio was the sixth of his eleven children.

Parsonage House, where Horatio was born seven weeks' premature in 1758, was demolished during his lifetime, but the pub (one of more than 200 hostelries across the country bearing the hero's name) has become a kind of shrine to Nelson's memory, its walls covered with portraits, battle scenes and other marine paintings.

There are more Nelson memorabilia in the church, among them a crucifix and lectern made with wood from HMS *Victory*, a great chest from the pulpit used by the Revd Nelson, and two flags from HMS *Nelson*.

A little over a mile to the south of Burnham Thorpe stand the picturesque ruins of **Creake Abbey** (English Heritage), an Augustinian monastery founded in 1206. The Abbey's working life came to an abrupt end in 1504

when, within a single week, every one of the monks died of the plague.

HOLKHAM

16 miles E of Hunstanton, on the A149

If the concept of the Grand Tour ever needed any justification, **Holkham Hall**, seat of eight generations of the Earls of Leicester, amply provides it. For six years, from 1712 to 1718, young Thomas Coke (pronounced Cook) travelled extensively in Italy, France and Germany, studying and absorbing at first hand the glories of European civilisation. And, wherever possible, buying them. When he returned to England, Coke realised that his family's modest Elizabethan manor could not possibly house the collection of treasures he had amassed. The manor would have to be demolished and a more worthy building erected in its place. During his travels in Italy, Coke had been deeply impressed by the cool, classical lines favoured by the Renaissance architect Andrea Palladio. Working with his friend Lord Burlington - another fervent admirer of Palladio - and the architect William Kent, Coke's monumental project slowly took shape. Building began in 1734 but was not completed until 1762, three years after Coke's death.

The completed building, its classical balance and restraint emphasised by the pale honey local brick used throughout, has been described as 'the ultimate achievement of the English

Every year on Trafalgar Day, October 21st, members of the Nelson Society gather at the riverside church in Burnham Thorpe for a service in commemoration of the man who had specified in his will that he wanted to be buried in its country graveyard 'unless the King decrees otherwise'. George III did indeed decree otherwise, and the great hero was interred in St Paul's Cathedral.

47 HOLKHAM HALL & BYGONES MUSEUM

Wells-next-the-Sea

In a lakeside deer park on the beautiful North Norfolk coast stands **Holkham Hall**, one of Britain's most majestic stately homes.

🏛 *see page 254*

61

Palladian movement'. As you step into the stunning entrance hall, the tone is set for the rest of the house. Modelled on a Roman Temple of Justice, the lofty coved ceiling is supported by 18 huge fluted columns of pink Derbyshire alabaster, transported to nearby Wells by river and sea.

Each room reveals new treasures: Rubens and Van Dyck in the Saloon (the principal reception room), the Landscape Room with its incomparable collection of paintings by Lorrain, Poussin and other masters, the Brussels tapestries in the State Sitting Room and, on a more domestic note, the vast, high-ceilinged kitchen that remained in use until 1939 and still displays the original pots and pans. Historically the most important room at Holkham is the Statue Gallery, which contains one of the finest collections of classical sculpture still in private ownership. In this sparsely furnished room there is nothing to distract one's attention from the sublime statuary that has survived for millennia, among it a bust of Thucydides (one of the earliest portrayals of man) and a statue of Diana, both of which have been dated to the 4th Century BC.

Astonishingly, the interior of the house remains almost exactly as Thomas Coke planned it, his descendants having respected the integrity of his vision. They concentrated their reforming zeal on improving the enormous estate. It was Coke's great-nephew, Thomas William Coke (1754-1842),

in particular who was responsible for the elegant layout of the 3,000-acre park visitors see today. Universally known as 'Coke of Norfolk', Thomas was a pioneer of the Agricultural Revolution, best known for introducing the idea of a four-crop rotation. William Coke, son of Thomas William, was the first man in England to wear a bowler hat, made specially for him by the Bowler firm of London hatters. Among some more traditionalist hat-makers a bowler hat is still apparently known as a Coke. As well as the Pottery in the former brickworks and its associated shop, Holkham's other attractions include an 18th century walled garden, a fascinating Bygones Museum and a History of farming Exhibition with thousands of domestic and agricultural artefacts. Gwyneth Paltrow walked on the lovely sands of Holkham Beach in the closing scenes of the film *Shakespeare in Love*.

WELLS-NEXT-THE-SEA

17 miles E of Hunstanton, on the A149

There's no doubt about the appeal of the picturesque quayside, narrow streets and ancient houses of Wells. It has been a working port since at least the 13th century, but over the years the town's full name of Wells-next-the-Sea has become increasingly inapt – its harbour now stands more than a mile from the sea. In 1859, to prevent the harbour silting up altogether, Lord Leicester of Holkham Hall built an Embankment cutting off some 600 acres of marshland. This now provides a pleasant walk down to the sea.

The Embankment gave no protection, however, against the great floods of 1953 and 1978. On the 11th January 1978 the sea rose 16 feet 1 inch above high tide, a few inches less than the 16 feet 10 inches recorded on the 31st January 1953, when the floodwaters lifted a ship on to the quay. A silo on the harbour is marked with these abnormal levels.

Running alongside the Embankment in Wells-next-the-Sea is the

Wells-next-the-Sea

Harbour Railway, which trundles from the quay to the lifeboat station by the beach. The nearby narrow-gauge Wells to Walsingham Light Railway carries passengers on a particularly lovely ride along the route of the former Great Eastern Railway to Little Walsingham. The four-mile journey takes about 30 minutes with stops at Warham St Mary and Wighton. Both the WWR and the Harbour Railway services are seasonal.

In a curious change of function, the former GER station at Wells is now home to the Old Station Pottery & Bookshop, the former signal box is now the station, while the old station at Walsingham is now a church!

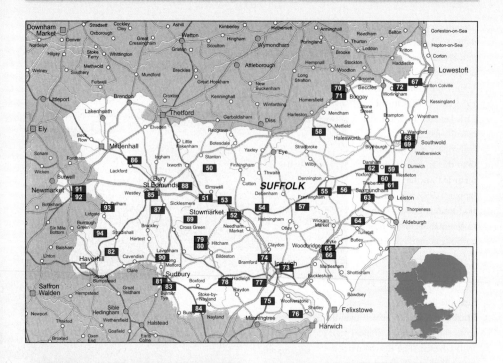

Suffolk

uffolk is known for its lovely countryside but is also very every much a maritime county, with over 50 miles of coastline. The whole coast is a conservation area, which the 50-mile Suffolk Coastal Path makes walkable throughout. Watery pursuits are naturally a popular pastime, and everything from sailing to scuba diving, angling to powerboat racing is available. Many of the museums also have a nautical theme, and the coast has long been a source of inspiration for artists, writers and composers. The sea brings its own dangers, even in human form, and it was against the threat of a Napoleonic invasion that Martello Towers were built in southeastern Suffolk, in the tradition of Saxon and Tudor forts and the precursors of concrete pillboxes. Starting just before the end of the 18th century, over 100 of these sturdy circular fortified towers were built along the coast from Suffolk to Sussex. Aldeburgh's at Slaughden is

the most northerly (and the largest), while the tower at Shoreham in Sussex the southernmost.

Inland Suffolk has few peers in terms of picturesque countryside and villages, and the area of central Suffolk between the heathland and the coast is a delightful place to get away from it all to the real countryside, with unspoilt ancient villages, gently flowing rivers and rich farmland. The Rivers Deben and Gipping run through much of the region, which also boasts a

Snape Maltings Riverside Centre

generous share of churches, museums, markets, fairs and festivals. The little market towns of Stowmarket and Needham Market are full of interest, and in this part of the county some of the best-preserved windmills and watermills are to be found. Southeast of Ipswich, the peninsula created by the Deben and the Orwell is one of the prettiest areas in Suffolk, its winding lanes leading through quiet rural villages and colourful riverside communities. John Constable, England's greatest landscape painter, was born at East Bergholt in 1776 and remained at heart a Suffolk man throughout his life. The Suffolk tradition of painting

Flatford Mill, East Bergholt

continues to this day, with many artists drawn particularly to Walberswick as well as what is known as Constable Country. Cambridgeshire, Norfolk, the A134 and the A14 frame the northern part of West Suffolk, which includes Bury St Edmunds, a pivotal player in the country's religious history, and Newmarket, one of the major centres of the horseracing world. Between and above them are picturesque villages, bustling market towns, rich farming country, the fens and the expanse of sandy heath and pine forest that is Breckland. The area south and west of Bury towards the Essex border contains some of Suffolk's most attractive and peaceful countryside. The visitor will come upon a succession of picturesque villages, historic churches, remarkable stately homes, heritage centres and nature reserves. In the south, along the River Stour, stand the historic wool towns of Long Melford, Cavendish and Clare.

CENTRAL AND EASTERN SUFFOLK

NORTH AND EAST OF BURY ST EDMUNDS

PAKENHAM

4 miles NE of Bury St Edmunds off the A143

On a side road just off the A143 (turn right just north of Great Barton) lies the village of Pakenham, whose long history has been unearthed in the shape of a Bronze Age barrow and kiln, and another kiln from Roman times.

Elsewhere in Pakenham is the 17th century **Nether Hall**, from whose lake in the park the village stream flows through the fen into the millpond. From the same period dates **Newe House**, a handsome Jacobean building with Dutch gables and a two-storey porch. Pakenham's **Church of St Mary** has an impressive carved Perpendicular font, and in its adjacent vicarage is the famous Whistler Window - a painting by Rex Whistler of an 18th century parish priest. The fens were an important source of reeds, and many of Pakenham's buildings show off the thatcher's art.

IXWORTH

5 miles NE of Bury St Edmunds on the A143

Ixworth played its part as one of the Iceni tribe's major settlements, with important Roman connections and, in the 12th century, the site of an Augustinian priory. The remains of the priory were incorporated into a Georgian house known as Ixworth Abbey, which stands among trees by the River Blackbourne. The village has many 14th century timber-framed dwellings, and the Church of St

Pakenham's current unique claim to fame is in being the last parish in England to have a working watermill and windmill, a fact proclaimed on the village sign. The Watermill was built around 1814 on a site mentioned in the Domesday Book (the Roman excavations suggest that there could have been a mill here as far back as the 1st century AD). The mill, which is fed from Pakenham fen, has many interesting features, including the Blackstone oil engine, dating from around 1900, and the Tattersall Midget rollermill from 1913, a brave but ultimately unsuccessful attempt to compete with the larger roller mills in the production of flour. The mill and the neighbouring recreation park are well worth a visit. No less remarkable is the Windmill, one of the most famous in Suffolk. The black-tarred tower was built in 1831 and was in regular use until the 1950s. One of the best preserved mills in the county, it survived a lightning strike in 1971. Both mills lie on the village's circular walks, and fresh flour is available from both.

Ixworth Abbey, Ixworth

50   THE WHITE HORSE

Badwell Ash, nr Bury St Edmunds

A friendly, family-run village inn serving traditional pub food.

see page 254

Mary dates from the same period, though with many later additions.

A variety of circular walks take in lovely parts of Ixworth, which is also the starting point of the Miller's Trail cycle route.

A little way north of the village, on the A1088, are a nature trail and bird reserve at Ixworth Thorpe Farm. At this point a brief diversion northwards up the A1088 is very worth while.

BARDWELL

7 miles NE of Bury St Edmunds just off the A1088

Bardwell offers another tower windmill. This one dates from the 1820s and was worked by wind for 100 years, then by an oil engine until 1941. It was restored in the 1980s, only to suffer severe damage in the great storm of October 1987, when its sails were torn off. Stoneground flour is still produced by an auxiliary engine, and there's an on-site bakery. Also in this delightful village are a 16th century inn and the Church of St Peter and St Paul, known particularly for its medieval stained glass.

HONINGTON

7 miles NE of Bury St Edmunds on the A1088

Back on the A1088, the little village of Honington was the birthplace of the pastoral poet Robert Bloomfield (1766-1823), whose best known work is *The Farmer's Boy*. The house where he was born is now divided, one part called Bloomfield Cottage, the other Bloomfield Farmhouse. A brass plaque to his memory can be seen in All Saints Church, in the graveyard of which his parents are buried.

EUSTON

9 miles N of Bury St Edmunds on the A1088

Euston Hall, on the A1088, has been the seat of the Dukes of Grafton for 300 years. It's open to the public on Thursday afternoons and is well worth a visit, not least for its portraits of Charles II and its paintings by Van Dyck, Lely and Stubbs. In the colourful landscaped grounds is an ice-house disguised as an Italianate temple, the distinguished work of John Evelyn and William Kent.

Euston's church, in the grounds of the Hall, is the only one in the county dedicated to St Genevieve. It's also one of only two Classical designs in the county, being rebuilt in 1676 on part of the original structure. The interior is richly decorated, with beautiful carving on the hexagonal pulpit, panelling around the walls and a carved panel of the Last Supper. Parts of this lovely wood carving are attributed by some to Grinling Gibbons. Behind the family pew is a marble memorial to Lord Arlington, who built the church.

Euston's watermill was built in the 1670s and rebuilt in 1730 as a Gothic church.

STANTON

7 miles NE of Bury St Edmunds on the A143

Stanton is mentioned in the *Domesday Book*; before that, the Romans were here. A double ration of medieval churches - All Saints and St John the Baptist - will satisfy the ecclesiastical scholar, while for more worldly indulgences **Wyken Vineyards** will have a strong appeal. The four acres of grounds around the Elizabethan Wyken Hall include herb, knot, rose, kitchen, edible and woodland gardens, a water garden, a nuttery, a gazebo and a hornbeam maze planted in 1991. The gardens are open from April to September.

BARNINGHAM

8 miles NE of Bury St Edmunds on the B1111

Near the Norfolk border, Barningham was the first home of the firm of Fisons, which started in the late 18th century. Starting with a couple of windmills, they later installed one of the earliest steam mills in existence. The engine saw service for nearly 100 years and is now in an American museum; the mill building exists to this day, supplying animal feed.

WALSHAM-LE-WILLOWS

9 miles NE of Bury St Edmunds off the A143

A pretty name for a pretty village, with weather-boarded and timber-framed cottages along the willow-banked river which flows throughout its length. **St Mary's Church** is no less pleasing to the eye, with its sturdy western tower and handsome windows in the Perpendicular style. Of particular interest inside is the superb tie and hammerbeam roof of the nave, and (unique in Suffolk, and very rare elsewhere) a tiny circular medallion which hangs suspended from the nave wall, known as a 'Maiden's Garland' or 'Virgin's Crant'. These

marked the pew seats of unmarried girls who had passed away, and the old custom was for the young men of the village to hang garlands of flowers from them on the anniversary of a girl's death. This particular example celebrates the virginity of one Mary Boyce, who died (so the inscription says) of a broken heart in 1685, just 20 years old. There is also a carving on the rood screen which looks rather like the face of a wolf: this may well be a reference to the benevolent creature that plays such an important role in the legend of St Edmund. A museum by the church has changing exhibitions of local history.

RICKINGHALL

12 miles NE of Bury St Edmunds on the A143

More timber-framed buildings, some thatched, are dotted along the streets of the two villages, Superior and Inferior, which follow an underground stream running right through them. Each has a church dedicated to St Mary and featuring fine flintwork and tracery. The upper church, now closed, was used as a school for London evacuees during the Second World War.

REDGRAVE

13 miles NE of Bury St Edmunds on the B1113

Arachnophobes beware! Redgrave and Lopham Fens form a 360-acre reserve of reed and sedge beds where one of the most interesting inhabitants is the Great Raft Spider. The village is the source of the Little Ouse and Waveney rivers, which rise on either side of the

•

The area around Barningham is marvellous walking country, and Knettishall Heath Country Park, on 400 acres of prime Breckland terrain, is the official starting place of the Peddars Way National Trail to Holme-next-the-Sea and of the Angles Way Regional Path that stretches 77 miles to Great Yarmouth by way of the Little Ouse and Waveney valleys.

•

A favourite Woolpit legend concerns the Green Children, a brother and sister with green complexions who appeared one day in a field, apparently attracted by the church bells. Though hungry, they would eat nothing until some green beans were produced. Given shelter by the lord of the manor, they learned to speak English and said that they came from a place called St Martin. The boy survived for only a short time, but the girl thrived, lost her green colour, was baptised and married a man from King's Lynn – no doubt leaving many a Suffolk man green with envy!

B1113 and set off on their seaward journeys in opposite directions.

THELNETHAM

12 miles NE of Bury St Edmunds off the B111

West of Redgrave between the B1113 and the B1111 lies Thelnetham – which boasts a windmill of its own. This one is a tower mill, built in 1819 to replace a post mill on the same site, and worked for 100 years. It has now been lovingly restored. Stoneground flour is produced and sold at the mill.

COTTON

16 miles E of Bury St Edmunds off the B1113

South of Finningham, where Yew Tree House displays some fine pargeting, and just by Bacton, a lovely village originally built round seven greens, lies the village of Cotton, which should be visited for several reasons, one of which is to see the splendid 14th century flint church of St Andrew, impressive in its dimensions and notable for its double hammerbeam roof with carved angels.

Cotton's **Mechanical Music Museum & Bygones** has an extensive collection that includes gramophones, music boxes, street pianos, fairground organs and polyphons, as well as the marvellous Wurlitzer Theatre pipe organ. Open summer Sundays. Tel: 01449 613876

HESSETT

4 miles E of Bury St Edmunds off the A14

Dedicated to St Ethelbert, King of East Anglia, Hessett's church has many remarkable features, particularly some beautiful 16th century glass and wall paintings, both of which somehow escaped the Puritan wave of destruction. Ethelbert was unlucky enough to get on the wrong side of the mighty Offa, King of the Mercians, and was killed by him at Hereford in AD 794.

WOOLPIT

6 miles E of Bury St Edmunds on the A14

The **Church of St Mary the Virgin** is Woolpit's crowning glory, with a marvellous porch and one of the most magnificent double hammerbeam roofs in the county. Voted winner of Suffolk Village of the Year in 2000, the village was long famous for its brick industry, and the majority of the old buildings are faced with 'Woolpit Whites'. This yellowish-white brick looked very much like more expensive stone, and for several centuries was widely exported. Some was used in the building of the Senate wing of the Capitol Building in Washington DC. Red bricks were also produced, and the village Museum, open in summer, has a brick-making display and also tells the story of the evolution of the village. Woolpit also hosts an annual music festival.

Nearby is a moated site known as **Lady's Well**, a place of pilgrimage in the Middle Ages. The water from the spring was reputed to have healing properties, most efficacious in curing eye troubles.

ELMSWELL

7 miles E of Bury St Edmunds off the A14

Clearly visible from the A14, the impressive church of St John the Baptist with its massive flint tower stands at the entrance to the village, facing Woolpit across the valley. A short drive north of Elmswell lies **Great Ashfield**, an unspoilt village whose now disused airfield played a key role in both World Wars. In the churchyard of the 13th century All Saints is a memorial to the Americans who died during the Second World War, as attested to by the commemorative altar. Some accounts say that Edmund was buried here in AD 903 after dying at the hands of the Danes; a cross was put up in his memory. The cross was replaced in the 19th century and now stands in the garden of Ashfield House.

HAUGHLEY

12 miles E of Bury St Edmunds off the A14

On the run into Stowmarket, Haughley once had the largest motte-and-bailey castle in Suffolk. All that now remains is a mound behind the church. **Haughley Park** is a handsome Jacobean redbrick manor house set in gardens, parkland and surrounding woodland featuring ancient oaks and splendid magnolias. Woodland paths take the visitor past a half-mile stretch of rhododendrons, and in springtime the bluebells and lilies of the valley are a magical sight. The gardens are open on Tuesdays between May and September, the house by appointment only.

HARLESTON

9 miles E of Bury St Edmunds off the A14

The churches of Shelland and Harleston lie in close proximity on a minor road between Woolpit and Haughley picnic site. At Shelland, the tiny church of King Charles the Martyr is one of only four in England to be dedicated to King Charles I. The brick floor is laid in a herringbone pattern, there are high box pews and a triple-decker pulpit, but the most unusual feature is a working barrel organ dating from the early 19th century.

The church of St Augustine at Harleston stands all alone among pine trees and is reached by a track across a field. It has a thatched roof, Early English windows and a tower with a single bell.

STOWMARKET

The largest town in the heart of Suffolk, Stowmarket enjoyed a period of rapid growth when the River Gipping was still navigable to Ipswich and when the railway arrived.

Much of the town's history and legacy are brought vividly to life in the splendid **Museum of East Anglian Life**, situated in the centre of town to the west of the marketplace (where markets are held twice a week), in a 70-acre meadowland site on the old Abbot's Hall Estate (the aisled original barn dates from the 13th century). Part of the open-air section features several historic buildings that have been moved from elsewhere in the

| 51 | KILN FARM GUEST HOUSE |

Elmswell, nr Bury St Edmunds

Quiet, comfortable B&B rooms in a guest house well placed for touring many of Suffolk's main attractions.

 see page 256

| 52 | MUSEUM OF EAST ANGLIAN LIFE |

Stowmarket

The Museum of East Anglian Life occupies a 75-acre site in the heart of Stowmarket.

see *page 256*

region and carefully re-erected on
site. These include an engineering
workshop from the 1870s, part of a
14th century farmhouse, a
watermill from Alton and a wind
pump which was rescued in a
collapsed state at Minsmere in
1977. There's also a collection of
working steam engines, farm
animals and year-round
demonstrations of all manner of
local arts and crafts, from
coopering to chandlery, from sheep
shearing to saddlery.

Stowmarket's church of St
Peter and St Mary acquired a new
spire in 1994, replacing the 1715
version (itself a replacement) which
was dismantled on safety grounds
in 1975.

The town certainly merits a
leisurely stroll, while for a peaceful
picnic the riverbank beckons.
Serious scenic walkers should make
for the **Gipping Valley River Park
Walk**, which follows the former
towpath all the way to Ipswich.

AROUND
STOWMARKET

BUXHALL

3 miles W of Stowmarket just off the B1115

The village church here is notable
for its six heavy bells, but the best-
known landmark in this quiet
village is undoubtedly the majestic
tower mill, without sails since a gale
removed them in 1929 but still
standing as a silent, sturdy reminder
of its working days. This is good
walking country, with an ancient
wood and many signposted
footpaths.

NEEDHAM MARKET

4 miles SE of Stowmarket off the A14

A thriving village whose greatest
glory is the wonderful carvings on
the ceiling of the **Church of St
John the Baptist**. The church's
ornate double hammerbeam roof is
nothing short of remarkable,
especially when bathed in light
from the strategically placed
skylight. The roof is massive, as
high as the walls of the church
itself; the renowned authority on
Suffolk churches, H Munro Cautley,
described the work at Needham as
'the culminating achievement of the
English carpenter'. The village also
boasts some excellent examples of
Tudor architecture.

The River Gipping flows to the
east of the High Street and its
banks provide miles of walks: the
towpath is a public right of way
walkable all the way from
Stowmarket to Ipswich. **Fen Alder**
Local Nature Reserve consists of
meadow, fen and alder carr – boggy
areas, with a canopy of alder trees,
a network of ditches and a pond.
Together they support an
abundance of wildlife.

Monthly farmers' markets are
held at Alder Carr Farm, where
there is also a pottery, crafts centre
and farm shop.

Barking, on the B1018 south
of Needham, was once more
important than its neighbour, being
described in 1874 as 'a pleasant
village … including the hamlet of
Needham Market'. This explains
the fact that Barking's church is
exceptionally large for a village

house of worship: it was the mother church to Needham Market and was used for Needham's burials when Needham had no burial ground of its own.

EARL STONHAM

6 miles E of Stowmarket on the A1120

A scattered village set around three greens in farming land, Earl Stonham's church of St Mary the Virgin boasts one of Suffolk's finest single hammerbeam roofs, and is also notable for its Bible scene murals, the 'Doom' (Last Judgement scene) over the chancel arch and a triple hour-glass, presumably to record just how protracted were some of the sermons.

STONHAM ASPAL

7 miles E of Stowmarket on the A1120

On the other side of the A140 lies Stonham Aspal, where in 1962 the remains of a Roman bath-house were unearthed. The parish church has an unusual wooden top to its tower, a necessary addition to house the ten bells that a keen campanologist insisted on installing.

EARL SOHAM

12 miles E of Stowmarket on the A1120

Earl Soham comprises a long, winding street that was once part of a Roman road. It lies in a valley, and on the largest of its three greens the village sign is a carved wooden statue of a falconer given as a gift by the Women's Institute in 1953. The 13th century church of St Mary is well worth a visit.

SAXTEAD GREEN

14 miles E of Stowmarket off the A1120

One of the prettiest sights in Suffolk is the white 18th century **Mill** that stands on the marshy green in Saxtead. This is a wonderful example of a post mill, perhaps the best in the world, dating back to 1796 and first renovated in the 19th century. It worked until 1947 and has since been kept in working order, with the sails turning even though the mill no longer grinds. In summer, visitors can climb into the buck (body) of this elegant weather-boarded construction and explore its machinery.

FRAMLINGHAM

18 miles NE of Stowmarket on the B1119

The marvellous **Castle**, brooding on a hilltop, dominates this agreeable market town, as it has since Roger Bigod, 2nd Earl of Norfolk, built it in the 12th century (his grandfather built the first a century earlier, but this wooden

At Stonham Barns, the British Birds of Prey and Nature Centre is home to every British owl, together with raptors from Britain and around the world. These wonderful birds flap their wings in regular flying displays, and in the Pets Paradise area children can meet and greet hamsters and horses, mice and meerkats, parrots and piglets.

54 THE MAGPIE

Little Stonham, nr Stowmarket

The **Magpie** attracts a loyal clientele with its family-friendly atmosphere, real ales and traditional home cooking.

see page 257

Framlingham Castle

55 THE CASTLE INN

Framlingham

A delightful pub next to the Castle, with a warm welcome for all the family.

 see page 258

56 HIGH HOUSE AND WOODLODGE

Cransford, nr Woodbridge

High House (B&B) and **Woodlodge** (self-catering) are ideally situated for exploring the heart of rural Suffolk.

 see page 258

construction was soon demolished). The Earls and Dukes of Norfolk, the Howards, were here for many generations before moving to Arundel in 1635. The castle is in remarkably good condition, partly because it was rarely attacked – though King John put it under siege in 1215. Its most famous occupant was Mary Tudor, who was in residence when proclaimed Queen in 1553. During the reign of Elizabeth I it was used as a prison for defiant priests and, in the 17th century after being bequeathed to Pembroke College, Cambridge, it saw service as a home and school for local paupers. Nine of the castle's 13 towers are accessible - the climb up the spiral staircase and walk round the battlements are well worth the effort. On one side the view is of the Mere, managed by the Suffolk Wildlife Trust and home to a diversity of wildlife, from marsh marigolds and ragged robin to water voles, kingfishers and barn owls. In the north wing is the **Lanman Museum**, devoted to agricultural, craftsman's tools and domestic memorabilia.

The castle brought considerable prestige and prosperity to Framlingham, evidence of which can be found in the splendid **Church of St Michael**, which has two wonderful works of art. One is the tomb of Henry Fitzroy, bastard son of Henry VIII and Elizabeth Blount, a lady-in-waiting to Catharine of Aragon, beautifully adorned with scenes from Genesis and Exodus and in a superb state of repair. The other is the tomb of the 3rd Duke, with carvings of the apostles in shell niches. Also of note is the Carolean organ of 1674, a gift of Sir Robert Hitcham, to whom the Howards sold the estate. Cromwell and the Puritans were not in favour of organs in churches, so this instrument was lucky to have escaped the mass destruction of organs at the time of the Commonwealth. Sir Robert is buried in the church.

DENNINGTON

2 miles N of Framlingham on the B1116

The pretty little village of Dennington boasts one of the oldest post offices in the country, this one having occupied the same site since 1830. The **Village Church** has some very unusual features, none more so than the hanging 'pyx' canopy above the altar. A pyx served as a receptacle for the Reserved Sacrament, which would be kept under a canopy attached to weights and pulleys so that the whole thing could be lowered when the sacrament was required for the sick and the dying. In the chapel at the top of the south aisle stands the tomb of Lord Bardolph, who fought at Agincourt, and of his wife, their effigies carved in alabaster. The most remarkable carving is that of a skiapod, the only known representation in this county of a mythical creature of the African desert, humanoid but with a huge boat-shaped foot with which it could cover itself and its family against the sun. This curious beast was 'known' to Herodotus and to Pliny, who remarked that it had 'great pertinacity in leaping'.

CHARSFIELD

5 miles S of Framlington off the B1078

A minor road runs from Framlingham through picturesque Kettleburgh and Hoo to Charsfield, best known as the inspiration for Ronald Blyth's book Akenfield, later memorably filmed by Sir Peter Hall. A cottage garden in the village displays the Akenfield village sign and is open to visitors in the summer.

OTLEY

7 miles SW of Framlingham on the B1079

The 15th century **Moated Hall** in Otley is open to the public at certain times of the year. Standing in ten acres of gardens that include a canal, a nuttery and a knot garden, the hall was long associated with the Gosnold family, whose coat of arms is also that of the village. The best-known member of that family was Bartholomew Gosnold, who sailed to the New World, coined the named 'Martha's Vineyard' for the island off the coast of Massachusetts, discovered Cape Cod and founded the settlement of Jamestown, Virginia. The 13th century church of St Mary has a remarkable baptistry font measuring 6 feet in length and 2 feet 8 inches in depth. Though filled with water, the font is not used and was only discovered in 1950 when the vestry floor was raised. It may have been used for adult baptisms.

FRAMSDEN

7 miles SW of Framlingham on the B1077

The scenery in these parts is real picture-postcard stuff, and in the village of Framsden the picture is completed by a fine **Post Mill**, built high on a hill in 1760, refitted and raised in 1836 and in commercial use until 1934. The milling machinery is still in place and the mill is open for visits (at weekends, by appointment only).

CRETINGHAM

4 miles SW of Framlingham off the A1120

The village sign is the unusual item here, in that it has two different panels: one shows an everyday Anglo-Saxon farming scene, the other a group (of Danes?) sailing up the River Deben, with the locals fleeing. The signs are made from mosaic tiles.

BRANDESTON

3 miles SW of Framlingham off the A1120

A further mile to the east, through some charming countryside, Brandeston is another delightful spot, with a row of beautiful thatched cottages and the parish **Church of All Saints** with its 13th century font.

DEBENHAM

10 miles E of Stowmarket on the B1077

Debenham is a sizable village of architectural distinction, with a profusion of attractive timber-framed buildings dating from the 14th to the 17th centuries. The River Deben flows beside and beneath the main street and, near

57 THE CRETINGHAM BELL

Cretingham

A neatly kept traditional village inn – free house, restaurant and B&B base.

see page 258

The best-known vicar of Brandeston was John Lowes (1572-1646) who was accused of witchcraft by the villagers, interrogated by Witchfinder General Matthew Hopkins and hanged at Bury St Edmunds. His sad end was made even sadder by the fact that before being strung up he had to read out the burial service of a condemned witch himself, as no priest was allowed to conduct the service. Hopkins made a handsome living out of this bizarre business, preying on the superstitions of the times and using the foulest means to obtain confessions. One account of Hopkins' end is that he himself was accused of being a witch and hanged. The less satisfactory alternative is that he died of tuberculosis.

•

Wetheringsett has had two well-known rectors, famous for very different reasons. Richard Hakluyt, incumbent from 1590 to 1616, is remembered for his major work Voyages (full title Principal Navigation, Voiages, Traffiques and Discoveries of the English Nation). The rector between 1858 and 1883 was a certain George Wilfrid Ellis, sometime tailor and butler, and finally a bogus clergyman. After he was unmasked as a sham, a special Act of Parliament was needed to validate the marriage ceremonies he had illegally performed, and to legitimise the issue of those marriages.

•

one of the little bridges, weavers still practise their craft. There is also a pottery centre. St Mary's Church is unusual in having an original Saxon tower, and the roof alternates hammerbeams with crested tie beams.

MENDLESHAM

6 miles NE of Stowmarket off the A140

On the green in Old Market Street, Mendlesham, lies an enormous stone which is said to have been used as a preaching stone, mounted by itinerant Wesleyan preachers. In the Church of St Mary there is a collection of parish armour assembled some 400 years ago, and also some fine carvings. The least hidden local landmark is a 1,000-feet TV mast put up by the IBA in 1959. The 34th Bomb Group operated from Mendlesham airfield, and an impressive memorial to personnel lost over the airfield was built in 1949.

WETHERINGSETT

7 miles NE of Stowmarket off the A140

On the other side of the A140, Wetheringsett is where visitors will find the **Mid-Suffolk Light Railway Museum**, open on Sundays and Bank Holidays from Easter to September. Tel: 01449 766899

THORNHAM MAGNA & PARVA

10 miles N of Stowmarket off the A140

The **Thornham Walks and Field Centre**, with 12 miles of walks and a herb garden and nursery, cater

admirably for hikers, horticulturists and lovers of the countryside. The tiny thatched **Church of St Mary** at Thornham Parva houses a considerable treasure in the shape of an exquisite medieval altar painting, known as a retable, with a central panel depicting the Crucifixion and four saints on each side panel. Its origins are uncertain, but it was possibly the work of the Royal Workshops at Westminster Abbey and made for Thetford Priory, or for a nearby Dominican monastery. When conservation work was urgently needed, the villagers of Thornham Parva managed to raise the money needed to save this national treasure; their successful efforts were rewarded when the work, carried out by the Hamilton Kerr Institute, part of the Fitzwilliam Museum in Cambridge, earned an allocation of funds from the Heritage Lottery Fund. Also to be admired is the 14th century octagonal font and a series of fascinating wall paintings. In the churchyard are the grave and monument of Sir Basil Spence (1907-76), architect of Coventry Cathedral.

YAXLEY

12 miles N of Stowmarket on the A140

Yaxley's **Church of St Mary** offers up more treasures. One is an extremely rare sexton's wheel, which hangs above the south door and was used in medieval times to select fast days in honour of the Virgin. When a pair of iron wheels were spun on their axle, strings attached to the outer wheel would catch on the inner, stopping both and indicating the chosen day. The 17th century pulpit is one of the finest in the country, with the most glorious, sumptuous carvings.

EYE

13 miles NE of Stowmarket on the B1117

The name of this excellent little town is derived from the Saxon for an island, as Eye was once surrounded by water and marshes. The **Church of St Peter and St Paul** stands in the shadow of a mound on which a castle once stood (the remains are worth visiting and the mound offers a panoramic view of the town – almost a bird's eye view, in fact). The church's 100-feet tower was described by Pevsner as 'one of the wonders of Suffolk' and the interior is a masterpiece of restoration, with all the essential medieval features in place. The rood screen, with painted panels depicting St Edmund, St Ursula, Edward the Confessor and Henry VI, is particularly fine.

Other interesting Eye sights are the ornate redbrick Town Hall; the timbered Guildhall, with the archangel Gabriel carved on a corner post; a crinkle-crankle wall fronting Chandos Lodge, where Sir Frederick Ashton once lived; and a tiny but thriving theatre.

HOXNE

4 miles NE of Eye on the B1118

Palaeolithic remains indicate the exceptionally long history of Hoxne (pronounced Hoxon), which stands along the banks of the River

Eye Castle

Waveney near the Norfolk border. It is best known for its links with King Edmund, who was reputedly killed here, though Bradfield St Clare and Shottisham have rival claims to this distinction. The Hoxne legend is that Edmund was betrayed to the Danes by a newlywed couple who were crossing the Goldbrook bridge and spotted his golden spurs reflected from his hiding place below the bridge. Edmund put a curse on all newlyweds crossing the bridge, and to this day some brides take care to avoid it.

The story continues that Edmund was tied to an oak tree and killed with arrows. That same oak mysteriously fell down in 1848 while apparently in good health, and a monument at the site is a popular tourist attraction. In the church of St Peter and St Paul an oak screen (perhaps that very same oak?) depicts scenes from the martyr's life. A more cheerful event is the Harvest Breakfast on the village green that follows the annual service. The East Anglian bishops

Wingfield's Church of St Andrew was built as the collegiate church and has an extra-large chancel to accommodate the college choir. The church contains three really fine monuments: to Sir John (in stone); to Michael de la Pole, 2nd Earl of Suffolk (in wood); and to John de la Pole, Duke of Suffolk (in alabaster). In the churchyard there is a 'hudd' – a shelter for the priest for use at the graveside in bad weather.

58   THE SWAN INN

Fressingfield

A traditional setting for enjoying Cask Marque-accredited ales and excellent home cooking.

see page 259

once had their seat at Hoxne, and the moated vicarage beside the church may have been the original location of the Bishops Palace.

HORHAM

6 miles E of Eye on the B1117

Three distinct musical connections distinguish this dapper little village. The Norman church has had its tower strengthened for the rehanging of the peal of eight bells, which is believed to be the oldest in the world. Benjamin Britten, later associated with the Aldeburgh Festival, lived and composed in Horham for a time. On a famous day during the Second World War, Glenn Miller brought his band to Horham to celebrate the 200th flying mission to set out from the American aerodrome. The 95th Bomb Group Hospital Museum contains some wonderful wartime paintings, and a memorial in Horham Church remembers the airfield's personnel.

WORLINGWORTH

8 miles SE of Eye off the B1118

It's well worth taking the country road to Worlingworth, a long, straggling village whose church of St Mary has a remarkable font cover reaching up about 30 feet. It is brilliantly coloured and intricately carved, and near the top is an inscription in Greek which translates as 'wash my sin and not my body only.' Note, too, the Carolean box pews, the carved pulpit and an oil painting of Worlingworth's Great Feast of 1810 to celebrate George III's jubilee.

WINGFIELD

6 miles E of Eye off the B1118

Wingfield College is one of the country's most historic seats of learning, founded in 1362 as a college for priests with a bequest from Sir John de Wingfield, Chief Staff Officer to the Black Prince. Sir John's wealth came from ransoming a French nobleman at the Battle of Poitiers in 1356. Surrendered to Henry VIII at the time of the Dissolution, the college became a farmhouse and is now in private hands. The façade is now Georgian, but the original medieval Great Hall still stands, and the college and its three acres of gardens are open to the public at weekends in summer. Attractions include regular artistic events and printing demonstrations.

On a hill outside the village are the imposing remains of a castle built by the 1st Earl.

FRESSINGFIELD

10 miles E of Eye on the B1116

Fressingfield's first spiritual centre was the **Church of St Peter and St Paul**. It has a superb hammerbeam roof and a lovely stone bell tower that was built in the 14th century. On one of the pews the initials A P are carved. These are believed to be the work of Alice de la Pole, Duchess of Norfolk and grand-daughter of Geoffrey Chaucer. Was this a work of art or a bout of vandalism brought on by a dull sermon?

The village sign is a pilgrim and a donkey, recording that

Fressingfield was a stopping place on the pilgrim route from Dunwich to Bury St Edmunds.

LAXFIELD

12 miles E of Eye on the B1117

Laxfield & District Museum, in the 16th century Guildhall, gives a fine insight into bygone ages with geology and natural history exhibits, agricultural and domestic tools, a Victorian kitchen, a village shop and a costume room. The museum is open on Saturday and Sunday afternoons in summer.

All Saints Church is distinguished by some wonderful flint 'flushwork' (stonework) on its tower, roof and nave. In the 1808 Baptist church is a plaque remembering John Noyes, burnt at the stake in 1557 for refusing to take Catholic vows. History relates that the villagers - with a single exception - dowsed their fires in protest. The one remaining fire, however, was all that was needed to light the stake.

A couple of miles east of Laxfield, **Heveningham Hall** is a fine Georgian mansion, a model of classical elegance designed by James Wyatt with lovely grounds by Capability Brown. As it runs through the grounds, the River Blyth widens into a lake.

ALONG THE COAST

DUNWICH

4 miles SW of Southwold off the B1105

Surely the hidden place of all hidden places, Dunwich was once the capital of East Anglia, founded by the Burgundian Christian missionary St Felix and for several centuries a major trading port (wool and grain out; wine, timber and cloth in) and a centre of fishing and shipbuilding. The records show that in 1241 no fewer than 80 ships were built here for the king. By the middle of the next century, however, the sea attacked from the east and a vast bank of sand and shingle silted up the harbour. The course of the river was diverted, the town was cut off from the sea and the town's trade was effectively killed off. For the next 700 years the relentless forces of nature continued to take their toll, and of the six churches, monasteries, mills and hospitals all that remains now of ancient Dunwich are the ruins of the Norman **Leper Hospital of St James**, the ruins of a clifftop **Friary** that was home to the Greyfriars, and a buttress of one of the nine churches which once served the community. The last church succumbed to the waves in 1920, but local legend says that the church bells can be heard beneath

Medieval Priory, Dunwich

the waves on stormy nights. Other tales tell of strange lights in the ruined priory and the eerie chanting of long-dead monks.

Today's village comprises a 19th century church and a row of Victorian cottages, one of which houses the **Dunwich Museum**. Local residents set up the museum in 1972 to tell the Dunwich story; the historical section has displays and exhibits from Roman, Saxon and medieval times, the centrepiece being a large model of the town at its 12th century peak. There are also sections devoted to natural history, social history and the arts. Extended and refurbished in 1998 after a generous grant from the national Lottery, Dunwich Museum has won numerous awards, including the coveted Gulbenkian Award.

Dunwich Forest, immediately inland from the village, is one of three – the others are further south at Tunstall and Rendlesham – named by the Forestry Commission as Aldewood Forest. Work started on these in 1920 with the planting of Scots pine, Corsican pine and some Douglas fir; oak and poplar were tried but did not thrive in the sandy soil. The three forests, which between them cover nearly 9,000 acres, were almost completely devastated in the hurricane of October 1987, Rendlesham alone losing more than a million trees.

South of the village lies **Dunwich Heath**, one of Suffolk's most important conservation areas, comprising the beach, splendid heather, a field study centre, a public hide and an information centre and restaurant in converted coastguard cottages.

Around Dunwich Heath are the attractive villages of **Westleton**, **Middleton**, **Theberton** and **Eastbridge**. During the First World War, German airships were used to spy on and bomb England. In the porch of Theberton church are remains of a Zeppelin that crashed in a nearby field in 1917.

In Westleton, the 14th century thatched **Church of St Peter**, built by the monks of Sibton Abbey, has twice seen the collapse of its tower. The first fell down in a hurricane in 1776; its smaller wooden replacement collapsed when a bomb fell during the Second World War. The village is also the main route of access to the RSPB-managed **Minsmere Bird Sanctuary**, the most important sanctuary for wading birds in eastern England. The marshland was flooded during the Second World War, and nature and this wartime emergency measure created the perfect habitat for innumerable birds. More than 100 species nest here, and a similar number of birds visit throughout the year, making it a birdwatcher's paradise. Minsmere is rich in other kinds of wildlife, and one of the best ways of discovering more is to join one of the guided walks. The Suffolk Coastal Path runs along the foreshore.

A little way inland from Westleton lies **Darsham**, where another nature reserve is home to many varieties of birds and flowers.

YOXFORD

10 miles SW of Southwold on the A12

Once an important stop on the London-to-Yarmouth coaching route, Yoxford now attracts visitors with its pink-washed cottages and its arts and crafts, antiques and food shops. Look for the cast-iron signpost outside the church, with hands pointing to London, Yarmouth and Framlingham set high enough to be seen by the driver of a stagecoach.

SAXMUNDHAM

12 miles SW of Southwold off the A12

A little town that was granted its market charter in 1272. On the font of the church in Saxmundham is the carving of a 'woodwose' - a tree spirit or green man. He, and others like him, have given their name to a large number of pubs in Suffolk and elsewhere. A major attraction is the **Saxmundham Museum**, housed in a former bakehouse. Among the many fascinating displays are a scale model of Saxmundham railway station as it was in the 1930s, complete with working trains; a re-creation of Saxmundham Playhouse; replicas of shops; costumes and dolls; and various memorabilia relating to the town.

BRUISYARD

4 miles NW of Saxmundham off the B1119

Just west of this village is the **Bruisyard Vineyard, Winery and Herb Centre**, a complex of a 10-acre vineyard with 13,000 Müller Thurgau grape vines, a wine-production centre, herb and water gardens, a tea shop and a picnic site.

PEASENHALL

6 miles NW of Saxmundham on the A1120

A little stream runs along the side of the main street in Peasenhall, whose buildings present several styles and ages. Most distinguished is the old timbered **Woolhall**, splendidly restored to its 15th century grandeur.

LEISTON

4 miles E of Saxmundham off the B1119

The first **Leiston Abbey** was built on Nunsmere marshes in 1182, but in 1363 the Earl of Suffolk rebuilt it on its present site away from the frequent floods. It became one of the largest and most prestigious monasteries in the country, and its wealth probably spelled its ruin, as it fell within Henry VIII's plan for the Dissolution of the Monasteries. The visible ruins are of a chapel built on the site of the monastic church. A new abbey was built using stone from the first abbey site, and the restored old hall is used as a base for PROCORDA, a group promoting musical excellence.

For 200 years the biggest name in Leiston was that of Richard Garrett, who founded an engineering works here in 1778 after starting a business in Woodbridge. In the early years ploughs, threshers, seed drills and other agricultural machinery were the main products, but the company later started one of the

62 THE GRIFFIN INN

Yoxford

A former Dutch river barge. A 14th century inn of great charm and character, serving real ales and generous home cooking.

see page 260

63 THE GEORGIAN GUEST HOUSE

Saxmundham

5 Star Silver Award accommodation in a Grade II listed house in the small market town of Saxmundham.

see page 261

•

The oddest building in Peasenhall is certainly a hall in the style of a Swiss chalet, built for his workers by James Josiah Smyth, grandson of the founder of James Smyth & Sons. This company, renowned for its agricultural drills, was for more than two centuries the dominant industrial presence in Peasenhall. On the south side of St Michael's churchyard stands the 1805 drill-mill where James Smyth manufactured his Nonpareil seed drills, one of which is on display in Stowmarket's museum.

•

Leiston Abbey

minibus, with a guide and videos, round Sizewell B.

ALDRINGHAM

4 miles E of Saxmundham on the B1122

Aldringham's church is notable for its superb 15th century font, and the village inn was once a haunt of smugglers. It now helps to refresh the visitors who flock to the Aldringham Craft Market, founded in 1958 and extending over three galleries, with a serious selection of arts and crafts, clothes and gifts, pottery, basketry, books and cards.

THORPENESS

6 miles E of Saxmundham on the B1353

Thorpeness is a unique holiday village with mock-Tudor houses and the general look of a series of eccentric film sets. Buying up a considerable packet of land called the Sizewell estate in 1910, the architect, barrister and playwright Glencairn Stuart Ogilvie created what he hoped would be a fashionable resort with cottages, some larger houses and a 65-acre shallow boating and pleasure lake called the Meare. Every August, following the Aldeburgh Carnival, a regatta takes place on the Meare, culminating in a splendid fireworks display. The 85-feet water tower, built to aid in the lake's construction, looked out of place, so Ogilvie disguised it as a house. Known ever since as the **House in the Clouds**, it is now available to rent as a holiday home. The neighbouring mill, moved lock, stock and millstones from Aldringham, stopped pumping in

country's first production lines for steam machines. The Garrett works are now the **Long Shop Museum**, the factory buildings having been lovingly restored, and many of the Garrett machines are now on display, including traction engines, a steam-driven tractor and a road roller. There's also a section where the history and workings of steam engines are explained. A small area of the museum recalls the USAAF's 357th fighter group, who flew from an airfield outside Leiston during the Second World War. One of their number, a Captain Chuck Yeager, was the first man to fly faster than the speed of sound.

The Garrett works closed in 1980, but what could have been a disastrous unemployment situation was alleviated to some extent by the nuclear power station at **Sizewell**. The coast road in the centre of Leiston leads to this establishment, where visitors can take tours - on foot with access to buildings at Sizewell A or by

1940 but has been restored and now houses a visitor centre. Thorpeness is very much a one-off, not at all typical Suffolk but with a droll charm that is all its own.

ALDEBURGH

6 miles SE of Saxmundham on the A1094

And so down the coast road to Aldeburgh, another coastal town that once prospered as a port with major fishing and shipbuilding industries. Drake's *Greyhound* and *Pelican* were built at Slaughden, now taken by the sea, and during the 16th century some 1,500 people were engaged in fishing. Both industries declined as shipbuilding moved elsewhere and the fishing boats became too large to be hauled up the shingle.

Suffolk's best-known poet, George Crabbe, was born at Slaughden in 1754 and lived through the village's hard times. He reflected the melancholy of those days when he wrote of his fellow townsmen:

> *Here joyless roam a wild*
> *amphibious race,*
> *With sullen woe displayed in every face;*
> *Who far from civil arts and social fly,*
> *And scowl at strangers with*
> *suspicious eye.*

He was equally evocative concerning the sea and the river, and the following lines written about the River Alde could apply to several others in the county:

> *With ceaseless motion comes*
> *and goes the tide*
> *Flowing, it fills the channel*
> *vast and wide;*
> *Then back to sea,*

> *with strong majestic sweep*
> *It- rolls, in ebb yet terrible and deep;*
> *Here samphire-banks*
> *and salt-wort bound the flood*
> *There stakes and seaweed*
> *withering on the mud;*
> *And higher up, a ridge of all things base,*
> *Which some strong tide*
> *has rolled upon the place.*

It was Crabbe who created the character of the solitary fisherman Peter Grimes, later the subject of an opera composed by another

View to the Sea from Aldeburgh

83

• At the very southern tip of the town of Aldeburgh, the Martello Tower serves as a reminder of the power of the sea: old pictures show it standing well back from the waves, but now the seaward side of the moat has disappeared and the shingle is constantly being shored up to protect it. This squat tower dates from 1814 and never saw action, although its guns were manned until the middle of the 19th century. It is the most northerly of 75 erected on the coast between Sussex and Suffolk as a defence against a possible attack by Napoleon's forces. The Martello Towers were named after the Torre della Mortella on the island of Corsica, which the English army saw in the war in 1793. Aldeburgh's tower was completed in 1810, and never saw action, although it had four guns at the ready and was manned until the middle of Queen Victoria's reign. Beyond the tower, a long strip of marsh and shingle stretches right down to the mouth of the river at Shingle Street. •

Aldeburgh resident, Benjamin Britten. Britten lived in the Red House, off the B1122 Leiston road opposite the golf course, from 1957 until hid death in 1976. Here he composed many of his greatest works, including the *War Requiem* and *Death in Venice*. Guided tours of the house take place on certain days in the summer; for details call 01728 451700.

Aldeburgh's role gradually changed into that of a holiday resort, and the Marquess of Salisbury, visiting early in the 19th century, was one of the first to be attracted by the idea of sea-bathing without the crowds. By the middle of the century the grand houses that had sprung up were joined by smaller residences, the railway had arrived, a handsome water tower was put up (1860) and Aldeburgh prospered once more. There were even plans for a pier, and construction started in 1878, but the project proved too difficult or too expensive and was halted, the rusting girders being removed some time later.

One of the town's major benefactors was Newson Garrett, a wealthy businessman who was the first mayor under the charter of the Local Government Act of 1875. This colourful character also developed the Maltings at Snape, but is perhaps best remembered through his remarkable daughter Elizabeth, who was the first woman doctor in England (having qualified in Paris at a time when women could not qualify here) and

the first woman mayor (of Aldeburgh, in 1908). This lady married the shipowner James Skelton Anderson, who established the golf club in 1884.

If Crabbe were alive today he would have a rather less cantankerous opinion of his fellows, especially at carnival time on a Monday in August when the town celebrates with a colourful procession of floats and marchers, a fireworks display and numerous other events. As for the arts, there is, of course, the **Aldeburgh Festival**, started in 1948 by Britten and others; the festival's main venue is **Snape Maltings**, but many performances take place in Aldeburgh itself.

The town's maritime connections remain very strong. There has been a lifeboat station here since 1851, when the RNLI took over from the Suffolk Shipwreck Association; it was the last station to operate the traditional 'double-ended' design of lifeboat. The very modern lifeboat station on Crag Path is one of the town's chief attractions for visitors, open daily from 10 to 4, and there are regular practice launches from the shingle beach. A handful of fishermen still put out to sea from the beach, selling their catch from their little wooden huts, while a thriving yacht club is the base for sailing on the river and the sea.

Back in town there are several interesting buildings, notably the **Moot Hall** and the parish **Church of St Peter and St Paul**. The

Moot Hall is a 16th century timber-framed building that was built in what was once the centre of town. It hasn't moved, but the sea long ago took away several houses and streets. Inside the Hall is a museum of town history and finds from the nearby Snape burial ship. The museum also recounts the story of the Aldeburgh lifeboat's rescue on the second Sunday of the Second World War of sailors from the SS *Magdapur*. Benjamin Britten set the first scene of *Peter Grimes* in the Moot Hall. A sundial on the south face of the Hall proclaims, in Latin, that it only tells the time when the sun shines.

The church, which stands above the town as a very visible landmark for mariners, contains a memorial to George Crabbe and a beautiful stained-glass window, the work of John Piper, depicting three Britten parables: *Curlew River*, *The Burning Fiery Furnace* and *The Prodigal Son*. Britten, his companion Peter Pears and the musician Imogen Holst are buried in the churchyard, part of which is set aside for the benefit of wildlife. The latest of the many tributes in Aldeburgh to Britten is a giant metal clam shell designed by Maggie Hambling. It stands on the beach at the north end of town, and the words on its rim – 'I hear those voices that will not be drowned' – are taken from Britten's opera *Peter Grimes*. Elizabeth Garrett Anderson (see above) is also buried in the churchyard, so too George and Mary Crabbe, the poet's parents.

Aldeburgh Moot Hall

FRISTON

3 miles SE of Saxmundham off the A1094

Friston's **Post Mill**, the tallest in England, is a prominent sight on the Aldeburgh-Snape road, moved from Woodbridge in 1812 just after its construction. It worked by wind until 1956, then by engine until 1972.

SNAPE

3 miles S of Saxmundham on the A1094

This 'boggy place' has a long and interesting history. In 1862 the remains of an Anglo-Saxon ship were discovered here, and since that time regular finds have been made, with some remarkable cases of almost perfect preservation. Snape, like Aldeburgh, has

Snape Maltings Riverside Centre

•

A short distance west of Snape, off the B1069, lies Blaxhall, famed for its growing stone. The Blaxhall Stone, which lies in the yard of Stone Farm, is reputed to have grown to its present size (5 tons) from a comparative pebble the size of a football, when it first came to local attention 100 years ago. Could there be more 'Blarney' than Blaxhall at work here?

•

benefited over the years from the philanthropy of the Garrett family, one of whose members built the primary school and set up the Maltings, centre of the Aldeburgh Music Festival.

The last 30-odd years have seen the development of the **Snape Maltings Riverside Centre**, a group of shops and galleries located in a complex of restored Victorian granaries and malthouses that is also the setting for the renowned Aldeburgh festival. The Maltings began their designated task of converting grain into malt in the 1840s, and continued thus until 1965, when the pressure of modern techniques brought them to a halt. There was a real risk of the buildings being demolished, but George Gooderham, a local farmer,

bought the site to expand his animal feeds business and soon saw the potential of the redundant buildings.

The Concert Hall came first, in 1967, and in 1971 the Craft Shop was established as the first conversion of the old buildings for retail premises. Conversion and expansion continue to this day, and in the numerous outlets visitors can buy anything from fudge to country-style clothing, from herbs to household furniture, silver buttons to top hats. Plants and garden accessories are also sold, and art galleries feature the work of local painters, potters and sculptors. The Centre hosts regular painting, craft and decorative art courses, and more recent expansion saw the creation of an impressive country-style store.

CAMPSEA ASHE
6 miles NE of Woodbridge on the B1078

On towards Wickham Market the road passes through Campsea Ashe in the parish of Campsey Ashe. The 14th century church of St John the Baptist has an interesting brass showing one of its first rectors in full priestly garb.

WICKHAM MARKET
5 miles N of Woodbridge off the A12

Places to see in this straggling village are the picturesque watermill by the River Deben and All Saints Church, whose 137-feet octagonal tower has a little roof to shelter the bell. In the little country churchyard at Boulge, a couple of miles southwest of Wickham Market, is the grave of Edward Fitzgerald (1809-1883), whose free translation of *The Rubaiyat of Omar Khayyam* is an English masterpiece. Tradition has it that on his grave is a rose bush grown from one found on Omar Khayyam's grave in Iran.

EASTON
5 miles N of Woodbridge off the B1078

A scenic drive leads to the lovely village of Easton, one of the most colourful, flower-bedecked places in the county.

Tucked away three miles off the A12 in the beautiful Deben Valley, **Easton Park Farm** is one of Suffolk's greatest attractions. Since it opened in 1973, more than a million visitors have passed through the gates to have a great day out; they leave knowing a lot more about the ways of the countryside than when they arrived. It's a marvellous place to bring the family, as the children can have endless fun feeding and making friends with the animals in Pets Paddock, riding ponies, seeing the Suffolk Punches or simply running around in the adventure playground. The showpiece of the park is the Victorian dairy, an ornate octagonal building, while the Dairy Centre is contrastingly modern, with walkways over the top of the stalls and a viewing gallery over the milking parlour.

PARHAM
8 miles N of Woodbridge on the B1116

Parham Airfield is now agricultural land, but in the museum in the control tower and an adjacent hut can be found memorabilia of the 390th Bomb Group of the USAAF. The airfield was built in 1942 for the RAF, but it was taken over by the USAAF in 1943. From here they flew Flying Fortresses on many successful missions, and the museum is a memorial to all the airmen who flew from here.

UFFORD
4 miles N of Woodbridge off the A12

Pride of place in a village that takes its name from Uffa (or Wuffa), the founder of the leading Anglo-Saxon dynasty, goes to the 13th century **Church of the Assumption**. The font cover, which telescopes from 5 feet to 18 feet in height, is a masterpiece of craftsmanship, its elaborate carving crowned by a pelican. Many 15th

64 THE SHIP INN AT BLAXHALL

Blaxhall, nr Snape

The **Ship** is a lovely country pub serving a fine choice of food, real ales and wines. Also chalet-style B&B rooms.

see page 262

•

A remarkable sight to the west of Easton is the two-mile-long Crinkle-Crankle Wall that surrounds Easton Park. This extraordinary type of wall, also known as a ribbon wall, weaves snake-like in and out and is much stronger than if it were straight. This particular wall, said to be the world's longest, was built by Lord of the Manor, the Earl of Rochford, in the 1820s.

•

65 YE OLDE COACH & HORSES INN

Melton, nr Woodbridge

A traditional inn offering superb hospitality and an outstanding choice of food (British classics and Indian specialities) and drink.

see page 263

century benches have survived, but Dowsing smashed the organ and most of the stained glass – what's there now is mainly Victorian, some of it a copy of 15th century work at All Souls College, Oxford. Ufford is where the Suffolk Punch originated, Crisp's 404 being, in 1768, the progenitor of this distinguished breed of horses.

BREDFIELD

3 miles N of Woodbridge off the A12

There's a plaque on the wall of the village pub in Bredfield commemorating a day in 1742 on which nothing at all happened. On a day in 1809, however, something did happen: Edward Fitzgerald was born. Something else happened in 1953: a wrought-iron canopy with a golden crown, made at the village forge, was put on the crossroads pump to celebrate Queen Elizabeth II's coronation.

WOODBRIDGE

Udebyge, Wiebryge, Wodebryge, Wudebrige ... just some of the ways of spelling this splendid old market town since it was first mentioned in writing in AD 970. As to what the name means, it could simply be 'wooden bridge' or 'bridge by the wood', but the most likely and most interesting explanation is that it is derived from Anglo-Saxon words meaning 'Woden's (or Odin's) town'. Standing at the head of the Deben estuary, it is a place of considerable charm with a wealth of handsome, often historic buildings and a

considerable sense of history, as both a market town and a port.

The shipbuilding and allied industries flourished here, as at most towns on the Suffolk coast, and it is recorded that both Edward III, in the 14th century, and Drake in the 16th sailed in Woodbridge ships. There's still plenty of activity on and by the river, though nowadays it is all leisure-orientated. The town's greatest benefactor was Thomas Seckford, who rebuilt the abbey, paid for the chapel in the north aisle of St Mary's Church and founded the original almshouses in Seckford Street. In 1575 he gave the town the splendid Shire Hall on Market Hill. Originally used as a corn exchange, it now houses the **Suffolk Punch Heavy Horse Museum**, with an exhibition devoted to the Suffolk Punch breed of heavy working horse, the oldest such breed in the world. The breed dates from the 16th century, but all animals alive today trace the male line back to one stallion called Crisp's Horse of Ufford, foaled in 1768. The history of the breed and its rescue from near-extinction in the 1960s is covered in fascinating detail, and a small section relates to other famous Suffolk breeds – the Red Poll cattle, the Suffolk sheep and the Large Black pigs. Tel: 01394 380643. Opposite the Shire Hall is **Woodbridge Museum**, a treasure trove of information on the history of the town and its more notable residents; from here it is a short stroll down the cobbled alleyway to the magnificent parish church of St Mary, where Seckford was buried in 1587.

Seckford naturally features prominently in the museum, along with the painter Thomas Churchyard, the map-maker Isaac Johnson and the poet Edward Fitzgerald. 'Old Fitz' was something of an eccentric and, for the most part, fairly reclusive. He loved Woodbridge and particularly the River Deben, where he often sailed in his little boat Scandal.

Woodbridge is lucky enough to have two marvellous mills, both in working order, and both great attractions for the visitor. The **Tide Mill**, on the quayside close to the town centre, dates from the late 18th century (though the site was mentioned 600 years previously) and worked by the power of the tide until 1957. It has been meticulously restored and the waterwheel still turns, fed by a recently created pond which replaced the original huge mill pond when it was turned into a marina. **Buttrum's Mill**, named after the last miller, is a tower mill standing just off the A12 bypass a mile west of the town centre. A marvellous sight, its six storeys make it the tallest surviving tower mill in Suffolk. There is a ground-floor display of the history and workings of the mill.

Many of the town's streets are traffic-free, so shopping is a real pleasure. If you should catch the Fitzgerald mood and feel like *'a jug of wine and a loaf of bread'*, Woodbridge can oblige with a good variety of pubs and restaurants.

Tide Mill, Woodbridge

AROUND WOODBRIDGE

SUTTON HOO

1 mile E of Woodbridge off the B1083

A mile or so east of Woodbridge on the opposite bank of the Deben is the **Sutton Hoo Burial Site**, a group of a dozen grassy barrows which hit the headlines in 1939 and are sometimes known as 'page one of the history of England'. Excavations, which initially unearthed ship's rivets, brought to light the outline of an 80-feet long Anglo-Saxon ship, filled with one of the greatest hoards of treasure ever discovered in Britain. The priceless find, which eluded grave robbers and lay undisturbed for over 1,300 years, includes gold coins and ornaments, silverware, weapons and armoury, drinking horns and leather cups; it is housed in the British Museum in London, but there are exhibitions, replicas and plenty of other items of interest at the site, along with special events throughout

66   SUTTON HOO

Sutton Hoo

Sutton Hoo kept its secret for more than 1300 years, until, on the very brink of war in 1939, an incomparable buried treasure was discovered here.

 see page 264

Rendlesham Forest, part of the Forest of Aldewood, was ravaged by the great hurricane of October 1987, when two-thirds of the trees, planted in the 1920s, were destroyed. Seven years before that, on Christmas night, another visitation had occurred. Security guards at RAF Woodbridge, at that time a front line NATO base, spotted strange lights in the forest and went to investigate. They came upon a nine-foot high triangular object with a series of lights around it. As they approached, it did what all good UFOs do and flew off before it could be photographed. The next day the guards returned to the spot where it had landed and found three depressions in the ground. The UFO was apparently sighted again two days later, and security in the area was heightened. No explanation has ever been forthcoming about the incident, but interest in it continues and from time to time guided walks to the landing site are arranged.

the year. Research continues, and it is now believed that the ship was the burial place of Raedwald, of the Wuffinga dynasty, King of East Anglia from about AD 610 to AD 625. Access to the site is on foot from the B1083.

RENDLESHAM

5 miles NE of Woodbridge on the A1152

The **Church of St Gregory the Great** dates from the 14th century, but there is evidence (not physical, unfortunately) of an earlier Christian presence in the shape of Raedwald's palace.

The only part still standing of **Rendlesham Hall**, built in 1871 and demolished in 1949, is the Gothic folly of Woodbridge Lodge, a remarkable edifice which loses little in comparison with some of the more extraordinary buildings designed by Gaudi in Barcelona.

BUTLEY

5 miles NE of Woodbridge on the B1084

At the northern edge of Rendlesham Forest, the village of Butley has a splendid 14th century gatehouse, all that remains of **Butley Priory**, an Augustinian priory founded by Ranulf de Glanville in 1171. The gatehouse is, by itself, a fairly imposing building, with some interesting flintwork on the north façade (1320) and baronial carvings. Butley still has a working mill, remarkable for its fine Regency porch, and the parish church is Norman, with a 14th century tower.

There are some splendid country walks around Butley, notably by **Staverton Thicks**,

which has a deer park and woods of oak and holly. The oldest trees date back more than 400 years. Butley Clumps is an avenue of beech trees planted in fours, with a pine tree at the centre of each clump – the technical term for such an arrangement is a quincunx. Butley has long been renowned for its oysters.

CHILLESFORD

6 miles E of Woodbridge on the B1084

Brick was once big business here, and while digging for clay the locals made many finds, including hundreds of varieties of molluscs and the skeleton of an enormous whale. Chillesford supplies some of the clay for Aldeburgh brickworks.

ORFORD

12 miles E of Woodbridge at the end of the B1084

Without doubt one of the most charming and interesting of all the places in Suffolk, Orford has something to please everyone. The ruins of the **Castle**, one of the most important in medieval England, are a most impressive sight, even though the keep is all that remains of the original building commissioned by Henry II in 1165. The walls of the keep are 90 feet high and 10 feet deep, and behind them are many rooms and passages in a remarkable state of preservation. A climb up the spiral staircase to the top provides splendid views over the surrounding countryside and to the sea.

St Bartholomew's Church was built at the same time, though the present church dates from the 14th century. A wonderful sight at night when floodlit, the church is regularly used for the performance of concerts and recitals, and many of Benjamin Britten's works were first heard here. At the east end lie the still-splendid Norman remains, all that is left of the original chancel.

These two grand buildings indicate that Orford was a very important town at one time. Indeed it was once a thriving port, but the steadily growing shingle bank of Orford Ness gradually cut it off from the sea, and down the years its appeal has changed.

The sea may have gone from Orford but the river is still there, and in summer the quayside is alive with yachts and pleasure craft. On the other side of the river is **Orford Ness**, the largest vegetated shingle spit in England which is home to a variety of rare flora and fauna. The lighthouse marks the most easterly point (jointly with Lowestoft) in Britain.

Access to the 10-mile spit, which is in the hands of the National Trust, is by ferry from Orford Quay. For many years the Ness was out of bounds to the public, being used for various military purposes, including pre-war radar research under Sir Robert Watson-Watt. Trails pass through the varied habitats found on the Ness, as well as areas and buildings of historic interest such as the First World War airfield site, firing ranges and the lighthouse. Boat trips also leave Orford Quay for the RSPB reserve at **Havergate Island**,

Orford Castle

haunt of avocet and tern (the former returned in 1947 after being long absent).

The **Dunwich Underwater Exploration Exhibition** in Front Street features exhibits on marine archaeology, coastal erosion and more, gleaned from the exploration of the ruins of the former town of Dunwich, now largely claimed by the sea.

Back in the market square are a handsome town hall, two pubs with a fair quota of smuggling tales, a

91

Lowestoft has some interesting literary and musical connections. The Elizabethan playwright, poet and pamphleteer Thomas Nash was born here in 1567. His last work, Lenten Stuffe, was a eulogy to the herring trade and specifically to Great Yarmouth. Joseph Conrad (Jozef Teodor Konrad Korzeniowski), working as a deckhand on a British freighter bound for Constantinople, jumped ship here in 1878, speaking only a few words of the language in which he was to become one of the modern masters. Benjamin Britten, the greatest English composer of the 20th century, is associated with several places in Suffolk, but Lowestoft has the earliest claim, for it is here that he was born in 1913.

well-loved restaurant serving Butley oysters and a smokehouse where kippers, salmon, trout, ham, sausages, chicken and even garlic are smoked over Suffolk oak.

BAWDSEY

7 miles SE of Woodbridge on the B1083

The B1083 runs from Woodbridge through farming country and several attractive villages (Sutton, Shottisham, Alderton) to Bawdsey, beyond which lies the mouth of the River Deben, the end of the Sussex Coastal Path, and the ferry to Felixstowe. The late-Victorian Bawdsey Manor was taken over by the Government and became the centre for radar development when Orford Ness was deemed unsuitable. By the beginning of the Second World War there were two dozen secret radar stations in Britain, and radar HQ moved from Bawdsey to Dundee. The manor is now a leisure centre.

RAMSHOLT

7 miles SE of Woodbridge off the B1083

Ramsholt is a tiny community on the north bank of the Deben a little way up from Bawdsey. The pub is a popular port of call for yachtsmen, and half a mile from the quay, in quiet isolation, stands the Church of All Saints with its round tower. Road access to Ramsholt is from the B1083 just south of Shottisham.

HOLLESLEY

5 miles SE of Woodbridge off the B1083

The Deben and the Ore turn this part of Suffolk almost into a peninsula, and on the seaward side

lie Hollesley and Shingle Street. The latter stands upon a shingle bank at the entrance to the Ore and comprises a row of little houses, a coastguard cottage and a Martello tower. Its very isolation is an attraction, and the sight of the sea rushing into and out of the river is worth the journey.

Brendan Behan did not enjoy his visit. Brought here on a swimming outing from the Borstal at Hollesley, he declared that the waves had 'no limit but the rim of the world'. Looking out to the bleak North Sea, it is easy to see what he meant.

LOWESTOFT

The most easterly town in Britain had its heyday as a major fishing port during the late 19th and early 20th centuries, when it was a mighty rival to Great Yarmouth in the herring industry. That industry has been in major decline since the First World War, but Lowestoft is still a fishing port and the trawlers still chug into the harbour in the early morning with the catches of the night. Guided tours of the **Fish Market** and the **Harbour** are available.

Lowestoft is also a popular holiday resort, the star attraction being the lovely South Beach with its golden sands, safe swimming, two piers and all the expected seaside amusements and entertainments. **Claremont Pier**, over 600 feet in length, was built in 1902, ready to receive day-trippers on the famous Belle steamers. The buildings near the pier were developed in mid-Victorian times by the company of Sir Samuel Morton Peto, also responsible for Nelson's Column, the statues in the Houses of Parliament, the Reform Club and Somerleyton Hall.

At the heart of the town is the old harbour, home to the Royal Norfolk & Suffolk Yacht Club and the Lifeboat Station. Further upriver is the commercial part of the port, used chiefly by ships carrying grain and timber. The history of Lowestoft is naturally tied up with the sea, and much of that history is recorded in fascinating detail in the **Lowestoft & East Suffolk Maritime Museum** with model boats, fishing gear, a lifeboat cockpit, paintings and shipwrights' tools. The setting is a flint-built fisherman's cottage in Sparrow's Nest Gardens. The **Royal Naval Patrol Museum** nearby remembers the minesweeping service in models, photographs, documents and uniforms. Lowestoft had England's first lighthouse, installed in 1609. The present one dates from 1874. Also in Sparrow's Nest Gardens is the War Memorial Museum, dedicated to those who served during the Second World War. There's a chronological photographic collection of the bombing of the town, aircraft models and a chapel of remembrance.

St Margaret's Church, notable for its decorated ceiling and copper-covered spire, is a memorial

Lowestoft Harbour

to seafarers, and the north aisle has panels recording the names of fishermen lost at sea from 1865 to 1923.

Just north of town, with access from the B1385, Pleasurewood Hill is the largest theme park in East Anglia.

Oulton Broad, on the western edge of Lowestoft, is a major centre of amusements afloat, with boats for hire and cruises on the Waveney. It also attracts visitors to Nicholas Everitt Park to look around **Lowestoft Museum**, housed in historic Broad House. Opened by the Queen and Prince Philip in 1985, the museum displays archaeological finds from local sites, some now lost to the sea, costumes, toys, domestic bygones and a fine collection of Lowestoft porcelain. (The porcelain industry lasted from about 1760 to 1800, using clay from the nearby Gunton Hall Estate. The soft-paste ware,

•

Lowestoft's Maritime Museum specialises in the history of the Lowestoft fishing fleet, from early sail to steam and through to the modern diesel-powered vessels. Methods of fishing are recorded, including trawling and the no longer practised driftnet fishing for herring, and other displays depict the town's association with the Royal Navy and the evolution of lifeboats. The state-of-the-art boathouse at South Pier was part of a £24 million project to redevelop Lowestoft's yacht basin; the all-weather Tyne class lifeboat is adjacent to the building with its own secure pontoon. An impressive 39 Medals for Gallantry have been awarded to the Lowestoft lifeboat crews, the last in 1997.

•

67 EAST ANGLIA TRANSPORT MUSEUM

Carlton Colville

At Carlton Colville you will find a museum unique to the last detail, for this is the only place in the British Isles where visitors can not only view but also ride on all three principal forms of public transport from the earlier part of the 20th century. .

 see page 264

resembling Bow porcelain, was usually decorated in white and blue.)

AROUND LOWESTOFT

CARLTON COLVILLE
3 miles SW of Lowestoft on the B1384

Many a transport enthusiast has enjoyed a grand day out at the **East Anglia Transport Museum**, where children young and old (and even very old!) can climb aboard wide-eyed to enjoy rides on buses, trams and trolleybuses (one of the resident trolleybuses was built at the Garrett works in Leiston). The East Suffolk narrow-gauge railway winds its way around the site, and there's a 1930s street with all the authentic accessories, plus lorries, vans and steamrollers.

Carlton Marshes is Oulton Broad's nature reserve, with grazing marsh and fen, reached by the Waveney Way footpath.

Church of St John the Baptist, Lound

BLUNDESTON
4 miles N of Lowestoft off the A12

Known chiefly as the village used by Charles Dickens as the birthplace of that writer's 'favourite child', David Copperfield, the morning light shining on the sundial of Blundeston's **Church** – which has the tallest, narrowest Saxon round tower of any in East Anglia – greeted young David as he looked out of his bedroom window in the nearby Rookery. He said of the churchyard: *"There is nothing half so green that I know anywhere, as the grass of that churchyard, nothing half so shady as its trees; nothing half so quiet as its tombstones."*

LOUND
5 miles N of Lowestoft off the A12

Lound's parish **Church of St John the Baptist**, in the very north of the county, is sometimes known as the 'golden church'. This epithet is the result of the handiwork of designer/architect Sir Ninian Comper, seen most memorably in the gilded organ-case with two trumpeting angels, the font cover and the rood screen. The last is a very elaborate affair, with several heraldic arms displayed. The surprise package here is the modern St Christopher mural on the north wall. It includes Sir Ninian at the wheel of his Rolls Royce – and in 1976 an aeroplane was added to the scene!

SOMERLEYTON
5 miles NW of Lowestoft on the B1074

Somerleyton Hall, one of the

grandest and most distinctive of stately homes, is a splendid Victorian mansion built in Anglo-Italian style by Samuel Morton Peto. The Oak Room, with 17th century panelling from the original Jacobean house, some outstanding wood carvings and an exquisite silver and gilt mirror made for the Doge's Palace in Venice, is one of several superb rooms in this most magnificent of houses; others include the elegant Library, its walls lined with over 3,500 books, the Dining Room and the sumptuous Ballroom. The grounds include a renowned yew-hedge maze, where people have been going round in circles since 1846, walled and sunken gardens, and a 300-feet pergola. There's also a sweet little miniature railway, and **Fritton Lake Countryworld**, part of the Somerleyton Estate, is a 10-minute drive away. The Hall is open to the public on most days in summer.

HERRINGFLEET

5 miles NW of Lowestoft on the B1074

Standing above the River Waveney, the parish **Church of St Margaret** is a charming sight with its Saxon round tower, thatched roof and lovely glass. Herringfleet Windmill is a beautiful black-tarred smock mill in working order, the last survivor of the Broadland wind pump, whose job was to assist in draining the marshes. This example was built in 1820 and worked regularly until the 1950s. It contains a fireplace and a wooden bench, providing a modicum of comfort for a millman on a cold night shift.

To arrange a visit call 01473 583352.

KESSINGLAND

3 miles S of Lowestoft off the A12

A small resort with a big history, Palaeolithic and Neolithic remains have come to light in Kessingland, and traces of an ancient forest have been unearthed on the sea bed. At the time of William the Conqueror, Kessingland prospered with its herring industry and was a major fishing port rivalled only by Dunwich. The estuary gradually silted up, sealing off the river with a shingle bank and cutting off the village's major source of wealth. The tower of the church of St Edmund reaches up almost 100 feet – not unusual on the coast - where it provides a conspicuous landmark for sailors and fishermen. Most of Kessingland's maritime trappings have now disappeared: the lighthouse on the cliffs was scrapped 100 years ago, the lifeboat lasted until 1936 (having saved 144 lives), and one of the several former coastguard stations was purchased by the writer Rider Haggard as a holiday home.

Kessingland's major tourist attraction is the **Suffolk Wildlife Park**, 100 acres of coastal parkland that are home to a wide range of wild animals, from aardvarks to zebras by way of bats, flamingos, giraffes, meerkats and sitatunga. The flamingos have their own enclosure. Burmese pythons are used for snake-handling sessions – an experience that's definitely not for everyone!

•

Samuel Morton Peto learned his skills as a civil engineer and businessman from his uncle, and was still a young man when he put the Reform Club and Nelson's Column into his CV. The Somerleyton Hall he bought in 1843 was a Tudor and Jacobean mansion. He and his architect virtually rebuilt the place, and also built Somerleyton village, a cluster of thatched redbrick cottages. Nor was this the limit of Peto's achievements, for he ran a company which laid railways all over the world and was a Liberal MP, first for Norwich, then for Finsbury and finally for Bristol. His company foundered in 1863 and Somerleyton Hall was sold to Sir Francis Crossley, one of three brothers who made a fortune in mass-producing carpets. Crossley's son became Baron Somerleyton in 1916, and the Baron's grandson is the present Lord Somerleyton.

•

'Church within a Church', Covehithe

not afford a replacement on the same grand scale, so in 1672 it was decided to remove the roof and sell off some of the material. From what was left a small new church was built within the old walls. The original tower still stands, spared by Cromwell for use as a landmark for sailors.

SOUTHWOLD

A town full of character and interest for the holidaymaker and for the historian. Though one of the most popular resorts on the east coast, Southwold has very little of the kiss-me-quick commercialism that spoils so many seaside towns. It's practically an island, bounded by creeks and marshes, the River Blyth and the North Sea, and has managed to retain the genteel atmosphere of the 19th century. There are some attractive buildings, from pink-washed cottages to elegant Georgian town houses, many of them ranged around a series of open spaces – the 'Southwold Greens' – which were left undeveloped to act as firebreaks after much of the town was lost in the great fire of 1659.

In a seaside town whose buildings present a wide variety of styles, shapes and sizes, William Denny's **Buckenham House** is among the most elegant and interesting. On the face of it a classic Georgian town house, it's actually much older, dating probably from the middle of the 16th century. Richard Buckenham,

COVEHITHE

7 miles S of Lowestoft off the A12

Leave the A12 at Wrentham and head for the tiny coastal village of Covehithe, remarkable for its 'church within a church'. The massive **Church of St Andrew**, partly funded by the Benedictine monks at Cluniac, was left to decline after being laid waste by Dowsing's men. The villagers could a wealthy Tudor merchant, was the man who had it built and it was truly impressive in size, as can be deduced from the dimensions of the cellar (now the Coffee House). Many fine features survive, including moulded cornices, carefully restored sash windows, Tudor brickwork and heavy timbers in the ceilings.

The town, which was granted its charter by Henry VII in 1489, once prospered, like many of its neighbours, through herring fishing, and the few remaining fishermen share the harbour on the River Blyth with pleasure craft. Also adding to the period atmosphere is the recently renovated 1900 pier, which was once named Pier of the Year by the National Piers Society; as a result of storm damage this is much shorter than in the days when steamers from London called in on their way up the east coast.

There are also bathing huts, and a brilliant white **Lighthouse** that's over 100 years old. It stands 100 feet tall and its light can be seen 17 miles out to sea. Guided tours of the lighthouse culminate in unrivalled views over the town and out to sea. Beneath the lighthouse stands a little Victorian pub, the **Sole Bay Inn**, whose name recalls a battle fought off Southwold in 1672 between the British and French fleets and the Dutch. This was an episode in the Third Anglo-Dutch War, when the Duke of York, Lord High Admiral of England and later to be crowned James II, used Sutherland House in

Southwold Beach

Southwold as his headquarters and launched his fleet (along with that of the French) from here. One distinguished victim of this battle was Edward Montagu, 1st Earl of Sandwich, great-grandfather of the man whose gambling mania did not allow him time for a formal meal. By inserting slices of meat between slices of bread, the 4th Earl ensured that his name would live on.

Southwold's maritime past is recorded in the **Museum** set in a Dutch-style cottage in Victoria Street. Open daily in the summer months, it records the famous battle and also features exhibits on local archaeology, geology and natural history, and the history of the Southwold railway. The **Southwold Sailors' Reading Room** contains pictures, ship models and other items, and at Gun Hill the Southwold **Lifeboat Museum** has a small collection of RNLI-related material with particular reference to Southwold. The main attraction at **Gun Hill** is a set of six 18-pounder guns,

68 COASTERS OF SOUTHWOLD

Southwold

Coasters is open seven days a week for breakfasts, lunches and evening meals using prime local produce.

⫙ see page 265

69 THE KINGS HEAD HOTEL

Southwold

A traditional family hostelry with home-cooked food and three spacious en suite rooms for B&B guests.

⫙ ⊨ see page 265

No visitor to Southwold should leave without spending some time in the splendid Church of St Edmund King and Martyr, which emerged relatively unscathed from the ravages of the Commonwealth. The lovely painted roof and wide screen are the chief glories, but the slim-stemmed 15th century pulpit and the Elizabethan Holy Table must also be seen. Inside the church there's also a splendid 'Jack o' the Clock' – a little wooden man in War of the Roses armour, holding a bell. A rope is pulled to sound the bell to mark the start of church services.

captured in 1746 at the Battle of Culloden and presented to the town (hitherto more or less undefended) by the Duke of Cumberland. Amber has been found on the beaches of Southwold for many years, and at the back of the Amber Shop in the market place is an **Amber Museum** with a large number of amber pieces, some in original form, others carved into beautiful pieces of jewellery.

AROUND SOUTHWOLD

WANGFORD

2 miles NW of Southwold off the A12

There's some great walking in the country around Southwold, both along the coast and inland. At Wangford, a mile or so inland, **Henham Walks** are waymarked paths through Repton Park, lake and woods. A splendid place for a ramble or a picnic, or to see the wildlife, rare-breed sheep and Highland cattle, the paths are open only on specific dates, and there's an entry fee.

Also at Wangford is the Perpendicular **Church of St Peter and St Paul**, built on the site of a Benedictine priory. Even closer to Southwold is **Reydon Wood Nature Reserve**.

BLYTHBURGH

2 miles SW of Southwold, A1095 then A12

Blythburgh's **Church of Holy Trinity** is one of the wonders of Suffolk, a stirring sight as it rises from the reed beds, visible for miles around and floodlit at night to spectacular effect. This 'Cathedral of the Marshes' reflects the days when Blythburgh was a prosperous port with a bustling quayside wool trade. With the silting up of the river, trade rapidly fell off and the church fell into decay. In 1577 the steeple of the 14th century tower was struck by lightning in a severe storm; it fell into the nave, shattering the font and taking two lives. The scorch marks visible to this day on the north door are said to be the claw

Church of Holy Trinity, Blythburgh

marks of the Devil in the guise of hellhound Black Shuck, left as he sped towards Bungay to terrify the congregation of St Mary's.

Disaster struck again in 1644, when Dowsing and his men smashed windows, ornaments and statues, blasted the wooden angels in the roof with hundreds of bullets and used the nave as a stable, with tethering rings screwed into the pillars of the nave. Luckily, the bench-end carvings escaped the desecration, not being labelled idolatrous. These depict the Labours of the Months, and the Seven Deadly Sins. Blythburgh also has a Jack o'the Clock, a brother of the figure at Southwold, and the priest's chamber over the south porch has been lovingly restored complete with an altar made with wood from HMS *Victory*. The angels may have survived, but the font was defaced to remove the signs of the sacraments.

The **Norman Gwatkin Nature Reserve** is an area of marsh and fen with two hides, walkways and a willow coppice.

WENHASTON

5 miles W of Southwold off the A12

The **Church of St Peter** is well worth a detour. Saxon stones are embedded in its walls, but the most remarkable feature is the Doom (Last Judgement scene), said to have been painted around 1500 by a monk from Blythburgh.

When the rood was ordered to be taken down during the reign of Edward VI, the doom painting was covered with whitewash and not rediscovered until 1892.

WALBERSWICK

1 mile SW of Southwold on the B1387

The story is familiar: flourishing fishing port; grand church; changing of the coastline due to erosion and silting; decline of fishing and trading; no money to maintain the church; church falls into disrepair. Towards the end of the 16th century, a smaller church was built within the original St Andrew's, by then in ruins through neglect. The situation in Walberswick had also been exacerbated by the seizing of church lands and revenues by the King, and by a severe fire.

Fishing hardly exists today, and boating in Walberswick is almost entirely a weekend and holiday activity. The tiny 'church within a church' is still in use, its churchyard a nature reserve. South of the village is the bird sanctuary of **Walberswick & Westleton Heaths**.

HALESWORTH

16 miles SW of Lowestoft on the A144

Granted a market in 1222, Halesworth reached the peak of its trading importance when the River Blyth was made navigable as far as the town in 1756. A stroll around the streets reveals several buildings of architectural interest. The Market Place has a handsome Elizabethan timber-framed house, but the chief attraction for the visitor is the **Halesworth and District Museum** at the railway station, in Station Road, where

A mile south of Blythburgh, at the junction of the A12 and the Walberswick road, Toby's Walks is an ideal place for a picnic and, like so many places in Suffolk, has its own ghost story. This concerns Tobias Gill, a dragoon drummer who murdered a local girl and was hanged here after a trial at Ipswich. His ghost is said to haunt the heath, but this should not deter picnickers.

For more than two centuries, Walberswick has been a magnet for painters, with the religious ruins, the beach and the sea being favourite subjects for visiting artists. The tradition continues unabated, and many academics have also made their homes here.

Close to the Church in Bungay is the famous octagonal Butter Cross, rebuilt after the great fire of 1688 and topped by Justice with her scales and sword. This building was once used as a prison, with a dungeon below.

exhibits feature local geology and archaeology, with various fossils and flints on display, and there's also a fascinating account of the Halesworth witchcraft trials of 1645.

Halesworth Gallery, at Steeple End, holds a collection of contemporary paintings, sculpture and other artwork in a converted row of 17th century almshouses.

BRAMFIELD

3 miles S of Halesworth on the A144

The massive Norman round tower of **St Andrew's Church** is separate from the main building and was built as a defensive structure, with walls over 3 feet thick. Dowsing ran riot here in 1643, destroying 24 superstitious pictures, one crucifix, a picture of Christ and 12 angels on the roof. The most important monument is one to Sir Arthur Coke, sometime Lord Chief Justice, who died in 1629, and his wife Elizabeth. Arthur is kneeling, resplendent in full armour, while Elizabeth is lying on her bed with a baby in her arms. This monument is the work of Nicholas Stone, the most important English mason and sculptor of his day. The Cokes at one time occupied Bramfield Hall, and another family, in residence for 300 years, were the Rabetts, whose coat of arms in the church punningly depicts rabbits on its shield.

BUNGAY

9 miles N of Halesworth on the A144

An ancient fortress town on the River Waveney, the river played an important part in Bungay's fortunes

until well into the 18th century, with barges laden with coal, corn, malt and timber plying the route to the coast. The river is no longer navigable above Geldeston, but is a great attraction for anglers and yachtsmen.

Bungay is best known for its Castle, built in its original form by Hugh Bigod, 1st Earl of Norfolk, as a rival to Henry II's castle at Orford. In 1173 Hugh took the side of the rebellious sons of Henry, but this insurrection ended with the surrender of the castle to the King. Hugh was killed not long after this episode while on the Third Crusade; his son Roger inherited the title and the castle, but it was another Roger Bigod who came to Bungay in 1294 and built the round tower and mighty outer walls that stand today.

To the north of the castle are Bungay's two surviving churches of note (the *Domesday Book* records five). The Saxon round tower of **Holy Trinity Church** is the oldest complete structure in the town, and a brass plate on the door commemorates the church's narrow escape from the fire of 1688 that destroyed much of the town (similar disasters overtook many other towns with close-set timber-and-thatch buildings). The **Church of St Mary** - now deconsecrated - was not so lucky, being more or less completely gutted. The tower survives to dominate the townscape, and points of interest in the church itself include a woodcarving of the Resurrection presented by Rider Haggard, and a

Bungay Butter Cross

Trust, on the banks of the Waveney, where the largest collection of otters in natural enclosures is bred for re-introduction into the wild. The British otter tends to be shy and retiring, but his cousins the Asian short-clawed otters are playful and extrovert and always delighted to welcome visitors. There are some lovely walks by the river and the lakes teeming with waterfowl and other wetland wildlife. The flock of free-flying Barnacle geese is probably the largest in the country. Also at home in the grounds are Muntjac and fallow deer.

FLIXTON

2 miles SW of Bungay on the B1062

Javelin, Meteor, Sea Vixen, Avro Anson C19, Dassault Mystère IVA, Westland Whirlwind: names that evoke earlier days of flying, and just four of more than 25 aircraft on show at the **Norfolk and Suffolk Aviation Museum**, on the site of a USAAF Liberator base during the Second World War. There's a lot of associated material, both civil and military, covering the period from the First World War to the present day. The museum incorporates the Royal Observer Corps Museum, RAF Bomber Command Museum, and the Museum and Memorial of the

monument to General Robert Kelso, who fought in the American War of Independence.

A century before the fire, the church received a visit, during a storm, from the devilish Black Shuck, a retriever-like hound who, hot from causing severe damage at Blythburgh, raced down the nave and killed two worshippers. A weather vane in the market place puts the legend into verse:

All down the church in midst of fire
The Hellish Monster Flew
And Passing onwards to the Quire
He many people slew.

EARSHAM

1 mile SW of Bungay off the A143

All Saints Church and **Earsham Hall** are well worth a visit, but what brings most people here is the **Otter**

101

72   THE SWAN INN

Barnby, nr Beccles

Visitors come from all over
the region to enjoy the
superb seafood dishes that
are the speciality of the
Swan Inn.

|| see page 266

*The parish Church of St
Michael in Beccles was
built in the second half of
the 14th century by the
Abbot of Bury. Its tower
stands separate, built in
the 16th century, rising
almost 100 feet and
containing a peal of
bells. An unusual feature
at the north façade is an
outside pulpit taking the
form of a small balcony.
The priest could enter the
pulpit from inside the
church and preach to
lepers, who were not
allowed inside. Nelson's
parents, the Reverend
Edmund Nelson and
Catherine Suckling, were
married in St Michael's,
as was the great Suffolk
poet George Crabbe.*

446th Bomb Group - the Bungay
Buckeroos. Tel: 01986 896644.
American airmen presented the
gates into Flixton churchyard.

MENDHAM

6 miles SW of Bungay off the A143

This pretty little village on the
Waveney was the birthplace of Sir
Alfred Munnings RA, who was
born at Mendham Mill, where his
father was the miller. Sir Alfred's
painting *Charlotte and her Pony* was
the inspiration for the village sign,
which was unveiled by his niece
Kathleen Hadingham.

BECCLES

9 miles W of Lowestoft on the A146

The largest town in the Waveney
district at the southernmost point
of the Broads, Beccles has in its
time been home to Saxons and
Vikings, and at one time the market
here was a major supplier of
herring (up to 60,000 a year) to the
Abbey at Bury St Edmunds. At the
height of its trading importance
Beccles must have painted a
splendidly animated picture, with
wherries constantly on the move
transporting goods from seaports
to inland towns. The same stretch
of river is still alive, but now with
the yachts and pleasure boats of the
holidaymakers and weekenders who
fill the town in summer. The regatta
in July and August is a particularly
busy time.

Fire, sadly such a common part
of small-town history, ravaged
Beccles at various times in the 16th
and 17th centuries, destroying
much of the old town. For that

reason the dwellings extant today
are largely Georgian in origin, with
handsome redbrick facades. One
that is not is **Roos Hall**, a gabled
building dating from 1583. Just
outside the town, far enough away
to escape the great fire of 1586, it
was built to a Dutch design,
underlining the links between East
Anglia and the Low Countries
forged by the wool and weaving
trades. Elizabeth I stayed at the
Hall just after it was completed,
when she visited Beccles to present
the town's charter; the occasion is
depicted in the town sign. One of
the hall's owners was Sir John
Suckling (later to become
Controller of the Household to
James I), one of whose
descendants was Lord Nelson. Any
old hall worth its salt has a ghost,
and the Roos representative is a
headless coachman who is said to
appear on Christmas Eve.

A fine building with Dutch-
style gables houses the **Beccles
and District Museum**, whose
contents include 19th century toys
and costume, farm implements,
items from the old town gaol and
memorabilia from the sailing
wherries, including a wealth of old
photographs.

RINGSFIELD

2 miles SW of Beccles off the A146

In a wooded valley away from the
main village, Ringfield's parish
Church of All Saints has a dual
appeal: the marvellous array of
spring flowers in the churchyard
and the story of the robins. A pair
nested in the lectern 50 years ago

and raised a family, an event recalled in carvings on the new lectern and on the porch gates. The original nest, in the old lectern, can still be found in the church.

SOUTH AND WEST SUFFOLK

IPSWICH

History highlights Ipswich as the birthplace of Cardinal Wolsey, but the story of Suffolk's county town starts very much earlier than that. It has been a port since the time of the Roman occupation, and by the 7th century the Anglo-Saxons had expanded it into the largest port in the country. King John granted a civic charter in 1200, confirming the townspeople's right to their own laws and administration, and for several centuries the town prospered as a port, exporting wool, textiles and agricultural products.

Thomas Wolsey arrived on the scene in 1475, the son of a wealthy butcher. Educated at Magdalen College, Oxford, he was ordained a priest in 1498 and rose quickly in influence, becoming chaplain to Henry VII and then Archbishop of York, a cardinal, and Lord Chancellor under Henry VIII. He was quite indispensable to the king and had charge of foreign policy as well as powerful sway over judicial institutions. He also managed to amass enormous wealth, enabling him to found a grammar school in Ipswich and Cardinal's College

(later Christ Church) in Oxford.

Cardinal Wolsey had long been hated by certain nobles for his low birth and arrogance, and they were easily able to turn Henry against him when his attempts to secure an annulment from the Pope of the king's marriage to Catherine of Aragon met with failure. Stripped of most of his offices following a charge of overstepping his authority as a legate, he was later charged with treason, but died while travelling from York to London to face the king. His death put an end to his plans for the grammar school - all that remains now is a redbrick gateway.

When the cloth market fell into decline in the 17th century, a respite followed in the following century, when the town was a food-distribution port during the Napoleonic Wars. At the beginning of the 19th century the risk from silting was becoming acute at a time when trade was improving and industries were springing up. The Wet Dock, constructed in 1842, solved the silting problem and, with the railway arriving shortly after,

Wolsey's Gate, Ipswich

73 SIDEGATE GUEST HOUSE

Ipswich

Award winning guesthouse on the site of the side gate to Round Wood, Lord Nelson's 'dream cottage' which he bought in 1797

see page 267

In a 1937-built one-time trolleybus depot on Cobham Road is the Ipswich Transport Museum, a fascinating collection dedicated to preserving the transport and engineering heritage of the Ipswich area. Among the more unusual exhibits are a monorail for transporting spoil, a road sweeper converted from a Morris car, a horse-drawn tower wagon for maintaining overhead wires, and what is thought to be the oldest trolleybus in the world (Ipswich no.2, built by Railless in 1923).

On the outskirts of Ipswich, signposted from Nacton Road, is Orwell Country Park, a 150-acre site of wood, heath and reed beds by the Orwell estuary. At this point the river is crossed by the imposing Orwell Bridge, a graceful construction in pre-stressed concrete that was completed in 1982 and is not far short of a mile in length.

Ipswich could once more look forward to a safe future. The Victorians were responsible for considerable development: symbols of their civic pride include the handsome **Old Custom House** by the Wet Dock, the Town Hall, and the splendid **Tolly Cobbold** brewery, rebuilt at the end of the 19th century, 150 years after brewing started on the site. Victorian enterprise depleted some of the older buildings, but a number survive, notably the house where Wolsey was born, and the Ancient House (also called Sparrowe's House) with its wonderful pargeting and Royal Arms of Charles II – perhaps painted after the King hid here after the Battle of Worcester. Fine former Tudor merchants' houses grace the town's historic waterfront, such as Isaac Lord's and The Neptune (the latter was once home of Thomas Eldred, who circumnavigated the world with Thomas Cavendish shortly after Drake). A dozen medieval churches remain, of which St Margaret's is the finest, boasting some very splendid flintwork and a double hammerbeam roof. Another, St Stephen's, today houses the town's Tourist Information Centre.

Christchurch Mansion is a beautiful Tudor home standing in 65 acres of attractive parkland a short walk from the town centre. Furnished as an English country house, it contains a major collection of works by Constable and Gainsborough, as well as many other paintings, prints and

sculptures by Suffolk artists from the 17th century onwards.

Wolsey Art Gallery is a purpose-built space entered through Christchurch Mansion which features changing displays including touring and national exhibitions. **Ipswich Museum** is in a Victorian building in the High Street. Displays include a natural history gallery, a wildlife gallery complete with a model of a mammoth, a reconstruction of a Roman villa, replicas of Sutton Hoo treasures and a display of elaborately carved timbers from the homes of wealthy 17th century merchants. There is also a rolling programme of exciting temporary exhibitions, events and displays.

Ipswich's position at the head of the River Orwell has always influenced the town's fortunes; today, a stroll along the waterfront should be included in any visit. Tudor houses and medieval churches stand alongside stylish new apartments which overlook the new marinas. An art gallery and choice of eateries enhance the experience, and there are regular pub cruises, leaving the Ipswich waterfront and travelling the pretty River Orwell as far as Felixstowe harbour.

Notables from the world of the arts with Ipswich connections include Thomas Gainsborough, who got his first major commissions here to paint portraits of local people; David Garrick, the renowned actor-manager, who made his debut here in 1741 as Aboan in Thomas Southerne's *Oroonoko*; and the peripatetic Charles Dickens, who stayed at the Great White Horse while still a young reporter with the Morning Chronicle. Soon afterwards, he featured the tavern in *The Pickwick Papers* as the place where Mr Pickwick wanders inadvertently into a lady's bedroom. Sir V S Pritchett was born in Ipswich, while Enid Blyton trained as a kindergarten teacher at Ipswich High School.

AROUND IPSWICH

BRAMFORD

2 miles NW of Ipswich off the A14

Bramford has a pretty little church, St Mary's, with a 13th century stone screen. It was once an important spot on the river route, when barges from Ipswich stopped to unload corn; the walls of the old lock are still visible. In the vicinity is **Suffolk Water Park**, where the lake welcomes canoeists and windsurfers.

BAYLHAM

5 miles NW of Ipswich off the B1113O

The Roman site of Combretrovium is home to **Baylham House Rare Breeds Farm**, and visitors (April-early October) will find displays and information relating to both Rome and rare animals. The farm's chief concern is the survival of rare breeds, and there are breeding groups of cattle, sheep, pigs, goats and poultry.

NACTON

4 miles SE of Ipswich off the A14

South of Nacton's medieval church lies **Orwell Park House**, which was built in the 18th century by Admiral Edward Vernon, sometime Member of Parliament for Ipswich. The admiral, who had won an important victory over the Spanish in the War of Jenkins Ear, was known to his men as 'Old Grog' because of his habit of wearing a cloak of coarse grogram cloth. His nickname passed into the language when he ordered that the rum ration dished out daily to sailors should be diluted with water to combat the drunkenness that was rife in the service. That was in 1740, but this allotted ration of 'grog' was officially issued to sailors right up until 1970.

Nacton Picnic Site in Shore Lane (signposted from the village) commands wonderful views of the Orwell and is a prime spot in winter for birdwatchers. The birds feed very well off the mud flats.

LEVINGTON

5 miles SE of Ipswich off the A14

A pretty village on the banks of the Orwell. Fisons established a factory here in 1956, and developed the now famous Levington Compost. On the foreshore below the village is an extensive marina which has brought a bustling air to the area. The coastal footpath along the bank of the Orwell leads across the nature reserve of **Trimley Marshes** and on to Felixstowe.

TRIMLEY ST MARY & TRIMLEY ST MARTIN

6 miles SE of Ipswich off the A14

Twin villages with two churches in the same churchyard, famous

74 THE BRAMFORD COCK

Bramford

A much-loved local with a popular landlord, Adnams ale, well-priced pub grub and a twice-weekly Indian buffet.

see page 267

•

George Tomline bought Orwell Park House in 1857 and made it even more splendid, adding a conservatory, a ballroom and towers. He also changed the façade along handsome Georgian lines. The house became the setting for some of the grandest shooting parties ever seen in this part of the world, and such was the power of the Tomlines that they were able to move the village away from the house to its present site.

•

Trimley Marshes were created from farmland and comprise grazing marsh, reed beds and wetland that's home to an abundance of interesting plant life and many species of wildfowl, waders and migrant birds. Access is on foot from Trimley St Mary.

The original fishing hamlet from which the Victorian resort of Felixstowe was developed lies beyond a golf course north of the town. This is Felixstowe Ferry, a cluster of holiday homes, an inn, a boatyard, fishing sheds and two Martello towers. The sailing club is involved mainly with dinghy racing, and the whole place becomes a hive of activity during the class meetings. A walk from Felixstowe Ferry takes in a boatyard, Falkenham Marshes, St Ethelbert's Church, and an inlet where Edward III assembled a fleet of ships ready to sail to France. A ferry takes foot passengers (plus bicycles) across to Bawdsey.

Trimley residents have included the Cavendish family, whose best-known member was the adventurer Thomas Cavendish. In 1590 he became the second man to sail round the world. Two years later he died while embarked on another voyage. He is depicted on the village sign.

NEWBOURNE

7 miles E of Ipswich off the A12

A small miracle occurred here on the night of the hurricane of October 1987. One wall of the ancient St Mary's Church was blown out, and with it the stained glass, which shattered into fragments. One piece, showing the face of Christ, was found undamaged and was later incorporated into the rebuilt wall.

Two remarkable inhabitants of Newbourne were the Page brothers, who both stood over 7 feet tall; they enjoyed a career touring the fairs, and are buried in Newbourne churchyard.

WALDRINGFIELD

7 miles E of Ipswich off the A12

Waldringfield lies on a particularly beautiful stretch of the Deben estuary, and the waterfront is largely given over to leisure boating and cruising. The quay was once busy with barges, many of them laden with coprolite. This fossilised dung, the forerunner of today's fertilisers, was found in great abundance in and around Waldringfield, and a number of exhausted pits can still be seen.

FELIXSTOWE

12 miles SE of Ipswich off the A14

Until the early 17th century, Felixstowe was a little-known village - but it was the good Colonel Tomline of Orwell Park who put it on the map by creating a port to rival its near neighbour Harwich. He also started work on the Ipswich-Felixstowe railway (with a stop at Nacton for the guests of his grand parties), and 1887 saw the completion of both projects. Tomline also developed the resort aspects of Felixstowe, rivalling the amenities of Dovercourt, and when he died in 1887 most of his dreams had become reality. (He was, incidentally, cremated, one of the first in the county to be so disposed of in the modern era.) The town has suffered a number of ups and downs since that time, but continues to thrive as one of England's busiest ports, having been much extended in the 1960s. The resort is strung out round a wide, gently curving bay, where the long seafront road is made even prettier with trim lawns and gardens.

The **Martello Tower** is a noted landmark, as is the **Pier**, which was once long enough to merit an electric tramway. It was shortened as a security measure during the Second World War. All kinds of attractions are provided for holidaymakers, including one very unusual one. This is the **Felixstowe Water Clock**, a curious piece assembled from dozens of industrial bits and pieces.

At the southernmost tip of the peninsula is Landguard Point, where a nature reserve supports rare plants and migrating birds.

Just north on this shingle bank is **Landguard Fort**, built in 1718 to protect Harwich harbour and replacing an earlier construction ordered by Henry VIII. It is now home to **Felixstowe Museum**. The museum is actually housed in the Ravelin Block (1878), which was used as a mine storage depot by the army when a mine barrier was laid across the Orwell during the First World War. A fascinating variety of exhibits includes local history, model aircraft and model paddle steamers, Roman coins and the history of the fort itself, which was the scene of the last invasion of English soil. In 1667 Captain Nathaniel Darell and 500 men defeated Admiral de Ruyter's Dutch force. The fort is open daily from May to October. Beyond the fort is an excellent viewing point for watching the comings and goings of ships.

FRESTON

3 miles S of Ipswich off the B1080

Freston is an ancient village on the south bank of the Orwell, worth visiting for some fine old buildings and some curiosities. The most curious and best known of these buildings is the six-storey Tudor tower by the river in **Freston Park** (it's actually best viewed from across the river). This redbrick house, built around 1570, has just six rooms, one per storey. It might be a folly, but it was probably put up as a lookout tower to warn of enemies sailing up the river. The nicest theory is that it was built for Ellen, daughter of Lord Freston, to study a different subject each day, progressing floor by floor up the tower (and with Sundays off, presumably). Studies started with charity at 7 am, and continued onwards and upwards with tapestry, music, painting, literature and astronomy.

Freston Tower

WOOLVERSTONE

4 miles S of Ipswich on the B1456

Dating back to the Bronze Age, Woolverstone has a large marina along the banks of the Orwell. One of the buildings in the complex is Cat House, where it is said that a stuffed white cat placed in the window would be the all-clear sign for smugglers. **Woolverstone House** was originally St Peter's Home for 'Fallen Women', run by nuns. It was designed by Sir Edwin Lutyens and has its own chapel and bell tower.

TATTINGSTONE

4 miles S of Ipswich off the A137

The **Tattingstone Wonder**, on the road between Tattingstone and Stutton, looks like a church from the front, but it isn't. It was built by a local landowner to provide accommodation for estate workers. He presumably preferred to look at a church from his mansion than some plain little cottages. Tattingstone lies at the western edge of Alton Water, a vast man-made lake created as a reservoir in the late 1970s. A footpath runs round the perimeter, and there's a wildlife sanctuary. On the water itself all sorts of leisure activities are on offer, including angling, sailing and windsurfing.

STUTTON

6 miles S of Ipswich on the B1080

The elongated village of Stutton lies on the southern edge of Alton Water. The *Domesday Book* records six manor houses standing here, and there are still some grand properties down by the Stour. St Peter's Church stands isolated overlooking Holbrook Bay, and a footpath from the church leads all the way along the river to Shotley Gate. A little way north, on the B1080, Holbrook is a large village with a brook at the bottom of the hill. Water from the brook once powered Alton Mill, a weather-boarded edifice on a site occupied by watermills for more than 900 years. The mill is now a restaurant.

CHELMONDISTON

5 miles SE of Ipswich on the B1456

The church here is modern, but incorporates some parts of the original, which was destroyed by a flying bomb in 1944. In the same parish is the tiny riverside community of **Pin Mill**, a well-known beauty spot and sailing centre. The river views are particularly lovely at this point, and it's also a favourite place for woodland and heathland walks.

Pin Mill was once a major manufacturer of barges, and those imposing craft can still be seen, sharing the river with sailing boats and pleasure craft. Each year veteran barges gather for a race that starts here, at Buttermans Bay, and ends at Harwich. Arthur Ransome, author of *Swallows and Amazons*, stayed here and had boats built to his specifications. His *We Didn't Mean to Go to Sea* starts aboard a yacht mooring here.

ERWARTON

6 miles SE of Ipswich off the B1456

An impressive redbrick Jacobean gatehouse with a rounded arch, buttresses and pinnacles is part of **Erwarton Hall**, the family home of the Calthorpes. Anne Boleyn was the niece of Philip Calthorpe, and visited as a child and as queen. Just before her execution Anne apparently requested that her heart be buried in the family vault at St Mary's Church. A casket in the shape of a heart was found there in 1836, but when opened contained only dust that could not be positively identified. The casket was resealed and laid in the Lady Chapel.

SHOTLEY

8 miles SE of Ipswich on the B1456

Right at the end of the peninsula, with the Orwell on one side and the Stour on the other, Shotley was the home of HMS *Ganges*, where generations of sailors received their training. A small museum records the history of the establishment from 1905 to 1976, when it became a police academy. At the very tip of the Shotley Peninsula is a large marina where a classic boat festival is an annual occasion.

HINTLESHAM

7 miles W of Ipswich on the A1071

Hintlesham's glory is a magnificent hall dating from the 1570s, when it was the home of the Timperley family. It was considerably altered during the 18th century, when it acquired its splendid Georgian façade. For some years the hall was owned by the celebrated chef Robert Carrier, who developed it into the county's leading restaurant. It still functions as a high-class hotel and restaurant.

HADLEIGH

10 miles W of Ipswich on the A1071

The old and not-so-old blend harmoniously in a variety of architectural styles in Hadleigh. Timber-framed buildings, often with elaborate plasterwork, stand in the long main street as a reminder of the prosperity generated by the wool trade in the 14th to 16th centuries, and there are also some fine houses from the Regency and Victorian periods. The 15th century Guildhall has two overhanging storeys, and together with the Deanery Tower and the church makes for a magnificent trio of huge appeal and contrasting

construction – timber for the Guildhall, brick for the tower and flint for the church.

Guthrun, the Danish leader who was captured by Alfred and pardoned on condition that he became a Christian, made Hadleigh his HQ and lived here for 12 years. He was buried in the church, then a wooden construction but subsequently twice rebuilt. In the south chapel of the present church is a 14th century bench-end carving depicting the legendary scene of the wolf guarding the head of St Edmund. The wolf is wearing a monk's habit, indicating a satirical sense of humour in the carpenter. Also of interest is the Clock Bell, which stands outside the tower.

KERSEY

12 miles W of Ipswich off the A1141

The ultimate Suffolk picture-postcard village, Kersey boasts a wonderful collection of timbered merchants' houses and weavers' cottages with paint and thatch. The main street has a **Water Splash**, which, along with the 700-year-old Bell Inn, has featured in many films and travelogues. The Church of St Mary, which overlooks the village from its hilltop position, is of massive proportions, testimony to the wealth that came with the wool and cloth industry. Kersey's speciality was a coarse twill broadcloth much favoured for greatcoats and army uniforms. Headless angels and mutilated carvings are reminders of the Puritans' visit to the church, though some treasures survive, including

•

There are two good walks from Hadleigh, the first being along the Brett with access over medieval Toppesfield Bridge. The other is a walk along the disused railway line between Hadleigh and Raydon through peaceful, picturesque countryside. At Raydon a few buildings survive from the wartime base of the 353rd, 357th and 358th Fighter Groups of the USAAF. Two miles east of Hadleigh is Wolves Wood, an RSPB reserve with woodland nature trails - and no wolves!

•

Kersey Water Splash

hump-backed bridge. The timbered houses and thatched cottages look much the same as when they were built, and every year the villagers open their gardens to the public.

MONKS ELEIGH

16 miles W of Ipswich on the A1141

The setting of thatched cottages, a 14th century church and a pump on the village green is so traditional that Monks Eleigh was regularly used on railway posters as a lure to this wonderful part of the country.

BILDESTON

14 miles W of Ipswich on the B1115

More fine old buildings here, including timber-framed cottages with overhanging upper floors. The Church of St Mary has a superb carved door and a splendid hammerbeam roof. A tablet inside the church commemorates Captain Edward Rotherham, Commander of the Royal Sovereign at the Battle of Trafalgar. He died in Bildeston while staying with a friend, and is buried in the churchyard. The local manor was once a royal estate owned by Queen Edith, consort of Edward the Confessor. The only trace of the manor is an ancient manorial wood, enclosed by a deep ditch.

BRENT ELEIGH

17 miles W of Ipswich off the A1141

The church at Brent Eleigh, on a side road off the A1141, is remarkable for a number of quite beautiful ancient wall paintings, discovered during maintenance work as recently as 1960. The most

the ornate flintwork of the 15th century south porch. Traditional craftsmanship can still be seen in practice at the Kersey Pottery, which sells many items of stoneware plus paintings by Suffolk artists.

CHELSWORTH

14 miles W of Ipswich off the A1141

Chelsworth is an unspoilt delight in the lovely valley of the River Brett, which is crossed by a little double striking and moving of the paintings is one of the Crucifixion.

LAVENHAM

18 miles W of Ipswich on the A1141

An absolute gem of a town, the most complete and original of the medieval 'wool towns', with crooked timbered and whitewashed buildings lining the narrow streets from the 14th to the 16th centuries Lavenham flourished as one of the leading wool and cloth-making centres in the land. With the decline of that industry, however, the prosperous times soon came to an end. It is largely due to the fact that Lavenham found no replacement industry that so much of its medieval character remains: there was simply not enough money for the rebuilding and development programmes that changed many other towns, often for the worse. The medieval street pattern still exists, complete with market place and market cross.

Lavenham Guildhall

More than 350 of Lavenham's buildings are officially listed as being of architectural and historical interest, and none of them is finer than the **Guildhall**. This superb 16th century timbered building was originally the meeting place of the Guild of Corpus Christi, an organisation that regulated the production of wool. It now houses exhibitions of local history and the wool trade, and has a walled garden with a special area devoted to dye plants. **Little Hall** is hardly less remarkable, a 15th century hall house with a superb crown post roof. It was restored by the Gayer Anderson brothers, and has a fine collection of their furniture. The Church of St Peter and St Paul dominates the town from its elevated position. It's a building of great distinction, perhaps the greatest of all the 'wool churches', and declared by the 19th century architect August Pugin to be the finest example of late-Perpendicular style in the world. It was built, with generous help from wealthy local families (notably the Spryngs and the de Veres) in the late 15th and early

The Priory originated in the 13th century as a farm for Benedictine monks; the beautiful timber-framed house on the site dates from about 1600. In the original hall, at the centre of the building, is an important collection of paintings and stained glass. The extensive grounds include a kitchen garden, a herb garden and a pond.

111

79 BOX TREE FARM

Kettlebaston, nr Lavenham

Comfortable, civilised B&B
farmhouse accommodation
in a quiet rural setting.

 see page 269

80 THE OLD
CONVENT

Kettlebaston, nr Lavenham

A thatched cottage for B&B
and a ground-floor self-
catering unit in a pretty
village setting.

 see page 269

16th centuries to celebrate the end
of the Wars of the Roses. Its flint
tower is a mighty 140 feet in
height, and it's possible to climb to
the top to take in the glorious
views over Lavenham and the
surrounding countryside. Richly
carved screens and fine (Victorian)
stained glass are eye-catching
features within.

John Constable went to school
in Lavenham, where one of his
friends was Jane Taylor, who wrote
the words to 'Twinkle Twinkle
Little Star'.

SUDBURY

Sudbury is another wonderful town,
the largest of the 'wool towns' and
still home to a number of weaving
concerns.

Sudbury boasts three medieval
churches, but what most visitors
make a beeline for is
Gainsborough's House in
Gainsborough Street. The painter
Thomas Gainsborough was born
here in 1727 in the house built by
his father John. Around 25 oil
paintings are on show, including a
magnificent landscape of 1782 and
a touching miniature of his wife,
and among the memorabilia to be
seen in the house are the artist's
studio cabinet, his swordstick and
his pocket watch. A changing
programme of contemporary art
exhibitions includes fine art,
photography and sculpture,
highlighting East Anglian artists in
particular, and the print workshop
hosts evening classes and summer
courses in the techniques of
etching, screenprinting, stone
lithography and relief printing. A
bronze statue of Gainsborough
stands in the square.

About those churches: All
Saints dates from the 15th century
and has a glorious carved tracery
pulpit and screens; 14th century St
Gregory's is notable for a
wonderful medieval font; and St
Peter's has some marvellous painted
screen panels and a piece of 15th
century embroidered velvet.

Other buildings of interest are
the Victorian **Corn Exchange**,
now a library; **Salter's Hall**, a 15th

Salter's Hall, Sudbury

century timbered house; and the **Quay Theatre**, a thriving centre for the arts.

Unlike Lavenham, Sudbury kept its weaving industry longer because it was a port, and the result is a much more varied architectural picture. The surrounding countryside is some of the loveliest in Suffolk, and the River Stour is a further plus, with launch trips and fishing available.

The decline of the cloth trade in East Anglia had several causes. Fierce competition came from the northern and western weaving industries, which generally had easier access to water supplies for fulling; the wars on the continent of Europe led to the closure of some trading routes and markets; and East Anglia had no supplies of the coal that was used to drive the new steam-powered machinery. In some cases, as at Sudbury, weaving or silk took over as smaller industries.

CONSTABLE COUNTRY

England's greatest landscape painter was born at East Bergholt in 1776 and remained at heart a Suffolk man throughout his life. His father, Golding Constable, was a wealthy man who owned both Flatford Mill and Dedham Mill, the latter on the Essex side of the Stour. The river was a major source of inspiration to the young John Constable, and his constant involvement in country matters gave him an expert knowledge of the elements and a

keen eye for the details of nature. He was later to declare

'I associate my careless boyhood with all that lies on the banks of the Stour. Those scenes made me a painter and I am grateful.'

His interest in painting developed early and was fostered by his friendship with John Dunthorne, a local plumber and amateur artist. Constable became a probationer at the Royal Academy Schools in 1799, and over the following years developed the technical skills to match his powers of observation. He painted the occasional portrait and even attempted a couple of religious works, but he concentrated almost entirely on the scenes that he knew and loved as a boy. Two quotations from Constable himself reveal much about his aims and philosophy:

'In a landscape I want to give one brief moment caught from fleeting time a lasting and sober existence.'

'I never saw any ugly thing in my life; in fact, whatever may be the shape of an object, light, shade or perspective can always make it beautiful.'

The most significant works of the earlier years were the numerous sketches in oil which were forerunners of the major paintings of Constable's mature years. He had exhibited at the Royal Academy every year since 1802, but it was not until 1817 that the first of his important canvases, *Flatford Mill on the River Stour*, was hung. This was succeeded by the six large paintings which became his best-known works. These were all set on a short

81 AMICI CUCINA ITALIANA

Sudbury

A stylish restaurant serving top-notch Southern Italian food with both traditional and contemporary elements.

see page 269

82 THE ROSE & CROWN

Hundon, nr Clare

A friendly family-run village pub serving good basic food.

see page 270

83 THE BROOK INN

Great Cornard, nr Sudbury

Excellent home cooking is a major magnet at this friendly pub on the edge of Sudbury.

see page 270

•

*A man equally
indomitable of spirit as
Gainsborough was Sir
Alfred Munnings, born at
Mendham in the north of
Suffolk in 1878. The last
of the great sporting
painters in the tradition
of Stubbs and Marshall,
Munnings was outspoken
in his opinions on
modern art. In 1949, as
outgoing President of the
Royal Academy, he
launched an animated
attack on modern art as
'silly daubs' and 'violent
blows at nothing'. The
occasion was broadcast
on the radio; in response
many listeners
complained about the
'strong language'
Munnings had used. In
1956, Munnings jolted
the art world again by
describing that year's
Summer Exhibition as
'bits of nonsense' hung on
the wall.*

•

stretch of the Stour, and all except *The Hay Wain* show barges at work. These broad, flat-bottomed craft were displayed in scenes remarkable for the realism of the colours, the effects of light and water and, above all, the beautiful depiction of clouds. His fellow-artist Fuseli declared that whenever he saw a Constable painting he felt the need to reach for his coat and umbrella. Though more realistic than anything that preceded them, Constable's paintings were never lacking soul, and his work was much admired by the painters of the French Romantic School.

At the time of his death in 1837, Constable's reputation at home was relatively modest, though he had many followers and admirers in France. Awareness and understanding of his unique talent grew only in the ensuing years, so that, today, his place as England's foremost landscape painter is rarely disputed.

Suffolk has produced many other painters of distinction. Thomas Gainsborough, born in Sudbury in 1727, was an artist of great versatility, innovative and instinctive, and equally at home with portraits and landscapes. He earned his living for a while from portrait painting in Ipswich before making a real name for himself in Bath. His relations with the Royal Academy were often stormy, however, culminating in 1784 in a major dispute over the height at which a painting should be hung. He withdrew his intended hangings from the exhibition and never again showed at the Royal Academy.

Mary Beale, born at Barrow in 1633, was a noted portrait painter and copyist; some of her work has been attributed to Lely and Kneller, and it was rumoured that Lely was in love with her.

Philip Wilson Steer (1860-1942) was among the most distinguished of the many painters who were attracted to Walberswick. He studied in Paris and acquired the reputation of being the best of the English impressionist painters.

The Suffolk tradition of painting continues to this day, with many artists drawn to this part of the county. While nowadays crowds congregate throughout the Stour valley at summer weekends, at other times the tranquillity and loveliness are just as unmatched as they were in Constable's day.

BRANTHAM

8 miles SW of Ipswich on the A137

Also known as 'Burnt Village' – possibly because it was sacked during a Danish invasion 1,000 years ago – Brantham's Church of St Michael owns one of the only two known religious paintings by Constable, *Christ Blessing the Children*, which he executed in the style of the American painter Benjamin West. It is kept in safety in Ipswich Museum.

EAST BERGHOLT

8 miles SW of Ipswich on the B1070

Narrow lanes lead to this picturesque and much-visited little village. The **Constable Country Trail** starts here, where the painter was born, and passes through Flatford Mill and on to Dedham in Essex. The actual house where he was born no longer stands, but the site is marked by a plaque on the fence of its successor, a private house called Constables. A little further along Church Street is Moss Cottage, which Constable once used as his studio. **St Mary's Church** is one of the many grand churches built with the wealth brought by the wool trade. This one should have been even grander, with a tower to rival that of Dedham across the river. The story goes that Cardinal Wolsey pledged the money to build the tower, but fell from grace before the funds were forthcoming. The tower got no further than did his college in Ipswich, and a bellcage constructed in the churchyard as a

Wooden Bellcage, East Bergholt

temporary house for the bells became their permanent home, which it remains to this day. In this unique timber-framed structure the massive bells hang upside down and are rung by hand by pulling on the wooden shoulder stocks - an

Flatford Mill, East Bergholt

Bridge Cottage at Flatford is a restored 16th century building housing a Constable display, a tea room and a shop. There's also a restored dry dock, and the whole area is a delight for walkers; it is easy to see how Constable drew constant inspiration from the wonderful riverside setting.

84 GLADWINS FARM

Nayland

Outstanding self-catering and B&B accommodation in a lovely quiet setting with glorious views

see page 270

arduous task, as the five bells are among the heaviest in England.

The church is naturally something of a shrine to Constable, his family and his friends. There are memorial windows to the artist and to his beloved wife Maria Bicknell, who bore him seven children and whose early death was an enormous blow to him. His parents, to whom he was clearly devoted, and his old friend Willy Lott, whose cottage is featured famously in The Hay Wain, are buried in the churchyard.

East Bergholt has an interesting mix of houses, some dating back as far as the 14th century. One of the grandest is **Stour House**, once the home of Randolph Churchill. Its gardens are open to the public, as is **East Bergholt Place Garden** on the B1070.

A leafy lane leads south from the village to the Stour, where two of Constable's favourite subjects, **Flatford Mill** and **Willy Lott's Cottage**, both looking much as they did when he painted them, are to be found. Neither is open to the public, and the brick watermill is run as a residential field study centre.

STRATFORD ST MARY
10 miles SW of Ipswich off the A12

Another of Constable's favourite locations, Stratford St Mary is the most southerly village in Suffolk. *The Young Waltonians* and *A House in Water Lane* (the house still stands today) are the best known of his works set in this picturesque spot. The village church is typically large

and imposing, with parts dating back to 1200. At the top of the village are two splendid half-timbered cottages called the Ancient House and the Priest's House. Stratford was once on the main coaching route to London, and the largest of the four pubs had stabling for 200 horses. It is claimed that Henry Williamson, author of *Tarka the Otter*, saw his first otter here.

NAYLAND
14 miles SW of Ipswich on the B1087

On a particularly beautiful stretch of the Stour in Dedham Vale, Nayland has charming colour-washed cottages in narrow, winding streets, as well as two very fine 15th century buildings in Alston Court and the Guildhall. Abels Bridge, originally built of wood in the 15th century by wealthy merchant John Abel, divides Suffolk from Essex. In the 16th century a hump bridge replaced it, allowing barges to pass beneath. The current bridge carries the original keystone, bearing the initial A. In the **Church of St James** stands an altarpiece by Constable entitled *Christ Blessing the Bread and Wine*.

One mile west of Nayland, at the end of a track off the Bures road, stands the Norman **Church of St Mary at Wissington**. The church has a number of remarkable features, including several 13th century wall paintings, a finely carved 12th century doorway and a tiebeam and crown post roof.

STOKE BY NAYLAND

12 miles SW of Ipswich on the B1087

The drive from Nayland reveals quite stunning views, and the village itself has a large number of listed buildings. The magnificent **Church of St Mary**, with its 120-feet tower, dominates the scene from its hilltop position. This church also dominates more than one Constable painting, the most famous showing the church lit up by a rainbow. William Dowsing destroyed 100 'superstitious pictures' here in his Puritan purges, but plenty of fine work is still to be seen, including several monumental brasses.

POLSTEAD

11 miles SW of Ipswich off the B1068

Polstead is a very pretty village set in wooded, hilly countryside, with thatched, colour-washed cottages around the green and a wide duck pond at the bottom of the hill. Standing on a rise above the pond are Polstead Hall, a handsome Georgian mansion, and the 12th century **Church of St Mary**. The church has two features not found elsewhere in Suffolk – a stone spire and the very early bricks used in its construction. The builders used not only these bricks, but also tiles and tufa, a soft, porous stone much used in Italy. In the grounds of the hall stand the remains of a 'Gospel Oak' said to have been 1,300 years old when it collapsed in 1953. Legend has it that Saxon missionaries preached beneath it in the 7th century; an open-air service

is still held here annually.

Polstead has two unique claims to fame. One is for Polstead Blacks, a particularly tasty variety of cherry which was cultivated in orchards around the village and which used to be honoured with an annual fair. The other is much less agreeable, for it was here that the notorious Red Barn murder hit the headlines in 1827. A young girl called Maria Marten, daughter of the local molecatcher, disappeared with William Corder, a farmer's son who was the girl's lover and father of her child. It was at first thought that they had eloped, but Maria's stepmother dreamt three times that she had been murdered and buried in a red barn. A search of the barn soon revealed this to be true. Corder was tracked down to Middlesex, tried and found guilty of Maria's murder and hanged. (Until August 2004 his skeleton was kept at the Royal College of Surgeons of England's Hunterian Museum in London, where it was taken in 1949. After a long campaign by a descendant of Corder, the skeleton was released and was cremated at London's Streatham crematorium.) The murder aroused a great deal of interest at the time, and today's visitors to the village will still find reminders of the ghastly deed: the thatched cottage where Maria lived stands, in what is now called Marten's Lane, and the farm where the murderer lived, now called Corder's Farm. Maria is buried in St Mary's Church in Polstead.

The Guildhall in Stoke by Nayland is another very fine building, now privately occupied but in the 16th century a busy centre of trade and commerce. When the wool trade declined, so did the importance of the Guildhall, and for a time this noble building saw service as a workhouse.

117

Bures has a long connection with the Waldegrave family, possibly from as far back as Chaucer's day. One of the Waldegrave memorials shows graphically the results of a visitation by Dowsing and the Puritan iconoclasts: all the figures of the kneeling children have had their hands cut off.

BOXFORD

12 miles W of Ipswich on the A1071

A gloriously unspoilt weaving village, downhill from anywhere, surrounded by the peaceful water meadows of the River Box, Boxford's **St Mary's Church** dates back to the 14th century. Its wooden north porch is one of the oldest of its kind in the country. In the church is a touching brass in memory of David Byrde, son of the rector, who died a baby in 1606. At the other end of the continuum is Elizabeth Hyam, four times a widow, who died in her 113th year.

BURES

17 miles W of Ipswich on the B1508

At this point the River Stour turns sharply to the east, creating a

natural boundary between Suffolk and Essex. The little village of Bures straddles the river, lying partly in each county. Bures St Mary in Suffolk is where the church is, overlooked by houses of brick and half-timbering.

Bures wrote itself very early into the history books when on Christmas Day AD 855 it is thought that our old friend Edmund the Martyr, the Saxon king, was crowned at the age of 15 in the Chapel of St Stephen. For some time after that momentous occasion, Bures was the capital seat of the East Anglian kings.

EDWARDSTONE

14 miles W of Ipswich off the A1071

Just to the north of Boxford and close to Edwardstone Hall and the Temple Bar Gate House, Edwardstone is now a 700-acre estate originally home to the Winthrop family. Winthrop was born in Edwardstone and emigrated to the New World, eventually becoming Governor of Massachusetts.

BURY ST EDMUNDS

'A handsome little town, of thriving and cleanly appearance'. Thus Charles Dickens described Bury in his *Pickwick Papers*.

A gem among Suffolk towns, rich in archaeological treasures and places of religious and historical interest, Bury St Edmunds takes its name from St Edmund, who was

Bures Mill

born in Nuremberg in AD 841 and came here as a teenager to become the last King of East Anglia. He was a staunch Christian, and his refusal to deny his faith caused him to be tortured and killed by the Danes in AD 870. Legend has it that although his body was recovered, his head (cut off by the Danes) could not be found. His men searched for it for 40 days, then heard his voice directing them to it from the depths of a wood, where they discovered it lying protected between the paws of a wolf. The head and the body were seamlessly united and, to commemorate the wolf's deed, the crest of the town's armorial bearings depicts a wolf with a man's head.

Edmund was possibly buried first at Hoxne, the site of his murder, but when he was canonised in about AD 910 his remains were moved to the monastery at Beodricsworth, which changed its name to St Edmundsbury. A shrine was built in his honour, later incorporated into the Norman Abbey Church after the monastery was granted abbey status by King Canute in 1032. The town soon became a place of pilgrimage, and for many years St Edmund was the patron saint of England, until replaced by St George. Growing rapidly around the great abbey, which became one of the largest and most influential in the land, Bury prospered as a centre of trade and commerce, thanks notably to the cloth industry.

The next historical landmark was reached in 1214, when on St Edmund's Feast Day the then Archbishop of Canterbury, Simon Langton, met with the Barons of England at the high altar of the Abbey and swore that they would force King John to honour the proposals of the Magna Carta. The twin elements of Edmund's canonisation and the resolution of the Barons explain the motto on the town's crest: '*sacrarium regis, cunabula legis*' – '*shrine of a king, cradle of the law*'.

Rebuilt in the 15th century, the Abbey was largely dismantled after its Dissolution by Henry VIII, but imposing ruins remain in the colourful Abbey Gardens beyond the splendid **Abbey Gate** and Norman Tower. **St Edmundsbury Cathedral** was originally the Church of St James, built in the 15th/16th century and accorded cathedral status (alone in Suffolk) in 1914. The original building has been much extended over the years (notably when being adapted for its role as a cathedral) and outstanding features include a magnificent hammerbeam roof, whose 38 beams are decorated with angels bearing the emblems of St

85 THE PRIORS INN

Bury St Edmunds

The **Priors** is a lively, popular 1930s pub with real ales, home cooking and live music Friday and Saturday.

see page 271

Abbey Gate, Bury St Edmunds

Perhaps the most fascinating building of all Bury's non-eccliastical buildings is Moyse's Hall Museum, located at one end of the Buttermarket. Built of flint and limestone about 1180, it has claims to being the oldest stone domestic building in England. Originally a rich man's residence, it later saw service as a tavern, gaol, police station and railway parcels office, but since 1899 it has been a museum. It houses some 10,000 items, including costumes and clocks, a 19th century doll's house and relics of the notorious Red Barn murder. One wing contains the Suffolk Regiment collection and education room.

James, St Edmund and St George. The monumental Bishop's throne depicts wolves guarding the crowned head of St Edmund, and there's a fascinating collection of 1,000 embroidered kneelers. Work was recently completed to crown the Cathedral with a 140feet Gothic-style tower. The Cathedral Centre houses the Song School, refectory and meeting rooms.

St Mary's Church, in the same complex, is also well worth a visit: an equally impressive hammerbeam roof, the detached tower standing much as Abbot Anselm built it in the 12th century, and several interesting monuments, the most important commemorating Mary Tudor, sister of Henry VIII, Queen of France and Duchess of Suffolk. Her remains were moved here when the Abbey was suppressed; a window in the Lady Chapel recording this fact was the gift of Queen Victoria.

The **Abbey Gardens**, laid out in 1831, have as their central feature a great circle of flower beds following the pattern of the Royal Botanical Gardens in Brussels. Some of the original ornamental trees can still be seen, and other - later - features include an Old English rose garden, a water garden and a garden for the blind where fragrance counts for all. Ducks and geese live by the little River Lark, and there are tennis courts, putting and bowls greens and children's play equipment.

Bury is full of fine non-ecclesiastical buildings, many with Georgian frontages concealing

medieval interiors. Among the most interesting are the Victorian **Corn Exchange** with its imposing colonnade; the **Athenaeum**, hub of social life since Regency times and scene of Charles Dickens's public readings; **Cupola House**, where Daniel Defoe once stayed; the **Angel Hotel**, where Dickens and his marvellous creation Mr Pickwick stayed; and the **Nutshell**, owned by Greene King Brewery and probably the smallest pub in the country; and the marvellous **Theatre Royal**, built in 1819 by William Wilkins (also responsible for the National Gallery in London), recently superbly renovated and one of the oldest working theatres in Europe. It once staged the first performance of *Charley's Aunt*.

One of Bury's oldest residents and a major attraction is the **Greene King Brewery Visitor Centre**. Greene King has been brewed here in Bury since 1799; the museum's informative storyboards, artefacts, illustrations and audio displays bring the history and art of brewing to life. Brewery tours include a look round the museum and beer-tasting (and the best view of Bury from the brewhouse roof). The shop sells a variety of memorabilia, souvenirs, gifts and clothing – as well, of course, as bottles and cans of the frothy stuff.

The **Bury St Edmunds Art Gallery** is housed in one of Bury's noblest buildings, built to a Robert Adam design in 1774. It has filled many roles down the years, and was rescued from decline in the 1960s to be restored to Adam's original plans. It is now one of the county's premier art galleries, with eight exhibitions each year and a thriving craft shop.

Outside the Spread Eagle pub on the western edge of town is a horse trough erected to the memory of the Victorian romantic novelist 'Ouida' (Maria Louisa Ramee, 1839-1908).

Steeped though it is in history, Bury also moves with the times, and its sporting, entertainment and leisure facilities are impressive. A mile and a half outside town on the A14 (just off the East Exit) is **Nowton Park**, 172 acres of countryside landscaped in Victorian style and supporting a wealth of flora and fauna; the avenue of limes, carpeted with daffodils in the spring, is a particular delight. There's also a play area and a ranger centre. **Hardwick Heath**, its sister park, features a tree gallery and 200-year-old Cedars of Lebanon.

Arriving in Bury in 1698, Celia Fiennes, the inveterate traveller and stern architecture critic, was uncharacteristically favourable in her remarks about Cupola House, which had just been completed at the time of her visit. William Cobbett (1763-1835), a visitor when chronicling his *Rural Rides*, did not disagree with the view that Bury St Edmunds was 'the nicest town in the world' - a view which would be endorsed by many of today's inhabitants and by many of the millions of visitors who have

Daffodil Fields, Bury St Edmunds

been charmed by this jewel in Suffolk's crown.

AROUND BURY ST EDMUNDS

HENGRAVE

3 miles NW of Bury St Edmunds on the A1101

A captivating old-world village of flint and thatch, excavations and aerial photography indicate that there has been a settlement at Hengrave since Neolithic times.

Those parts of the village that are of archaeological interest are now protected. Hengrave Hall is a rambling Tudor mansion built partly of Northamptonshire limestone and partly of yellow brick by Sir Thomas Kytson, a wool merchant. A notable visitor in the early days was Elizabeth I, who brought her court here in 1578. Several generations of the Gage family were later the owners of Hengrave Hall - one of them, with a particular interest in horticulture,

121

The villages of West Stow, Culford, Ingham, Timworth and Wordwell were for several centuries part of a single estate covering almost 10,000 acres. Half the estate was sold to the Forestry Commission in 1935 and was renamed the King's Forest in honour of King George V's Jubilee in that year.

86 WEST STOW ANGLO-SAXON VILLAGE

West Stow

Between 1965 and 1972 the low hill by the River Lark in Suffolk was excavated to reveal several periods of occupation, but in particular, over 70 buildings from an early Anglo Saxon village.

 see page 271

imported various kinds of plum trees from France. Most of the bundles were properly labelled with their names, but one had lost its label. When it produced its first crop of luscious green fruit, someone had the bright idea of calling it the Green Gage. The name stuck, and the descendants of these trees, planted in 1724, are still at the Hall, which is not open to the public.

FLEMPTON

4 miles NW of Bury St Edmunds on the A1101

An interesting walk from this village just north of the A1101 follows the **Lark Valley Park** through Culford Park, providing a good view of Culford Hall, which has been a school since 1935. A handsome cast-iron bridge dating from the early 19th century - and recently brought to light from among the reeds - crosses a lake in the park.

WEST STOW

6 miles NW of Bury St Edmunds off the A1101

An Anglo-Saxon cemetery was discovered in the village in 1849; subsequent years have revealed traces of Roman settlements and the actual layout of the original **Anglo-Saxon Village**. A trust was established to investigate further the Anglo-Saxon way of life and their building and farming techniques. Several buildings were constructed using, as accurately as could be achieved, the tools and methods of the 5th century. The

undertaking has become a major tourist attraction, with assistance from guides both human (in Anglo-Saxon costume) and in the form of taped cassettes. There are pigs and hens, growing crops, craft courses, a Saxon market at Easter, a festival in August and special events all year round. This fascinating village, which is entered through the Visitor Centre, is part of the 125-acre **West Stow Country Park**, a large part of which is designated a Site of Special Scientific Interest (SSSI). Over 120 species of birds and 25 species of animals have been sighted in this Breckland setting, and a well-marked 5-mile nature trail links this nature reserve with the woods, a large lake and the River Lark. The Park is open daily all year.

ICKLINGHAM

8 miles NW of Bury St Edmunds on the A1101

The village of Icklingham boasts not one but two churches - the parish **Church of St James** (mentioned in the *Domesday Book*) and the deconsecrated thatched-roofed **Church of All Saints**, with medieval tiles on the chancels and beautiful east windows in the south aisle. At the point where the Icknield Way crosses the River Lark, Icklingham has a long history, brought to light in frequent archaeological finds, from pagan bronzes to Roman coins. The place abounds in tales of the supernatural, notably of the white rabbit who is seen at dusk in the company of a witch, causing –

it is said - horses to bolt and men to die.

GREAT WELNETHAM

2 miles S of Bury St Edmunds off the A134

One of the many surviving Suffolk windmills is to be found here, just south of the village. The sails were lost in a gale 80 years ago, but the tower and a neighbouring old barn make an attractive sight.

THE BRADFIELDS

7 miles SE of Bury St Edmunds off the A134

The Bradfields - St George, St Clare and Combust - and Cockfield thread their way through a delightful part of the countryside and are well worth a little exploration, not only to see the picturesque villages themselves but for a stroll in the historic **Bradfield Woods**. These woods stand on the eastern edge of the parish of Bradfield St George and have been turned into an outstanding nature reserve, tended and coppiced in the same way for more than 700 years, and home to a wide variety of flora and fauna. They once belonged to the Abbey of St Edmundsbury, and one area is still today called Monk's Park Wood.

Coppicing involves cutting a tree back down to the ground every ten years or so. Woodlands were managed in this way to provide an annual crop of timber for local use and fast regrowth. After coppicing, as the root is already strongly established, regrowth is quick. Willow and hazel are the trees most commonly coppiced. Willow is often also pollarded, a less drastic form of coppicing where the trees are cut far enough from the ground to stop grazing animals having a free lunch.

Bradfield St Clare, the central of the three Bradfields, has a rival claim to that of Hoxne as the site of the martyrdom of St Edmund. The St Clare family arrived with the Normans and added their name to the village, and to the church, which was originally All Saints but was then rededicated to St Clare; it is the only church in England dedicated to her. Bradfield Combust, where the pretty River Lark rises, probably takes its curious name from the fact that the local hall was burnt to the ground during the 14th century riots against the Abbot of St Edmundsbury's crippling tax demands.

COCKFIELD

8 miles SE of Bury St Edmunds off the A1141

Cockfield is perhaps the most widely spread village in all Suffolk, its little thatched cottages scattered around and between no fewer than nine greens. Great Green is the largest, with two football pitches and other recreation areas, while Parsonage Green has a literary connection: the **Old Rectory** was once home to a Dr Babbington, whose nephew Robert Louis Stephenson was a frequent visitor and who is said to have written Treasure Island while staying there. Cockfield also shelters one of the last windmills to have been built in Suffolk (1891). Its working life was very short but the tower still stands, now in use as a private residence.

87 THE METCALFE ARMS

Hawstead, nr Bury St Edmunds

Excellent home cooking brings appreciative diners to a friendly village pub south of Bury.

see *page 271*

88 THE VICTORIA

Thurston, nr Bury St Edmunds

A popular, comfortable restaurant with a long menu of home-cooked dishes.

see *page 272*

89 WINES BAR & KITCHEN AT THE SIX BELLS

Felsham, nr Bury St Edmunds

Wines Bar & Kitchen offers an interesting range of dishes in the setting of a traditional village inn.

see *page 272*

In the village of Alpheton, two oak trees were planted and a pump installed in 1887, to commemorate Queen Victoria's 50th year on the throne. Another of the village's claims to fame is that its American airfield was used as the setting for the classic film Twelve o'Clock High, *in which Gregory Peck memorably plays a Second World War flight commander cracking under the strain of countless missions. Incidentally, one of the reasons for constructing the A134 was to help in the development of the airfield. The A134 continues south to Long Melford. An alternative road from Bury to Long Melford is the B1066, quieter and more scenic, with a number of pleasant places to visit en route.*

THORPE MORIEUX

9 miles SE of Bury St Edmunds off the B1071

St Mary's Church in Thorpe Morieux is situated in as pleasant a setting as anyone could wish to find. With water meadows, ponds, a stream and a fine Tudor farmhouse to set it off, this 14th century church presents a memorable picture of old England. Look at the church, then take the time to wander round the peaceful churchyard with its profusion of springtime aconites, followed by the colourful flowering of limes and chestnuts in summer.

LAWSHALL

8 miles S of Bury St Edmunds off the A134

A spread-out village first documented in AD 972 but regularly giving up evidence of earlier occupation, Lawshall was the site where a Bronze Age sword dated at around 600 BC was found (the sword is now in Bury Museum). The Church of All Saints, Perpendicular with some Early English features, stands on one of the highest points in Suffolk. Next to it is Lawshall Hall, whose owners once entertained Queen Elizabeth I. An interesting site in Lawshall is the Wishing Well, a well-cover on the green put up in memory of Charles Tyrwhitt Drake, who worked for the Royal Geographic Society and was killed in Jerusalem.

ALPHETON

10 miles S of Bury St Edmunds on the A134

There are several points of interest in this little village straddling the main road. It was first settled in AD 991 and its name means 'the farm of Aefflaed'. That lady was the wife of Ealdorman Beorhtnoth of Essex, who was killed resisting the Danes at the Battle of Maldon and is buried in Ely Minster.

The hall, the farm and the church stand in a quiet location away from the main road and about a mile from the village. This remoteness is not unusual: some attribute it to the villagers moving during times of plague, but the more likely explanation is simply that the scattered cottages, originally in several tiny hamlets, centred on a more convenient site than that of the church. Equally possible is that the church was located here to suit the local landed family (who desired to have the church next door to their home). The main features at the **Church of St Peter and St Paul** are the flintwork around the parapet (the exterior is otherwise fairly undistinguished), the carefully restored 15th century porch and some traces of an ancient wall painting of St Christopher with the Christ Child. All in all, it's a typical country church of unpretentious dignity and well worth a short detour from the busy main roads.

HARTEST

9 miles S of Bury St Edmunds on the B1066

Hartest, which has a history as long as Alpheton's, celebrated its millennium in 1990 with the erection of a village sign (the hart, or stag). It's an agreeable spot in the valley, with colour-washed houses and chestnut trees on the green. Also on the green are All Saints Church (mentioned in the *Domesday Book*) and a large glacial stone, the **Hartest Stone**, which was dragged by a team of 45 horses from where it was found in a field in neighbouring Somerton. Just outside the village is **Gifford's Hall**, a smallholding which includes 14 acres of nearly 12,000 grapevines, as well as a winery producing white and rosé wines and fruit liqueurs. There are also organic vegetable gardens, wildflower meadows, black St Kilda sheep, black Berkshire pigs, goats and free-range fowl, together with a trailer ride ('The Grape Express') and children's play area. The Hall is particularly famous for its sweet peas and roses, and an annual festival is held on the last weekend in June. Open from Easter to the end of October. From 1789 until the 1930s, Hartest staged a St George's Day Fair, an annual event celebrating King George III's recovery from one of his spells of illness.

SHIMPLING

9 miles S of Bury St Edmunds off the B1066

Shimpling is a peaceful farming community whose church, St George's, is approached by a lime avenue. It is notable for Victorian stained glass and a Norman font, and in the churchyard is the **Faint House**, a small stone building where ladies overcome by the tightness of their stays could decently retreat from the service.

The banker Thomas Hallifax built many of Shimpling's cottages, as well as the village school and Chadacre Hall, which Lord Iveagh later turned into an agricultural college (a role it ceased to hold in 1989 - the Hall is today again in private hands).

GLEMSFORD

12 miles S of Bury St Edmunds off the B1066

Driving in from the north on the B1066, the old Church of St Mary makes an impressive sight on what, for Suffolk, is quite a considerable hill. Textiles and weaving have long played a prominent part in Glemsford's history, and thread from the silk factory, which opened in 1824 and is still going strong, has been woven into dresses and robes for various members of the royal family, including Princess Diana's wedding dress.

LONG MELFORD

13 miles S of Bury St Edmunds off the A134

The heart of this atmospheric wool town is its very long and, in stretches, fairly broad main street, set on an ancient Roman site in a particularly beautiful part of south Suffolk. In Roman times the Stour was a navigable river, and trade flourished. Various Roman finds have been unearthed, notably a blue glass vase which is now on display in the British Museum in London. The street is filled with antique shops, book shops and art galleries, and is a favourite place for collectors and browsers. Some of the houses are washed in the characteristic Suffolk pink, which

During the last century several factories in Glemsford produced matting from coconut fibres, and in 1906 the town was responsible for the largest carpet in the world, used to cover the floor at London's Olympia. To this day one factory processes horse hair for use in judges' wigs, sporrans and busbies.

90 KENTWELL HALL

Long Melford
Kentwell Hall, a romantic, mellow, moated redbrick Tudor mansion in a tranquil parkland setting, has a great deal to offer the visitor.

 see page 272

might originally have been achieved by mixing ox blood or sloe juice into the plaster.

Holy Trinity Church, on a 14-acre green at the north end of Hall Street, is a typically exuberant manifestation of the wealth of the wool and textile trade. It's big enough to be a cathedral, but served (and still serves) comparatively few parishioners. John Clopton, grown rich in the woollen business, was largely responsible for this magnificent Perpendicular-style edifice of Holy Trinity, which has a 180-feet nave and chancel and half timbers, flint 'flushwork' (stonework) of the highest quality, and 100 large windows to give a marvellous sense of light and space. Medieval glass in the north aisle depicts religious scenes and the womenfolk of the Clopton family. There are many interesting monuments and brasses, and in the chantry entrance is a bas relief of the Three Wise Men, the Virgin and Child, and St Joseph. In the Lady Chapel, reached by way of the churchyard, a children's multiplication table written on one wall is a reminder that the chapel served as the village school for a long period after the Reformation.

The tower was struck by lightning in the early 18th century; the present brick construction dates from around 1900. The detail of this great church is of endless fascination, but it's the overall impression that stays in the memory, and the sight of the building floodlit at night is truly spectacular. The distinguished 20th century poet Edmund Blunden spent his last years at Hall Mill in Long Melford and is buried in the churchyard. The inscription on his gravestone reads *'I live still to love still things quiet and unconcerned.'*

Melford Hall, east of town beyond an imposing 16th century gateway, was built around 1570 by Sir William Cordell on the site of an earlier hall that served as a country retreat, before the Dissolution of the Monasteries, for the monks of St Edmundsbury Abbey. There exists an account of Cordell entertaining Queen Elizabeth I at the Hall in 1578, when she was welcomed by '200 young gentlemen in white velvet, 300 in black and 1,500 serving men'. Much of the fine work of Sir William (whose body lies in Holy Trinity Church) has been altered in restoration, but the pepperpot chimneys are original, as is the panelled banqueting hall. The rooms are in various styles, some with ornate walnut furniture, and there's a notable collection of

Gateway, Long Melford Hall

126

Chinese porcelain on show.

Most delightful of all the rooms at Melford Hall is the Beatrix Potter room, with some of her watercolours, first editions of her books and, among the toys, the original of Jemima Puddleduck. She was a frequent visitor here (her cousins, the Hyde Parkers, were then the owners), bringing small animals to draw. The Jeremy Fisher illustrations were mostly drawn at Melford Hall's fishponds, and the book is dedicated to Stephanie Hyde Parker. The Hall, which is a National Trust property, stands in a lovely garden with some distinguished clipped box hedges. On the green near the hall is a vast brick conduit built to supply water to the hall and the village. William Cordell was also responsible for the red-brick almshouses, built in 1593 for '12 poor men', which stand near Holy Trinity.

Kentwell Hall is a red-brick Tudor moated mansion approached by a long avenue of limes. Its grounds include a unique Tudor rose maze, and are set out to illustrate and re-create Tudor times, with a walled garden, a bakery, a dairy and several varieties of rare-breed farm animals. The buildings include a handsome 14th century aisle barn. The Hall was the setting for a film version of *Toad of Toad Hall*.

Long Melford is a great place for leisurely strolls, and for the slightly more energetic there's a scenic 3-mile walk along a disused railway track and farm tracks that leads straight into Lavenham.

Cavendish

CAVENDISH

3 miles W of Long Melford on the A1092

A most attractive village, where the Romans stayed awhile - the odd remains have been unearthed - and the Saxons settled, Cavendish is splendidly traditional, with its church, thatched cottages, almshouses, Nether Hall and the **Sue Ryder Foundation Museum** spread around the green. The last, in a 16th century rectory by the pond, illustrates the work of the Sue Ryder Foundation, and was formally opened by Queen Elizabeth II in 1979. Once a refuge for concentration camp victims, it houses abundant war photographs and memorabilia. **Nether Hall** is a well-restored 16th century building and the headquarters of Cavendish Vineyards.

In the **Church of St Mary**, whose tower has a pointed bellcote

In 1381 Wat Tyler, leader of the Peasants' Revolt, was killed at Smithfield, in London, by John Cavendish, son of Sir John Cavendish, then lord of the manor and Chief Justice of England. Sir John was then hounded by the peasants, who caught him and killed him near Bury St Edmunds. He managed en route to hide some valuables in the belfry of St Mary's here in Cavendish, and bequeathed to the church £40, sufficient to restore the chancel. A later Cavendish – Thomas – sailed round the world in the 1580s and perished on a later voyage. In the shadow of the church, on the edge of the village green, is a cluster of immaculate thatched cottages at a spot known as Hyde Park Corner. Pink-washed and pretty as a picture, they look almost too good to be true – and they almost are, having been rebuilt twice since the Second World War due to unhappy forces that included fires and dilapidation.

and a room inside complete with fireplace and shuttered windows, look for the two handsome lecterns, one with a brass eagle (15th century), the other with two chained books; and for the Flemish and Italian statues.

CLARE

6 miles W of Long Melford on the A1092

'A little town with a lot of history'.

A medieval wool town of great importance, Clare repays a visit today with its fine old buildings and some distinguished old ruins. Perhaps the most renowned tourist attraction is **Ancient House**, a timber-framed building dated 1473 and remarkable for its pargeting. This is the decorative treatment of external plasterwork, usually by dividing the surface into rectangles and decorating each panel. It was very much a Suffolk speciality, particularly in the 16th and 17th centuries, with some examples also being found in Cambridgeshire and Essex. The decoration could be simple brushes of a comb, scrolls or squiggles, or more elaborate, with religious motifs, guild signs or family crests. Some pargeting is incised, but the best is in relief – pressing moulds into wet plaster or shaping it by hand. Ancient House sports some splendid entwined flowers and branches, and a representation of two figures holding a shield. The best-known workers in the unique skill of pargeting had their own distinctive styles, and the expert eye could spot the particular 'trademarks' of each man (the same is the case with

the master thatchers). Ancient House is now a museum, open during the summer months and housing an exhibition on local history.

Another place of historical significance is **Nethergate House**, once the workplace of dyers, weavers and spinners. The Swan Inn, in the High Street, has a sign which lays claim to being the oldest in the land. Ten feet in length and carved from a solid piece of wood, it portrays the arms of England and France.

Clare Castle was a motte-and-bailey fortress that sheltered a household of 250. Clare Castle Country Park, with a visitor centre in the goods shed of a disused railway line, contains the remains of the castle and the moat, the latter now a series of ponds and home to varied wild life. At the Prior's House, the original cellar and infirmary are still in use.

Priests House, Clare

Established in 1248 by Augustine friars and used by them until the Dissolution of 1538, the priory was handed back to that order in 1953 and remains their property.

A mile or so west of Clare on the A1092 lies **Stoke-by-Clare**, a pretty village on one of the region's most picturesque routes. It once housed a Benedictine priory, whose remains are now in the grounds of a school. There's a fine 15th century church and a vineyard: Boyton Vineyards at Hill Farm, Boyton End, is open early April to the end of October for a tour, a talk and a taste.

HORRINGER

3 miles SW of Bury St Edmunds on the A143

Rejoining the A143 by Chedburgh, the motorist will soon arrive at Horringer, whose village green is dominated by the flintstone Church of St Leonard. Beside the church are the gates of one of the country's most extraordinary and fascinating houses, now run by the National Trust. **Ickworth House** was the brainchild of the eccentric 4th Earl of Bristol and Bishop of Derry, a collector of art treasures and an inveterate traveller (witness the many Bristol Hotels scattered around Europe). His inspiration was Belle Isle, a house built on an island in Lake Windermere, and the massive structure is a central rotunda linking two semi-circular wings. It was designed as a treasure house for his art collection, and work started in 1795. Sadly, the first collection of the Earl's treasures was seized by Napoleon

in 1798, so never reached England.

Derry died in 1803 and his son, after some hesitation, saw the work through to completion in 1829. Its chief glories are some marvellous paintings by Titian, Gainsborough, Hogarth, Velasquez, Reynolds and Kauffman, but there's a great deal more to enthral the visitor: late Regency and 18th century French furniture, a notable collection of Georgian silver, friezes and sculptures by John Flaxman, frescoes copied from wall paintings discovered at the Villa Negroni in Rome in 1777.

Arable land surrounds Horringer, with a large annual crop of sugar beet grown for processing at the factory in Bury, the largest of its kind in Europe.

HAVERHILL

18 miles SW of Bury St Edmunds on the A604

Notable for its fine Victorian architecture, Haverhill also boasts one fine Tudor gem. Although many of Haverhill's buildings were destroyed by fire in 1665, **Anne of Cleves House** was restored and is well worth a visit. Anne was the fourth wife of Henry VIII and, after a brief political marriage, she was given an allowance and spent the remainder of her days at Haverhill and Richmond.

Haverhill Local History Centre, in the Town Hall, has an interesting collection of memorabilia, photographs and archive material.

East Town Park is an attractive country park on the east side of Haverhill.

The Italian garden at Ickworth, where Mediterranean species have been bred to withstand a distinctly non-Mediterranean climate, should not be missed, with its hidden glades, orangery and temple rose garden, and in the park landscaped by Capability Brown there are designated walks and cycle routes, bird hides, a deer enclosure and play areas. Other attractions include the vineyard and plant centre.

Following the Stour along the B1061, the visitor will find a number of interesting little villages. In Little Wratting, Holy Trinity Church has a shingled oak-framed steeple (a feature more usually associated with Essex churches). John Sainsbury was a local resident, while in Great Wratting another magnate, W H Smith, financed the restoration of St Mary's Church in 1887. This church boasts some diverting topiary in the shape of a church, a cross and – somewhat comically - an armchair.

KEDINGTON

2 miles N of Haverhill on the B1061

Haverhill intrudes somewhat, but the heart of the old village of Kedington gains in appeal by the presence of the River Stour. Known to many as the 'Cathedral of West Suffolk', the **Church of St Peter and St Paul** is the village's chief attraction. Almost 150 feet in length, it stands on a ridge overlooking the Stour Valley. It has several interesting features, including a 15th century font, a Saxon cross in the chancel window, a triple-decker pulpit (with a clerk's desk and a reading desk) and a sermon-timer, looking rather like a grand egg-timer. The foundations of a Roman building have been found beneath the floorboards.

The Bardiston family, one of the oldest in Suffolk, had strong links with the village and many of the family tombs are in the church. In the church grounds is a row of ten elm trees, each, the legend says, with a knight buried beneath its roots.

GREAT AND LITTLE THURLOW

3 miles N of Haverhill on the B1061

Great and Little Thurlow form a continuous village on the west bank of the River Stour a few miles north of Haverhill. Largely undamaged thanks to being in a conservation area, together they boast many 17th century cottages and a Georgian manor house. In the main street is a schoolhouse built in 1614 by Sir Stephen Soame,

one-time Lord Mayor of London, whose family are commemorated in the village church.

A short distance further up the B1061 stands the village of **Great Bradley**, divided in two by the River Stour, which rises just outside the village boundary. Chief points of note in the tranquil parish church are a fine Norman doorway sheltering a Tudor brick porch and some beautiful stained glass poignantly depicting a soldier in the trenches during the First World War. The three bells in the tower include one cast in the 14th century, among the oldest in Suffolk.

DENSTON

6 miles NE of Haverhill just off the A143

Denston lies just east of the A143 on the River Glem, and is notable chiefly for its magnificent Perpendicular church, one of 18 dedicated to St Nicholas, patron saint of sailors. Stop and admire the fan vaulting in the roof (a comparative rarity in Suffolk), the outstanding brasses and the wide variety of carved animals.

HAWKEDON

7 miles NE of Haverhill off the A143

Hawkedon is designated a place of outstanding natural beauty. Here the Church of St Mary is located atypically in the middle of the village green. The pews and intricately carved bench-ends take the eye here, along with a canopied stoup (a recess for holding holy water) and a Norman font. There is a wide variety of carved animals, many on the bench-ends but some also on the roof cornice. One of the stalls is decorated with the carving of a crane holding a stone in its claw: legend has it that if the crane were on watch and should fall asleep, the stone would drop and the noise would wake it.

WICKHAMBROOK

8 miles NE of Haverhill on the B1063

Wickhambrook is a series of tiny hamlets with no fewer than 11 greens and three manor houses. The greens have unusual names - Genesis, Nunnery, Meeting, Coltsfoot - whose origins keep local historians busy. One of the two pubs has the distinction of being officially half in Wickhambrook and half in Denston.

NEWMARKET

On the western edge of Suffolk, Newmarket is home to some 17,000 human and 4,000 equine inhabitants. The historic centre of British racing lives and breathes horses, with 73 training establishments, 70 stud farms, the top annual thoroughbred sales and two racecourses (the only two in Suffolk). Thousands of the population are involved in the trade, and racing art and artefacts fill the shops, galleries and museums; one of the oldest established saddlers even has a preserved horse on display - 'Robert the Devil', runner-up in the Derby in 1880.

History records that Queen Boudica of the Iceni, to whom the six-mile Devil's Dyke stands as a memorial, thundered around these parts in her lethal chariot behind her shaggy-haired horses. She is said to have established the first stud here. In medieval times the chalk heathland was a popular arena for riders to display their skills. In 1605, James I paused on a journey northwards to enjoy a spot of hare coursing. He enjoyed the place and said he would be back. By moving the royal court to his Newmarket headquarters, he began the royal patronage which has remained strong throughout the years. James' son, Charles I, maintained the royal connection, but it was Charles II who really put the place on the map when he, too, moved the Royal court here in the spring and autumn of each year. He initiated the Town Plate, a race which he himself won twice as a rider and which, in a modified form, still exists.

One of Newmarket's two racecourses, the **Rowley Mile**,

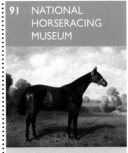

91 NATIONAL HORSERACING MUSEUM

Newmarket

"The Newmarket Experience" comprises two separate attractions: **The National Horseracing Museum** and **The National Stud**.

🏛 see page 273

Newmarket Gallops

In Newmarket High Street is the National Horseracing Museum. Opened by Her Majesty the Queen in 1983, its five galleries chronicle the history of the Sport of Kings from its royal beginnings through to the top trainers and jockeys of today. Highlights include the head of Persimmon, who won the Derby in 1896, a special display about Fred Archer, and items associated with many human and equine heroes of the turf. Visitors can ride a mechanical horse, try on racing silks, record a race commentary, ask questions and enjoy a snack in the café, whose walls are hung with murals of racing personalities.

92 BYERLEY HOUSE

Newmarket

One of the very best B&B establishments in the region, a perfect base for racegoers.

 see page 273

takes its name from Old Rowley, a favourite horse of the Merry Monarch. Here the first two classics of the season, the 1,000 and 2,000 Guineas, are run, together with important autumn events including the Cambridgeshire and the Cesarewich. There are some 18 race days at this track, while on the leafy July course, with its delightful garden-party atmosphere, a similar number of race days take in all the important summer fixtures.

The visitor to Newmarket can learn almost all there is to know about flat racing and racehorses by making the grand tour of the several establishments open to the public (sometimes by appointment only). The Jockey Club, which was the first governing body of the sport and, until recently, its ultimate authority, was formed in the mid-18th century and occupied an imposing building which was restored and rebuilt in Georgian style in the 1930s. Originally a social club for rich gentlemen with an interest in the turf, it soon became the all-powerful regulator of British racing, owning all the racing and training land. When holding an enquiry the stewards sat round a horseshoe-shaped table while the jockey or trainer under scrutiny faces them on a strip of carpet by the door - hence the expression 'on the mat'.

A few steps away is **Palace House**, which contains the remains of Charles II's palace and which, as funds allow, has been restored over the years for use as a visitor centre and museum. In the same street is

Nell Gwynn's House, which some say was connected by an underground passage beneath the street to the palace. The diarist John Evelyn spent a night in (or on?) the town during a royal visit, and declared the occasion to be 'more resembling a luxurious and abandoned rout than a Christian court'.

Other must-sees on the racing enthusiast's tour are **Tattersalls**, where leading thoroughbred sales take place from February to December; the **British Racing School**, where budding jockeys are taught the ropes; the **National Stud**, open from March till the end of September (plus race days in October - booking essential); and the **Animal Health Trust** based at Lanwades Hall, where there's an informative Visitor Centre. The National Stud at one time housed no fewer than three Derby winners - Blakeney, Mill Reef, and Grundy.

Horses aren't all about racing, however. One type of horse you won't see in Newmarket is the wonderful Suffolk Punch, a massive yet elegant working horse which can still be seen at work at Rede Hall Park Farm near Bury St Edmunds and at Kentwell Hall in Long Melford. All Punches descend from Crisp's horse, foaled in 1768. The Punch is part of the Hallowed Trinity of animals at the very centre of Suffolk's agricultural history; the others being the Suffolk Sheep and the Red Poll Cow. It is entirely appropriate that the last railway station to employ a horse for shunting wagons should have been at Newmarket. That hardworking one-horse-power shunter retired in 1967. Newmarket also has things to offer the tourist outside the equine world, including the churches of St Mary and All Saints, and St Agnes, and a landmark at each end of the High Street - a Memorial Fountain in honour of Sir Daniel Cooper and the Jubilee Clock Tower commemorating Queen Victoria's Golden Jubilee.

AROUND NEWMARKET

EXNING

2 miles NW of Newmarket on the A14

A pause is certainly in order at this ancient village, whether on your way from Newmarket or arriving from Cambridgeshire on the A14. Anglo-Saxons, Romans, the Iceni and the Normans were all here, and the *Domesday Book* records the village under the name of Esselinga. The village was stricken by plague during the Iceni occupation, so its market was moved to the next village along - thus Newmarket acquired its name.

KENTFORD

5 miles E of Newmarket by the A14

At the old junction of the Newmarket-to-Bury road stands the grave of a young boy who hanged himself after being accused of sheep-stealing. It was a well-established superstition that suicides should be buried at a crossroads to prevent their spirits from wandering. Flowers are still

sometimes laid at the **Gypsy Boy's Grave**, sometimes by punters hoping for good luck at Newmarket races.

MOULTON

4 miles E of Newmarket on the B1085

This most delightful village lies in wonderful countryside on chalky downland in farming country; its proximity to Newmarket is apparent from the racehorses which are often to be seen on the large green. The River Kennett flows through the green before running north to the Lark, a tributary of the Ouse. Flint walls are a feature of many of the buildings, but the main point of interest is the 15th century Four-arch Packhorse Bridge on the way to the church.

DALHAM

5 miles E of Newmarket on the B1063

Eighty per cent of the buildings in Dalham are thatched (the highest proportion in Suffolk) and there are many other attractions in this pretty village. Above the village on one of the county's highest spots stands **St Mary's Church**, which dates from the 14th century. Its spire toppled over during the gales which swept the land on the night that Cromwell died, and was replaced by a tower in 1627. Sir Martin Stutteville was the leading light behind this reconstruction; an inscription at the back of the church notes that the cost was £400. That worthy's grandfather was Thomas Stutteville, whose memorial near the altar declares that 'he saw the New World with Francis Drake.' (Drake

Exning's written history begins when Henry II granted the manor to the Count of Boulogne, who divided it between four of his knights. References to them and to subsequent Lords of the Manor are to be found in the little Church of St Martin, which might well have been founded by the Burgundian Christian missionary monk St Felix in the 7th century. Water from the well used by that saint to baptise members of the Saxon royal family is still used for baptisms by the current vicar.

Dalham Hall was constructed in the first years of the 18th century at the order of the Bishop of Ely, who decreed that it should be built up until Ely Cathedral could be seen across the fens on a clear day. That view was sadly cut off in 1957 when a fire shortened the hall to only two storeys high. Wellington lived here for some years, and much later it was bought by Cecil Rhodes, who unfortunately died before taking up residence. His brother Francis erected the village hall in the adventurer's memory, and he himself is buried in the churchyard.

133

93 THE AFFLECK ARMS

Dalham

The **Affleck Arms** is a
delightful old thatched
village pub serving
interesting real ales and
traditional home-cooked
meals.

 see page 273

94 HILL FARM

Kirtling, nr Newmarket

Hill Farm is a comfortable
B&B base in a 400-year-old
farmhouse surrounded by
arable farmland.

 see page 274

•

*Sir Henry North built a
manor house on the north
side of Mildenhall's St
Mary's Church in the
17th century. His
successors included a
dynasty of the Bunbury
family, who were Lords
of the Manor from 1747
to 1933. Sir Henry
Edward Bunbury was
the man chosen to let
Napoleon Bonaparte
know of his exile to St
Helena, but the best-
known member of the
family is Sir Thomas,
who in 1780 tossed a
coin with Lord Derby to
see whose name should
be borne by a race to be
inaugurated at Epsom.
Lord Derby won, but Sir
Thomas had the
satisfaction of winning
the first running of the
race with his colt,
Diomed.*

•

did not survive that journey - his
third to South America.) Thomas'
grandson died in the fullness of his
years (62 wasn't bad for those times)
while hosting a jolly evening at The
Angel Hotel in Bury St Edmunds.

MILDENHALL

8 miles NE of Newmarket off the A11

On the edge of the Fens and
Breckland, Mildenhall is a town
which has many links with the past.
It was once a port for the
hinterlands of West Suffolk, though
the River Lark has long ceased to be
a trade route. Most of the town's
heritage is recorded in the excellent
Mildenhall & District Museum in
King Street. Here will be found
exhibits of local history (including
the distinguished RAF and USAAF
base), crafts and domestic skills, the
natural history of the Fens and
Breckland and, perhaps most
famously, the chronicle of the
'**Mildenhall Treasure**'. This was a
cache of 34 pieces of 4th century
Roman silverware - dishes, goblets
and spoons - found by a ploughman
in 1946 at Thistley Green and now
on display in the British Museum in
London, while a replica makes its
home here where it was found.
There is evidence of much earlier
occupation than the Roman era, with
flint tools and other artefacts being
unearthed in 1988 on the site of an
ancient lake.

The parish of Mildenhall is the
largest in Suffolk, so it is perhaps
fitting that it should boast so
magnificent a parish church as **St
Mary's**, built of Barnack stone; it
dominates the heart of the town and

indeed its west tower commands the
flat surrounding countryside. Above
the splendid north porch (the largest
in Suffolk) are the arms of Edward
the Confessor and of St Edmund.
The chancel, dating back to the 13th
century, is a marvellous work of
architecture, but pride of place goes
to the east window, divided into
seven vertical lights. Off the south
aisle is the Chapel of St Margaret,
whose altar, itself modern, contains
a medieval altar stone. At the west
end, the font, dating from the 15th
century, bears the arms of Sir Henry
Barton, who was twice Lord Mayor
of London and whose tomb is
located on the south side of the
tower. Above the nave and aisles is a
particularly fine hammerbeam roof
whose outstanding feature is the
carved angels. Efforts of the
Puritans to destroy the angels failed,
though traces of buckshot and
arrowheads remain and have been
found embedded in the woodwork.

The other focal point in
Mildenhall is the Market Place, with
its 16th century timbered cross.

BARTON MILLS

1 mile S of Mildenhall off the A11

Known as Barton Parva (Little
Barton) in Saxon times, this village
changed its name during the 18th
century. St Mary's Church can trace
its origins back to at least 1150, and
one of its early rectors had the
Pope as his patron. Sir Alexander
Fleming had a country house in the
village of Barton Mills, and it is
possible that he worked on the
invention of penicillin in a shed in
the garden.

WORLINGTON

2 miles W of Mildenhall on the B1102

Worlington is a small village near the River Lark, known chiefly as the location of **Wamil Hall**, an Elizabethan mansion which stands on the riverbank. Popular lore has it that a person called Lady Rainbow haunts the place, though the spot she once favoured for appearances, a flight of stairs, was destroyed in one of the many fires the mansion has suffered. Cricket is very much part of the village scene (there's a splendid village green), and has been since the early days of the 19th century.

BRANDON

9 miles NE of Mildenhall on the A1065

On the edge of **Thetford Forest** by the Little Ouse, Brandon was long ago a thriving port, but flint is what really put it on the map. The town itself is built mainly of flint, and flint was mined from early Neolithic times to make arrowheads and other implements and weapons of war. The gun flint industry brought with it substantial wealth, and a good flint-knapper could produce up to 300 gun flints in an hour. The invention of the percussion cap killed off much of the need for this type of work, however, so they turned to shaping flints for church buildings and ornamental purposes. **Brandon Heritage Centre**, in a former fire station in George Street, provides visitors with a splendid insight into this industry, while for an even more tangible feel, a visit to

Grime's Graves, just over the Norfolk border, reveals an amazing site covering 35 acres and 300 pits (one of the shafts is open to visitors). With the close proximity of numerous warrens and their rabbit population, the fur trade also flourished here, and that, too, along with forestry, is brought to life in the Heritage Centre (see also under Thetford in the Norfolk chapter).

The whole of this northwestern corner of Suffolk, know as Breckland, offers almost unlimited opportunities for touring by car, cycling or walking. A mile south of town on the B1106 is **Brandon Country Park**, a 30-acre landscaped site with a tree trail, forest walks, a walled garden and a visitor centre. There's also an orienteering route leading on into Thetford Forest, Britain's largest lowland pine forest. Three miles west of Brandon on the county border lies the Norfolk Wildlife Trust's **Weeting Heath**, famous for its extraordinary-looking stone curlews.

The High Lodge Forest Centre, near Santon Downham (off the B1107), also attracts with walks, cycle trails and adventure facilities.

ELVEDEN

5 miles S of Brandon on the A11

The road from Brandon leads south through the forest to a historic estate village with some unusual architectural features. Where the three parishes of Elveden, Eriswell and Icklingham meet, a tall war memorial in the form of a Corinthian column is a landmark.

*Elveden Hall became more remarkable than its builders intended when Prince Duleep Singh, the last Maharajah of Punjab and a noted sportsman, crack shot and the man who handed over the Koh-I-Noor diamond to Queen Victoria, arrived on the scene. Exiled to England with a handsome pension, he bought the Georgian house in 1863 and commissioned John Norton to transform it into a palace modelled on those in Lahore and Delhi. Although it is stated that in private Duleep Singh referred to Queen Victoria as 'Mrs Fagin ... receiver of stolen goods', he kept close contact with the royal household and the Queen became his son's godmother. The Guinness family (Lord Iveagh) later took the Hall over and joined in the fun, adding even more exotic adornments including a replica Taj Mahal, while at the same time creating the largest arable farm in the whole of the country. In recent times, Stanley Kubrick's last film, **Eyes Wide Shut**, was shot here, as was **Tomb Raider**.*

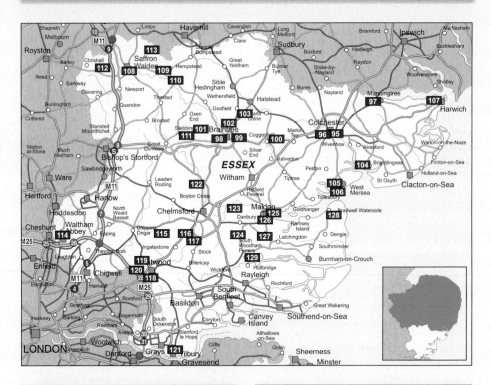

Essex

Northeast Essex has the true feel of East Anglia, particularly around the outstanding villages of the Stour Valley - which has come to be known as Constable Country (along with its near neighbour southern Suffolk.) The inland villages and small towns here are notably historic and picturesque, offering very good touring and walking opportunities.

A plethora of half-timbered medieval buildings, farms and churches mark this region out as of particular historical interest. Monuments to engineering feats past and present include Hedingham Castle, Chappel Viaduct and the postmill at Bocking Church Street. Truly lovely villages such as Finchingfield abound, rewarding any journey to this part of the county. There are also many lovely gardens to visit, and this region's principal town, Colchester, is a mine of interesting sights and experiences.

The North Essex coast has a

distinguished history and a strong maritime heritage, as exemplified in towns like Harwich, Manningtree and Mistley. Further examples are the fine Martello Towers - circular brick edifices built to provide a coastal defence against Napoleon's armies - along the Tendring coast at Walton and Clacton. Dating from 1808 to 1812, each is mounted with a gun on the roof.

River Stour, Dedham

The Tendring Peninsula has a rich and varied heritage ranging from prehistoric remains to medieval churches and elegant Victorian villas. The Tendring Coast contains an interesting mix of extensive tidal inlets, sandy beaches and low cliffs. Place names include the Danish ending 'by', meaning a settlement, and the Old English 'ea' and 'ey' for an island. Among the many attractive villages in the district are Thorpe-le-Soken, Kirby-le-Soken and Great Bentley - the last reputed to have the largest village green in England. The Stour Estuary, Hamford Water and the Colne Estuary are all renowned for seabirds and other wildlife, and many areas are protected nature reserves. The Manningtree-Ramsey

Danbury Village

road passes through some of the best coastal scenery in Essex, with some outstanding views of the Suffolk shore.

This is, of course, also the part of the county known as 'the sunshine holiday coast', where the resorts of Clacton, Frinton and Walton-on-the-Naze are to be found.

The small northwest Essex towns of Saffron Walden, Thaxted, Great Dumnow and Stansted Mountfichet are among the loveliest and most interesting in the land. This area is also home to a wealth of picturesque villages boasting weatherboarded houses and pargeting. The quiet country lanes are perfect for walking, cycling or exploring. Here can be seen three historic windmills, at Stansted Mountfichet, Aythorpe Roding and Thaxted. Visitors to southwest Essex and Epping Forest will find a treasure-trove of woodland, nature reserves, superb gardens and other rural delights. Epping Forest dominates much of the far western corner, but all this part of the county is rich in countryside, forests and parks, including the magnificent Lee Valley regional Park, Thorndon Country Park at Brentwood and Weald Country Park at South Weald. Bordering the north bank of the Thames, the borough of Thurrock has long been a gateway to London but also affords easy access to southwest Essex and Kent. Along the 18 miles of Thames frontage there are many important marshland wildlife habitats. History, too, abounds in this part of the county. Henry VIII built riverside block houses at East and West Tilbury, and it was at West Tilbury that Elizabeth I gave her famous speech to her troops, gathered to meet the threat of the Spanish Armada. At the extreme southeast of the county, Southend is a popular seaside resort with a wealth of sights and amenities. The area surrounding the Rivers Blackwater and Crouch contains a wealth of ancient woodland and other natural beauty, particularly along the estuaries of the Chelmer & Blackwater Canal. This part of Essex affords some marvellous sailing, walking, cycling, birdwatching and other outdoor activities.

COLCHESTER AND NORTH EAST ESSEX

COLCHESTER

This ancient market town and garrison stands in the midst of rolling East Anglian countryside. England's oldest recorded town, it has over 2,000 years of history, there to be discovered by visitors. First established during the 7th century BC, west of town there are the remains of the massive earthworks built to protect Colchester in pre-Roman times. During the 1st century, Colchester's prime location made it an obvious target for invading Romans. The Roman Emperor Claudius accepted the surrender of 11 British Kings in Colchester. In AD 60, Queen Boudica helped to establish her place in history by taking revenge on the Romans and burning the town to the ground, before going on to destroy London and St Albans. Here in this town that was once capital of Roman Britain, Roman walls - the oldest in Britain - still surround the oldest part of town. Balkerne Gate, west gate of the original Roman town, is the largest surviving Roman gateway in the country, and remains magnificent to this day.

The town affords plenty to see and explore. There are many guided town walks available, as well as bus tours. The local Visitor Information Centre on Queen Street has details of the many places to visit. Market days in this thriving town are Friday and Saturday. Today, Colchester is presided over by its lofty town hall and enormous Victorian Water Tower, nicknamed 'Jumbo' after London Zoo's first African elephant, an animal sold to P T Barnum (causing some controversy) in 1882. The tower has four massive pillars made up of one-and-a-quarter million bricks, 369 tons of stone and 142 tons of iron, all working to support the 230,000-gallon tank.

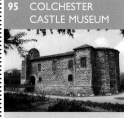

95 COLCHESTER CASTLE MUSEUM

Colchester

Colchester Castle is undeniably one of the most important historic buildings in the country.

 see page 274

Balkerne Gate, Colchester

Dutch Protestants arrived in Colchester in the 16th century, fleeing Spanish rule in the Netherlands, and revitalised the local cloth industry. The houses of these Flemish weavers in the Dutch Quarter to the west of the castle, and the Civil War scars on the walls of Siege House in East Street, bear testimony to their place in the town's history. The Dutch Quarter west of the castle remains a charming and relatively quiet corner of this bustling town. Close to the railway station are the ruins of St Botolph's Priory, the oldest Augustinian priory in the country. Its remains are a potent reminder of the bitterness of Civil War times, as it was here that Royalists held out for 11 weeks during the siege of Colchester, before finally being starved into submission.

96 HOLLYTREES MUSEUM

Colchester

Hollytrees is a beautiful Georgian town house in the grounds of the award-winning Castle Park.

  see page 275

A good place to start any exploration of the town is **Colchester Castle** and its museum. When the Normans arrived, Colchester (a name given the town by the Saxons) was an important borough. The Normans built their castle on the foundations of the Roman temple of Claudius. Having used many of the Roman bricks in its construction, it boasts the largest Norman keep ever built in Europe - the only part still left standing. The keep houses the **Castle Museum**, one of the most exciting hands-on historical attractions in the country. Its fascinating collection of Iron Age, Roman and medieval relics is one of the most important in the country. Among the numerous attractions are a Roman bronze statue of Mercury; the original charter granted to Colchester in 1413; the Colchester Vase, one of the most important examples of Roman pottery found in Britain; the Colchester Sphinx, once part of a Roman tomb; gold coins of King Cunobelin; and a new interactive gallery affording a walk through virtual Colchester. Visitors can try on a toga and medieval hats and shoes, feel the weight of Roman armour and experience the town's murkier past by visiting the Castle prisons, where witches were interrogated by the notorious Witchfinder General Matthew Hopkins.

Hollytrees Museum in the High Street is located in a fine Georgian home dating back to 1718. This award-winning museum, found on the edge of Castle Park,

houses a wonderful collection of toys, costumes, curios and antiquities from the last two centuries. Purchased for the town by Viscount Cowdray it first opened as a museum in 1920. Also nearby, housed in the former All Saints' Church, is the **Natural History Museum**, with many hands-on displays illustrating the natural history of Essex from the Ice Age right up to the present day.

Housed in the Minories Art Gallery, **First Site** features changing exhibitions of contemporary visual art, housed in a converted Georgian town house with beautiful walled garden. An arch in Trinity Street leads to **Tymperleys Clock Museum**, the 15th century timber-framed home of William Gilberd, who entertained Elizabeth I with experiments in electricity. Today this fine example of architectural splendour houses a magnificent collection of 18th and 19th century Colchester-made clocks. The **Colchester Arts Centre**, not far from Balkerne Gate, features a regular programme of visual arts, drama, music, poetry and dance; the Mercury Theatre is the town's premier site for stage dramas, comedies and musical theatre.

Colchester Zoo, just off the A12 outside the town, stands in the 40-acre park of Stanway Hall, with its 16th century mansion and church dating from the 14th century. Founded in 1963, the Zoo has a wide and exciting variety of attractions. The Zoo has gained a well-deserved reputation as one of the best in Europe. Its award-winning enclosures allow visitors closer to the animals and provide naturalistic environments for upwards of 200. The daily displays include the chance to help feed elephants and giraffes, and watch the free-flying birds of prey. Other attractions include the African Zone, the Penguin Parade, the Tiger Taiga enclosure and the sea lion pool with a viewing tunnel.

Just north of the centre of town, **High Woods Country Park** offers 330 acres of woodland, grassland, scrub and farmland. A central lake is fed by a small tributary of the River Colne. The land originated as three ancient farms, and forms part of a Royal hunting forest. Large numbers of musket balls dating from the Civil War period have been unearthed, indicating that the woods served as a base for the Roundheads. On Bourne Road, south of the town centre just off the B1025, there's a striking stepped-and-curved gabled building known as **Bourne Mill**, now owned by the National Trust. Built in 1591 from stone taken from the nearby St John's Abbeygate, this delightful restored building near a lovely millpond was originally a fishing lodge, later converted (in the 19th century) into a mill - and still in working order.

AROUND COLCHESTER

ABBERTON

3 miles S of Colchester off the B1026

Abberton Reservoir Nature Reserve is a 1,200-acre reservoir and wildlife centre, ideal for birdwatching. Designated a Site of Special Scientific Interest, it is home to hundreds of goldeneye, wigeon, gadwall and shovellers, as well as a resting colony of cormorants; the site has a conservation room, shop, toilets and hides.

•

Colchester has been famous in its time for both oysters and roses. Colchester oysters are still cultivated on beds in the lower reaches of the River Colne, which skirts the northern edge of town. A visit to the Oyster Fisheries on Mersea Island is a fascinating experience, and the tour includes complimentary fresh oysters and a glass of wine.

•

Bourne Mill, Colchester

GREAT WIGBOROUGH

6 miles S of Colchester off the B1026 or B1025

This area had a number of experiences with Zeppelins during the First World War. In September 1916 Zeppelin L33, which had been hit over Bromley, crashed near here. The event is commemorated in an account in St Stephen's Church, framed by metal from the wreck. Another part of L33 can be seen in the Church of St Nicholas in neighbouring Little Wigborough.

COPFORD GREEN & COPFORD

3½ miles SW of Colchester off the B1022

Copford is home to the wonderful Norman **Church of St Michael and All Angels**, with its magnificent, well-restored medieval wall paintings, while Copford Green, a lovely and peaceful village, is home to **Springfields at Copford** with 17 acres of gardens and parkland. Here visitors will find old established south gardens with roses and shrubbery, as well as a parterre planted in 1997 with 330 rose bushes. Other attractions include a rare Maidenhair Gingko tree, ancient mulberry, woodland walks, spring-fed water gardens and lake, and croquet and putting greens. The Church of St Mary the Virgin also repays a visit.

LAYER BRETON

5½ miles SW of Colchester off the B1026

On the right side of Layer Breton Heath there's Stamps and Crows, a must for gardening enthusiasts. Two and a half acres of moated garden surrounding a 15th century farmhouse boast herbaceous borders, mixed shrubs, old roses and good ground cover. There is also a bog garden and dovecote.

LAYER MARNEY

6 miles SW of Colchester off the B1022

The mansion, which was planned to rival Hampton Court, was never completed, but its massive 8-storey Tudor gatehouse, known as **Layer Marney Tower**, is very impressive. Built between 1515 and 1525, it is

Layer Marney Tower

one of the most striking examples of 16th century architecture in Britain. Its magnificent four red brick towers, covered in 16th century Italianate design, were built by Lord Marney, Henry VIII's Lord Privy Seal. As well as spectacular views from the top of the towers, they are surrounded by formal gardens designed at the turn of the century, with lovely roses, yew hedges and herbaceous borders. There is also on site a rare breeds farm, farm shop and tea room.

TIPTREE
7 miles SW of Colchester on the B1023

As all true jam-lovers will know, Tiptree is famed as the home of the **Wilkin and Son Ltd** jam factory, a Victorian establishment which now boasts a fascinating visitors' centre in the grounds of the original factory.

CHAPPEL
5 miles W of Colchester off the A604

Here, on an open-air site with beautiful valley views beside Chappel and Wakes Colne Station, is the **East Anglian Railway Museum**, a comprehensive collection spanning 150 years of railway history, with period railway architecture, engineering and memorabilia in beautifully restored station buildings. For every railway buff, young or old, this is the place to try your hand at being a signalman and admire the handsome restored engines and carriages. They also run special railway experience courses in driving and firing a steam

locomotive. Platform 1 of the station is still used by 'One' Great Eastern services between Marks Tey and Sudbury. Easy to find on the A1124 (off the A12), the Museum is open daily from 10 to 4.30.

Chappel Galleries (free entry) is a commercial gallery with a programme of changing exhibits of fine art.

EARLS COLNE
7 miles W of Colchester off the A604

The de Veres, Earls of Oxford, and the River Colne bestowed this village with its name. Aubery de Vere founded a Benedictine priory here in the 12th century, and both he and his wife, sister of William the Conqueror, were buried there. Today the site is marked by a redbrick Gothic mansion. Though the commuter culture has spread modern housing around the village, the cluster of timbered cottages hearkens back to this village's distinguished past. At Pound Green, on the Coggeshall road, stands a pump erected in 1853 by benefactor Mary Gee in thanks for the absence of cholera in the village.

DEDHAM
6 miles NE of Colchester off the A14

This is true Constable country, along the border with Suffolk, the county's prettiest area. The village has several fine old buildings, especially the 15th century flint church, its pinnacled tower familiar from so many Constable paintings. There's also the school Constable

The dramatic 32-arched Chappel Viaduct standing 75 feet above the Colne Valley, a designated European Monument, was begun in 1846 and opened in 1849.

97 THE MARLBOROUGH HEAD INN

Dedham

A historic inn with a happy, relaxed ambience, good ales, home cooking and comfortable, characterful rooms for B&B.

see page 275

River Stour, Dedham

At Castle House, approximately three-quarters of a mile from the centre of Dedham on the corner of East Lane and Castle Hill, the Sir Alfred Munnings Art Museum is housed in the former home, studios and grounds of the famous painter, who lived here between 1898 and 1920. The museum prides itself on the diversity of paintings and sculptures on view. The house itself is a mixture of Tudor and Georgian periods, carefully restored. Munnings' original furniture is still in place. The spacious grounds boast well-maintained gardens.

went to, and good walks through the protected riverside meadows of Dedham Vale to **Flatford**, where Bridge Cottage is a restored thatched 16th century building housing a display about Constable, who featured this cottage in several of his paintings (his father's mill is across the river lock in Dedham).

The Art & Craft Centre on Dedham's High Street is well worth a visit. Marlborough Head, a wool merchant's house dating back to 1475, is now a pub. The **Toy Museum** has a fascinating collection of dolls, teddy bears, toys, games, doll houses and other artefacts of childhoods past.

Dedham Vale Family Farm on Mill Street is a nicely undeveloped 16-acre farm boasting a comprehensive collection of British farm animals, including many different breeds of livestock such as pigs, sheep, cattle, Suffolk horses, goats and poultry. Children may enter certain of the paddocks

to stroke and feed the animals (bags of feed provided).

WIVENHOE
4 miles SE of Colchester off the A133

This riverside town on the banks of the River Colne was once renowned as a smugglers' haunt, and there is a very pretty quayside that is steeped in maritime history. There are still strong connections with the sea, with boat-building having replaced fishing as the main industry. The pretty church, with its distinctive cupola atop a sturdy tower, stands on the site of the former Saxon church and retains some impressive 16th century brasses.

The small streets lead into each other and end at the picturesque waterfront, where fishing boats and small sailing craft bob at their moorings. On the Quay visitors will find the **Nottage Institute**, the River Colne's nautical academy; classes here teach students about knots, skippering and even how to build a boat! It is open to visitors on Sundays in summer. The Wivenhoe Trail, by the river, is an interesting cycle track starting at the railway station and continuing along the river to Colchester Hythe. Wivenhoe Woods is dotted with grassy glades set with tables, the perfect place for a picnic.

East of Wivenhoe quay, the public footpath takes visitors to the **Tidal Surge Barrier**, one of only two in the country. Volunteers run a ferry service operating across the River Colne between the Quay at Wivenhoe, Fingringhoe and

Rowhedge. Nearby Wivenhoe Park has been the site of the campus for the University of Essex since 1962. Visitors are welcome to stroll around the grounds.

BRAINTREE

This town and its close neighbour Bocking are sited at the crossing of two Roman roads and were brought together by the cloth industry in the 16th century. Flemish weavers settled here, followed by many Huguenots. One, Samuel Courtauld, set up a silk mill in 1816 and, by 1866, employed over 3,000 Essex inhabitants.

The magnificent former Town Hall is one of the many Courtauld legacies in the town. It was built in 1928 with panelled walls, murals by Grieffenhagen showing stirring scenes of local history, and a grand central tower with a five-belled striking clock. A smaller but no less fascinating reminder of Courtauld's generosity is the 1930s bronze fountain, with bay, shell and fish, near St Michael's Church.

Huguenot names such as Courtauld are connected with international enterprises to this day. Their reason for coming to Britain is a fascinating and poignant tale. Formed in France in 1559 as an organised Protestant group taking direction from Calvin and the Calvinistic Reformation in Geneva, the Huguenots were at first allowed to live and worship freely. However, as political and religious rivalries grew in France, the Catholic majority started to

persecute them; a century of war, massacre and bloodshed followed. Finally in 1685 all their rights were stripped. In the chaos that ensued, many died and thousands fled. It was to turn out to be France's loss, for the Huguenots were among the most industrious and economically advanced elements in French society. Others gained at France's expense; Huguenots poured into England, and especially East Anglia, where their skills soon made them welcome and valued members of the community.

The **Braintree District Museum**, housed in a converted Victorian school in the historic market square tells the story of Braintree's diverse industrial heritage and traditions; exhibits include a re-created Victorian classroom, the wool and silk industries and various country crafts. The **Town Hall Centre** is a Grade II listed building housing the Tourist Information Centre and the Art Gallery, which boasts a continuous changing programme of exhibitions and works.

AROUND BRAINTREE

COGGESHALL

5 miles E of Braintree on the A120

This medieval hamlet, a pleasant old cloth and lace town, has some very fine timbered buildings. **Paycocke's House** on West Street, a delightful timber-framed medieval merchant's home dating from about 1500, boasts unusually rich

98 THE ANGEL

Bocking, nr Braintree

A fine old coshing inn at the heart of the local community, equally popular for a drink, a meal or a game of pool.

🍴 see page 275

99 BALLAGLASS

Stisted, nr Braintree

Luxurious holiday accommodation centrally located for touring the picturesque Essex countryside and villages.

🛏 see page 276

100 THE KINGS ARMS

Coggeshall

A welcoming free house open all day for well-kept ales and excellent home cooking

🍴 see page 277

145

Paycocke's House, Coggeshall

Marks Hall fell on hard times in the 19th and early 20th century, but owner Thomas Phillips Price began an association with Kew Gardens and left the estate to be held and used for 'advancement in the National interest of Agriculture, Aboriculture and Forestry'. The Thomas Phillips Price Trust was formed and registered as a charity in 1971, and a major programme of revitalisation and restoration began. The estate now flourishes with native plants and wildlife, ornamental lakes, a 17th century walled garden, arboretum, cascades, coach house and Information Centre. This last is housed in a painstakingly refurbished 15th century barn, and features informative displays as well as a gift shop and tea room.

panelling and wood carvings, and is owned by the National Trust. Inside there's a superb carved ceiling and a display of Coggeshall lace. Outdoors there's a lovely garden. The village also has some good antique shops and a working pottery.

Located in Stoneham Street, **Coggeshall Heritage Centre** displays items of local interest and features changing exhibitions on themes relating to the past of this historic wool town.

The National Trust also owns the restored **Coggeshall Grange Barn**, which dates from around 1140 and is the oldest surviving timber-framed barn in Europe. Built for the monks of the nearby Cistercian Abbey, it is a magnificent example of this type of architecture.

Marks Hall is a historic estate and arboretum that began life in Saxon times, and is mentioned in the *Domesday Book*. In the 15th century, then-owner Sir Thomas Honywood was a leading Parliamentarian who commanded

the Essex Regiment during the Civil War. Local legend has it that the two artificial lakes on the grounds were dug by Parliamentary troops during the siege of Colchester in 1648. One of his successors, General Philip Honywood, in 1758 forbade (under the terms of his will) any of his successors to fell timber - thus his lasting legacy of avenues of mature oaks, limes and horse chestnuts, surrounded by one of the largest continuous areas of ancient woodland in the county.

CRESSING

4 miles E of Braintree off the B1018

Cressing Temple Barns, set in the centre of an ancient farmstead, are two splendid medieval timber barns commissioned in the 12th century by the Knights Templar. They contain the timber of over 1,000 oak trees; an interpretive exhibition explains to visitors how the barns were made, as a special viewing platform brings visitors up into the roof of the magnificent Wheat Barn for a closer look. There's also a beautiful walled garden re-creating the Tudor style, with an arbour, fount and physic garden. Special events are held throughout the year.

FEERING

6 miles E of Braintree off the A12

Feeringbury Manor near Feering has a fine, extensive riverside garden with ponds, streams, a little waterwheel, old-fashioned plants and bog gardens, and fascinating sculpture by artist Ben Coode-Adams.

ESSEX

KELVEDON

6 miles SE of Braintree off the A12

This village alongside the River Blackwater houses the **Feering and Kelvedon Museum**, which is dedicated to manorial history and houses artefacts from the Roman settlement of Canonium, agricultural tools through the ages and other interesting exhibits.

FAIRSTEAD

4 miles S of Braintree off the A131

Fairstead (or Fairsted) is an undulating parish about three miles east of the A131. The **Church of St Mary and St Peter** is an ancient building of flint, in the Norman style, consisting of chancel, nave, north porch and a western tower with a lofty shingled spire with four bells, one of which dates back to before the Reformation. During restoration in the late 1800s various handsome mural paintings were discovered, including, over the chancel arch, those entitled Our Lord's Triumphal Entry into Jerusalem, The Last Supper, The Betrayal, Our Lord being crowned with thorns, and Incidents on the way to Calvary.

BLAKE END

3 miles W of Braintree off the A120

The **Great Maze** at Blake End is one of the most challenging in the world. Set in over 10 acres of lovely North Essex farmland, it is grown every year from over half a million individual maize and sunflower seeds, and is open every summer. Continuing innovations

bring with them extra twists and turns, making this wonderful maze, with more than five miles of pathways, even more of a brain teaser. A viewing platform makes it easy to help anyone hopelessly lost! Ten per cent of all profits go to the Essex Air Ambulance service.

GREAT SALING

4 miles NW of Braintree off the A120

Saling Hall Garden is a 12-acre garden including a walled garden dating from 1698. The small park boasts a collection of fine trees, and there are ponds, a water garden and an extensive collection of unusual plants with an emphasis on rare trees.

WETHERSFIELD

5 miles NW of Braintree on the B1053

Boydells Dairy Farm is a working farm where visitors are welcome to join in with tasks such as milking, feeding and more. A guided tour mixes fun with education, and all questions are most welcome. From bees to llamas, just about every kind of farm animal can be found here

GREAT BARDFIELD

6 miles NW of Braintree off the B1053

This old market town on a hill above the River Pant is a pleasant mixture of cottages and shops, nicely complemented by the 14th century **Church of St Mary the Virgin**. Perhaps Great Bardfield's most notable feature is, however, a restored windmill that goes by the strange name of Gibraltar.

Blake House Craft Centre comprises carefully preserved farm buildings centred round a courtyard. Visitors will find a fine array of craft shops and a restaurant serving breakfast and morning coffee, lunch and afternoon tea.

101 THE WHITE HART

Great Saling, nr Braintree

Well-kept ales and serious cooking in an atmospheric village inn.

see page 277

147

Spains Hall, Finchingfield

Here in one of the prettiest villages in all of Essex, **Great Bardfield Museum** occupies a 16th century charity cottage and 19th century village lockup (the Cage), and features exhibits of mainly 19th and 20th century domestic and agricultural artefacts and some fine examples of rural crafts such as corn dollies and straw-plaiting.

FINCHINGFIELD

6 miles NW of Braintree off the B1053

This charming village is graced with thatched cottages spread generously around a sloping village green that dips to a stream and duck pond at the centre of the village. Nearby stands an attractive small 18th century Post Mill with one pair of stones and tailpole winding. Extensively restored, today's visitors can climb up the first two floors.

Just up the hill, visitors will find the Norman **Church of St John the Baptist**, the Guildhall (mentioned in the *Domesday Book*), which has a small museum open Sundays and also houses a local heritage centre with displays of artwork, paintings, pottery, sewing and weaving.

Finchingfield is easily one of the most picturesque and most photographed villages in Essex, featured in many television programmes and the home of the series Lovejoy. Here visitors will also find the privately owned Tudor stately home, **Spains Hall**, which has a lovely flower garden containing a huge Cedar of Lebanon planted in 1670 and an Adams sundial. Many good roses surround the kitchen garden, which contains an ancient Paulonia tree and a bougainvillea in the greenhouse.

Dodie Smith, author of *101 Dalmatians*, lived for many years in a 17th century cottage in the village.

GOSFIELD

4 miles N of Braintree off the A1017

Gosfield Lake Leisure Resort, the county's largest freshwater lake, lies in the grounds of Gosfield Hall. This Tudor mansion was remodelled in the 19th century by its owner Samuel Courtauld. He also built the attractive mock-Tudor houses in the village.

HALSTEAD

The name 'Halstead' comes from the Anglo-Saxon for healthy place. Like Braintree and Coggeshall, Halstead was an important weaving centre. **Townsford Mill** is certainly the most picturesque reminder of Halstead's industrial heritage. Built in the 1700s, it remains one of the most handsome buildings in a town with a number of historic buildings. This white, weather-boarded three-storey mill across the River Colne at the Causeway was once a landmark site for the Courtauld empire, producing both the famous funerary crepe and rayon. Today the Mill is an antiques centre, one of the largest in Essex, with thousands of items of furniture, porcelain, collectibles, stamps, coins, books, dolls, postcards, costume, paintings, glass and ceramics, old lace and clocks.

Halstead's most famous product was once mechanical elephants. Life-sized and weighing half a ton, they were built by W Hunwicks. Each one consisted of 9,000 parts and could carry a load of eight adults and four children at speeds of up to an impressive 12 miles per hour.

There are several historic buildings in the shopping centre of Halstead, which is part of a designated conservation area. Markets are held every Friday and Saturday.

AROUND HALSTEAD

CASTLE HEDINGHAM
3 miles NW of Halstead off the B1058

This town takes its name from its **Norman Castle**, which dominates the landscape. One of England's strongest fortresses in the 11th century, even now it is impossible not to sense its power and strength.

The impressive stone keep is one of the tallest in Europe, with four floors and rising over 100 feet, with 12-feet thick walls. The banqueting hall and minstrels' gallery can still be seen. It was owned by the Earls of Oxford, the powerful de Vere family, one of whom was among the barons who forced King John to accept the Magna Carta. Among those entertained at the castle were Henry VII and Elizabeth I.

The village itself is a maze of narrow streets radiating from Falcon Square, named after the

103 FROYZ HALL BARN

Halstead

Superb self-catering accommodation for up to 8 guests in a beautifully converted barn on a large country estate.

see *page 277*

Castle Hedingham Castle

At the Colne Valley Railway and Museum, on the A1017 between Sible Hedingham and Great Yeldham, a mile of the Colne Valley and Halstead line between Castle Hedingham and Great Yeldham has been restored and now runs steam and heritage diesel trains operated by enthusiasts. These lovingly restored Victorian railway buildings feature a collection of vintage engines and carriages; short steam train trips are available. Colne Valley Farm Park, set in 30 acres of traditional river meadows, is home to sheep, pigs, poultry, cattle and natural flora and fauna.

Swan Street is the main thoroughfare of the charming village of Sible Hedingham, boasting several delightful establishments devoted to providing visitors and natives of the town with places to shop, dine, enjoy a quiet drink and even stay for the night.

half-timbered Falcon Inn. Attractive buildings include many Georgian and 15th century houses comfortably vying for space, and the **Church of St Nicholas**, built by the de Veres, which avoided Victorian 'restoration' and is virtually completely Norman, with grand masonry and interestingly carved choir seats. There is a working pottery in St James' Street.

SIBLE HEDINGHAM

3 miles NW of Halstead off the A1017

Mentioned in the *Domesday Book* as the largest parish in England, Sible Hedingham was the birthplace of Sir John Hawkwood, one of the 14th century's most famous soldiers of fortune. He led a band of mercenaries to Italy, where he was paid to defend Florence and where he married the daughter of the Duke of Milan. He died in Italy and was buried in Florence Cathedral, where a commemorative fresco was painted by Uccello. His body was returned to Essex and was reputedly buried in the south aisle of Sible Hedingham's **Church of St Peter**. A monument to him in the church is decorated with hawks and various other beasts.

GESTINGTHORPE

5 miles N of Halstead off the A131

The **Church of St Mary the Virgin** in Gestingthorpe is distinctive in many respects. Witness to centuries of Christian worship, the *Domesday Book* of 1086 tells that 'Ghestingetorp' was held by Ledmer the priest before 1066. The oldest part extant of the

existing building is the blocked-up lancet window in the north wall of the chancel, which dates back to the 1200s. Apart from this, most of the chancel, nave and south aisle dates from the 14th century. The tower, constructed in about 1500, is 66 feet high. Of the six bells hung in the tower, four were cast in 1658-9 by Miles Gray, a Colchester bellfounder. The 16th century fifth and sixth bells were cast in Bury St Edmunds, and recast in 1901. The west door, set in a stepped brick arch, is the original. The unusual tracery in the East window consists of arches placed atop the apexes of the arches beneath them. The late 15th century/early 16th century nave roof is of the double hammer-beam type, and one of the finest in Essex. The font is late 14th century. One of the handsome memorials in Gestinthorpe's church commemorates Captain L E G Oates, who died in an attempt to save the lives of his companions on an ill-fated expedition to the Antarctic in 1912.

LITTLE MAPLESTEAD

3 miles NE of Halstead off the A131

Little Maplestead has an unusual **round church**, dedicated to St John the Baptist, modelled on the Holy Sepulchre in Jerusalem, and used as a stopping-point for pilgrims on their way there. Built more than 600 years ago by the military order of the Knights Hospitallers, their 'Perceptory' at Little Maplestead was suppressed more than 400 years ago by Henry VIII.

THE NORTH ESSEX COAST

CLACTON-ON-SEA

16 miles SE of Colchester on the A133

Clacton is a traditional sun-and-sand family resort with a south-facing, long sandy beach, lovely gardens on the seafront and a wide variety of shops and places to explore. It also boasts a wide variety of special events and entertainment taking place throughout the year.

Settled by hunters during the Stone Age - which is borne witness to by the wealth of flint implements and the fossilised bones of the cave lion, straight-tusked elephant and wild ox unearthed on the Clacton foreshore and at Lion Point - the town grew over the centuries from a small village into a prosperous seaside resort in the 1800s, when the craze for the health benefits of coastal air and bathing was at its peak. The **Pier** was constructed in 1871; at first paddle steamers provided the only mode of transport to the resort, the railway arriving in 1882. The Pier was widened from 30 to over 300 feet in the 1930s. On the pier, apart from the marvellous traditional sideshows, big wheel, restaurants and fairground rides, there is the fascinating **Seaquarium and Reptile Safari**.

Amusement centres include the arcades and Clacton Pavilion. The two theatres, Princes Theatre and West Cliff, are open all year. Clacton Pavilion boasts a range of attractions, including crazy golf and dodgems. The Clifftop Public Gardens also repay a visit.

Great Clacton is the oldest part of town, comprising an attractive grouping of shops, pubs and restaurants within the shadow of the 12th century parish church.

HOLLAND-ON-SEA

1½ miles NE of Clacton off the B1032

This attractive community is home to **Holland Haven Country Park**, 100 acres of open space near the seashore, ideal for watching the marine birds and other wildlife of the region. Throughout the area there are a number of attractive walks which take full advantage of the varied coastal scenery.

FRINTON-ON-SEA

3 miles NE of Clacton off the B1032

Once a quiet fishing village, this town was developed as a select resort by Sir Richard Cooper, and expanded in the 1880s to the genteel family resort it is today. Situated on a long stretch of sandy beach, Frinton remains peaceful and unspoilt. The tree-lined residential avenues sweep elegantly down to the Esplanade and extensive clifftop greensward. The **Church of Old St Mary** in Frinton contains some panels of stained glass in the East window designed by the Pre-Raphaelite artist Burne-Jones. A good example of 20th century English vernacular architecture is The Homestead at the corner of Second Avenue and Holland Road, built in 1905 by C F Voysey.

Along Frinton's main shopping street in Connaught Avenue, the

A walk round the town of Clacton-on-Sea rewards the visitor with some very handsome sights, while just south of town Jaywick Sands is an ideal spot for a picnic by the sea, wih one of the finest natural sandy beaches in the county. There are three Martello Towers along this part of the Essex coast.

151

Oakwood Crafts Resource Centre in Little Clacton provides an environment for people with learning disabilities to learn and develop work skills, motivation, responsibility, team spirit, self-esteem and confidence through horticulture, woodwork, ceramics, crafts and catering. As a horticultural centre, it sells a wide range of bedding plants, shrubs and hanging baskets seasonally, along with a selection of wooden garden implements, furnishings and other items, and ceramics.

'Bond Street' of the East Coast, shopkeepers maintain a tradition of friendly and courteous service. Summer theatre and other open-air events take place throughout the season, and there are also some excellent tennis and golf clubs in the town. The grace and elegance of this sophisticated resort is evidenced at every turn, as are hints of its distinguished past: Victorian beach huts still dot the extensive beach.

The area south of Frinton Gates has a unique local character, being laid out with detached houses set along broad tree-lined avenues.

WEELEY
5 miles NW of Clacton off the A133

St Andrew's Church is the handsome parish church just south of the centre of this picturesque village. There is a lovely tree-lined path that passes Weeleyhall Wood and Weeley Lodge, with its beautifully kept gardens. Here visitors will also pass a navigational beacon that forms part of Aircraft Flight Operations for both civil and military flights.

A mile south, off the B1411, Weeley Heath is a small and attractive community boasting a lovely village green and stunning surrounding countryside.

LITTLE CLACTON
3 miles NW of Clacton off the A133

Though it shares its name with its near neighbour, this is a town apart. Quiet and secluded, multiple-winner of the Best Kept Village award, Little Clacton features a lovely Jubilee Oak, planted to celebrate

Victoria's 50th year on the throne.

The fine **Church of St James** has been described as one of the most beautiful medieval churches in Essex, and sits at the heart of the village.

TENDRING
7 miles NW of Clacton off the A133

This village that gives its name to both the peninsula and the district council contains the handsome **Church of St Edmund**, whose elegant spire can be seen for miles around. The church is dedicated to the last King of independent East Anglia, martyred by the Danes in the 9th century.

WALTON-ON-THE-NAZE
8 miles NE of Clacton on the B1034

Walton is all the fun of the fair. It is a traditional, singular and cheerful resort which focuses on the pier and all its attractions, including a ten-pin bowling alley. The gardens at the seafront are colourful and the beach has good sand. The Backwaters to the rear of Walton are made up of a series of small harbours and saltings, which lead into Harwich harbour.

Walton has an outstanding sandy beach. The town's seafront was developed in 1825 and provides a fine insight into the character of an early Victorian seaside resort. The charming narrow streets of the town contain numerous shops, restaurants and pubs overlooking the second longest pier in the country. **Marine Parade**, originally called The Crescent, was built in 1832. The

Pier, first built in 1830, was originally constructed of wood and measured 330 feet long. It was extended to its present length of 2,610 feet in 1898, at the same time as the electric train service began. The Old Lifeboat House Museum at East Terrace, in a building over 100 years old, houses an interpretive museum of local history and development, rural and maritime, covering Walton, Frinton and the Sokens

The wind-blown expanse of **The Naze** just north of Walton is an extensive coastal recreation and picnic area, pleasant for walking, especially out of season when the visitor is likely to have all 150 acres virtually to him or herself, with great views out over the water. The shape of the Naze is constantly changing, eroded by wind, water and tide.

The year 1796 saw the demise of the medieval church, and somewhere beyond the 800-feet pier lies medieval Walton. The sandstone cliffs are internationally important for their shell fossil deposits. Inhabitants have been enjoying the bracing sea air at Walton since before Neolithic times: flint-shaping instruments have been found here, and the fossil teeth and the ears of sharks and whales have been discovered in the Naze's red crag cliffs. The Naze Tower is brick built and octagonal in shape, originally built as a beacon in 1720 to warn seamen of the West Rocks off shore. A nature trail has been created nearby, and the Essex Skipper butterfly and Emperor moth can be seen here.

The Marina and Harbour, Walton-on-the-Naze

BRIGHTLINGSEA

7 miles W of Clacton on the B1029

Brightlingsea enjoys a long tradition of shipbuilding and seafaring. In 1347, 51 men and five ships were sent to the siege of Calais. Among the crew members of Sir Francis Drake's fleet which vanquished the Spanish Armada was one 'William of Brightlingsea'. Brightlingsea has the distinction of being the only limb of the Cinque Ports outside Kent and Sussex.

All Saints Church, which occupies the highest point of the town on a hill about a mile from the centre, is mainly 13th century. Here are to be found some Roman brickwork and a frieze of ceramic tiles commemorating local residents whose lives were lost at sea. Its 97-

There are plenty of superb walks along Brightlingsea Creek and the River Colne, which offer a chance to watch the birdlife on the saltings and the plethora of boats on the water. Today the town is a haven for the yachting fraternity and is the home of national and international sailing championships, with one of the best stretches of sailing on the East Coast. Day and half-day sailing and canoeing sessions are held at the Brightlingsea Outdoor Education Centre.

feet tower can be seen from 17 miles out to sea. A light was once placed in the tower to guide the town's fishermen home

The **Town Hard** is where you can see all the waterfront comings and goings, including the activities of the Colne Smack Preservation Society, which maintains a seagoing link with the past. The 13th century **Jacobes Hall** in the centre of Brightlingsea is one of the oldest occupied buildings in Essex. It is timber-framed with an undulating tile roof and an external staircase. Used as a meeting hall during the reign of Henry III, its name originates from its first owner, Edmund, Vicar of Brightlingsea, who was known locally as Jacob le Clerk. **Brightlingsea Museum** in Duke Street offers an insight into the lives, customs and traditions of the area, housing a collection of exhibits relating to the town's maritime connections and the oyster industry.

ELMSTEAD MARKET
6 miles N of Brightlingsea off the A120

The **Church of St Anne and St Lawrence** to the north of this village has a rare carved oak recumbent effigy of a knight in armour.

Elmstead Market is perhaps best known as the location of **Beth Chatto Gardens**, at White Barn House. Here visitors will find six acres of gravel, water and woodland gardens, five large ponds, shady walks and a Mediterranean-style garden where aromatic drought-loving plants thrive. The adjoining

nursery contains a wide variety of plants for sale. Close by is the **Rolts Nursery Butterfly Farm**.

THORRINGTON
3 miles NW of Brightlingsea off the B1027

Thorrington Tide Mill, built in the early 19th century, is the only remaining Tide Mill in Essex, and one of very few left in East Anglia. It has been fully restored, and although no longer in use, the Wheel can be run for guided groups. A public footpath runs along the creek here.

POINT CLEAR
2 miles SE of Brightlingsea off the B1027

The **East Essex Aviation Society & Museum**, located in the Martello Tower at Point Clear, not only retains its original flooring and roof, but today contains interesting displays of wartime aviation, military and naval photographs, uniforms and other memorabilia with local and US Air Force connections. There are artefacts on show from the crash sites of wartime aircraft in the Tendring area, including the engine and fuselage section of a recovered P51D Mustang fighter. The museum also explores civil and military history from both World Wars. There are very good views from the tower over the Colne Estuary and Brightlingsea.

ST OSYTH
3 miles SE of Brightlingsea off the B1027

This pretty little village has a fascinating history and centres around its Norman church and the

St Osyth Priory

• Cudmore Grove Country
Park on Bromans Lane,
East Mersea, boasts fine
views across the Colne
and Blackwater
estuaries. Grassland
adjoining a sandy beach,
it's an ideal spot for
shore walks and picnics.
There's also a pathway
on the sea wall and a
birdwatching hide. •

ancient ruins of **St Osyth Priory**, founded in the 12th century. The village and Priory were named by Augustinian Canons after St Osytha, martyred daughter of Frithenwald, first Christian King of the East Angles, who was beheaded by Diceian pirates AD 653. Little of the original Priory remains, except for the magnificent late-15th century flint gatehouse, complete with battlements. The Church of St Peter and St Paul in the village centre has unusual internal red brick piers and arches. The nearby creek has a small boatyard.

MERSEA ISLAND

2 miles SW of Brightlingsea off the B1025

Much of this island is a National Nature Reserve, home to its teeming shorelife. The island is linked to the mainland by a narrow causeway which is covered over at high tide. The towns of both East and West Mersea have excellent facilities for sailing enthusiasts, and

East Mersea is also a haven for birdwatchers. **Mersea Island Museum** contains exhibits on Mersea's social and natural history, archaeology and the fishing industry, including a fisherman's cottage. Visitors to **Mersea Island Vineyard** can enjoy tours and tastings.

HARWICH

Harwich's name probably originates from the time of King Alfred, when 'hare' meant army, and 'wic' a camp. This attractive old town was built in the 13th century by the Earls of Norfolk to exploit its strategic position on the Stour and Orwell estuary; the town has an important and fascinating maritime history, the legacy of which continues into the present.

During the 14th and 15th century French campaigns, Harwich was an important naval base. The famous Elizabethan seafarers

105 THE COAST INN

West Mersea

A popular bar and restaurant overlooking the Blackwater estuary.

🍴 see page 279

106 THE VICTORY AT MERSEA

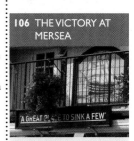

West Mersea

A family-run, waterfront pub serving excellent home-cooked food, with superior en-suite B & B rooms.

🍴 🛏 see page 280

155

•

Harwich remains popular as a vantage point for watching incoming and outgoing shipping in the harbour and across the waters to Felixstowe. Nowadays, lightships, buoys and miles of strong chain are stored along the front, and passengers arriving on North Sea ferries at Harwich International Port see the 90-feet high, six-sided High Lighthouse as the first landmark. Now housing the National Vintage Wireless and Television Museum, it was built in 1818 along with the Low Lighthouse. When the two lighthouses were in line they could indicate a safe shipping channel into the harbour. Each had replaced earlier wooden structures, and were themselves replaced by cast iron structures (both of which still stand on the front in nearby Dovercourt) in 1863 when the shifting sandbanks altered the channel. Shipping now relies on light buoys to find its way. The Low lighthouse is now the town's Maritime Museum, with specialist displays on the Royal Navy and commercial shipping.

•

Hawkins, Frobisher and Drake sailed from Harwich on various expeditions; in 1561 Queen Elizabeth I visited the town, describing it *'a pretty place and want[ing] for nothing'*. Christopher Newport, leader of the Goodspeed expedition which founded Jamestown, Virginia, in 1607, and Christopher Jones, master of the Pilgrim ship *The Mayflower*, lived in Harwich (the latter just off the quay in King's Head Street), as did Jones' kinsman John Alden, who sailed to America in 1620. The famous diarist Samuel Pepys was MP for the town in the 1660s, thus it was also during this time headquarters for the King's Navy. Charles II took the first pleasure cruise from Harwich's shores. Other notable visitors included Lord Nelson and Lady Hamilton, who are reputed to have stayed at The Three Cups in Church Street.

The **Lifeboat Museum** off Wellington Road contains the last Clacton offshore 34-feet lifeboat

and a history of the lifeboat service in Harwich. Harwich is a very busy lifeboat station with around 100 call-outs a year; the all-weather lifeboat often goes far out into the North Sea, while the inshore boat attends the rivers and coal areas. The station can be visited between 10 and 4 daily. The **Ha'penny Pier Visitor Centre**, also on the Quay, has information on just about everything in Harwich and a small heritage exhibition.

The **Treadwell Crane** now stands on Harwich Green, but for over 250 years it was sited in the Naval Shipyard. It is worked by two people walking in two 16-feet diameter wheels, and is the only known British example of its kind. Amazingly, it was operational up until the 1920s.

The importance of Harwich's port during the 19th century is confirmed by **The Redoubt**, a huge grey fort built between 1808 and 1810. Its design is an enlarged version of the Martello towers

Treadwell Crane, Harwich

which dotted the English coast, awaiting a Napoleonic invasion that never came (some of these towers, of course, still exist). Today the Harwich Society has largely restored it and opened it as a small museum.

The old town also contains many ancient buildings, including the Guildhall, which was rebuilt in 1769 and is located in Church Street. The Council chamber, Mayor's Parlour and other rooms may be viewed. The former gaol contains unique graffiti of ships, probably carved by prisoners, and is well worth putting aside a morning to explore (by appointment only). Documents on show include those detailing the connection of Harwich with Pepys, the Pilgrim Fathers, and the Virginia settlement.

A fascinating piece of Harwich's history is the **Electric Palace Cinema**, built in 1911 and now the oldest unaltered purpose-built cinema in Britain. It was restored by a trust and re-opened in 1981.

heads found here (now in Colchester Museum). The Romans found the town a useful source of the stone 'Septaria', taken from the cliffs and used in building. The town that visitors see today developed primarily in Victorian times as a fashionable resort.

MISTLEY

7 miles W of Harwich off the B1352

Here at the gateway to Constable Country, local 18th century landowner and MP Richard Rigby had grand designs to develop Mistley into a fashionable spa to rival Harrogate and Bath, adopting the swan as its symbol. Sadly, all that remains of Rigby's ambitious scheme is the Swan Fountain, a small number of attractive Georgian houses and **Mistley Towers**, the remains of a church (otherwise demolished in 1870) designed by the flamboyant architect Robert Adams. From the waterfront, noted for its colony of swans, there are very pleasant views across the estuary to Suffolk.

AROUND HARWICH

DOVERCOURT

1 mile S of Harwich off the A120

This residential and holiday suburb of Harwich has Market Day on Fridays. With its attractive cliffs and beach, it also boasts the Iron Lighthouse or 'Leading Lights' located just off lower Marine Parade. The town has been settled from prehistoric times, as attested to by the late-Bronze Age axe-

107 HOME BAY B&B

Dovercourt

A cosy little home from home for B&B guests with three quiet, comfortable bedrooms.

see *page 280*

•

A curiosity in Dovercourt's All Saints Church is a stained-glass window presented by the German Kaiser as a memorial to the thousands of British troops killed in an aborted expedition to Walcheren in Holland, sent to secure the area and prevent the French navy from operating from Antwerp – Britain and Germany were both at war with Napoleon's France at the time.

•

Mistley Towers

Mistley Place Park Environmental & Animal Rescue Centre is set in 25 acres of parkland with country walks, wildlife habitats, lake, farm animals and great views across the Stour Estuary. Over 2,000 rescued animals including rabbits, Vietnamese pigs and horses roam free.

Mistley Quay Workshops in the High Street feature a pottery workshop, lute/cello maker, harpsichord maker, wood worker, bookbinder, and stained-glass window maker and restorer. There is also a tea shop on the premises.

MANNINGTREE

9 miles W of Harwich off the B1352

The Walls, on the approach to Manningtree along the B1352, offer unrivalled views of the Stour estuary and the Suffolk coast, and the swans for which the area is famous. Lying on the River Stour amid beautiful rolling countryside, the scene has oft been depicted by artists over the centuries.

Back in Tudor times, Manningtree was the centre of the cloth trade, and later a port filled with barges carrying their various cargoes along the coast to London. Water still dominates today and the town is a centre of leisure sailing.

Manningtree has been a market town since 1238, and is still a busy shopping centre. It is the smallest town in Britain, and a stroll through the streets reveals the diversity of its past. There are still traditional (and mainly Georgian) restaurants, pubs and shops, as well as handcraft and specialist outlets.

The views over the river are well known to birdspotters, sailors and ramblers. The town has an intriguing past - as a river crossing, market, smugglers' haven and home of Matthew Hopkins, the reviled and self-styled Witchfinder General who struck terror into the local community during the 17th century.

Some of his victims were hanged on Manningtree's small village green.

It is believed that the reference in Shakespeare's Henry IV to Falstaff as 'that roasted Manningtree ox' relates to the practice of roasting an entire ox, as was known at that time to be done at the town's annual fair.

Manningtree Museum in the High Street opened in the late 1980s and mounts two exhibitions a year, together with permanent photographs and pieces relating to the heritage of Manningtree, Lawford, Mistley and the district. Manningtree railway station is an alternative to Dedham as a start point of a walk to Constable Country, taking in Cattawade Marshes (SSSI), Willy Lot's Cottage and Flatford Mill. In the station itself is a buffet serving a range of excellent traditional English dishes.

ARDLEIGH

10 miles W of Harwich off the A137

Tendring's westernmost village comprises an attractive group of 16th and 17th century cottages grouped around the fine 15th century **Butterfield Church**. Spring Valley Mill, a now privately owned 18th century timber-framed and weather-boarded edifice, was once a working watermill, later adapted to steam. Day and half-day canoeing and sailing lessons can be taken at the Ardleigh Outdoor Education Centre.

Nearby is Ardleigh Reservoir, offering many opportunities for water sports and trout fishing.

SOUTH AND WEST ESSEX

SAFFRON WALDEN

Named after the Saffron crocus - grown in the area to make dyestuffs and fulfil a variety of other uses in the Middle Ages - Saffron Walden has retained much of its original street plan, as well as hundreds of fine old buildings, many of which are timbered and have overhanging upper floors and decorative plastering (also known as pargeting). Gog and Magog (or, in some versions, folk-hero Tom Hickathrift and the Wisbech Giant) battle forever in plaster on the gable of the **Old Sun Inn**, where, legend has it, Oliver Cromwell and General Fairfax both lodged during the Civil War.

A typical market town, Saffron Walden's centrepiece is its magnificent church. At the **Saffron Walden Museum**, a glove reputedly worn by Mary Queen of Scots on the day she died can be seen. The museum first opened to the public at its present location in 1835, and was founded 'to gratify the inclination of all who value natural history'. It remains faithful to this credo, while widening the museum's scope in the ensuing years. The museum has won numerous awards, including joint winner of the Museum of the Year Award for best museum of Industrial or Social History in 1997. At this friendly, family-sized museum visitors can try their hand

at corn grinding with a Romano-British quern, see how a medieval timber house would have been built, admire the displays of Native American and West African embroidery, and come face to face with Wallace the Lion, the museum's faithful guardian. Over two floors, exhibits focus on town and country, with furniture and woodwork, costumes, ancient Egyptian artefacts, geology exhibits, and ceramics and glass. In the 'ages of man' gallery, the history of northwest Essex is traced from the Ice Age to the Middle Ages, while the Discovery Centre offers a personal encounter with natural history. The ruins of historic **Walden Castle** are also here.

On the local Common, once known as Castle Green, is the largest surviving **Turf Maze** in England. Only eight ancient turf mazes survive in England – there were many more in the Middle Ages, but if they are not looked after they soon become overgrown and are

•

Henry Winstanley - inventor, engineer and engraver, and builder of the first Eddystone Lighthouse at Plymouth - was born in the town in 1644. His design for the lighthouse drew heavily on his previously constructed wooden 'lantern' which then crowned the 16th century parish church. The Lighthouse, and Winstanley with it, were swept away in a fierce storm in 1703.

•

Saffron Walden Turf Maze

159

108 THE GATE

Saffron Walden

A newly refurbished pub
serving real ales and a good
choice of snacks and meals.

see page 280

*The gardens at Audley
House are managed by
the Henry Doubleday
Research Association,
who grow and sell a
wide range of organic
produce in the shop.
Within the rolling
parkland of the grounds
there are several elegant
outbuildings, some of
which were designed by
Robert Adam. Among
these are an icehouse, a
circular temple and a
Springwood Column.
The Audley End
Miniature Railway is 1.5
miles long and takes
visitors along Lord
Braybrooke's private
10¼-inch gauge railway
through beautiful private
woods.*

lost. This one is believed to be some 800 years old, a circular labyrinth of medieval Christian design.

To the north of the town are the **Bridge End Gardens**, a wonderfully restored example of early Victorian gardens, complete with the wonderful **Hedge Maze**, which was planted in 1840 in the Italian Renaissance style and has 610 metres of paths. Close to Bridge End is the Anglo-American War Memorial dedicated by Field Marshal the Viscount Montgomery of Alamein in 1953 to the memory of all the American flyers of the 65th Fighter Wing who lost their lives in the Second World War.

Next to the gardens is the **Fry Public Art Gallery**, with a unique collection of work by 20th century artists and designers such as Edward Bawden, Michael Rothenstein, Eric Ravilious, John Aldridge and Sheila Robinson. It also exhibits work by contemporary artists working in Essex today, demonstrating the area's continuing artistic tradition. The gallery was purpose-designed and opened in 1856 to house the collection of Francis Gibson. The gallery also houses the Lewis George Fry RBA, RWA (1860-1933) Collection, which is exhibited each summer, along with works by Robert Fry (1866-1934) and Anthony Fry.

Audley End House was built by the first Earl of Suffolk, and was at one time owned by Charles II. The original early 17th century house, with its two large courtyards, had a magnificence claimed to match that of Hampton Court. Remodelled in the 18th century by Robert Adam, unfortunately the subsequent earls lacked their forebears' financial resources, and much of the house was demolished as it fell into disrepair. Nevertheless it remains today one of England's most impressive Jacobean mansions; its distinguished stone façade set off perfectly by Capability Brown's lake. The remaining state rooms retain their palatial magnificence and the exquisite state bed in the Howard Room is hung with the original embroidered drapes. The silver, the Jacobean Screen and Robert Adam painted Drawing Room are among the many sights to marvel at. The natural history collection features more than 1,000 stuffed animals and birds. To complement this, there are paintings by Holbein, Lely and Canaletto. Fascinating introductory talks help visitors get the most from any visit to this, one of the most magnificent houses in England. This jewel also has a kitchen garden and grounds landscaped by Capability Brown, including the 'Temple of Concord' dedicated to George III. There is a lovely parterre, lake and Pond Garden. Circular walks help visitors make the most of all there is to see. The organic kitchen garden was recently opened to the public for the first time in 250 years.

AROUND SAFFRON WALDEN

RADWINTER

4 miles E of Saffron Walden off the B1053

Radwinter boasts a fine church, which was largely renovated and rebuilt in the 19th century by architect William Eden Nesfield and has a fine Tudor porch with a room above. The village also has cottages and almshouses designed by Nesfield.

HEMPSTEAD

5 miles E of Saffron Walden off the B1054

The highwayman, Dick Turpin, was born here in 1705 in what was then the Bell Inn, which was kept by his parents at the time. Dick Turpin trained as a butcher before turning to cattle and deer stealing, smuggling and robbery. Narrowly avoiding capture, he fled to Yorkshire and carried on his nefarious ways as John Palmer. He was captured while horse-stealing and was hanged in York in 1739.

Inside the 14th/15th century Hempstead village church, an impressively life-like bust carved by Edward Marshall recalls the town's rather worthier son, William Harvey (1578-1657), who is buried in a white marble sarcophagus in the crypt. Harvey was chief physician to Charles I and the discoverer of the circulation of blood, as recorded in his De Motu Cordis of 1628. Like many other villages, Hempstead once boasted a village cockpit; its faint outline can still be traced, though the steep banks are now crowned with trees.

THAXTED

7 miles SE of Saffron Walden on the B184

This small country town has a recorded history that dates back to before the *Domesday Book*. Originally a Saxon settlement, it

developed around a Roman road. The town's many beautiful old buildings contribute to its unique character and charm. To its credit Thaxted has no need of artificial tourist attractions, and is today what it has been for the last ten centuries: a thriving and beautiful town.

Thaxted has numerous attractively pargeted and timber-framed houses, and a magnificent **Guildhall**, built as a meeting-place for cutlers around 1390. The demise of the cutlery industry in this part of Essex in the 1500s led it to becoming the administrative centre of the town. Restored in Georgian times, it became the town's Grammar School, as well as remaining a centre of administration. Once more restored in 1975, the Parish council still holds its meetings here.

The town's famous **Tower Windmill** was built in 1804 by John Webb. In working order until 1907, it had fallen into disuse and disrepair but work is in progress to restore it to full working order. It contains a rural life museum, well worth a visit. Close to the windmill are the town's Almshouses, which continued to provide homes for the elderly even 250 years after they were built for that purpose.

Thaxted's **Church of St John** stands on a hill and soars cathedral-like over the town's streets. It has been described as the finest parish church in the country and, though many towns may protest long and loud at this claim, it certainly is magnificent. Gustav Holst,

109 THE BLUEBELL INN

Hempstead, nr Saffron Walden

Excellent hospitality, real ales and good food in the pub where Dick Turpin was born.

see page 281

110 THE RED LION

Great Sampford, nr Saffron Walden

A cosy, traditional inn serving a good choice of dishes cooked by the hosts. Also 2 rooms for B&B.

see page 281

161

The church at Thaxted was the somewhat unlikely setting for a pitched battle in 1921. The rather colourful vicar and secretary of the Church Socialist League, the Revd Conrad Noel, displayed the red flag of communism and the Sinn Fein flag in the church. Incensed Cambridge students tore them down and substituted the Union Jack; Noel in turn ripped that down, and his friends are said to have slashed the tyres of the students' cars and motorbikes. A fine bronze in the church celebrates this adventurous man of the cloth. Conrad Noel's wife is remembered for encouraging Morris dancing in the town. Today, the famous Morris Ring is held annually in early June, attracting over 300 dancers from all over the country, who dance through the streets. Dancing can also be seen around the town on most Bank Holiday Mondays, usually in the vicinity of a pub!

Thaxted Moot Hall and Church

composer of, among other pieces, the renowned 'Planets' Suite', lived in Thaxted from 1914 to 1925, and often played the church organ. To celebrate his connection with the town there is a music festival in late June/early July which attracts performers of international repute.

GREAT EASTON

10 miles SE of Saffron Walden off the B184

Great Easton boasts a wealth of cottages and farmhouses with ornamental plasterwork, clustered Tudor chimneys and half-timbering. Great Easton's well-known and very popular Green Man pub occupies a handsome building dating back to the 15th century.

LITTLE EASTON

10 miles SE of Saffron Walden off the B184

The charming 12th century **Church of St Mary** is rich in historic features. Its Maynard Chapel features some outstanding

marble monuments of the family that gives the chapel its name, as well as some famous brasses. The church's oldest treasures are, however, a well-preserved and priceless 12th century wall painting and several 15th century frescoes. Two more recent additions, a pair of stained glass windows, were unveiled in 1990. The 'Window of the Crusaders' and the 'Window of Friendship and Peace' are a lasting memorial to the American 386th Bomb Group. Known as 'The Crusaders', they were stationed nearby for 13 months and lost over 200 of their number in battle overseas during that short time. They flew from an airstrip created in the park of **Easton Lodge**, the favourite home of Frances, Countess of Warwick – Edward VII's 'Darling Daisy'. Harold Peto designed the gardens for her in 1902. The house was demolished in 1950 but the pavilions were restored in 1996 and much other restoration has taken place in the garden, including the sunken Italian garden; the Glade, formerly Peto's Japanese garden; and the living sundial with a border featuring every plant mentioned in Shakespeare's plays and sonnets. The 17th century dovecote houses an exhibition of photography, prints and writings on the history of the Lodge since 1950.

BROXTED

10 miles SE of Saffron Walden off the B1051

The parish Church of St Mary the Virgin here in the handsome village of Broxted has two remarkably lovely stained glass windows commemorating the captivity and release of John McCarthy and the other Beirut hostages, dedicated in January 1993. Though just a few minutes drive from Stansted Airport off the M11, it is a welcoming haven of rural tranquillity.

GREAT DUNMOW

13 miles SE of Saffron Walden on the A120

The town is famous for the 'Flitch of Bacon', an ancient ceremony which dates back as far as the early 12th century. A prize of a flitch, or side, of bacon was awarded to the local man who '*does not repent of his marriage nor quarrel, differ or dispute with his wife within a year and a day after the marriage*'.

Amidst great ceremony, the winning couple would be seated and presented with their prize. The custom, which lapsed on the Dissolution of the Monasteries, was briefly revived in the 18th century,

and became established again after 1885. 'Trials' to test the truth are all in good fun, and carried out every leap year. The successful couple are carried through the streets on chairs and then presented with the Flitch. The original 'bacon chair' can be seen in Little Dunmow parish church.

Other places of historical interest include the parish church of St Mary at Church End, Great Dunmow, dating back to 1322. The Clock House, a private residence built in 1589, was the home of St Anne Line, martyred for sheltering a Jesuit priest. Clock House was subsequently occupied by Sir George Beaumont. He used it to store and display his extensive art collection, which he bequeathed to the nation and which forms the nucleus of the National Gallery collection in London. H G Wells lived at Brick House in Great Dunmow, overlooking the Doctor's Pond, where in 1784 Lionel Lukin is reputed to have tested the first unsinkable lifeboat.

The **Great Dunmow Maltings**, opened to the public in 2000 after restoration costing £750,000, is the most complete example of a medieval timber-framed building of its type in the United Kingdom, and a focal point for local history in the shape of **Great Dunmow Museum**, with changing displays illustrating the history of the town from Roman times to the present day.

The **Flitch Way** is a 15-mile country walk along the former Bishop's Stortford-to-Braintree

•

The Barn Theatre at Little Easton Manor is situated in one of the finest and oldest tithe barns in the country, with magnificent oak timbers and ancient tiled roof. It was visited by some of the most distinguished actors and impresarios of the early 20th century, including Ellen Terry, Hermione Baddeley, Charlie Chaplin, George Formby, Basil Dean (who married Daisy's daughter) and George Bernard Shaw.

•

III THE WHITE HART

Stebbing, nr Great Dunmow

A convivial old village inn serving traditional pub foods, real ales, good house wines and a selection of malts.

see page 281

Hatfield Forest is a rare surviving example of a medieval Royal hunting forest. It has wonderful 400-year-old pollard trees, two ornamental lakes and an 18th century shell house. Once covering a great deal more land, the remaining 400 hectares are now protected by the National Trust and offer splendid woodland walks along with good chases and rides.

railway, taking in Victorian stations, impressive views, and a wealth of woodland wildlife.

PLESHEY

18 miles SE of Saffron Walden off the A130

Pleshey, midway between Chelmsford and Great Dunmow, is surrounded by a mile-long earthen rampart, protecting its castle, of which only the motte with its moat and two baileys survive. There are good views from the mound, which although only 60 feet high, is nonetheless one of the highest points in Essex. The village is truly delightful, with a number of thatched cottages, and the area is excellent for walkers and ramblers.

WIDDINGTON

4 miles S of Saffron Walden off the B1383

Covering over 20 acres, **Mole Hall Wildlife Park** offers visitors the chance to come close to a range of wild and domesticated animals. With the private fully-moated 13th century manor house as a backdrop, the wide variety of animals in this excellent park include South American llamas, flamingos, Formosa Sika deer (which are extinct in the wild), chimpanzees, muntjac, Arctic fox, wallabies, red squirrels and much more. Mole Hall is also home to two species of otters: Short-clawed and North American. Domesticated animals such as guinea pigs, rabbits, goats, pigs and sheep can also be seen. The Butterfly Pavilion offers a tropical experience where brilliantly coloured butterflies flit about

freely. Within the tropical pavilion you can also find lovebirds and small monkeys, along with a variety of snakes, spiders and insects (safe behind glass). The pools are home to goldfish, toads and terrapins.

Widdington is also home to **Priors Hall Barn**, one of the finest surviving medieval 'aisled' barns in all of southeast England, and owned by English Heritage.

TAKELEY

13 miles S of Saffron Walden off the A120

The village is built on the line of the old Roman Stane Street. There are plenty of pretty 17th century timbered houses and barns to be seen in the village, and the church still has many of its original Norman features along with some Roman masonry. Rather unusually, it has a modern font that is surmounted by a six-feet-high medieval cover.

HATFIELD BROAD OAK

15 miles S of Saffron Walden off the B184

This very pretty village has many notable buildings for visitors to enjoy, including a church dating from Norman times, some delightful 18th century almshouses and several distinctive Georgian houses.

AYTHORPE RODING

15 miles S of Saffron Walden off the B184

Aythorpe Roding Windmill is the largest remaining post mill in Essex. Four storeys high, it was built around 1760 and remained in use up until 1935. It was fitted in the

1800s with a fantail which kept the sails pointing into the wind.

STANSTED MOUNTFICHET

8 miles SW of Saffron Walden off the B1383

Pilots approaching the airport may be surprised at the sight of a Norman Village, complete with domestic animals, and the reconstructed motte-and-bailey **Mountfichet Castle**, standing just two miles from the runway. The original castle was built after 1066 by the Duke of Boulogne, a cousin of the Conqueror. Siege weapons on show include two giant catapults. The Castle was voted Essex attraction of the year in 2002 by the Good Britain Guide, and visitors can take a trip to the top of the siege tower and tiptoe into the baron's bed chamber while he sleeps!

Next door to the castle is the **House on the Hill Museum Adventure**, where there are three museums for the price of one. The **Toy Museum** is the largest of its kind in the world, and here children of every age are treated to a unique and nostalgic trip back to their childhood. There is every toy imaginable here, many of them now highly prized collectors' items. There is a shop selling new toys and a collectors' shop with many old toys and books to choose from. The Rock 'n' Roll, Film and Theatre Experience and the End-of-the-pier Amusement machine displays also contribute to a grand day out here in Stansted Mountfichet.

HADSTOCK

6 miles N of Saffron Walden off the B1052

As well as claiming to have the oldest church door in England, at the parish **Church of St Botolph**, Hadstock also has a macabre tale to tell. The church's north door was once covered with a piece of skin, now to be seen in Saffron Walden Museum. Local legend says it is a 'Daneskin', from a Viking flayed alive, but recent DNA analysis has disproved this legend. Lining doors with animal leather was common in the Middle Ages, and many so-called 'Daneskins' are just that. The door itself is Saxon, as are the 11th century carvings, windows and arches, rare survivors that predate the Norman Conquest. **Linton Zoo** near Hadstock village is a privately owned collection of wild animals set in 10½ acres of gardens. A free car park, children's play area, picnic areas and a café are on site.

BARTLOW

5 miles NE of Saffron Walden off the B1052

Bartlow Hills are reputed to be the largest burial mounds in Europe dating from Roman times, one 15 metres high. They date back to the 2nd century.

WALTHAM ABBEY

The town of Waltham began as a small Roman settlement on the site of the present-day Market Square. The early Saxon kings maintained a

---

Stansted Windmill is one of the best-preserved tower mills in the country. Dating back to 1787 and in use until 1910, most of the original machinery has survived. It is open on Sunday and Monday afternoons from April to October.

112 THE CHAFF HOUSE

Littlebury Green, nr Saffron Walden

The **Chaff House** offers a true taste of country farmhouse living in three well-appointed bedrooms on a 900-care working farm.

see page 282

113 THE ROSE & CROWN

Ashdon, nr Saffron Walden

A country pub well worth seeking out for its super food, well-kept ales and fine wines.

see page 282

Waltham Abbey

114 WALTHAM ABBEY CHURCH

Waltham Abbey

Come and visit Waltham Abbey Church. Enjoy more than one thousand years of history and beautiful setting

see page 282

hunting lodge here; a town formed round this, and the first church was built in the 6th century. By the 8th, during the reign of Cnut, the town had a stone minster church with a great stone crucifix that had been brought from Somerset, where it had been found buried in land owned by Tovi, a trusted servant of the king. This cross became the focus of pilgrims seeking healing. One of those cured of a serious illness, Harold Godwinsson, built a new church, the third on the site, which was dedicated in 1060 - and

it was this self-same Harold who became king and was killed in the battle of Hastings six years later. Harold's body was brought back to Waltham to be buried in his church. The church that exists today was built in the first quarter of the 12th century. It was once three times its present length, and incorporated an Augustinian Abbey, built in 1177 by Henry II. The town became known for the Abbey, which was one of the largest in the country and the last to be the victim of Henry VIII's Dissolution of the Monasteries, in 1540.

The Abbey's **Crypt Centre** houses an interesting exhibition explaining the history of both the Abbey and the town, highlighting the religious significance of the site. Some visible remains of the Augustinian Abbey include the chapter house and precinct walls, cloister entry and gateway in the surrounding Abbey Gardens. The Abbey Gardens are also host to a Sensory Trail exploring the highlights of hundreds of years of the site's history; there's also a delightful Rose Garden. Along the Cornhill Stream, crossed by the impressive stone bridge, Waltham Abbey's **Dragonfly Sanctuary** is home to over half the native British species of dragonflies and damselflies. It is noted as the best single site for seeing these species in Greater London, Essex and Hertfordshire.

Sun Street is Waltham Abbey's main thoroughfare, and it is pedestrianised. It contains many buildings from the 16th century onwards. The Greenwich Meridian (0 degrees longitude) runs through the street, marked out on the pavement and through the Abbey Gardens.

In spite of its proximity to London and more recent development, the town retains a peaceful, traditional character, with its timber-framed buildings and small traditional market which has been held here since the early 12th century (now every Tuesday and Saturday). The whole of the town centre has been designated a conservation area. The Market Square boasts many fine and interesting buildings such as the lych-gate and The Welsh Harp, dating from the 17th and 16th centuries respectively.

The **Town Hall** offers a fine example of Art Nouveau style design, and houses the Waltham Abbey Town Council Offices and Epping Forest District Council Information Desk. The Tourist Information Centre is in Highbridge Street, opposite the entrance to the Abbey Church.

Gunpowder production became established in Waltham as early as the 1660s, and in 1787 the **Royal Gunpowder Mills** were acquired by the Crown. They became the pre-eminent powder works in Britain, employing up to 500 workers; production did not cease until 1943, after which time the factory became a research facility. In the spring of 2000, however, all this changed and much of the site is open to the public; some of the rest is a Site of Scientific Interest and the largest heronry in Essex.

Lee Valley Regional Park is a leisure area stretching for 26 miles along the River Lea (sometimes also spelled Lee) from East India Dock Basin, on the north bank of the River Thames in East London, to Hertfordshire. There's a range of facilities ideal for anglers, walkers and birdwatchers. The Lee Valley is an important area of high biodiversity, sustaining a large range of wildlife and birds. Two hundred species of birds, including internationally important populations of Gadwall and Shoveler ducks, can be seen each year on the wetlands and water bodies along the Lea. Of national importance for over-wintering waterbirds including rare species of bittern and smew, this fine park makes an ideal place for a picnic. Guided tours by appointment.

Lee Valley Park Farms, along Stubbins Hall Lane, boasts two farms on site: Hayes Hill and Holyfield Hall. At Hayes Hill Farm, visitors can interact with the animals and enjoy a picnic or the children's adventure playground. This traditional farm also boasts old-fashioned tools and equipment, an exhibition in the medieval barn and occasional craft demonstrations. At Holyfield Hall Farm, a working farm and dairy, visitors can see milking and learn about modern farming methods. Seasonal events such as sheep-shearing and harvesting are held, and there's an attractive farm tea room and a toy shop. A farm trail is

A Tudor timber-framed house forms part of the Epping Forest District Museum in Sun Street. The wide range of displays includes exhibits covering the history of the Epping Forest District from the Stone Age to the 20th century. Tudor and Victorian times are particularly well represented, with some magnificent oak panelling dating from the reign of Henry VIII, and re-creations of Victorian rooms and shops. There is also an archaeological display and temporary exhibitions covering such subjects as contemporary arts and crafts. The museum has several hands-on displays which help to bring history to life, and features special events and adult workshops throughout the year.

At the southern end of Lee Valley Park, the House Mill, one of two tidal mills still standing at this site, has been restored by the River Lea Tidal Mill Trust. It was built in 1776 in the Dutch style, and was used to grind grain for gin distilling. Myddelton House Gardens within Lee Valley Park is the place to see the work of the famous plantsman who created them – E A Bowles, an expert botanist, author, artist and Fellow of the Royal Horticultural Society.. Breathtaking colours and interesting plantings - such as the National Collection of award-winning bearded iris, the Tulip Terrace and the Lunatic Asylum (home to unusual plants) - are offset by a beautiful carp lake, two conservatories and a rock garden.

another of the site's attractions, offering wonderful views of the Lee Valley, an expanse of open countryside dotted with lakes and wildflower meadows attracting a wide range of wildlife including otters, bats, dragonfly, kingfisher, great-crested grebe and little-ringed plover. The area is ideal for walking or fishing, and the bird hides are open to all at weekends; permits available for daily access. Guided tours by arrangement. To the west of town, the **Lee Navigation Canal** offers opportunities for anglers, walkers, birdwatching and pleasure craft. Once used for transporting corn and other commercial goods to the growing City of London, and having associations with the town's important gunpowder industry for centuries, the canal remains a vital part of town life.

AROUND WALTHAM ABBEY

LOUGHTON

5 miles SE of Waltham Abbey off the A121

Corbett Theatre in Rectory Lane in Loughton is a beautiful Grade I listed converted medieval tithe barn, where classical, modern and musical theatre productions are performed. The theatre is set in a five-acre site with lovely gardens.

Loughton borders **Epping Forest**, a former Royal hunting forest stretching for over 12 miles from east London into southwest Essex. There are miles of leafy walks and rides (horses can be hired locally), with some rough grazing

and occasional distant views. Just off the A104 running through the forest, in the middle of a field called The Warren, stands an obelisk that is a memorial to the horse of General Thomas Grosvenor, who lived here and died at the Battle of Waterloo in 1815.

ABRIDGE

7 miles SE of Waltham Abbey off the A113

The **BBC Essex Garden** at Crowther Nurseries, Ongar Road, is a working garden consisting of a vegetable plot, two small greenhouses, lawns and herbaceous and shrub borders. The garden is also home to a range of farmyard animals which visitors are welcome to see and interact with, and there's a delightful tea shop filled with homemade cakes.

CHIGWELL

8 miles SE of Waltham Abbey off the A113

Hainault Forest Country Park is an ancient woodland covering 600 acres, with a lake and rare breeds farm, managed by the London Borough of Redbridge and the Woodland Trust for Essex County Council.

CHINGFORD

6 miles S of Waltham Abbey off the A11

Queen Elizabeth's Hunting Lodge is a timber-framed building covered in brightly coloured heraldic banners and standing on a hill above the plains and trees of Epping Forest. Originally called the Great Standing, it was built in 1543 on the orders of Henry VIII for the staging of royal deer hunts and entertainments in the forest. Displays include the handiwork of Tudor carpenters and food made from authentic recipes. The Lodge and the countryside around once provided a day out for thousands of Londoners, with buses arriving every few minutes and huge (and in those days orderly) queues waiting for the homeward journey in the early evening.

HODDESDON
6 miles NW of Waltham Abbey off the A10

Rye House Gatehouse in Rye Road was built by Sir Andre Ogard, a Danish nobleman, in 1443. It is a moated building and a fine example of early English brickwork. Now restored, visitors can climb up to the battlements. A permanent exhibition covers the architecture and history of the Rye House Plot to assassinate Charles II in 1683. Guided tours by prior arrangement. The building lies adjacent to a Royal Society for the Protection of Birds reserve. Other features include an information centre, shop, and circular walks around the site.

HARLOW

The 'New Town' of Harlow sometimes gets short shrift, but it is in fact a lively and vibrant place with a great deal more than excellent shopping facilities. There are some very good museums and several sites of historic interest. The **Gibberd Collection** in Harlow Town Hall offers a delightful collection of British

Epping Forest

watercolours featuring works by Blackadder, Sutherland, Frink, Nash and Sir Frederick Gibberd, Harlow's master planner and the founder of the collection. Gibberd Gardens, on the eastern outskirts of Harlow in Marsh Lane, Gilden Way, is well worth a visit, reflecting as it does the taste of Sir Frederick. This 7-acre garden was designed by Sir Frederick on the side of a small valley, with terraces, wild garden, landscaped vistas, pools and streams and some 80 sculptures. Marsh Lane is a turning off the B183.

The **Museum of Harlow** in Passmores House, Third Avenue, occupies a Georgian manor house

169

Harlow Study and Visitors Centre in Netteswellbury Farm is set in a medieval tithe barn and 13th century church. The site has displays outlining the story of Harlow New Town. Parndon Wood Nature Reserve, Parndon Wood Road in Harlow, is an ancient woodland with a fine variety of birds, mammals and insects. Facilities include two nature trails with hides for observing wildlife, and a study centre.

set in picturesque gardens which includes a lovely pond and is home to several species of butterfly. The museum has extensive and important Roman, post-medieval and early 20th century collections, as well as a full programme of temporary exhibitions.

Mark Hall Cycle Museum and Gardens, incorporated in the Museum of Harlow, contains a unique collection of cycles and cycling accessories illustrating the history of the bicycle from 1818 to the present day, including one made of plastic, one that folds, and one where the seat tips forward and throws its rider over the handlebars if the brakes were applied too energetically.

AROUND HARLOW

ROYDON

3 miles W of Harlow off the A414

Preserved in this handsome village are the old parish cage, stocks and a whipping post. Just about 1 mile southwest of Roydon are the ruins of Tudor **Nether Hall**, a manor house that once belonged to the Coates family. Here Thomas More came to woo and win the elder daughter of John Coates.

CHIPPING ONGAR

8 miles SE of Harlow on the A414

Today firmly gripped in the commuter belt of London, Chipping Ongar began as a Saxon market town protected beneath the walls of a Norman castle. The motte and bailey were built by Richard de Lucy in 1155. Indeed,

the town's name comes from 'cheaping', meaning market. Only the mound and moat of the castle remain, but the contemporary **Church of St Martin of Tours** still stands. Built in 1080, it has fine Norman flint walls and an anchorite's recess.

The explorer David Livingstone was a pupil pastor at Chipping Ongar's United Reform Church, and lived in what are now called Livingstone Cottages before his missionary work in Africa began.

BOBBINGWORTH

2 miles NW of Chipping Ongar off the A414

Blake Hall Gardens at Bobbingworth near Chipping Ongar incorporates a Tropical House, an Ice House, Bog garden, wild gardens, herbaceous borders, rose garden, sunken garden, duck pond and an ornamental wood. The south wing of Blake Hall itself houses the Airscene Aviation Museum run by local RAF enthusiasts. A short drive to the north of Bobbingworth is the village of **High Laver**, where the philosopher John Locke (1632-1704) is buried in the churchyard of All Saints.

WILLINGALE

3 miles NE of Chipping Ongar off the B184

St Christopher's and St Andrew's, churches of the respective parishes of Willingale Doe and Willingale Spain, stand side by side in the same churchyard in the heart of this lovely village. St Andrew's is the older, dating back to the 12th century.

FYFIELD

2 miles N of Chipping Ongar off the B184

The name 'Fyfield' means five river meadows. Originally a Saxon enclave, the village Church of St Nicholas is Norman. There's a beautiful mill house with flood gates in the village. Fyfield Hall, opposite the church, is said to be the oldest inhabited timber frame building in England (it dates from AD 870).

BEAUCHAMP RODING

3 miles NE of Chipping Ongar off the B184

One of the eight Rodings, it was at Beauchamp Roding that a local farm labourer, Isaac Mead, worked and saved enough to become a farmer himself in 1882. To show his gratitude to the land that made him his fortune, he had a corner of the field consecrated as an eternal resting place for himself and his family. Their graves can still be seen in the undergrowth. Beauchamp's **Church of St Botolph** stands alone in the fields, marked by a tall 15th century tower and reached by a track off the B184. Inside, the raised pews at the west end have clever space-saving wooden steps, pulled out of slots by means of iron rings.

GOOD EASTER AND HIGH EASTER

5 miles NE of Chipping Ongar off the B184

A quiet farming village, now in the commuter belt for London, Good Easter's claim to fame is the making of a world-record daisy chain (6,980 feet 7 inches) in 1985. The village's interesting name is probably derived from 'Easter', the Old English for 'sheepfolds' and 'Good' from a Saxon lady named Godiva.

Close to Good Easter, and thus named because it stands on higher ground than its neighbour, High Easter is a quiet and very picturesque village not far from the impressive **Aythorpe Post Mill**.

BLACKMORE

3 miles E of Chipping Ongar off the A414

The plague almost totally destroyed the village of Blackmore. Red Rose Lane was so-named because a red rose had to be given at the toll to indicate clear health from the dreaded disease. Henry VIII's mistress Bessie Blount lived in Jericho Priory in the village. Her son by Henry, the Earl of Rochford, also made his home here.

INGATESTONE

6 miles E of Chipping Ongar off the B1002

Ingatestone Hall on Hall Lane is a 16th century mansion set in 11 acres of grounds that include a fine walled garden and extensive lawns with specimen trees. It was built by Sir William Petre, Secretary of State to four monarchs, whose family continue to reside here. The Hall contains family portraits, furniture and memorabilia accumulated over the centuries. The Church of St Edmund and St Mary is notable for its magnificent redbrick tower and the many monuments to Sir William, who rebuilt the south chapel, and other members of the Petre family.

115 THE CRICKETERS

Mill Green, nr Ingatestone

Outstanding food in a fine village pub with plenty of seats inside and out on the terrace.

see page 282

116 THE SPREAD EAGLE

Margaretting

Live music at the weekend add another dimension to traditional hospitality and good food at a classic roadside inn.

 see page 284

117 THE WHITE HART INN

Margaretting Tye

With an excellent reputation as a really good place to eat this attractive pub also serves a fine selection of real Ales..

see page 283

Just north of Ingatestone, at Fryerning, the 16th century Church of St Mary contains a memorial to the MP Airey Neave, a native of the parish who was killed by the IRA in 1979. The window was designed by his cousin Penelope and shows St Michael and St Christopher, with roundels depicting Colditz, where he was a prisoner of war, and the Houses of Parliament.

MARGARETTING TYE

6 miles E of Chipping Ongar off the A12/B1007

The nickname of this town is 'Tigers Island'. Legend has it that in bygone days, bare-knuckle fights known as 'Tigers' would take place on Fridays, and the 'island' part of its soubriquet derives from the fact that in ancient times the area was subject to flooding all round the village.

MOUNTNESSING

6 miles SE of Chipping Ongar off the A12

This village has a beautifully restored early-19th century windmill as its main landmark, though the isolated church also has a massive beamed belfry. **Mountnessing Post Mill** in Roman Road is open to the public. This traditional weather-boarded post mill was built in 1807 and restored to working order in 1983. Visitors can see the huge wooden and iron gears; one pair of stones have been opened up for viewing.

Mountnessing Post Mill

KELVEDON HATCH

4 miles S of Chipping Ongar off the A128

A nondescript bungalow in the rural Essex village of Kelvedon Hatch is the deceptively simple exterior for the **Kelvedon Secret Nuclear Bunker**. In 1952, 40,000 tons of concrete were used to create a base some 80 feet underground for up to 600 top Government and civilian personnel, possibly including the Prime Minister, in the event of nuclear war. Visitors can explore room after room to see communications equipment, a BBC studio, a sick bay and surgery, massive kitchens and dormitories, military supplies stores, power and filtration plants, a government administration room and the scientists' room, where nuclear fall-out patterns would have been measured. Tel: 01277 364883

GREENSTED

1½ miles SW of Chipping Ongar off the A414

St Andrew's Church in Greensted is almost certainly the world's oldest wooden church, dating from the 9th to 11th centuries, with a later Tudor chancel. It is famous as the only surviving example of a Saxon log church extant in the world, built from split oak logs from Epping Forest, held together with dowells. Over the centuries the church has been enlarged and restored; later additions include the simple weather-boarded tower, Norman flint walls, the Tudor tiled roof, Victorian stone coping, porch and stained glass windows. The body of King Edmund (later

St Andrew's Church Greensted

canonised a saint) is believed to have rested here in 1013.

The village of Greensted has associations with the Tolpuddle Martyrs - six Dorset farm labourers who were taken to court on a legal technicality because they agitated for better conditions and wages, and formed a Trades Union. After their conviction in 1834 they were condemned to transportation to Australia for seven years. There was a public outcry for their release,

173

Thorndon Country Park, on the outskirts of Brentwood, boasts historic parkland, lakes and woods. The site, formerly a royal deer park, also features a wildlife exhibition and gift shop; fishing is also available.

The Peasants' Revolt of 1381 saw the massacre of hundreds of rebels just northeast of Billericay, at Norsey Wood. Today this area of ancient woodland is a country park, managed by coppicing (the traditional way of ensuring the timber supply), which also encourages plant and birdlife.

and their sentences were commuted in 1837. Unable to return to Dorset, they were granted tenancies in Greensted and High Laver. One of the martyrs, James Brine, of New House Farm (now Tudor Cottage, on Greensted Green), married Elizabeth Standfield, daughter of one of his fellow victims - the record of their marriage in 1839 can be seen in the parish register.

NORTH WEALD

3 miles W of Chipping Ongar off the A414

North Weald Airfield Museum and Memorial at Ad Astra House, Hurricane Way, North Weald Bassett is a small, meticulously detailed 'House of Memories' displaying the history of the famous airfield and all who served at RAF North Weald from 1916 to the present. Collections of photos and artefacts such as uniforms and the detailed records of all flying operations are on display. There is also a video exhibit recounting a day-to-day account of North Weald history. Guided tours of the airfield can be arranged for large groups.

BRENTWOOD

Brentwood is a busy shopping and entertainment centre, with quite a distinguished past. The town was on the old pilgrim and coaching routes to and from London. Mainly post-war in character, the town is the setting for the UK headquarters of Ford Motors.

Brentwood Cathedral on Ingrave Road was built in 1991.

This classically-styled church incorporates the original Victorian church that stood on this spot. It was designed by the much-admired architect Quinlan Terry, with roundels by Raphael Maklouf (who also created the relief of the Queen's head used on current coins).

Brentwood Centre on Doddinghurst Road is one of the top entertainment venues in the UK, with an extensive programme of concerts, shows, bands and top comedy names, and extensive sports and fitness facilities.

Brentwood Museum at Cemetery Lode in Lorne Road, in the Warley Hill area of Brentwood, is a small and picturesque cottage museum concentrating on local and social interests during the late 19th and early 20th centuries.

AROUND BRENTWOOD

BILLERICAY

6 miles E of Brentwood off the A129

There was a settlement here as far back as the Bronze Age, though there is to date no conclusive explanation of Billericay's name. There is no question about the attraction of the High Street, though, with its timber weather-boarding and Georgian brick. The **Chantry House**, built in 1510, was the home of Christopher Martin, treasurer to the Pilgrim Fathers.

Barleylands Farm Museum and Visitor Centre features a glass-blowing studio, blacksmith's and other craft shops, a wealth of farm animals, chick hatchery, duck pond and one of the largest collections of vintage farm machinery in the country, together with a play area, picnic area and, on Sunday afternoons, a steam railway.

GREAT WARLEY

1 mile S of Brentwood on the B186

Warley Place was formerly home to one of the most famous female gardeners, Ellen Willmott, who died in 1934. She introduced to Warley - and to Britain - many exotic plants. A trail takes visitors through what is now Warley Place Nature Reserve, with 16 acres of what was once domesticated garden but has now reverted to woodland. A fascinating selection of trees, shrubs and wildlife makes this well worth a visit.

SOUTH WEALD

2 miles W of Brentwood off the A12

This very attractive village has, at its outskirts, **Weald Country Park**, a former estate with medieval deer park, partially landscaped in the 1700s. Featuring lake and woodland, visitors' centre, landscapes exhibition and gift shop, with facilities for fishing and horse-riding, there are guided events and activities programmes held throughout the year.

Another good day out in the open air can be had at **Old Macdonald's Educational Farm Park**, where visitors can see the largest selection of pure-bred British farm animals and poultry in the southeast of England.

THE NORTH THAMES CORRIDOR

Bordering the north bank of the Thames, the borough of **Thurrock** has long been a gateway to London but also affords easy access to southwest Essex and to Kent. This thriving borough encompasses huge swathes of green belt country, and along its 18 miles of Thames frontage there are many important marshland wildlife habitats. This stretch of Essex affords some marvellous walking, cycling, birdwatching and other nature pursuits. The area has many bridleways, footpaths and country parks, including Davy Down within the Mardyke Valley. The river's flood plain is a broad tract of grassland which is an important feature of the landscape of the area.

GRAYS

4 miles S of Brentwood off the M25

Thurrock Museum is in the Thameside Complex in Grays. It collects, conserves and displays items of archaeology and local history from prehistoric times to the end of the 20th century. The archaeological items include flint and metal tools of people who lived in prehistoric Thurrock and pottery, jewellery and coins from the Roman and Saxon period.

WEST THURROCK

1½ miles SW of Grays off the A13

Immortalised by the film Four Weddings and a Funeral, little **St**

118 THE HORSE & GROOM

Great Warley

Excellent home cooking brings an appreciative clientele to this popular, convivial pub.

 see page 284

119 THE ROSE & CROWN

Pilgrim's Hatch, nr Brentwood

A traditional tavern where a good variety of food is served in the restaurant overlooking the garden.

 see page 285

120 WEALD COUNTRY PARK

South Weald, nr Brentwood

Weald Country Park is steeped in history. It was once a deer park, and used for hunting by the Abbots of Waltham in around 1063.

see page 286

The Purfleet Heritage and Military Centre is a heritage and military museum featuring displays of many items of interest and memorabilia in the setting of the No 5 Gunpowder Magazine on Centurion Way. This remaining magazine was built in the 1770s for testing and issuing gun powder to the army and navy. Purfleet Conservation Area includes several buildings which were part of a planned village built by the one-time owners of the chalk quarry, the Whitbread family.

Clement's Church occupies a striking location and is one of a number of picturesque ancient churches in the borough. Although this 12th century church is now deconsecrated, it was in its day a stopping point for pilgrims; visitors can see the remains of its original round tower. There is also a mass grave to the boys of the reformatory ship Cornwall who were drowned in an accident off Purfleet.

PURFLEET

3 miles W of Grays off the M25/A13

Fans of Bram Stoker's novel *Dracula* will know that in this book the famous vampire buys a house called 'Carfax' in Purfleet. The town's esteemed Royal Hotel, by the Thames, is said to have played host to Edward VII, while still Prince of Wales in the 1880s and 1890s, at which time the hotel was called Wingrove's.

AVELEY

3 miles NW of Grays off the A13

Mardyke Valley is an important wildlife corridor running from Ship Lane in Aveley to Orsett Fen. Many pleasant views can be had along the seven-mile stretch of footpaths and bridleways. Davy Down within Mardyke Valley consists of riverside meadows, ponds and wetland. The Visitors' Centre is in the well-preserved water pumping station on the B186 near South Ockendon.

Aveley's 12th century St Michael's Church features many Flemish brasses and other items of historical interest.

SOUTH OCKENDON

3 miles N of Grays off the A13/A1306

South Ockenden's Church of St Nicholas has one of only six round church towers in Essex. This one was built in the 13th century and used to have a spire, which was sadly destroyed by lightning in the 17th century.

Belhus Woods Country Park covers approximately 250 acres and contains an interesting variety of habitats, including woodland, two lakes and the remains of a pond designed by 'Capability' Brown. The Visitors' Centre to this superb park can be found at the main entrance off Romford Road. Belhus Park Golf Course is a well-established 18-hole course set within this beautiful parkland.

Grangewaters Country Park in South Ockendon has two lakes. Managed by Thurrock Environmental and Outdoor Education Centre, it offers watersports such as windsurfing, sailing and canoeing, as well as off-road biking, climbing and other outdoor pursuits. Brannetts Wood is one of the oldest recorded ancient woodlands in South Essex. It can be reached from the Mardyke Way, or from South Road in South Ockendon.

HORNDON-ON-THE-HILL

6 miles NE of Grays off the B1007/A13

Listed in the *Domesday Book* as Horninduna, a name which also appears on a Saxon coin of Edward the Confessor (1042-1066), it is said to have once been the site of a Royal Anglo-Saxon mint. The town's 16th century **Woolmarket** indicates the importance of the wool trade to the region, and is one of the area's historical treasures. The upper room served as Horndon's manor courtroom, while the lower, open area was used for trading in woollen cloth.

The main entrance and Visitors' Centre for **Langdon Hills Conservation Centre and Nature Reserve** are located off the Lower Dunton Road north of Horndon-on-the-Hill. A bridleway and footpaths lead visitors to meadows, a pond and outstanding ancient woods. Also within the reserve is the **Plotlands Museum**, housed in an original 1930s plotland bungalow known as the Haven.

LINFORD
3 miles NE of Grays off the A13/A1013

Walton Hall Museum on Walton Hall Road has a large collection of historic farm machinery in a 17th century barn. It affords visitors the opportunity to watch traditional craftsmen, such as a blacksmith, saddlemaker, printer and wheelwright, together with a printing shop, baker's, dairy and nursery.

STANFORD-LE-HOPE
4 miles NE of Grays off the A1014

Stanford Marshes is an area to the south of Stanford-le-Hope, next to the Thames. The Marshes are home to a variety of wildlife and are an ideal location for birdwatching. **Grove House Wood** in Stanford-le-Hope is a nature reserve managed by Essex Wildlife Trust and the local Girl Guides. A footpath here leads to reed beds, a pond and a brook as well as an area of woodland.

The graveyard of **St Margaret's Church** has an unusual half-barrelled tomb, for one James Adams (d. 1765), that is decorated with a gruesome stone-carved symbol of death.

CANVEY ISLAND
10 miles NE of Grays off the A130

Canvey Island is a picturesque stretch of land overlooking the Thames estuary with views to neighbouring Kent.

The island boasts two unusual museums: **Dutch Cottage Museum** is an early 17th century eight-sided cottage built by Dutch workmen for Dutch workmen and boasting many traditional Flemish features.

The Canvey Miniature Railway at the Waterside Farm Centre has two steam miniature railways guaranteed to delight the child in all of us.

WEST TILBURY
3 miles E of Grays off the A1089

West Tilbury was the site chosen for the Camp Royal in 1588, to prepare for the threatened Spanish invasion. Queen Elizabeth I visited the army here, and made her famous speech,

'I know I have the body but of a weak and feeble woman: but I have the heart and stomach of a king, and a king of England too.'

Castle Point Transport Museum is housed in a 1930s bus garage on Canvey Island. It houses an interesting collection of historic and modern buses and coaches, mainly of East Anglian origin.

Coalhouse Fort is set in a lovely riverside park with walks and a children's play area, as well as other items of military history including a Quick Fire Battery and Minefield Control box. You can also follow the old railway tracks from the Fort to the side of the old jetty, where many of the armaments and supplies for the fort were shipped in.

Hidden away in rural tranquillity over-looking the Thames estuary, West Tilbury remains unspoilt in spite of its proximity to busy, industrial Tilbury. The former local church (now a private dwelling) in West Tilbury is a nautical landmark used for navigation. The list of Rectors of the church, dating from 1279-1978, when the church was disestablished, can be seen in The Kings Head Pub.

EAST TILBURY

5 miles E of Grays off the A13

Coalhouse Fort is considered to be one of the best surviving examples of a Victorian Casement fortress in the country. As such it is a protected Scheduled Ancient Monument. Built between 1861 and 1874 as a first line of defence to protect the Thames area against invasion, it stands on the site of other defensive works and fortifications dating back to around 1400. Even before the Middle Ages, this was an important site.

Part of the construction work on the Fort was overseen by Gordon of Khartoum. It was constructed to be a dedicated Artillery casement fortress, which meant that the guns were housed in large vaulted rooms with armour-plated frontages. Beneath these rooms lies an extensive magazine tunnel system to service the artillery.

Over the years many alterations were made to the Fort to accommodate new artillery. The Fort was manned during both

World Wars, and is now owned by Thurrock Borough Council and administered by The Coalhouse Fort Project, a registered charity manned entirely by volunteers. Open to the public, it contains reconstructions of period guns and other displays, and also houses the Thameside Aviation Museum, with a large collection of local finds and other aviation material. In the two parade grounds visitors will find various artillery pieces and military vehicles. One recent addition to the many pieces of historical military equipment is a Bofor Anti-Aircraft Gun of the Second World War. The site also offers visitors the chance to handle period equipment or try on a period uniform.

During the year the Fort hosts a range of shows, including an historic artillery rally when various big guns are fired by crews in the uniforms of the period, including a Second World War crew firing a 1940 25-pounder field gun. A guided tour (included in the price of admission) allows visitors to see the magazine tunnels beneath the gun casements and offers a feel for the work and conditions of a Victorian gunner. The tour also takes in the roof of the Fort, from which you will be able to judge for yourself the value of a fortification at this point along the Thames. The view from here is outstanding, taking in the two sister forts in Kent and, on a clear day, Southend.

The Bata Estate at East Tilbury is a conservation area of architectural and historical interest. Established in 1933, the British

Bata Shoe Company was the creation of Czech-born Thomas Bata, who also developed a housing estate for his workforce. The uniform flat-roofed houses can still be seen on the site.

TILBURY

3 miles SE of Grays off the A1089

Tilbury Fort is a well-preserved and unusual 17th century structure with double moat. The largest and best example of military engineering in England at that time, the fort also affords tremendous views of the Thames estuary. The most violent episode in the fort's history occurred in 1776, during a particularly vociferous cricket match which left three people dead. For a small fee visitors to the fort can fire a 1943 3.7mm anti-aircraft gun - a prospect most children and many adults find irresistible! Owned by English Heritage, the site was used for a military Block House during the reign of Henry VIII and was rebuilt in the 17th century. It remains one of Britain's finest examples of a star-shaped bastion fortress. Extensions were made in the 18th and 19th centuries, and the Fort was still being used in the Second World War.

Tilbury Festival is held every year in July in the field near the fort, and features arena events, craft and food stalls, and living history re-enactments. **Tilbury Energy and Environment Centre** at Tilbury Power Station provides a nature reserve and study centre for schools and community education.

There is a flat two-mile nature trail leading to and from the Centre.

SOUTHEND-ON-SEA

Beside the seaside in Southend-on-Sea there is always plenty to do and see, and many events are held throughout the year to ensure its continuing interest and popularity. The town is one of the best loved and most friendly resorts in Britain, featuring the very best ingredients for a break at the seaside. With seven miles of beaches, this treasure trove boasts Adventure Island theme park, Cliffs Bandstand, Cliffs Pavilion, a distinguished art gallery and several interesting museums.

Southend Pier and Museum brings to life the fascinating past of the longest Pleasure Pier in the world. The Pier itself is well over a

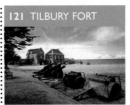

121 TILBURY FORT

Tilbury

Discover the history of this most impressive of English artillery forts, from Henry VIII's time right up to World War II.

🏛 see page 286

Western Esplanade Gardens, Southend-on-Sea

Sealife Adventure employs the most advanced technology to bring visitors incredibly close to the wonders of British marine life, offering fun ways of exploring life under the waves, with concave bubble windows helping to make it seem you're actually part of the sea-creatures' environment. Another exhibit features a walk-through tunnel along a reconstructed seabed. The Shark Exhibition is not to be missed.

mile in length and visitors can either enjoy a leisurely walk along to the end or take advantage of the regular electric railway service that plies up and down the pier alongside the walkway.

Central Museum, Planetarium and Discovery Centre on Victoria Avenue features local history exhibits, archaeology and wildlife exhibits, while **Beecroft Art Gallery** boasts the work of four centuries of artistic endeavour, with some 2,000 works on display.

A floral trail guided tour around the parks and gardens will reveal why Southend has won the Britain in Bloom Awards so often, as well as winning medals at the Chelsea Flower Show.

The **Kursaal** on the Eastern Esplanade is an indoor entertainment complex, one of the largest in the country, with indoor bowling, synthetic ice and roller rink, a fun casino, children's play area, snooker and pool, arts and crafts, retail units and theme restaurants.

Boat trips in summer include occasional outings on a vintage paddle steamer. Ferry trips to Felixstowe are also available from Southend.

The **Southchurch Hall Museum** in Park Lane is a delightful 13th to 14th century timber-framed manor house with various displays and landscaped gardens. Period room settings are among this museum's many delights.

Prittlewell Priory Museum, slightly north of Southend town

centre in Priory Park, is a well-preserved 12th century Cluniac Priory set in lovely grounds and housing collections of the Priory's history, natural history and the Caten collection of radios and communications equipment.

AROUND SOUTHEND

OLD LEIGH
½ mile W of Southend off the A13

The unspoilt fishing village of Old Leigh has a long and distinguished history. It is picturesque, with seafront houses and narrow winding alleys. It has also earned its place in history: The pilgrim ship *The Mayflower* restocked here en route to the New World of America back in the mid-17th century, and the Dunkirk rescue embarked from here, as commemorated in a framed poem on the wall of the local pub, The Crooked Billet.

LEIGH-ON-SEA
2 miles W of Southend off the A13

Leigh-on-Sea has a character quite different from Southend, being more intimate and serene, with wood-clad buildings and shrimp boats in the working harbour. The shellfish stall on the harbourside is justly famous. The **Leigh Heritage Centre**, housed in a former ancient blacksmith's in the waterside High Street of the Old Town, now houses historical artefacts including a photographic display of the history of Leigh-on-Sea.

HADLEIGH

5 miles NW of Southend off the A13

Hadleigh Castle, built originally for Edward III, is owned by English Heritage and once belonged to Anne of Cleves, Catherine of Aragon and Katherine Parr. The ruins were also immortalised in a painting by Constable. The remains of this once impressive castle can still be seen. The curtain walls towers, which survive almost to their full height, overlook the Essex marshes and the Thames estuary. Hadleigh Castle Country Park offers a variety of woodland and coastal walks in grounds overlooking the Thames estuary. A Guided Events programme runs throughout the year.

HULLBRIDGE

8 miles NW of Southend off the A132

Jakapeni Rare Breed Farm at Burlington Gardens in Hullbridge is a pleasant smallholding set in 30 acres of rolling countryside. Specialising in sheep and pigs, with other pets and wildlife, there's also a fishing lake, country walk and pets corner. Snacks and light refreshments are available from the café, and there's an attractive shop.

HOCKLEY

6 miles NW of Southend off the A129

Hockley Woods is a 280-acre ancient woodland, managed for the benefit of wildlife and for the public. Traditional coppice management encourages a diverse array of flora and fauna, including the nationally rare Heath Fritillary butterfly.

Hadleigh Castle

RAYLEIGH

6 miles NW of Southend off the A1016

Dutch Cottage at Crown Hill in Rayleigh is a tiny traditional Flemish eight-sided cottage based on a 17th century design created by Dutch settlers.

Rayleigh Mount is a prominent landmark in this part of the county. Once a motte-and-bailey castle built in the 11th century, it was abandoned some 200 years later. **Rayleigh Windmill**, in Bellingham Lane close to Rayleigh Mount, was built around 1809; the tower mill houses a fascinating collection of bygones mostly used in and around Rayleigh. Refreshments are available from the coffee shop adjacent to the mill.

ROCHFORD

3 miles N of Southend off the B1013

The **Old House**, at 17 South Street, is an elegant, lovingly restored house originally built in 1270. The twisting corridors and handsome rooms of this fine structure offer a glimpse into the past; the building now houses some District Council offices, and is said to be haunted.

CHELMSFORD

Roman workmen cutting their great road linking London with Colchester built a fort at what is today called Chelmsford. Then called Caesaromagus, it stands at the confluence of the Rivers Chelmer and Can. The town has always been an important market centre and is now the bustling county town of Essex. It is also directly descended from a new town planned by the Bishop of London in 1199. At its centre are the principal inn, the Royal Saracen's Head, and the elegant **Shire Hall** of 1791. Three plaques situated high up on the eastern face of the Hall overlooking the High Street represent Wisdom, Justice and Mercy. The building now houses the town magistrates court.

Christianity came to Essex with the Romans and again, later, with St Cedd (AD 654); in 1914 the diocese of Chelmsford was created. **Chelmsford Cathedral** in New Street dates from the 15th century and is built on the site of a church constructed 800 years ago. The cathedral is noted for the harmony and unity of its perpendicular architecture. It was John Johnson, the distinguished local architect who designed both the Shire Hall and the 18th century Stone Bridge over the River Can, who also rebuilt the Parish Church of St Mary when most of its 15th century tower fell down. The church became a cathedral when the new diocese of Chelmsford was created. Since then it has been enlarged and re-organised inside. The cathedral boasts memorial windows dedicated to the USAAF airmen who were based in Essex from 1942 to 1945.

Three modern technologies - electrical engineering, radio, and ball and roller bearings - began in Chelmsford. At the **Engine House Project** at Sandford Mill

Chelmsford Cathedral

Waterworks, museum collections from the town's unique industrial story provide a fun and fascinating insight into the science of everyday things. Moulsham Mill Business & Craft Centre, set in a renovated early 18th century water mill at Parkway, houses a variety of craft workshops and businesses. Crafts featured include jewellery, pottery, flowers, lace-making, dolls houses and bears, and decoupage work. There is a charming picnic area nearby, and a good café.

AROUND CHELMSFORD

GREAT BADDOW

1 mile S of Chelmsford off the A12/A130

Baddow Antiques Centre at The Bringy, Church Street, is one of the leading antiques centres in Essex. Here, 20 dealers offer a wide selection of silver, porcelain, glass, furniture, paintings and collectibles.

SANDON

2 miles SE of Chelmsford off the A414

The village green here in Sandon has produced a notable Spanish oak tree, the biggest in the country, planted in the centre of the village green. This oak tree is remarkable not so much for its height as for the tremendous horizontal spread of its branches. Around the green are a fine church and a number of attractive old houses, some dating back to the 16th century when Henry VIII's Lord Chancellor, Cardinal Wolsey, was Lord of the Manor of Sandon.

SOUTH HANNINGFIELD

6 miles S of Chelmsford off the A130

The placid waters of nearby **Hanningfield Reservoir** were created by damming Sandford Brook, and transformed the scattered rural settlement of Hanningfield into a lakeside village. Now on the shores of the lake, the 12th century village church's belfry has been a local landmark in the flat Essex countryside for centuries. Some of the timbers in the belfry are said to have come from Spanish galleons, wrecked in the aftermath of Sir Francis Drake's defeat of the Armada.

The Visitor Centre at the Reservoir overlooks the 870-acre reservoir and the gateway to the 100-acre woodland beyond. The Centre also offers refreshments, a gift shop and toilet.

WRITTLE

2 miles W of Chelmsford off the A414

Hylands House was built in 1728; this beautiful neo-Classical Grade II listed villa is set in over 500 acres of parkland landscaped by Repton. Rooms that are open to the public include the Blue Room, Entrance Hall, Library, Saloon, Boudoir and Drawing Room. Host to many outdoor events, including the annual 'V' concerts and the Chelmsford Spectacular, Hylands Park features lawns, rhododendron bushes, woodland paths, ornamental ponds and Pleasure Gardens adjacent to the House.

Writtle's parish **Church of St John** features a cross of charred

•

The Marconi Company, pioneers in the manufacture of wireless equipment, set up the first radio company in the world in Chelmsford, in 1899. Exhibits of those pioneering days of wireless can be seen in the Chelmsford Museum in Oaklands Park, Moulsham Street, as can interesting displays of Roman remains and local history. Fine and decorative arts (ceramics, costume, glass), coins, natural history (live beehive, animals, geological exhibits) rub shoulders with displays exploring the history of the distinguished Essex Regiment. This section relates the history of the 44th and 56th Regiments from 1741 to the modern Royal Anglian Regiment. Exhibits include regimental colours and silver and four Victoria Crosses. The museum is set in a lovely park complete with children's play area.

•

122 THE ROSE & CROWN

Great Waltham, nr Chelmsford

A friendly, convivial inn serving a fine choice of real ales and country cooking.

see page 286

123 THE GENERALS ARMS

Little Baddow

Well-kept ales and excellent bar and restaurant menus in a cheerful pub in a village east of Chelmsford.

🍴 see page 287

---

timbers, a reminder of the fire which gutted the chancel in 1974. Ducks swim on the pond of the larger and quite idyllic main village green, which is surrounded by lovely Tudor and Georgian houses. From a tucked-away corner of St John's Green came Britain's first regular broadcasting service, an experimental 15-minute programme beamed out nightly by Marconi's engineers.

WITHAM
6 miles NE of Chelmsford off the A12/B1018

The River Brain flows through this delightful town; a continuous walk has been created along its length for a distance of about three miles. The settlement dates back to at least the 10th century; remains of a Roman temple have been found at Ivy Chimneys, off Hatfield Road.

Blackwater Lane leads to Whetmead, a nature reserve of 25 acres between the rivers Blackwater and Brain.

The **Dorothy L Sayers Centre** in Newland Street houses a collection of books by and about Sayers, the theologian, Dante scholar and novelist/creator of the Lord Peter Wimsey mysteries, who lived in Witham for many years.

LITTLE BRAXTED
6 miles NE of Chelmsford off the A12/B1018

Little Braxted has been voted the best-kept village on a regular basis since 1973. The privately owned St Mary's chapel was built in 1888, and can accommodate only 12 people at a time. The village church of St Nicholas, mentioned in the *Domesday Book*, is famous for its murals.

LITTLE BADDOW
5 miles E of Chelmsford off the A414

Blakes Wood is a designated Site of Special Scientific Interest, an ancient woodland of hornbeam and sweet chestnut renowned for its bluebells. There is a good circular way-marked one-and-a-half mile walk.

DANBURY
5 miles E of Chelmsford off the A414

This village is said to take its name from the Danes who invaded this part of the country in the Dark Ages. In the fine church, under a rare 13th century carved effigy, a crusader knight was found when the tomb was opened in 1779, perfectly preserved in the pickle

Danbury Village

184

which filled his coffin. Fine carving is also a feature of the bench ends; the oldest among them have inspired modern craftsmen to continue the same style of carving on all the pews. In 1402, 'the devil appeared in the likeness of Firor Minor, who entered the church, raged insolently to the great terror of the parishioners ... the top of the steeple was broken down and half the chancel scattered abroad.' And, in 1941, another harbinger of disaster, a 500-lb German bomb, reduced the east end to ruins.

At **Danbury Common**, acres of gorse flower in a blaze of golden colour for much of the year. Along with Lingwood Common, Danbury Common is at the highest point of the gravel ridge between Maldon and Chelmsford. There is evidence here of Napoleonic defences and old reservoirs. Circular nature trails make exploring the area easily accessible. To the west, **Danbury Country Park** offers another pleasant stretch of open country, boasting woodland, a lake and ornamental gardens.

WOODHAM WALTER
6 miles E of Chelmsford off the B1010

Woodham Walter is a small village which lies two and a half miles west of the ancient market town and coastal port of Maldon. It is rumoured that Henry VIII hunted in Woodham Walter during his reign. During the troubled times after Henry's death, Mary Tudor was concealed in Woodham Walter Hall, from where she was planning

to escape from England in 1550. The church in Woodham Walter, St Michael's, was consecrated in April 1564 and is said to one of the oldest Elizabethan churches still standing in England.

MALDON
10 miles E of Chelmsford on the A414

Maldon's High Street has existed since medieval times, and the alleys and mews leading from it are full of intriguing shops, welcoming old inns and good places to eat. One of the most distinctive features of the High Street is the **Moot Hall**. Built in the 15th century for the D'Arcy family, this building passed into the hands of the town corporation and was the seat of power in Maldon for over 400 years. The original brick spiral staircase (the best-preserved of its kind in England) and the 18th century courtroom are of particular interest. Guided tours are available on Saturdays in summer and by appointment with Maldon Town Council (01621 857373) at other times.

A colourful appliquéd embroidery made to commemorate the 1,000th anniversary of the crucial Battle of Maldon in AD991 (see Northey Island, below) is on display at the **Maeldune Heritage Centre** (Maeldune being the Saxon name for Maldon). The Centre is housed in the Grade I listed St Peter's Building, erected in the 17th century by a local benefactor when the nave of the church that had once stood on this site collapsed. It can be found at the junction of the

Promenade Park lies adjacent to Hythe Quay. This attractive park next to the River Blackwater was opened in 1885. The Edwardian-style gardens include an ornamental lake, water splash park, adventure playground with a sandy play area and a play galleon, an aerial runway, an amphitheatre for outdoor events, a picnic site, tennis courts and mini-golf. A varied programme of events takes place in the park throughout the year, including the Mad Maldon Mud Race and the RNLI Rowing Race, both held annually over the Christmas and New Year holidays. A statue of Byrhtnoth, earldorman of Essex at the time of the Battle of Maldon in AD 991, stands at the end of the promenade.

High Street and the steep and architecturally interesting Market Hill. The benefactor, one Thomas Plume, erected the building to house his collection of 6,000 books and a school; the **Plume Library** in St Peter's Building is open to the public.

A few minutes' walk down one of the small roads leading from the High Street brings you to the waterfront, where the old wharfs and quays are still active. Moored at **Hythe Quay** are several Thames Sailing Barges, all over 100 years old and still boasting their traditional rigging and distinctive tan sails. The barges and Quay are overlooked by two pubs, the Queen's Head and the Jolly Sailor. Maldon, famous for its sea salt, is the only place in England still making salt from sea water. Salt production in Maldon dates from Roman times, and from its current premises on the waterfront has continued uninterrupted since 1882.

Housed in what was originally the park-keeper's lodge, by the park gates, **Maldon District Museum** looks back on the colourful history of the town through permanent and changing displays of exhibits and objects associated with the area and the people of Maldon. A new attraction is the Combined Military Services Museum in Station Road, where the displays include armour and ancient weaponry, uniforms, a spy collection and many items brought home from the Gulf Wars. A Chieftain tank is among the external exhibits.

Ruins are all that remain of the **St Giles the Leper Hospital**, founded by King Henry II in the 12th century. As with all monastic buildings, it fell into disuse after Henry VIII's Dissolution of the Monasteries, though it retained its roof and was used as a barn until the late 19th century. Many other buildings in Maldon, almost as old,

Maldon Leper Hospital

fortunately remain - including two fine churches.

LANGFORD

2 miles NW of Maldon on the B1019

The **Museum of Power**, Hatfield Road, covers all aspects of power, from domestic batteries to the massive machines that powered British industry. It includes the steam-powered pumping-station machinery of the redundant waterworks in which the museum is housed. Recent additions include a miniature steam railway and model village.

NORTHEY ISLAND

1 mile SE of Maldon off the B1018

This small island, comprising mainly salt-marsh, is owned by the National Trust. Access to this nature reserve is on foot via a causeway passable at low tide with prior arrangement with the warden. It is a Site of Special Scientific Interest, important to over-wintering birds.

TOLLESBURY

9 miles NE of Maldon on the B1023

Located at the mouth of the River Blackwater is the marshland village of Tollesbury. Tollesbury Marina has been designed as a family leisure centre for the crews and passengers of visiting yachts. The Marina, with its tennis courts, heated covered swimming pool, bar and restaurant is ideally located for exploring the Blackwater and the neighbouring estuaries of the Crouch, Colne, Stour and Orwell.

Tollesbury Wick is a 600-acre nature reserve owned and run by Essex Wildlife Trust; it lies at one end of the North Blackwater Trail, which runs for 12 miles along the estuary to Heybridge Basin.

MUNDON

3 miles S of Maldon off the B1018

Mundon and the surrounding area boasts some excellent walking. **St Peter's Way**, a long-distance path from Ongar to St Peter's Chapel, Bradwell-on-Sea, leads through the village and past the disused Church of St Mary. This 14th century church is no longer open to the public as the building is unsafe following a fall of masonry. Tolstoy is known to have visited the village.

ALTHORNE

6 miles SE of Maldon on the B1012

The **Church of St Andrew**, some 600 years old, has a fine flint and stone tower, built in the perpendicular style. Inside the church there's a 15th century font which retains its original carvings of saints and angels. A brass plaque dated 1508 records that William Hyklott 'Paide for the werkemanship of the wall'; an inscription over the west door remembers John Wylson and John Hyll, who probably paid for the tower.

To the south, where Station Road meets Burnham Road, stands the villagers' own **War Memorial**. This solid structure of beams and tiles lends dignity and honour to the tragic roll-call of names listed on it.

To the north of the village is

●

The sea walls of Northey Island make for an interesting walk, and were used as the camp base for the Viking army in AD 991, when Byrhtnoth led the Saxons against the invading army. A fierce three-day battle took place, with Byrhtnoth's head eventually being cut off and the Viking warriors retreating despite their victory, leaving the English King Ethelred the Unready to pay an annual tribute, 'danegold', to the Danes to prevent further incursions.

●

127 THE ROUND BUSH

Mundon, nr Maldon

A friendly, family-run country pub serving an excellent variety of snacks and meals; an attached café is a good spot for breakfast.

see page 288

A ferry still links Burnham with Wallasea at weekends during the summer, and a programme of boat trips to see the seals on Foulness Sands operates from Burnham Quay. Near the Yacht Harbour, west of the town and accessible along the sea-wall path is Riverside Park (previously known as Burnham Country Park), which won the Green Flag award for the first time in 2007. Millfield Recreation ground is adjacent to the Park.

the golden-thatched and white-walled Huntsman and Hounds, an alehouse since around 1700.

STEEPLE AND ST LAWRENCE

8 miles SE of Maldon off the B1018

Public footpaths lead down to the water from the village of Steeple; the houses of St Lawrence stand close to the water. Several sailing clubs and some waterside caravan and camping parks ensure that there is plenty of activity on the adjacent stretch of the River Blackwater. **St Lawrence Rural Discovery Church**, on high ground further inland, overlooks the villages and the River Blackwater to the north; it also offers views over the River Crouch to the south. Exhibitions with local themes are held in the church during the summer months.

BURNHAM-ON-CROUCH

12 miles SE of Maldon on the B1012

Burnham-on-Crouch is attractively old-fashioned, and probably best known as a yachting venue. It is lively in summer, especially at the end of August when the town hosts one of England's premier regattas, Burnham Week. This week of racing and shore events attracts many visiting craft and landlubbers alike. In winter many yachts are left to ride at anchor offshore, and the sound of the wind in their rigging is ever-present.

Behind the gaily-coloured cottages along the Quay lie the High Street and the rest of the town, its streets lined with a

delightful assortment of old cottages and Victorian and Georgian houses and shops.

In past times, working boats thronged the estuary where yachts now ply to and fro. Seafarers still come ashore to buy provisions, following a tradition that goes back to medieval times when Burnham was the market centre for the isolated inhabitants of Wallasea and Foulness Islands in the estuary.

Burnham-on-Crouch & District Museum on The Quay features agricultural, maritime and social history exhibits relating to the Dengie Hundred. There is also a small archaeological collection. Special exhibitions are mounted periodically.

Mangapps Railway Museum on the edge of town offers an extensive collection of railway relics of all kinds, including steam and diesel engines, carriages and wagons, relocated railway buildings, one of the largest collections of signalling equipment open to the public, a complete country station and items of East Anglian railway history. New displays for 2007 include a London Underground carriage and Canadian and French memorabilia. A lineside walk between Mangapps and Old Heat station provides a great opportunity for photographers and those who want to enjoy the countryside and its wildlife.

St Mary's Church is constructed of Kentish ragstone that was transported to Burnham by sea. Construction was begun in the 12th century and was

188

Chapel of St Peter's on the Wall, Bradwell-on-Sea

128 THE KINGS HEAD

Bradwell-on-Sea

Quaint, homely and friendly country pub with super cooking by the leaseholder.

see *page 288*

completed in the 14th, but since that time the nucleus of the town has moved closer to the waterfront. The arches and pillars are particularly fine examples of medieval craftsmanship, hence the church being known as 'The Cathedral of the Dengie'.

SOUTHMINSTER

3 miles N of Burnham on the B1021

The old market town of Southminster was important as the economic centre for the isolated marshland communities of the Dengie Peninsula.

BRADWELL-ON-SEA/ BRADWELL WATERSIDE

12 miles NE of Burnham off the B1021

A visit to Bradwell-on-Sea (the name derives from the Saxon words brad pall, meaning 'broad wall') is well worth the long drive for its sense of being right out on the edge of things – the timeless emptiness is, if anything,

exaggerated by the distant views of buildings across the water on Mersea Island and the bulk of the nearby (now decommissioned) nuclear power station. A walk eastwards along the old Roman road across the marshes takes you to the site of their fort, 'Othona', on which the visitors of today will find the **Chapel of St Peter's on the Wall**, built by St Cedd and his followers in AD 654 using rubble from the ruined fort. In the 14th century the chapel was abandoned as a place of worship, and over the following centuries used at various times as a barn and a shipping beacon. Restored and re-consecrated in 1920, it is well worth the half-mile walk from the car park to reach it. It is the site of a pilgrimage each July. It has claims to be the oldest church in the land, with St Martin's in Canterbury and St Paul's in Jarrow as other contenders. St Cedd did not survive all that long after founding this

189

To the south of Bradwell village lie the remote marshes of the Dengie Peninsula, parts of which are important nature reserves. The salty tang of sea air, brought inland on easterly winds, gives an exhilarating flavour to the marshlands. Like the Cambridgeshire and Lincolnshire fens, this once-waterlogged corner of Essex was reclaimed from the sea by 17th century Dutch engineers. The views across the marshes take in great sweeps of countryside inhabited only by wildfowl and seabirds.

129 MARSH FARM COUNTRY PARK

South Woodham Ferrers

Marsh Farm Country Park overlooks the River Crouch and is surrounded by its creeks on three sides.

 see page 290

chapel, dying of a fever in Yorkshire in AD 664. Bradwell Lodge, in the village centre, is a part-Tudor former rectory that has known some famous visitors. Gainsborough, the Suffolk artist, used rooms as a studio, while the Irish writer Erskine Childers, who was shot by the Irish Free State in 1920 because he fought for the IRA, wrote *The Riddle of the Sands* here.

An unusual war memorial marks the site of the **Bradwell Bay Secret Airfield**, used during the Second World War for aircraft unable to return to their original base.

At **Bradwell Waterside**, a large marina has berths for 300 boats. The now-decommissioned nuclear power station no longer has a visitor centre, but a waymarked nature trail within the grounds is accessible to visitors.

PURLEIGH

5 miles SW of Maldon on the B1010

The first recorded vineyard in Purleigh was planted in the early 12th century, only 400 yards from the site of **New Hall Vineyards** in Chelmsford Road. It covered three acres of land next to **Purleigh Church**, where first US president George Washington's great-great-grandfather was the rector - until the time he was removed from this office for sampling too much of the local brew! Purleigh Vineyard became Crown property in 1163; subsequently the wines produced were taken each year to London to be presented to the monarch.

SOUTH WOODHAM FERRERS

5 miles SW of Maldon off the B1012

The empty marshland of the Crouch estuary, a yachtsman's paradise, was chosen by Essex County Council as the site for one of its most attractive new towns schemes. At its centre, this successful 20th century new town boasts a traditional market square surrounded by pleasant arcades and terraces built in the old Essex style with brick, tile and weather-board.

Marsh Farm Country Park in Marsh Farm Road, South Woodham Ferrers, is a working farm and country park adjoining the River Crouch. Sheep, pigs, cattle and hens roam; visitors can also partake of the adventure play area, farm trail, Visitors' Centre, gift shop and tea rooms. Guided tours are available by prior arrangement. Special events are held throughout the year.

RETTENDON

6 miles SW of Maldon off the A130

The **Royal Horticultural Society Garden** at Hyde Hall comprises 28 acres of year-round hillside colour, with a woodland garden, large rose garden, ornamental ponds with lilies and fish, herbaceous borders, shrubs, trees, and a National Collection of viburnums. 3,000 trees have recently been planted, and a dry garden features huge boulders from Scotland. New for 2007 are the Ronbinson Garden dedicated to the original owners of Hyde Hall and themed vegetable plots.

BATTLESBRIDGE

7 miles SW of Maldon off the A132

Battlesbridge Antiques Centre at Hawk Hill in Battlesbridge is the largest in Essex. Housed in five period buildings, more than 70 dealers display and sell their wares. The heart of the Centre is Cromwell House, its ground floor dedicated to specialist dealers with individual units. They will advise, value and give an expert opinion free of charge. They offer a wide variety of old and interesting pieces and collectibles.

The Centre's Haybarn Cottages were constructed as dwellings, while, alongside, The Bridgebarn began life as a barn with thatched roof and dates from the 19th century, at which time there were lime kilns nearby. It was converted to its present tiled roof in the 1930s. The building retains some fine oak beam work, and houses a small 'penny arcade' with working model roundabout, fortune teller, and 'What the Butler Saw' as well as a large collection of antiques for sale. From the top floor there are superb views of the River Crouch and the surrounding area.

This location is also the site of a **Classic Motor Cycle Museum**, with displays evoking the history of motorcycling through the ages and some interesting memorabilia. Open on Sundays or by appointment. Three classic vehicle events are held annually.

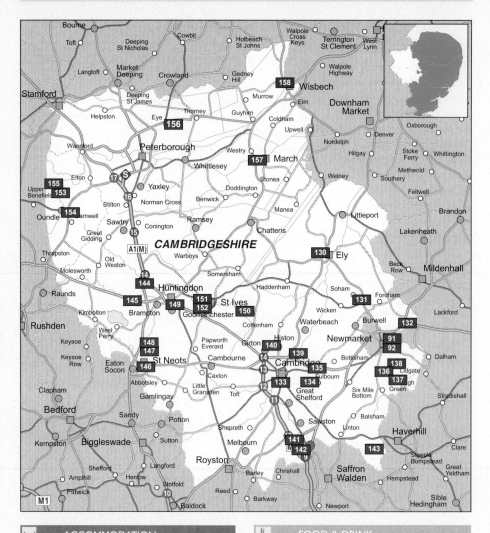

Cambridgeshire

ambridgeshire is a county with a rich rural heritage, with attractive villages strung along the banks of the Great Ouse and the flat land of the Fens. Far removed from the hustle and bustle of modern life, the Fens are like a breath of fresh air. Extending over much of Cambridgeshire from the Wash, these flat, fenland fields contain some of the richest soil in England. Villages such as Fordham and small towns like Ely rise out of the landscape on low hills.

Before the Fens were drained, this was a land of mist, marshes and bogs, of small islands inhabited by independent folk, their livelihood the fish and waterfowl of this eerie, watery place. The region is full of legends of web-footed people, ghosts and witchcraft.

Today's landscape is the result of human ingenuity, with its constant desire to tame the wilderness and create farmland. This fascinating story spans the centuries from the earliest Roman and Anglo-Saxon times, when the first embankments and drains were constructed to lessen the frequency of flooding. Throughout the Middle Ages large

Hartford Marina, Huntingdon

areas were reclaimed, with much of the work being undertaken by the monasteries. The first straight cut bypassed the Great Ouse, allowing the water to run out to sea more quickly. After the Civil War, the New Bedford River was cut parallel to the first. These two still provide the basic drainage for much of Fenland.

St Ives

The significant influence of the Dutch lives on in some of the architecture and place names of the Fens. Over the years it became necessary to pump rainwater from the fields up into the rivers and, as in the Netherlands, windmills took on this task. They could not always cope with the height of the lift required, but fortunately the steam engine came along, to be replaced eventually by the electric pumps that can raise thousands of gallons of water a second to protect the land from the ever-present threat of rain and tide.

The Fens today offer unlimited opportunities for exploring on foot, by car, bicycle or by boat. Anglers are well catered for, and visitors with an interest in wildlife will be in their element. The jewel in the crown of the Fens is Ely, with its magnificent cathedral. A few miles to the south, Wicken Fen is the oldest nature reserve in the country – 600 acres of undrained fenland that is famous for its varied plant, insect and bird life.

Southeastern Cambridgeshire covers the area around the city of Cambridge and is rich in history, with a host of archaeological sites and monuments to visit, as well as many important museums. The area is fairly flat, so it makes for great walking and cycling tours, and offers a surprising variety of landscapes. The Romans planted vines here, and to this day the region is among the main producers of British wines.

At the heart of it all is Cambridge itself, one of the leading academic centres in the world and a city which deserves plenty of time to explore - on foot, by bicycle or by the gentler, more romantic option of a punt.

The old county of Huntingdonshire is the heartland of the rural heritage of Cambridgeshire. Here, the home of Oliver Cromwell beckons with a wealth of history and pleasing landscapes. Many motorists follow the Cromwell Trail, which guides tourists around the legacy of buildings and places in the area associated with the man. The natural start of the Trail is Huntingdon itself, where he was born the son of a country gentleman.

The Ouse Valley Way (26 miles long) follows the course of the Great Ouse through pretty villages and a variety of natural attractions. A gentle cruise along this area can fill a lazy day to perfection, but for those who prefer something more energetic on the water there are excellent, versatile facilities at Grafham Water.

The Nene-Ouse Navigation Link, part of the Fenland Waterway, provides the opportunity for a relaxed look at a lovely part of the region. It travels from Stanground Lock near Peterborough to a lock at the small village of Salters Lode in the east, and the 28-mile journey passes through several Fenland towns and a rich variety of wildlife habitats.

ELY

Ely is the jewel in the crown of the Fens, in whose history the majestic **Cathedral** and the Fens themselves have played major roles. The Fens' influence is apparent even in the name: Ely was once known as Elge or Elig ('eel island') because of the large number of eels which lived in the surrounding fenland.

Ely owes its existence to St Etheldreda, wife of King Egfrid and Queen of Northumbria, who in AD 673 founded a monastery on the 'Isle of Ely', where she remained as abbess until her death in AD 679.

It was not until 1081 that work started on the present Cathedral, and in 1189 this remarkable example of Romanesque architecture was completed. The most outstanding feature in terms of both scale and beauty is the Octagon, built to replace the original Norman tower, which collapsed in 1322.

Alan of Walsingham was the inspired architect of this massive work, which took 30 years to complete and whose framework weighs an estimated 400 tons. Many other notable components include the 14th century Lady Chapel, the largest in England, the Prior's Door, the painted nave ceiling and St Ovin's cross, the only piece of Saxon stonework in the building.

The Cathedral, sometimes known as the 'Ship of the Fens', is set within the walls of the monastery, and many of the ancient buildings still stand as a tribute to

Etheldreda was also known as St Awdrey, and an annual fair was held in her memory. The cheap jewellery and lace sold at the fair were known as St Awdrey's lace, later corrupted into 'tawdry', a word now applied to anything cheap and showy.

Ely Cathedral

195

130 THE KINGS ARMS

Ely

A sociable inn close to the centre, serving a good selection of real ales and hot and cold snacks and meals.

🍴 *see page 290*

the incredible skill and craftsmanship of their designers and builders. Particularly worth visiting among these are the monastic buildings in the College, the Great Hall and Queens Hall.

Just beside the Cathedral is the Almonry, in whose 12th century vaulted undercroft visitors can take coffee, lunch or tea - outside in the garden if the weather permits. The **Stained Glass Museum**, housed in the south Triforium of the Cathedral, is the only museum of stained glass in the country and contains over 100 original panels from every period, tracing the complete history of stained glass. The cannon on Palace Green opposite the Cathedral was captured from the Russians in Sebastopol and was given to the citizens of Ely by Queen Victoria after the Crimean War. The gift was made in recognition of the formation of the Ely Rifle Volunteers.

Ely's **Tourist Information Centre** is itself a tourist attraction, since it is housed in a pretty black-and-white timbered building that was once the home of Oliver Cromwell. It is the only remaining house, apart from Hampton Court, where Oliver Cromwell and his family are known to have lived; parts of it trace back to the 13th century, and its varied history includes periods when it was used as a public house and, more recently, a vicarage. There are eight period rooms, exhibitions and videos to enjoy.

The Old Gaol, in Market Street, houses **Ely Museum**, with nine galleries telling the Ely story from the Ice Age to modern times. The tableaux of the condemned and debtors' cells are particularly fascinating and poignant.

Ely is not just the past, and its fine architecture and sense of history blend well with the bustle of the streets and shops and the riverside. That bustle is at its most fervent on Thursdays, when the largest general market in the area is held. Every Saturday there's a craft and collectibles market, and on the second and fourth Saturdays of the month Ely hosts a Farmers' Market.

The Riverside Trail takes in the Babylon Gallery in a converted 18th century brewery warehouse, where visitors will find an exciting collection of contemporary arts and crafts, in a programme of changing local and international exhibitions; the Jubilee Gardens; Ely Park, and the Quai d'Orsay, named after the twinning of East Cambridgeshire with the town of Orsay in France in 1981.

Bishops Old Palace, Ely

AROUND ELY

PRICKWILLOW

4 miles NE of Ely on the B1382

On the village's main street is the **Prickwillow Drainage Engine Museum**, which houses a unique collection of large engines associated with the drainage of the Fens. The site had been in continuous use as a pumping station since 1831, and apart from the engines there are displays charting the history of Fens drainage, the effects on land levels and the workings of the modern drainage system.

LITTLEPORT

6 miles N of Ely on the A10

St George's Church, with its very tall 15th century tower, is a notable landmark here in Littleport. Of particular interest are two stained-glass windows depicting St George slaying the dragon. Littleport was the scene of riots in 1861, when labourers from Ely and Littleport, faced with unemployment or low wages, and soaring food prices, attacked houses and people in this area, causing several deaths. Five of the rioters were hanged and buried in a common grave at St Mary's church. A plaque commemorating the event is attached to a wall at the back of the church.

LITTLE DOWNHAM

3 miles N of Ely off the A10

Little Downham's **Church of St Leonard** shows the change from Norman to Gothic in church building at the turn of the 13th century. The oldest parts are the Norman tower and the elaborately carved south door. Interior treasures include what is probably the largest royal coat of arms in the country. At the other end of the village are the remains (mainly the gatehouse and kitchen) of a 15th century palace built by a Bishop of Ely.

COVENEY

3 miles W of Ely off the A10/A142

A Fenland hamlet on the Bedford Level just above West Fen, Coveney's **Church of St Peter-ad-Vincula** has several interesting features, including a colourful German screen dating from around 1500 and a painted Danish pulpit. Unusual figures on the bench ends and a fine brass chandelier add to the opulent feel of this atmospheric little church.

SUTTON

6 miles W of Ely off the A142/B1381

A very splendid 'pepperpot' tower with octagons, pinnacles and spire tops marks out Sutton's grand **Church of St Andrew**. Inside, take time to look at the 15th century font and a fine modern stained-glass window.

The reconstruction of the church was largely the work of two Bishops of Ely, whose arms appear on the roof bosses. One of the Bishops was Thomas Arundel, appointed at the age of 21.

A mile further west, there's a great family attraction in the Mepal Outdoor Centre, an outdoor leisure

The Church of St Andrew stands on a hillside in Haddenham. Look for the stained-glass window depicting two souls entering Heaven, and the memorial (perhaps the work of Grinling Gibbons) to Christopher Wren's sister, Anne Brunsell.

centre with a children's playpark, an adventure play area and boat hire.

HADDENHAM

5 miles SW of Ely on the A1123

More industrial splendour: **Haddenham Great Mill**, built in 1803 for a certain Daniel Cockle, is a glorious sight, and one definitely not to be missed. It has four sails and three sets of grinding stones, one of which is working. The mill last worked commercially in 1946 and was restored between 1992 and 1998. Open on the first Sunday of each month and by appointment.

STRETHAM

5 miles S of Ely off A10/A1123

The **Stretham Old Engine**, a fine example of a land-drainage steam engine, is housed in a restored, tall-chimneyed brick engine house. Dating from 1831, it is one of 90 steam pumping engines installed throughout the Fens to replace some 800 windmills. It is the last to survive, having worked until 1925 and still under restoration. During the great floods of 1919 it really earned its keep by working non-stop for 47 days and nights.

This unique insight into Fenland history and industrial archaeology is open to the public on summer weekends, and on certain dates the engine and its wooden scoop-wheel are rotated (by electricity, alas!). The adjacent stoker's cottage contains period furniture and photographs of fen drainage down the years.

WICKEN

9 miles S of Ely off the A1123

Owned by the National Trust, **Wicken Fen** is the oldest nature reserve in the country, 600 acres of undrained fenland famous for its rich plant, insect and bird life and a delight for both naturalists and ramblers ever since it opened in 1899. Features include boardwalk and nature trails, hides and watchtowers, a workman's cottage with 1930s furnishings, a working wind pump (the oldest in the country), a visitor centre and a shop. It is also home to Highland cattle and wild Konik ponies. Open daily, dawn to dusk. Wicken Windmill is a fine and impressive smock windmill restored back to working order. One of only four smock windmills making flour by windmill in the UK, it is open the first weekend of every month and every Bank Holiday (except Christmas and Good Friday) from 11 until 5, and also over the

Wicken

National Mills Weekend, the second week in May.

St Lawrence's Church in Wicken is well worth a visit, small and secluded among trees. In the churchyard are buried several members of Oliver Cromwell's family, including his fourth son Henry. One of Cromwell's many nicknames was 'Lord of the Fens': he defended the rights of the Fenmen against those who wanted to drain the land without providing adequate compensation.

SOHAM

6 miles SE of Ely off the A142

Downfield Windmill was built in 1726 as a smock mill, destroyed by gales and rebuilt in 1890 as an octagonal tower mill. It still grinds corn and produces a range of flours and breads for sale (open Sundays and Bank Holidays).

St Andrew's church is a fine example of the Perpendicular style of English Gothic architecture. Very grand and elaborate, it was built on the site of a 7th century cathedral founded by St Felix of Burgundy. The 15th century west tower has an ornate parapet and two medieval porches. Note, too, the chancel with its panelling and stained glass.

A plaque in Soham commemorates engine driver Ben Gimbert and fireman James Nightall, who were taking an ammunition train through the town when a wagon caught fire. They uncoupled it and began to haul it into open country. The wagon exploded, killing the fireman and a signalman.

ISLEHAM

10 miles SE of Ely off the B1104

The remains of a Benedictine priory, with a lovely Norman chapel under the care of English Heritage, are a great draw here in Isleham. Also well worth a visit is the church of St Andrew, a 14th century cruciform building entered by a very fine lychgate. The 17th century eagle lectern is the original of a similar lectern in Ely Cathedral.

FORDHAM

10 miles SE of Ely off the A142

A small village on the Newmarket Cycle Way. The poet James Withers spent most of his life in Fordham and is buried in the churchyard; a stained-glass window in the church is inscribed in his memory.

SNAILWELL

12 miles SE of Ely off the A142

Snailwell's pretty, mainly 14th century church of St Peter on the banks of the River Snail boasts a 13th century chancel, a hammerbeam and tie beam nave roof, a 600-year-old font, pews with poppy heads and two medieval oak screens. The Norman round tower is unusual for Cambridgeshire.

CAMBRIDGE

Cambridge was an important town many centuries before the scholars arrived, standing at the point where forest met fen, at the lowest fording point of the river. The Romans took over a site previously settled

There are many Cambridges spread around the globe, but this, the original, is the one that the whole world knows as one of the leading university cities.

King's College, Cambridge

This was **Peterhouse**, founded by the Bishop of Ely, and in the next century Clare, Pembroke, Gonville & Caius, Trinity Hall and Corpus Christi followed. One of the modern Colleges is Robinson College, the gift of self-made millionaire David Robinson. The Colleges represent various architectural styles, the grandest and most beautiful being King's. Robinson has the look of a fortress; its concrete structure covered with a 'skin' of a million and a quarter hand-made red Dorset bricks.

The Colleges are all well worth a visit, but places that simply must not be missed include **King's College Chapel** with its breathtaking fan vaulting, glorious stained glass and Peter Paul Rubens' *Adoration of the Magi*; **Pepys Library**, including his diaries, in Magdalene College; and Trinity's wonderful **Great Court**. A trip by punt along the 'Backs' of the Cam brings a unique view of many of the Colleges and passes under six bridges, including the **Bridge of Sighs** (St John's) and the extraordinary wooden **Mathematical Bridge** at Queens'. It is not only the bricks and mortar and the treasures within that bring visitors to the colleges, as many of them have gardens of particular interest, some of them open to the public at various times. Notable among these is **Christ's College**, where the trees include an ancient mulberry and a cypress grown from seed from the tree on Shelley's grave in Rome. Oliver Cromwell's

by an Iron Age Belgic tribe, to be followed in turn by the Saxons and the Normans. Soon after the Norman Conquest, William I built a wooden motte-and-bailey castle; Edward I built a stone replacement: a mound still marks the spot. The town flourished as a market and river trading centre, and in 1209 a group of students fleeing the Oxford riots arrived. These students made their own arrangements for accommodation, and it was not until 1284 that the first residential college was opened.

final resting place is an unmarked grave near the chapel in Sidney Sussex College. The **University Botanic Garden** in the south of the city covers 40 acres and has a triple role of research, education and amenity.

The Colleges apart, Cambridge is packed with interest for the visitor, with a wealth of grand buildings both religious and secular, and some of the country's leading museums, many of them run by the University. The **Fitzwilliam Museum** is renowned for its art collection, which includes works by Titian, Rembrandt, Gainsborough, Hogarth, Turner, Renoir, Picasso and Cezanne, and for its antiquities from Egypt, Greece and Rome. **Kettle's Yard** has a permanent display of 20th century art in a house maintained just as it was when the Ede family donated it, with the collection, to the University in 1967. The **Museum of Classical Archaeology** has 500 plaster casts of Greek and Roman statues, and the **University Museum of Archaeology and Anthropology** covers worldwide prehistoric archaeology with special displays relating to Oceania and to the Cambridge area. The **Museum of Technology**, housed in a Victorian sewage pumping station, features an impressive collection of steam, gas and electric pumping engines and examples, great and small, of local industrial technology. Anyone with an interest in fossils should make tracks for the **Sedgwick Museum of Earth Sciences**, while in the same street

(Downing) the **Museum of Zoology** offers a comprehensive and spectacular survey of the animal kingdom. The **Whipple Museum of the History of Science** tells about science through instruments; and the **Scott Polar Research** Institute has fascinating, often poignant exhibits relating to Arctic and Antarctic exploration.

The work and life of the people of Cambridge and the surrounding area are the subject of the **Cambridge and County Folk Museum**, housed in a 15th century building that for 300 years was the White Horse Inn. Topics include Crafts & Trades, Town & Gown, and Skating & Eels, and throughout the year themed talks and exhibitions take place. One of the city's greatest treasures is the **University Library**, one of the world's great research libraries with 6 million books, a million maps and 350,000 manuscripts. The Library was built between 1930 and 1934 to a design of Giles Gilbert Scott.

Hobson Street, which runs between Sidney Sussex and Christ's Colleges, remembers the 16th century notable Thomas Hobson, sometime Mayor of Cambridge and benefactor. He was also a carrier, hiring out horses, but his customers could only choose the horse that happened to be standing next to the stable door – giving rise to the expression Hobson's Choice, ie no choice at all.

Cambridge also has many fine churches, some of them used by the Colleges before they built their own chapels. Among the most

Cambridge has nurtured more Nobel Prize winners than most countries - 32 from Trinity alone - and the list of celebrated alumni covers every sphere of human endeavour and achievement: Byron, Tennyson, Milton and Wordsworth; Marlowe and Bacon; Samuel Pepys; Sir Isaac Newton and Charles Darwin; Charles Babbage, Bertrand Russell and Ludwig Wittgenstein; actors Sir Ian McKellen, Sir Derek Jacobi and Stephen Fry; Lord Burghley; Harold Abrahams, who ran for England in the Olympics; and Burgess, Maclean, Philby and Blunt, all Trinity men who spied for Russia.

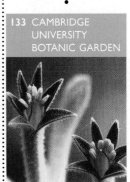

133 CAMBRIDGE UNIVERSITY BOTANIC GARDEN

Cambridge

Opened in 1846 by Professor John Henslow, Charles Darwin's teacher and mentor, this heritage-listed Botanic Garden Displays over 8,000 plant species

 see page 291

134 THE BAKERS ARMS

Fulbourn, nr Cambridge

Home cooking and well-kept ales keep the customers happy at a handsome inn a short drive east of Cambridge.

see page 291

135 THE WHEATSHEAF

Stow-cum-Quy, nr Cambridge

A smartly refurbished 1920s village pub with a restaurant serving super home-cooked food.

see page 292

136 THE THREE BLACKBIRDS

Woodditton, nr Newmarket

A great favourite with locals and racegoers, with real ales and fine wines to accompany super food.

see page 292

137 THE RED LION

Kirtling, nr Newmarket

The **Red Lion** provides a feel and flavour of Spain in a pleasant village close to Newmarket.

see page 292

St Benet's Church, Cambridge

notable are **St Andrew the Great** (note the memorial to Captain Cook); **St Andrew the Less**; **St Benet's** (its 11th century tower is the oldest in the county); **St Mary the Great**, a marvellous example of Late Perpendicular Gothic; and **St Peter Castle Hill**. This last is one of the smallest churches in the country, with a nave measuring just 25 feet by 16 feet. Originally much larger, the church was largely demolished in 1781 and rebuilt in its present diminished state using the old materials, including flint rubble and Roman bricks. The **Church of the Holy Sepulchre**, always known as the Round Church, is one of only four surviving circular churches in England.

AROUND CAMBRIDGE

BOTTISHAM

5 miles E of Cambridge on the A1303

John Betjeman ventured that Bottisham's Holy Trinity Church was 'perhaps the best in the county', so time should certainly be made for a visit. Among the many interesting features are the 13th century porch, an 18th century monument to Sir Roger Jenyns and some exceptionally fine modern woodwork in Georgian style.

SWAFFHAM PRIOR

8 miles NE of Cambridge on the B1102.

Swaffham Prior gives double value to the visitor, with two churches in the same churchyard and two fine old windmills. The **Churches of St Mary and St Cyriac** stand side by side, a remarkable and dramatic sight in the steeply rising churchyard. One of the mills, a restored 1850s tower mill, still produces flour and can be visited by appointment.

At Swaffham Bulbeck, a little way to the south, stands another **Church of St Mary**, with a 13th century tower and 14th century arcades and chancel. Look for the fascinating carvings on the wooden benches and a 15th century cedarwood chest decorated with biblical scenes.

LODE

6 miles NE of Cambridge on the B1102

Anglesey Abbey dates from 1600 and was built on the site of an Augustinian priory, but the house and the 100-acre garden came together as a unit thanks to the vision of the 1st Lord Fairhaven. The garden, created in its present form from the 1930s, is a wonderful place for a stroll, with 98 acres of landscaped gardens including wide grassy walks, open lawns, a riverside walk, a working water mill and one of the finest

collections of garden statuary in the country. There's also a plant centre, shop and restaurant. In the house itself is Lord Fairhaven's magnificent collection of paintings, sumptuous furnishings, tapestries and clocks.

BURWELL

10 miles NE of Cambridge on the B1102

Burwell is a village of many attractions with a history going back to Saxon times. **Burwell Museum** reflects many aspects of a village on the edge of the Fens up to the middle of the 20th century. A general store, model farm, local industries and children's toys are among the displays. Next to the museum is the famous **Stephens Windmill**, built in 1820 and extensively restored.

The Devil's Dyke runs through Burwell on its path from Reach to Woodditton. This amazing dyke, 30 yards wide, was built, it is thought, to halt Danish invaders.

138 THE REINDEER

Saxon Street, nr Newmarket

A handsome country inn with a fine reputation for hospitality, good food and well-kept ales. Two rooms for B&B.

❙❙ ⊨ see page 293

The man who designed parts of King's College Chapel, Reginald Ely, is thought to have been responsible for Burwell's beautiful St Mary's Church, which is built of locally quarried clunch stone and is one of the finest examples of the Perpendicular style. Notable internal features include a 15th century font, a medieval wall painting of St Christopher and roof carvings of elephants, while in the churchyard a gravestone marks the terrible night in 1727 when 78 Burwell folk died in a barn fire while watching a travelling Punch & Judy show. Behind the church are the remains of Burwell Castle, started in the 12th century but never properly completed.

Anglesey Abbey, Lode

139 THE CROWN & PUNCHBOWL

Horningsea

Quality to the fore in hospitality, food and accommodation in an immaculate 400-year-old hostelry a short drive from Cambridge.

🍴 🛏 see page 294

140 THE KING WILLIAM

Histon, nr Cambridge

A distinctive old coaching inn serving real ales and a fine selection of home-cooked food.

🍴 see page 295

REACH

8 miles NE of Cambridge off the A4280

The charming village of Reach is home to the oldest fair in England, which celebrated its 800th anniversary on 1st May, 2000.

WATERBEACH

5 miles N of Cambridge off the A10

Denny Abbey, easily accessible on the A10, is an English Heritage Grade I listed Abbey with ancient earthworks. On the same site, and run as a joint attraction, is the **Farmland Museum**. The history of Denny Abbey runs from the 12th century, when it was a Benedictine monastery. It was later home to the Knights Templar, Franciscan nuns and the Countess of Pembroke, and from the 16th century was a farmhouse. The old farm buildings have been splendidly renovated and converted to tell the story of village life and Cambridgeshire farming up to modern times. The museum is ideal for family outings, with plenty of hands-on activities for children and a play area, gift shop and weekend tearoom. Among the top displays are a village shop, agricultural machinery, a magnificent 17th century stone barn, a traditional farmworker's cottage and the workshops where various crafts are practised.

MILTON

3 miles N of Cambridge off the A10

Milton Country Park offers fine walking and exploring among acres of parkland, lakes and woods.

There's a visitor centre, a picnic area and a place serving light refreshments.

COTTENHAM

5 miles NW of Cambridge on the B1049

All Saints Church has an unusual tower of yellow and pink Jacobean brick topped with four pinnacles that look like pineapples. The original tower fell down in a gale, and its replacement was partially funded by former US President Calvin Coolidge, one of whose ancestors had lived in the village at the time when the tower fell down.

RAMPTON

6 miles N of Cambridge off the B1050/B1049

A charming village in its own right, with a tree-fringed village green, Rampton is also the site of one of the many archaeological sites in the area. This is **Giant's Hill**, a motte castle with part of an earlier medieval settlement.

GIRTON

3 miles NW of Cambridge off the A14

The first Cambridge College for women was founded in 1869 in Hitchin, by Emily Davies. It moved here to Girton in 1873, to be 'near enough for male lecturers to visit but far enough away to discourage male students from doing the same'. The problem went away when Girton became a mixed College in 1983.

MADINGLEY

4 miles W of Cambridge on the A428

The American Cemetery is one of the loveliest, most peaceful and most moving places in the region, a place of pilgrimage for the families of the American servicemen who operated from the many wartime bases in the county. The cemetery commemorates service personnel who lost their lives in World War II serving as crew members of British-based American aircraft. The tablet of the missing records 5,126 missing in action, lost or buried at sea, and the graves area contains 3,812 headstones.

CAXTON

6 miles W of Cambridge
off the A12198/A428

Caxton is home to Britain's oldest surviving **Postmill**, and at **Little Gransden**, a couple of miles further southwest on the B1046, another venerable mill has been restored. A scheduled ancient monument, it dates from the early 17th century and was worked well into the early years of the 20th century.

BARTON

3 miles SW of Cambridge off the A603/B1046

Looking south from this pleasant village you can see the impressive array of radio telescopes that are part of Cambridge University's Mullard Radio Astronomy Observatory.

GRANTCHESTER

2 miles SW of Cambridge off the A603

A pleasant walk by the Cam, or a punt on it, brings visitors from the bustle of Cambridge to the famous village of Grantchester, where Rupert Brooke lived and Byron swam. The walk passes through **Paradise Nature Reserve**.

'Stands the church clock at ten to three
And is there honey still for tea?'

The **Orchard**, with its Brooke connections, is known the world over. Brooke spent two happy years in Grantchester, and immortalised afternoon tea in The Orchard in a poem he wrote while homesick in Berlin.

Brooke also wrote the memorable lines

'If I should die, think only this of me,
That there's some corner of a foreign field
That is forever England'

Brooke died aged 28 on service to his country in 1915 in the Dardanelles.

Time should also be allowed for a look at the **Church of St Andrew and St Mary**, in which the remains of a Norman church have been incorporated into the 1870s main structure.

ARRINGTON

8 miles SW of Cambridge
off the A603/A1198

Arrington's 18th century **Wimpole Hall**, owned by the National Trust, is probably the most spectacular country mansion in the whole county, and certainly the largest 18th century country house in Cambridgeshire. The lovely interiors are the work of several celebrated architects, and there's a fine collection of furniture and pictures. The mansion's state and private rooms show how the last owner Mrs Elsie Bambridge, a daughter of Rudyard Kipling, lived

A brilliant attraction for all the family is Wimpole Home Farm, a working farm that is the largest rare breeds centre in East Anglia. The animals include Bagot goats, Tamworth pigs, Soay sheep and Longhorn cattle, and there's also a pets corner and horse-drawn wagon ride. Children can spend hours with the animals or in the adventure playground.

205

141 THE WHEATSHEAF

Duxford

A friendly, sociable pub open all day every day, with a warm welcome for all the family.

 see page 296

142 THE ICKLETON LION

Ickleton, nr Saffron Walden

An atmospheric old inn serving a fine selection of snacks and meals, with the bonus of a super lawned garden.

 see page 296

143 THE COCK INN

Castle Camps, nr Linton

A delightful country inn serving real ales and a fine variety of home-cooked dishes. Also 3 rooms for B&B.

see page 296

at Wimpole trying to restore the house and estate to its former glory. The magnificent formally laid-out grounds include a Victorian parterre (with some surprising modern sculptures), a rose garden and a walled garden. The park provides miles of wonderful walking and is perfect for anything from a gentle stroll to a strenuous hike.

SHEPRETH

8 miles S of Cambridge off A10

A paradise for lovers of nature and gardens and a great starting point for country walks, **Shepreth L Moor Nature Reserve** is an L-shaped area of wet meadowland - now a rarity - that is home to birds and many rare plants. The nearby **Shepreth Wildlife Park** started life as a refuge for injured and orphaned British birds and mammals. It now houses a collection of wild and domestic animals including wolves, monkeys, birds and reptiles. In the Water World and Bug City visitors can see insects and fish including the amazing leaf cutter ants. Surrounding 18th century **Docwra's Manor** at Shepreth is a series of enclosed gardens with multifarious plants that is open for visits Wednesday and Friday all year and the first Sunday afternoons from April to October. **Fowlmere**, on the other side of the A10, is an 86-acre nature reserve designed as a Site of Special Scientific Interest, with hides and trails for bird-watching.

DUXFORD

8 miles S of Cambridge off A505 by J10 of M11

Part of the Imperial War Museum, **Duxford Aviation Museum** is probably the leader in its field in Europe, with an outstanding collection of over 150 historic aircraft from biplanes through Spitfires, Concorde and Gulf War fighters. The American Air Museum, where aircraft are suspended as if in flight, is part of this terrific place, which was built on a former RAF and USAAF fighter base. Major air shows take place several times a year, and among the permanent features are a reconstructed wartime operations room, a hands-on exhibition for children and a dramatic land warfare hall with tanks, military vehicles and artillery. Everyone should take time to see this marvellous show - and it should be much more than a flying visit! A free bus service operates from Cambridge City Centre.

At nearby **Hinxton**, a few miles further south, is another mill: a 17th century water mill that is grinding once more.

LINTON

10 miles SE of Cambridge on the B1052

The village is best known for its zoo, but visitors will also find many handsome old buildings and the Church of St Mary the Virgin, built mainly in Early English style.

A world of wildlife set in 16 acres of spectacular gardens, **Linton Zoo** is a major wildlife breeding centre and part of the inter-zoo breeding programme for endangered species. Among the rare and exotic creatures to be seen are Grevy's zebra, snow leopards, tigers, lions, tapirs, lemurs, binturongs, owls, parrots, giant tortoises and tarantulas. The gardens also include picnic areas, a children's play area and, in summer, pony rides and a bouncy castle.

Chilford Hall Vineyard, on the B1052 between Linton and Balsham, comprises 18 acres of vines, with tours and wine-tastings available.

Some two miles further off the A1307, **Bartlow Hills** are the site of the largest Roman burial site to be unearthed in Europe.

HUNTINGDON

The former county town of Huntingdonshire is an ancient place first settled by the Romans. It boasts many grand Georgian buildings, including the handsome three-storeyed **Town Hall**.

Oliver Cromwell was born in Huntingdon in 1599 and attended Huntingdon Grammar School. The schoolhouse was originally part of the Hospital of St John the Baptist, founded during the reign of Henry II by David, Earl of Huntingdon. Samuel Pepys was also a pupil here.

Cromwell was MP for Huntingdon in the Parliament of 1629, was made a JP in 1630 and moved to St Ives in the following year. Rising to power as an extremely able military commander in the Civil War, he raised troops

from the region and made his headquarters in the Falcon Inn.

Appointed Lord Protector in 1653, Cromwell was ruler of the country until his death in 1658. The school he attended is now the **Cromwell Museum**, located on Huntingdon High Street, housing the only public collection relating specifically to him, with exhibits that reflect many aspects of his political, social and religious life. The museum's exhibits include an extensive collection of Cromwell family portraits and personal objects, among them a hat and seal, contemporary coins and medals, an impressive Florentine cabinet - the gift of the Grand Duke of Tuscany - and a surgeon's chest made by Kolb of Augsburg. This fine collection helps visitors interpret the life and legacy of Cromwell and the Republican movement.

All Saints Church, opposite the Cromwell Museum, displays many architectural styles, from medieval to Victorian. One of the

Hartford Marina, Huntingdon

About half a mile southwest of Huntingdon stands Hinchingbrooke House, which today is a school but which has its origins in the Middle Ages, when it was a nunnery (ghostly nuns are said to haunt the building to this day). The remains of the Benedictine nunnery can still be seen. It was given to the Cromwell family by Henry VIII in 1538. Converted by the Cromwell family in the 16th century and later extended by the Earls of Sandwich, it displays examples of every period of English architecture from the 12th to early 20th centuries. King James I was a regular visitor, and Oliver Cromwell spent part of his childhood here. The 1st Earl of Sandwich was a central figure in the Civil War and subsequent Restoration, while the 4th Earl (inventor of the lunchtime favourite that bears his name) was one of the most flamboyant politicians of the 18th century.

two surviving parish churches of Huntingdon (there were once 16), All Saints was considered to be the church of the Hinchingbrooke part of the Cromwell family, though no memorials survive to attest to this. The Cromwell family burial vault is contained within the church, however, and it is here that Oliver's father Robert and his grandfather Sir Henry are buried. The church has a fine chancel roof, a very lovely organ chamber, a truly impressive stained glass window and the font in which Cromwell was baptised, as it's the old font from the destroyed St John's church, discovered in a local garden in 1927!

Huntingdon's other important church, **St Mary's**, dates from Norman times but was almost completely rebuilt in the 13th century. It boasts a fine Perpendicular west tower, which partially collapsed in 1607. The damage was extensive, and the tower was not completely repaired until 1621. Oliver Cromwell's father Robert was one of two bailiffs who contributed to the cost of the repairs, as recorded on the stone plaque fixed to the east wall on the nave, north of the chancel arch.

Cowper House (No 29 High Street) has an impressive early 18th century frontage. A plaque commemorates the fact that the poet William Cowper (pronounced 'Cooper') lived here between 1765 and 1767. "Huntingdon is one of the neatest towns in England" wrote Cowper, so it's not surprising that he made it his home. Among

Huntingdon's many fine former coaching inns is the **George Hotel**. Although badly damaged by fire in 1865, the north and west wings of the 17th century courtyard remain intact, as does its very rare wooden gallery. The inn was one of the most famous of all the posting houses on the old Great North Run. It is reputed that Dick Turpin used one of the rooms here. The medieval courtyard, gallery and open staircase are the scene of annual productions of Shakespeare.

Along the south side of the Market Square, the Falcon Inn dates back in parts to the 1500s. Oliver Cromwell is said to have used this as his headquarters during the Civil War.

Huntingdon is twinned with Salon de Provence in France, Wertheim am Main in Germany and Szentendre in Hungary.

Hinchingbrooke Country Park covers 180 acres of grassy meadows, mature woodland, ponds and lakes. There is a wide variety of wildlife including woodpeckers, herons, kestrels, butterflies and foxes. The network of paths makes exploring the park easy, and battery-powered wheelchairs are provided for less able visitors. The Visitor Centre serves refreshments at peak times. Half a mile north of Hinchingbrooke, **Spring Common** offers another chance to enjoy some marvellous Cambridgeshire countryside. Covering 13 acres, its name comes from the natural spring that runs constantly and has long been a gathering place. The town developed around rather than within this area of rural tranquillity, which boasts a range of diverse habitats including marsh, grassland, scrub and streams. Plant life abounds, providing food and shelter for a variety of animals, amphibians, birds and invertebrates.

AROUND HUNTINGDON

BRAMPTON

2 miles SW of Huntingdon off the A1

Brampton is where Huntingdon racecourse is situated. An average of 18 meetings (all jumping) are scheduled every year, including Bank Holiday fixtures (extra-special deals for families). In November, the Grade II Peterborough Chase is the feature race.

Brampton's less speculative attractions include the 13th century church of St Mary, and Pepys House, the home of Samuel's uncle, who was a cousin of Lord Sandwich and who got Samuel his job at the Admiralty.

ALCONBURY

3 miles NW of Huntingdon off the A1

Fenland walks can be interspersed with pauses at the local inns and a look at the **Church of St Peter and St Paul**, whose steeple and chancel are particularly noteworthy. This long village has a large green, an ancient village pump and a 15th century bridge crossing the brook that runs through Alconbury.

BARHAM

6 miles W of Huntingdon off the A1/A14

This delightful hamlet boasts 12 houses and an ancient church with box pews, surrounded by undulating farmland. Nearby attractions include angling and sailing on Grafham Water, go-karting at Kimbolton and National Hunt racing at Huntingdon.

RAMSEY

9 miles NE of Huntingdon on the B1040

A pleasant market town with a broad main street down which a river once ran, Ramsey is home to the medieval **Ramsey Abbey**, founded in AD 969 by Earl Ailwyn as a Benedictine monastery. The Abbey became one of the most important in England in the 12th and 13th centuries, and as it prospered, so did Ramsey, so that by the 13th century it had become a town with a weekly market and an annual three-day festival at the time of the feast of St Benedict. After the Dissolution of the Monasteries in 1539, the Abbey and its lands were sold to Sir Richard Williams, great-grandfather of Oliver Cromwell. Most of the buildings

144 THE MANOR HOUSE

Alconbury, nr Huntingdon

A handsome hostelry with a fine reputation for its hospitality, home cooking and comfortable B&B rooms.

see page 297

Ramsey Abbey Gatehouse

Most of Ramsey Rural Museum is housed in an 18th century farm building and several barns set in open countryside. Among the many fascinating things to see are a Victorian home and school, a village store, and restored farm equipment, machinery, carts and wagons. The wealth of traditional implements used by local craftsmen such as the farrier, wheelwright, thatcher, dairyman, animal husbandman and cobbler offer an insight into bygone days. The Museum is open Thursday, Sunday and Bank Holiday afternoons between April and September.

were then demolished, the stones being used to build Caius, Kings and Trinity Colleges at Cambridge, the towers of Ramsey, Godmanchester and Holywell churches, the gate at Hinchingbrooke House and several local properties. In 1938 the house was converted for use as a school, which it remains to this day. To the northwest are the ruins of the once magnificent stone gatehouse of the late 15th century - only the porter's lodge remains, but inside can be seen an unusual large carved effigy made of Purbeck marble and dating back to the 14th century. It is said to represent Earl Ailwyn, founder of the Abbey. The gatehouse, now in the care of the National Trust, can be visited daily from April to October.

The **Church of St Thomas à Becket of Canterbury** forms an impressive vista at the end of the Ramsey High Street. Dating back to about 1180, it is thought to have been built as a hospital or guesthouse for the Abbey. It was converted, perhaps a century later, to a church to accommodate the many pilgrims who flocked to Ramsey. The church has what is reputed to be the finest nave in Huntingdonshire, dating back to the 12th century and consisting of seven bays. The church's other treasure is a 15th century carved oak lectern, thought to have come from the Abbey. Oliver Cromwell's uncle Sir Oliver is buried in the church.

The unusual **Ramsey War Memorial**, standing almost at the end of Church Green, is a listed

Grade II memorial consisting of a fine bronze statue of St George slaying the dragon atop a tall, octagonal pillar crafted of Portland stone.

UPWOOD
8 miles NE of Huntingdon off the B1040

Upwood is a pleasant, scattered village in a very tranquil and picturesque setting. Woodwalton Fen nature reserve is a couple of minutes' drive to the west.

SAWTRY
8 miles NW of Huntingdon on the A1

The main point of interest here has no point! **All Saints Church**, built in 1880, lacks both tower and steeple, and is topped instead by a bellcote. Inside the church are marvellous brasses and pieces from ancient Sawtry Abbey.

Just south of Sawtry, **Aversley Wood** is a conservation area with abundant birdlife and plants.

HAMERTON
9 miles NW of Huntingdon off the A1

Hamerton Zoological Park has hundreds of animals from tortoises to tigers. Specially designed enclosures make for unrivalled views of the animals, and the park features meerkats, marmosets and mongooses, lemurs, gibbons, possums and sloths, snakes and even creepy-crawlies such as cockroaches!

GREAT GIDDING
10 miles NW of Huntingdon off the B660

Stained-glass windows are a notable feature of **St Michael's Church** in this, the largest of the three Giddings. A fire ravaged the village in the 1860s and the church was one of the few buildings to survive. Today the church is the atmospheric setting for concerts and plays.

STILTON

12 miles NW of Huntingdon off the A1

Stilton has an interesting main street with many fine buildings, and is a good choice for the hungry or thirsty visitor, as it has been since the heyday of horse-drawn travel. Journeys were a little more dangerous then, and Dick Turpin is said to have hidden at the Bell Inn. The famous cheese is still produced and sold here.

ELLINGTON

4 miles W of Huntingdon off the A14

Ellington is a quiet village just south of the A14 and about a mile north of Grafham Water. Both Cromwell and Pepys visited, having relatives living in the village, and it was in Ellington that Pepys' sister Paulina found a husband, much to the relief of the diarist, who had written: 'We must find her one, for she grows old and ugly.' **All Saints Church** at Ellington is magnificent, like so many in the area, and among its many fine features are the 15th century oak roof and the rich carvings in the nave and the aisles. The church and its tower were built independently.

SPALDWICK

6 miles W of Huntingdon off the A14

A sizable village that was once the site of the Bishop of Lincoln's manor house, Spaldwick boasts the grand **Church of St James**, which dates from the 12th century and has seen restoration in most centuries, including the 20th, when the spire had to be partly rebuilt after being struck by lightning.

Two miles further west, **Catworth** is another charming village, regularly voted Best Kept Village in Cambridgeshire and well worth exploring.

KEYSTON

12 miles W of Huntingdon off the A14

A delightful village with a pedigree that can be traced back to the days of the Vikings, Keyston has major attractions both sacred and secular: the **Church of St John the Baptist** is impressive in its almost cathedral-like proportions, with one of the most magnificent spires in the whole county.

GRAFHAM

5 miles SW of Huntingdon on the B661

Created in the mid-1960s as a reservoir, **Grafham Water** offers a wide range of outdoor activities for visitors of all ages, with 1,500 acres of beautiful countryside, including the lake itself. The ten-mile perimeter track is great for jogging or cycling, and there's excellent sailing, windsurfing and fly-fishing. The area is a Site of Special Scientific Interest, and an ample nature reserve at the western edge is run jointly by Anglian Water and the Wildlife Trust. There are nature trails, information boards, a wildlife garden and a dragonfly pond. Bird-

145 THE MERMAID INN

Ellington, nr Huntingdon

A friendly village inn with traditional cooking and 2 spacious rooms for B&B guests.

see page 298

The gatehouse at Kimbolton Castle was added by Robert Adam in 1764. Henry VIII's first wife Catherine of Aragon spent the last 18 months of her life imprisoned here, where she died in 1536. She is buried in Peterborough Cathedral.

Buckden Towers

212

watchers have the use of six hides, three of them accessible to wheelchairs. An exhibition centre has displays and video presentations of the reservoir's history, a gift shop and a café.

KIMBOLTON

8 miles SW of Huntingdon on the B645

History aplenty here, and a lengthy pause is in order to look at all the interesting buildings. St Andrew's Church would head the list were it not for **Kimbolton Castle**, which, along with its gatehouse, dominates the village. Parts of the original Tudor building are still to be seen, but the appearance of the castle today owes much to the major remodelling carried out by Vanbrugh and Nicholas Hawksmoor in the first decade of the 18th century.

BUCKDEN

4 miles SW of Huntingdon on the A1

This historic village was an important coaching stop on the old Great North Road. It is known particularly as the site of **Buckden Towers**, the great palace built for the Bishops of Lincoln. In the splendid grounds are the 15th century gatehouse and the tower where Henry VIII imprisoned his first wife, Catherine of Aragon, in 1533 (open only on certain days of the year).

ST NEOTS

10 miles SW of Huntingdon off the A1

St Neots dates back to the founding of a Saxon Priory, built on the outskirts of Eynesbury in AD 974. Partially destroyed by the Danes in 1010, it was re-established as a Benedictine Priory in about 1081 by St Anselm, Abbot of Bec and later Archbishop of Canterbury. For the next two centuries the Priory flourished. Charters were granted by Henry I to hold fairs and markets. The first bridge over the Great Ouse, comprising 73 timber arches, was built in 1180. The name of the town comes from the Cornish saint whose remains were interred in the Priory some time before the Norman Conquest. With the Dissolution of the Monasteries, the Priory was demolished. In the early 17th century the old bridge was replaced by a stone one. This was then the site of a battle between the Royalists and Roundheads in 1648 - an event sometimes re-enacted by Sealed Knot societies.

St Neots repays a visit on foot, since there are many interesting sites and old buildings tucked away. The famous Market Square is one of the largest and most ancient in the country. A market has been held here every Thursday since the 12th century.

The magnificent parish **Church of St Mary the Virgin** is a very fine edifice, known locally as the Cathedral of Huntingdonshire. It is an outstanding example of Late Medieval architecture. The gracious interior complements the 130-feet Somerset-style tower, with a finely carved oak altar, excellent Victorian stained glass and a Holdich organ, built in 1855. **St Neots Museum** – opened in 1995 – tells the story of the town and the surrounding area. Housed in the former magistrates' court and police station, it still has the original cells. Eye-catching displays trace local history from prehistoric times to the present day. Open Tuesday to Saturday.

LITTLE PAXTON

2½ miles N of St Neots off the A1/A428

Fewer than three miles north of St Neots at Little Paxton is Paxton Pits Nature Reserve. Created alongside gravel workings, the Reserve attracts thousands of water birds for visitors to observe from hides. The wealth of wildlife means that the area is an SSSI (Site of Special Scientific Interest) and ensures a plethora of colour and activity all year round. The site also features nature trails and a visitors' centre. It has thousands of visiting waterfowl, including one of the largest colonies of cormorants, and is particularly noted for its wintering wildfowl, nightingales in late spring and kingfishers. There are about four miles of walks, some suitable for wheelchairs. Spring and summer also bring a feast of wildflowers, butterflies and dragonflies.

EYNESBURY

1 mile S of St Neots on the A428

Eynesbury is actually part of St Neots, with only a little stream separating the two. Note the 12th century **Church of St Mary** with its Norman tower. Rebuilt in the Early English period, it retains some well-preserved locally sculpted 14th century oak benches.

History has touched the quiet lovely village of Eynesbury from time to time: it was the home of the famous giant James Toller, who died in 1818 and is buried in the middle aisle of the church. Only 21 when he died, he measured some 8 feet tall - it is said he was buried here to escape the attention of body-snatchers, whose activities were widespread at the time. Eynesbury was also the birthplace of the Miles Quads, the first-ever surviving quadruplets in Britain.

BUSHMEAD

4 miles W of St Neots off the B660

The remains of **Bushmead Abbey**, once a thriving Augustinian community, are well worth a detour. The garden setting is delightful, and the surviving artefacts include some interesting stained glass. Open weekends in July and August.

GODMANCHESTER

2 miles SW of Huntingdon off the A1

Godmanchester is linked to Huntingdon by a 14th century bridge across the River Ouse. It was a Roman settlement and one that continued in importance down the years, as the number of handsome buildings testifies. One such is **Island Hall**, a mid-18th century mansion built for John Jackson, the Receiver General for Huntingdon; it contains many

147 THE ANCHOR

Little Paxton

Superb home cooking, including fish specials, bring appreciative crowds to **The Anchor**.

see *page 298*

148 PAXTON PITS NATURE RESERVE

Little Paxton

At Paxton Pits Nature Reserve you can enjoy gently strolls as well as longer walks.

see *page 298*

149 THE WHITE HART

Godmanchester

Fine dining, excellent service and a friendly, relaxed ambience in a superbly renovated coaching inn.

see *page 299*

Godmanchester

the First World War. Another site of considerable natural activity is **Godmanchester Pits**, accessed along the Ouse Valley Way and home to a great diversity of flora and fauna.

PAPWORTH EVERARD

6 miles S of Huntingdon on the A1198

One of the most recent of the region's churches, St Peter's dates mainly from the mid-19th century. Neighbouring **Papworth St Agnes** has an older church in St John's, though parts of that, too, are Victorian. Just up the road at Hilton is the famous **Hilton Turf Maze**, cut in 1660 to a popular medieval design.

BOXWORTH

7 miles SE of Huntingdon off the A14

A village almost equidistant from Huntingdon and Cambridge, and a pleasant base for touring the area, Boxworth's **Church of St Peter** is unusual in being constructed of pebble rubble.

A mile south of Boxworth is **Overhall Grove**, one of the largest elm woods in the country and home to a variety of wildlife.

THE GREAT OUSE VALLEY

HEMINGFORD ABBOTS

3 miles SE of Huntingdon off the A14

Once part of the Ramsey Abbey Estate, Hemingford Abbots is set around the 13th century church of St Margaret, along the banks of the Great Ouse. Opportunities for

Wood Green Animal Shelter at Kings Bush Farm, Godmanchester, is a purpose-built, 50-acre centre open to the public all year round. Cats, dogs, horses, donkeys, farm animals, guinea pigs, rabbits, llamas, red deer and ferrets are among the many creatures for visitors to see, and there is a specially adapted nature trail and restaurant.

interesting pieces. This family home has lovely Georgian rooms, with fine period detail and fascinating possessions relating to the owners' ancestors since their first occupation of the house in 1800. The tranquil riverside setting and formal gardens add to the peace and splendour - the house takes its name from the ornamental island that forms part of the grounds. Octavia Hill was sometimes a guest, and wrote effusively to her sister that Island Hall was 'the loveliest, dearest old house, I never was in such a one before.' Open only to pre-booked groups.

A footpath leads from the famous Chinese Bridge (1827) to **Port Holme Meadow**, at 225 acres one of the largest in England and the site of Roman remains. It is a Site of Special Scientific Interest, with a huge diversity of botanical and bird species. Huntingdon racecourse was once situated here, and it was a training airfield during angling and boating facilities, including rowing boats for hire, as well as swimming, country walks, golf and a recreation centre are all within a couple of miles. The village hosts a flower festival every two years. Just to the east of Hemingford Abbots is Hemingford Grey, with its church on the banks of the Ouse. **Hemingford Grey Manor** is reputedly the oldest continuously inhabited house in England, built around 1130. One of the owners was the author Lucy Boston, who used it as the house of Green Knowe in her children's books. This remarkable lady made a collection of exquisite patchworks, most of which are on display, and she also designed the garden, including topiary in the form of chess pieces in the garden. The garden is open daily, the house by appointment.

Hemingford Grey Manor

FENSTANTON

7 miles SE of Huntingdon off the A14 bypass

Capability Brown was Lord of the Manor from 1768, and he, his wife and his son are buried in the medieval church. Lancelot Brown (1716-1783) acquired his nickname from assuring innumerable clients that he could see the capabilities in their lands. He became head gardener and clerk of works at Stowe in 1741, where he helped in executing the designs of William Kent. He branched out on his own as an 'improver of gardens' in 1751, creating more than 140 splendid parks: Blenheim, Burghley and Badminton are among his many masterpieces – and that's just a few

of the Bs! Any visit here should also take in the 17th century manor house and the red-brick Clock Tower.

SWAVESEY

10 miles SE of Huntingdon off the A14

Look for the large 14th century church and the windmill a little way west, on the way to Fen Drayton, whose church is built of pebble rubble.

WYTON

2 miles E of Huntington off the A1123

Wyton is mentioned in the *Domesday Book* and is thought to have been founded in the 8th century. It is a popular tourist destination thanks to its proximity to **Houghton Mill** and opportunities for riverside walks, as well as its charming thatched buildings and shops. The large, impressive, timber-built water mill dates from the 17th century and is owned by the National Trust. Potto Brown, a Quaker merchant and non-conformist, was one of its famous millers. Milling days are

---

150 THE EXHIBITION

Over

A handsome inn with a fine reputation for food, drink and hospitality.

see page 300

151 SLEPE HALL

St Ives

A former Victorian girls'
boarding school is now a
splendidly appointed hotel
with all the modern
amenities.

 see page 301

152 FLOODS TAVERN

St Ives

A traditional pub with a
warm, friendly ambience,
real ales, decent wines and
great food.

see page 302

held on Sundays and Bank
Holidays.

HOUGHTON
5 miles E of Huntingdon on the A1123

Houghton Meadows is a Site of
Special Scientific Interest with an
abundance of hay meadow species.
One of the most popular walks in
the whole area links Houghton with
St Ives.

ST IVES
6 miles E of Huntingdon off the A1123

'As I was going to St Ives
I met a man with seven wives.
Each wife had seven sacks,
each sack had seven cats,
each cat had seven kits.
Kits, cats, sacks and wives,
how many were there going to St Ives?'

Just the story teller, of course,
but today's visitors are certain to
have a good time while they are
here.

This is an ancient town on the
banks of the Great Ouse which
once held a huge annual fair; it is
named after St Ivo, said to be a

Persian bishop who came here in
the Dark Ages to spread a little
light. In the Middle Ages, kings
bought cloth for their households
at the village's great wool fairs and
markets, and a market is still held
every Monday. The Bank Holiday
Monday markets are particularly
lively affairs, and the Michaelmas
fair fills the town centre for three
days.

Seagoing barges once navigated
up to the famous six-arched **River
Bridge** that was built in the 15th
century and has a most unusual
chapel in its middle: the two-storey
Chapel of St Leger is one of only
four surviving bridge chapels in the
country. Oliver Cromwell lived in
St Ives in the 1630s; his statue on
Market Hill, with its splendid hat, is
one of the village's most familiar
landmarks. It was made in bronze,
with a Portland stone base, and was
erected in 1901. It was originally
designed for Huntingdon, but they
wouldn't accept it!

The beautiful **All Saints
Church** in its yard beside the river
is well worth a visit. The quayside
provides a tranquil mooring for
holidaymakers and there are
wonderful walks by the riverside.

Clive Sinclair developed his tiny
TVs and pocket calculators in the
town, and another famous son of
St Ives was the great Victorian
rower John Goldie, whose name is
remembered each year by the
second Cambridge boat in the Boat
Race.

The **Norris Museum**, founded
in 1933 by the St Ives historian
Herbert Norris in a delightful

St Ives

setting by the river, tells the story of Huntingdonshire from the age of the dinosaurs to flint tools, Roman artefacts and Civil War armour, lace-making and ice-skating displays, and contemporary works of art. Exhibitions include a life-size replica of a 160-million-year-old ichthyosaur. There are remains of woolly mammoths from the Ice Ages, tools and pottery from the Stone Age to Roman times and relics from the medieval castles and abbeys. Also on show are toys and models made by prisoners of the Napoleonic Wars. Open all year; free admission.

River Bridge, St Ives

EARITH

4 miles E of St Ives on the A1123

The **Ouse Washes**, a special protection area, run northeast from the village to Earith Pits, a well-known habitat for birds and crawling creatures; some of the pits are used for fishing. The Washes are a wetland of major international importance supporting such birds as ruffs, Bewick and Whooper swans, and hen harriers. The average bird population is around 20,000. Some of the meadows flood in winter, and ice-skating is popular when the temperature really drops. There's a great tradition of ice-skating in the Fens, and Fenmen were the national champions until the 1930s.

WOODHURST

2 miles NE of St Ives off the B1040

The **Raptor Foundation** is a bird of prey rescue centre set in 20 acres of woodland and home to 300 birds of prey, mostly injured, orphaned or unwanted. Attractions include regular falconry displays, a flower garden, tea room, art gallery, craft village and picnic area. Nearby **Somersham** once had a palace for the Bishops of Ely, and its splendid Church of St John would have done them proud.

PETERBOROUGH

The second city of Cambridgeshire has a long and interesting history that can be traced back to the Bronze Age, as can be seen in the archaeological site at Flag Fen. Although a cathedral city, it is also a New Town (designated in 1967), so modern development and expansion have vastly increased its facilities while retaining the quality of its historic heart.

Peterborough's crowning glory is, of course, the Norman **Cathedral**, built in the 12th and 13th centuries on a site that had seen Christian worship since AD

Just outside St Ives are Wilthorn Meadow, a Site of Natural History Interest where Canada geese are often to be seen, and Holt Island Nature Reserve, where high-quality willow is being grown to reintroduce the traditional craft of basket-making. Take some time for spotting the butterflies, dragonflies and kingfishers.

Peterborough Cathedral

153 THE WHITE SWAN

Woodnewton, nr Oundle

A beautifully kept village inn with a welcome for all the family and a good choice of home cooking.

🍴 see page 302

154 ARCHIES

Oundle

Archies attracts lovers of good food from a wide area with its extensive choice of home-cooked dishes of worldwide inspiration.

🍴 see page 303

155 THE KINGS HEAD

Apethorpe, nr Peterborough

A fine old village inn with a high-class restaurant.

🍴 see page 303

museum at Wansford. A feature on the main railway line at Peterborough is the historic Iron Bridge, part of the old Great Northern Railway and still virtually as built by Lewis Cubitt in 1852.

Just outside the city, by the river Nene, is **Thorpe Meadows Sculpture Park**, one of several open spaces in and around the city with absorbing collections of modern sculpture.

AROUND PETERBOROUGH

LONGTHORPE

2 miles W of Peterborough off the A47

Longthorpe Tower, part of a fortified manor house, is graced by some of the very finest 14th century domestic wall paintings in Europe, featuring scenes both sacred and secular: the Nativity, the Wheel of Life, King David, the Labours of the Months. The paintings were discovered during renovations after the Second World War.

ELTON

6 miles SW of Peterborough on the B671

Elton is a lovely village on the river Nene, with stone-built houses and thatched roofs. **Elton Hall** is a mixture of styles, with a 15th century tower and chapel, and a major Gothic influence. The grandeur is slightly deceptive, as some of the battlements and turrets were built of wood to save money. The hall's sumptuous rooms are filled with art treasures (Gainsborough, Reynolds, Constable) and the library has a

655. Henry VIII made the church a cathedral, and his first queen, Catherine of Aragon, is buried here, as for a while was Mary Queen of Scots after her execution at Fotheringay. Features to note are the huge (85-feet) arches of the West Front, the unique painted wooden nave ceiling, some exquisite late 15th century fan vaulting, and the tomb of Catherine, who died at Kimbolton Castle.

Though the best-known of the city's landmarks, the Cathedral is by no means the only one. The **Peterborough Museum and Art Gallery** covers all aspects of the history of Peterborough from the Jurassic period to Victorian times.

There are twin attractions for railway enthusiasts in Peterborough in the shape of Railworld, a hands-on exhibition dealing with modern rail travel, and the wonderful Nene Valley Railway, which operates 15-mile steam-hauled trips between Peterborough and its HQ and wonderful collection of antique tomes.

THORNHAUGH

8 miles NW of Peterborough off the A1/A47

Hidden away in a quiet valley is **Sacrewell Farm and Country Centre**, whose centrepiece is a working watermill. All kinds of farming equipment are on display, and there's a collection of farm animals, along with gardens, nature trails and general interest trails, play areas, a gift shop and a restaurant serving light refreshments.

PEAKIRK

7 miles N of Peterborough off the A15

Peakirk boasts a village church of Norman origin that is the only one in the country dedicated to St Pega, the remains of whose hermit cell can still be seen.

CROWLAND

10 miles NE of Peterborough off the A1073

It is hard to imagine that this whole area was once entirely wetland and marshland, dotted with inhospitable islands. Crowland was one such island, then known as Croyland, and on it was established a small church and hermitage back in the 7th century, which was later to become one of the nation's most important monasteries. The town's impressive parish church was just part of the great edifice which once stood on the site. A wonderful exhibition can be found in the **Abbey** at Crowland, open all year round. The remains cover a third of the Abbey's original extent.

Crowland's second gem is the unique **Trinity Bridge** - set in the centre of town on dry land! Built in the 14th century, it has three arches built over one over-arching structure. Before the draining of the Fens, this bridge crossed the point where the River Welland divided into two streams.

THORNEY

8 miles E of Peterborough on the A47

Thorney Abbey, the **Church of St Mary and St Botolph**, is the dominating presence even though

156 THE SPADE & SHOVEL

Eye, nr Peterborough
A cheerful village pub appealing equally to locals and tourists.

see page 304

Crowland Abbey

Whittlesey was the birthplace of the writer L P Hartley (The Go Between) and of General Sir Harry Smith, hero of many 19th century campaigns in India. He died in 1860, and the south chapel of St Mary's Church (note the beautiful spire) was restored and named after him.

what now stands is but a small part of what was once one of the greatest of the Benedictine abbeys. Gravestones in the churchyard are evidence of a Huguenot colony that settled here after fleeing France in the wake of the St Bartholomew's Day massacre of 1572. The **Thorney Heritage Museum** is a small, independently-run museum of great fascination, describing the development of the village from a Saxon monastery, via Benedictine Abbey to a model village built in the 19th century by the Dukes of Bedford. The main innovation was a 10,000-gallon water tank that supplied the whole village; other villages had to use unfiltered river water.

WHITTLESEY

5 miles E of Peterborough off the A605

The market town of Whittlesey lies close to the western edge of the Fens and is part of one of the last tracts to be drained. Brick-making was a local speciality, and 180-feet brick chimneys stand as a reminder of that once-flourishing industry. The **Church of St Andrew** is mainly 14th century, with a 16th century tower; the chancel, chancel chapels and naves still have their original roofs.

A walk round this charming town reveals an interesting variety of buildings: brick, of course, and also some stone, thatch on timber frames, and rare thatched mud boundary walls.

Whittlesey Museum, housed in the grand 19th century Town Hall in Market Street, features an

archive of displays on local archaeology, agriculture, geology, brick-making and more. Reconstructions include a 1950s corner shop and post office, blacksmith's forge and wheelwright's bench.

A highlight of Whittlesey's year is the Straw Bear Procession that is part of a four-day January festival. A man clad in a suit of straw dances and prances through the streets, calling at houses and pubs to entertain the townspeople. The origins are obscure: perhaps it stems from pagan times when corn gods were invoked to produce a good harvest; perhaps it is linked with the wicker idols used by the Druids; perhaps it derives from the performing bears which toured the villages until the 17th century. What is certain is that at the end of the jollities the straw suit is ceremoniously burned.

FLAG FEN

6 miles E of Peterborough signposted from the A47 and A1139

Flag Fen Bronze Age Centre comprises massive 3,000-year-old timbers that were part of a major settlement and have been preserved in peaty mud. The site includes a Roman road with its original surface, the oldest wheel in England, re-creations of a Bronze Age settlement, a museum of artefacts, rare breed animals, and a visitor centre with a shop and restaurant. Ongoing excavations, open to the public, make this one of the most important and exciting sites of its kind.

MARCH

14 miles E of Peterborough off the A141

March once occupied the second-largest 'island' in the great level of Fens. As the land was drained the town grew as a trading and religious centre, and in more recent times as a market town and major railway hub. **March and District Museum**, in the High Street, tells the story of the people and the history of March and the surrounding area, and includes a working forge and a reconstruction of a turn-of-the-century home.

The uniquely dedicated **Church of St Wendreda**, at Town End, is notable for its magnificent timber roof, a double hammerbeam with 120 carved angels, a fine font and some impressive gargoyles. John Betjeman declared the church to be 'worth cycling 40 miles into a headwind to see'.

The **Nene-Ouse Navigation Link** runs through the town, affording many attractive riverside walks and, just outside the town off the B1099, Dunhams Wood comprises four acres of woodland set among the fens. The site contains an enormous variety of trees, along with sculptures and a miniature railway.

CHATTERIS

8 miles S of March off the A141

A friendly little market town, where the **Chatteris Museum and Council Chamber** features a series of interesting displays on Fenland life and the development of the town. Themes include education, agriculture, transport and local trades, along with temporary exhibitions and local photographs, all housed in five galleries.

The church of St Peter and St Paul has some 14th century features but is mostly more modern in appearance, having been substantially restored in 1909.

STONEA

3 miles SE of March off the B1098

Stonea Camp is the lowest 'hill'-fort in Britain. Built in the Iron Age, it proved unsuccessful against the Romans. A listed ancient monument whose banks and ditches were restored after excavations in 1991, the site is also an increasingly important habitat for wildlife.

WELNEY

4 miles SE of March off the A1101

The **Wildfowl & Wetlands Trust** in Welney is a nature reserve that attracts large numbers of swans and ducks in winter. Special floodlit 'swan evenings' are held, and there is also a wide range of wild plants and butterflies to be enjoyed.

WISBECH

One of the largest of the Fenland towns, a port in medieval times and still enjoying shipping trade with Europe, Wisbech is at the centre of a thriving agricultural region. The 18th century in particular saw the building of rows of handsome houses, notably in North Brink and South Brink, which face each other across the

157 THE ACRE

March

The Acre is a fine riverside inn open long hours every day for food and drink.

¶ see page 305

•

Wisbech is the stage for East Anglia's premier church flower festival, with flowers in four churches, strawberry teas, crafts, bric-a-brac, plants and a parade of floats. The event takes place at the beginning of July. The most important of the churches is the church of St Peter and St Paul, with two naves under one roof and an independent tower with a peal of ten bells. Note the royal arms of James I and the 17th century wall monuments in the chancel.

•

221

Wisbech

158 PECKOVER HOUSE & GARDEN

Wisbech

This lovely Georgian brick townhouse, built c. 1722, is renowned for its very fine plaster and wood rococo decoration.

 see page 303

river. The finest of all the properties is undoubtedly **Peckover House**, built in 1722 and bought at the end of the 18th century by Jonathan Peckover, a member of the Quaker banking family. The family gave the building to the National Trust in 1948. Behind its elegant brick façade are splendid panelled rooms, Georgian fireplaces with richly carved overmantels, and ornate plaster decorations. At the back of the house is a beautiful walled garden with summerhouses, a Victorian fernery, pond and rose garden and an orangery with 300-year-old orange trees.

No 1 South Brink Place is the birthplace of Octavia Hill (1838-1912), co-founder of the National Trust, campaigner for open spaces and a tireless worker for the cause of the poor, particularly in the sphere of housing. The house is now the **Octavia Hill's**

Birthplace House with displays and exhibits commemorating her work.

More Georgian splendour is evident in the area where the Norman castle once stood. The castle was replaced by a bishop's palace in 1478, and in the 17th century by a mansion built for Cromwell's Secretary of State, John Thurloe. Local builder Joseph Medworth built the present Regency villa in 1816; of the Thurloe mansion, only the gate piers remain.

The **Wisbech and Fenland Museum** is one of the oldest purpose-built museums in the country, and in charming Victorian surroundings visitors can view displays of porcelain, coins, rare geological specimens, Egyptian tomb treasures and several items of national importance, including the manuscript of Charles Dickens' *Great Expectations*, Napoleon's Sèvres breakfast set captured at Waterloo, and an ivory chess set that belonged to Louis XIV.

Another Wisbech attraction is the impressive 68-feet limestone memorial to Thomas Clarkson, one of the earliest leaders of the abolitionist movement. The **Clarkson Monument** was designed by Sir George Gilbert Scott in Gothic style.

Still a lively commercial port, Wisbech boasts a yacht harbour with facilities for small craft that include floating pontoons with berths for 75 yachts.

The **Angles Theatre** – one of the oldest working theatres in

Britain – is a vibrant centre for the arts located in a Georgian building with a history stretching back over 200 years. Some of the best talent in the nation, from poets and musicians to dance, comedy and theatrical troupes – come to perform in the intimate 112-seat auditorium.

Wisbech's **Lilian Ream Photographic Collection** is named after a daughter of Wisbech born in the late 19th century who at the time of her death in 1961 had amassed a collection of over 200,000 photographs of Wisbech people, places and events, making for a unique and fascinating insight into the history and culture of the town. The collection is housed in the Tourist Information Centre in Bridge Street, and offers changing exhibitions from this treasure trove of pictorial memorabilia.

On the B1101 between march and Wisbech in the village of Friday Bridge is a new family attraction: **Woodhouse Farm Park** is a genuine working farm where visitors can meet a wide variety of animals, including rabbits, guinea pigs, sheep, pigs, goats, horses, donkeys, peacocks, chickens and turkeys.

AROUND WISBECH

WEST WALTON AND WALTON HIGHWAY

3 miles NE of Wisbech off the A47/B198

Several attractions can be found here, notably the **Church of St Mary the Virgin** in West Walton with its magnificent 13th century detached tower that dominates the landscape. Walton Highway is home to the Fenland and West Norfolk Aviation Museum, whose exhibits include Rolls-Royce Merlin engines, a Lightning jet, a Vampire and a Jumbo jet cockpit simulator. The museum is open on summer weekends.

LEVERINGTON

1 mile NW of Wisbech off the A1101

The tower and spire of the **Church of St Leonard** date from the 13th and 14th centuries. The most exceptional feature of an exceptionally interesting church is the 15th century stained-glass Jesse window in the north aisle. There are many fine memorials in the churchyard. Oliver Goldsmith wrote *She Stoops to Conquer* while staying in Leverington.

PARSON DROVE

6 miles W of Wisbech on the B1187

Parson Drove is a Fenland village which Samuel Pepys visited in 1663. He stayed at the village's Swan Inn and mentions it in his diaries, though he was not complimentary. The village was a centre of the woad industry until 1914, when the last remaining woad mill was demolished. Parson Drove is most certainly not the 'heathen place' once described by Pepys!

Parson Drove Visitor Centre is set in the old Victorian lock-up on the village green, a building with an unusual 170-year history. Photographs and documents trace the story of this lovely Fenland village.

Sights to see in Wisbech include Elgoods Brewery, a classic Georgian brewery on the banks of the River Nene. Visitors can see traditional brewing methods and sample the excellent brews, savour award-winning ales and enjoy a walk in the four-acre garden, which includes a rockery and a maze planted with laurel and thuja.

223

Accommodation, Food & Drink and Places of Interest

The establishments featured in this section includes hotels, inns, guest houses, bed & breakfasts, restaurants, cafes, tea and coffee shops, tourist attractions and places to visit. Each establishment has an entry number which can be used to identify its location at the beginning of the relevant chapter or its position in this section.

In addition full details of all these establishments and many others can be found on the Travel Publishing website - www.travelpublishing.co.uk. This website has a comprehensive database covering the whole of Britain and Ireland.

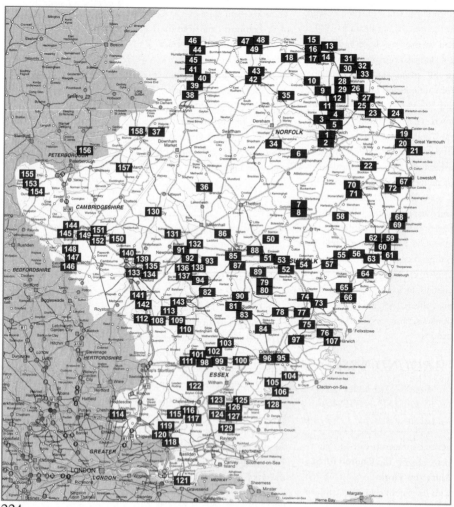

1 NORWICH CATHEDRAL

12 The Close, Norwich, Norfolk NR1 4DH
☎ 01603 218300

The splendour and tranquillity of **Norwich Cathedral** have attracted visitors and pilgrims for over 900 years.

The building remains a place of quiet reflection and prayer as well as for participation in daily worship or the rich pageantry of the Church's festivals.

For those with an interest in architecture, Norwich Cathedral boasts several superlatives. It is one of the finest complete Romanesque buildings in Europe. It has the second highest spire and largest monastic cloister in England.

The achievements of people, who have prayed, worked and even fought for their beliefs within its walls, live on. Bishop Herbert de Losinga, who began building the Cathedral in 1096, Sir Thomas Erpingham, whose archers secured victory for Henry V at the Battle of Agincourt, and more recently Nurse Edith Cavell, who was executed during WW I for helping prisoners of war to escape, are all buried here. They contribute their part to the living history of Norwich Cathedral.

The Cathedral Close is the largest in England (44 acres). This oasis of tranquillity nestles as a village in the heart of the city. Here can be found a rich mix of domestic buildings ranging from Norman to Dutch gables, flinted frame cottages and Georgian terracing. The Close is often used as a location for period drama.

2 DRAGON HALL

115-123 King Street, Norwich, NR1 1QE
☎ 01603 663 922
e-mail: info@dragonhall.org
🌐 www.dragonhall.org

Dragon Hall is a Grade 1 listed medieval trading hall and one of Norwich's most important historic buildings. It was built as a showroom and warehouse by a wealthy merchant called Robert Toppes around 1430.

Over the following 600 years many changes took place. By the 20th century the magnificent timber roof frame of the hall had been hidden from view in the attics of a row of terraced houses.

Dragon Hall has now been fully restored and developed. The timber-framed roof of the Great Hall is one of the most spectacular in Europe and Dragon Hall gets its name from a beautiful carved and painted dragon in the roof timbers. The ground floor rooms show how the building was later split into separate dwellings. Underground, in the cellars and undercroft, there is evidence of a thousand years of human history.

Visitors can enjoy the wonders of this unique building and discover its fascinating history through individual audio tours, group guided tours, interactive displays and a dragon trail for children. A new extension houses modern facilities and a lift to the first floor whilst a stunning new contemporary glass extension creates a Gallery overlooking the courtyard garden. Dragon Hall is fully accessible, apart from the cellars which are reached by steep steps.

Opening hours: Monday – Saturday, 10am–5pm (last admission 4pm)

3 BECKLANDS GUEST HOUSE

105 Holt Road, Horsford, nr Norwich,
Norfolk NR10 3AB
☎ 01603 898582
e-mail: becklands@aol.com

A friendly, welcoming owner, good personal service, comfortable bedrooms and a pleasant village setting bring guests back year after year to **Becklands Guest House**. The redbrick villa, which stands in neat, well-kept gardens, has eight graciously appointed guest bedrooms, tastefully and comfortably furnished; two are located on the ground floor. The house has a charming, spacious residents' lounge where guests can relax after a day's sightseeing and plan their next day's outings. Angela Magnus sets guests off with a heart breakfast and plenty of information on what to see and do in the area. Away from the bustle of Norwich, it's nonetheless within an easy drive and an ideal base for exploring the numerous attractions of the city.

Many other places of interest are easily reached, including Caldicott Horse Sanctuary, the charming Bure Valley Railway and Blickling Hall. With Norwich Airport nearby, Becklands is also an ideal choice for travellers and business people. The airport is home to the fascinating City of Norwich Aviation Museum, a must for anyone who wants to find out all about the history of flying in Norfolk.

Horsham St Faith, nr Norwich,
Norfolk NR10 3JP
☎ 01603 898911
⊕ www.kingsheadhorshamstfaith.co.uk

Brown tourist signs lead from the A140 to the City of Norwich Aviation Museum, an attraction that brings visitors in their thousands throughout the year. Close by, in the village of Horsham St Faith, is another popular place to visit. The **Kings Head** is a delightful pub dating from the early 17th century. The frontage, on an easy-to-find corner site, is adorned in summer with hanging baskets, and inside it's equally appealing. The locals love it, and visitors to Norwich and its northern surrounds are also beginning to appreciate the friendly ambience created by owners Alli Hall and Mandy Proctor and their staff. The busy public bar is a cheerful spot for enjoying a drink and a chat with the regulars – Adnams Brewery provides the resident real

ales – and in the two little dining areas good honest food is served at kind prices in generous platefuls. Across-the-board menus provide plenty of choice, and diners can end their meal in style with something scrumptious like chocolate fudge cake or butterscotch bananas. Food times are from 12 to 3pm and 7pm to 9.30pm Monday to Saturday and 12.30 to 3pm Sunday. The pub has a pleasant little beer garden and good off-road parking.

5 CITY OF NORWICH AVIATION MUSEUM 🏛

Old Norwich Road, Horsham St Faiths,
Norwich, Norfolk NR10 3JF
☎ 01603 893080

Follow the brown tourist signs from the A140 Norwich-Cromer road to find the **City of Norwich Aviation Museum**, a museum dedicated to keeping Norfolk's aviation heritage alive. Dominating the museum's collection is a massive Avro Vulcan bomber, a veteran of the Falklands War of 1982.

Eight other military and civilian aircraft are on show, and although they are the main attraction for many visitors, the most fascinating feature is the display within the main exhibition building showing the development of aviation in Norfolk. From the pioneering days of aviation to present-day civilian and military operations, every aspect is covered in a number of displays that are constantly being revised and expanded.

The major roles played by Norfolk-based aircraft during the great air battles of World War II are remembered by exhibitions on the USAAF 8th Air Force and the role of the Royal Air Force in this conflict.

A special section is dedicated to the operations of RAF Bomber Command's 100 Group which flew on electronic counter measure, deception and night intruder missions from a number of Norfolk airfields.

HIDDEN PLACES GUIDES

Explore Britain and Ireland with *Hidden Places* guides - a fascinating series of national and local travel guides.

Packed with easy to read information on hundreds of places of interest as well as places to stay, eat and drink.

Available from both high street and internet booksellers

For more information on the full range of *Hidden Places* guides and other titles published by Travel Publishing visit our website on

www.travelpublishing.co.uk
or ask for our leaflet by phoning
01752 276660 or emailing
info@travelpublishing.co.uk

7 THE WATERFRONT INN 🍴 🛏

43 Mere Street, Diss, Norfolk IP32 4AG
☎ 01379 652695
e-mail: 6516@greeneking.co.uk
⊕ www.greeneking.com

The **Waterfront** is a friendly Greene King public house in a prime position in Sir John Betjeman's favourite Norfolk town. It is open all day, every day, and food is served until 10 o'clock Sunday to Thursday and until 7 Friday and Saturday. A DJ does his stuff on Friday evenings, and there's a karaoke night every other Thursday. The Waterfront owes its name to The Mere, and in fine weather a decked area with plenty of tables and chairs is a pleasant spot overlooking this six-acre lake.

229

6 THE WYMONDHAM CONSORT HOTEL

28 Market Square, Wymondham,
Norfolk NR18 0BB
☎ 01953 606721

No hotel member group has more experience than Best Western, with more than 300 hotels worldwide, and that experience shows in every outlet. **Wymondham Consort Hotel** is no exception, priding itself justifiably on offering comfort, amenities and top-quality service with a personal touch from managers John and Rose Marie Bryer and their staff.

Occupying a prime site in the centre of the historic town of Wymondham, the 18th century redbrick residence has been transformed into an elegant townhouse hotel providing all the facilities expected by today's clientele. It's equally well set up for leisure and business guests, whether they are here for an overnight stop or a longer stay, and the well-appointed en suite bedrooms, including some on the ground floor with access for guests with mobility difficulties, offer every comfort; some rooms have queen-size beds, while some others boast four-posters. The informal, relaxing Café and Wine Bar, open all day, every day, is a pleasant place to meet for a drink – perhaps a beer, a glass of wine or a cocktail – and enjoy a good variety of Mediterranean-style dishes. It's also a favourite spot for local residents and business people to take a break from the day's engagements.

For diners in the hotel's restaurant, the chefs prepare a first-class choice of dishes to cater for all tastes and appetites: some dishes are old favourites, such as garlicky prawns or succulent steaks, while others are less familiar but equally tempting, like beef stifado of Greek inspiration, a house special chicken dish with garlic, rosemary and white wine, or an exotic red snapper with egg noodles and a sweet chilli and citrus sauce.

Residents can stroll in the hotel's garden or enjoy a walk along the River Tiffey, and the town of Wymondham itself is well worth taking time to explore. Among the sights not to be missed are the magnificent Abbey, the Market Cross (Friday is market day), Becket's Chapel, the Heritage Museum in the old House of Correction and the splendidly restored railway station, built in 1845 on the Great Eastern Railway's Norwich-Ely line. There are many other places of interest in the vicinity, and the fine city of Norwich is only a 15-minute drive away.

8 THE PARK HOTEL

**29 Denmark Street, Diss,
Norfolk IP22 4LE**

☎ 01379 642244 Fax: 01379 644218

e-mail: info@parkhotel-diss.co.uk

www.parkhotel-diss.co.uk

Ideally located on the Norfolk Suffolk border, ideal for exploring the Waveney Valleys and the Norfolk Broads, **The Park Hotel** is in the perfect position, within walking distance of the historic bustling market town of Diss.

The ideal venue to meet up with friends, family or colleagues, the privately owned Park Hotel has an informal atmosphere, friendly staff and an abundance of wines, beers, spirits and coffees, plus English & Continental food.

A combination of three old and new buildings home 19 bedrooms, all recently refurbished to create warm and welcoming accommodation. All rooms are en-suite with colour TV, hairdryers, ironing facilities, hospitality tray & complimentary products. Ground floor rooms are available upon request.

Along side our informal bar, we have introduced a fine dining experience, situated within the Hotel with a recently restored fireplace and original oak flooring. Our menu reflects our passion for fresh foods, and where possible fresh local produce. In addition to a selection of traditional dishes, we can cater for a more discerning palate with a varying menu to accommodate seasonal changes and interesting food combinations ~ Traditional food with a contemporary twist.

We can cater for private dining to large corporate events within our selection of onsite function rooms.

We are open for breakfast, lunch and dinner. Children are welcome. All major credit cards are accepted. For the comfort of our guests, this is a non-smoking hotel.

Real Food ~ Real People ~ Real Prices

9 THE OLD PUMP HOUSE

2 Holman Road, Aylsham,
Norfolk NR11 6BY
☎ 01263 733789
e-mail: theoldpumphouse@btconnect.com
🌐 www.theoldpumphouse.com

The **Old Pump House** is a delightful retreat for those who appreciate quality, a comfortable, characterful Georgian house standing in fine mature gardens and grounds close to the market square in Aylsham. Built some 250 years ago, it was originally a farmhouse and later saw life as a boarding school and a rectory. It takes its name from the historic thatched town pump that still stands nearby. The resident hosts are Charles Kirkman, formerly a banker, and Marc James, ex-antiques dealer. Both also had careers in the luxury hotel business and they put that experience to excellent use in this civilised, refined house. Sympathetically restored and traditionally appointed in keeping with its age and pedigree, the house has five superb guest bedrooms, totally refurbished at the beginning of 2007, with en suite bathrooms, LCD televisions, alarm clock-radios, tea/coffee making facilities and hairdryers. Quality is the keynote throughout, and the finest local produce is the basis of the excellent breakfasts cooked to order and served in the elegant pine-shuttered Georgian Room overlooking the lovely tranquil garden and pond. Evening meals are available with a little notice. The house lies within easy reach of many places of interest in the region. Aylsham is at the northern end of the narrow-gauge Bure Valley Railway, which runs down to Wroxham by way of Brampton, Buxton and Coltishall. The magnificent 17th century Blickling Hall, with grounds landscaped by Humphry Repton, is close by, and two other stately homes, Mannington and Wolterton Park, are a short drive away. Norwich is less than half an hour's drive away, and it's a similar drive to the Norfolk Broads and the North Norfolk coast at Cromer.

The Common, Itteringham, nr Norwich,
Norfolk NR11 7AR
☎ 01263 587258
e-mail: goodfood@thewalpolearms.co.uk
🌐 www.thewalpolearms.co.uk

The owners' philosophy that enjoying fine food and wine should be an adventure, a voyage of discovery, is shared by the discerning diners who have declared the **Walpole Arms** one of the very best eating places in the region. Tucked away down the little lanes of North Norfolk in a village signposted off the B1354, this handsome redbrick pub started life in the 17th century as a farmhouse. The pub is owned and run by Richard Bryan and Keith Reeves, both long-term Norfolk residents. Richard is a writer and broadcaster who for 10 years produced the popular TV *Masterchef* series, while Keith is a wine merchant with contacts to many top restaurants. Their obvious passion for food and drink is shared by head chef Andy Parle and his talented team. Andy's CV includes spells at top restaurants Adlard's in Norwich and Le Pont de la Tour by the Thames in London. Together they

have made the Walpole Arms the leading pub restaurant in the region and the winner of numerous awards. These include East Anglia Dining Pub of the Year from Les Routiers, Country Pub of the Year in the Norfolk Food Awards and Bib Gourmand from Michelin every year since 2003. Andy's

menus showcase the very finest Norfolk produce – fruit and vegetables, seafood and game: mussels come from Morston, the game is reared, slaughtered and hung at Gunton Hall. Typical dishes – the choice changes constantly – include braised lamb shanks, Gloucester Old Spot pork pie, sea bass with a saffron mash, paella and Oriental specials. A well-chosen wine list complements the outstanding food at this gem of a dining pub. The Walpole Arms also fulfils its traditional role as a village local, and in the cosy oak-beamed public bar or outside in the spacious landscaped garden regulars and visitors enjoy Adnams Bitter and Broadside, Woodfordes Wherry, Walpole Ale and a wide variety of other beers, wines and bar snacks.

11 THE OLD CROWN

Buxton, nr Aylsham, Norfolk NR10 5EN
☎ 01603 279958
e-mail: burnhamalison@hotmail.com

Alison and Tony Burnham are the affable hosts at the **Old Crown**, which stands at Buxton on the B1354, which runs from Aylsham through to Coltishall and Wroxham. Alison was previously in adult education and Tony can teach anyone about keeping great ale. Starting life as a dairy farmhouse in the 17th century, it was converted to a pub by the Coltishall Brewery in the following century. The two comfortable bars provide a delightful atmosphere for meeting or making friends over a glass of Woodfordes Wherry, Adnams Bitter, Old Speckled Hen or a regularly changing guest ale. The bars are open every day of the week, and food is served in the neat, cosy little restaurant from 12 to 2 and 6 to 9, and from 12 to 3 for the traditional Sunday roasts. The home-cooked dishes appeal to all tastes, with familiar favourites to the fore: beef & onion pie, steak & Guinness pie, chilli con carne,

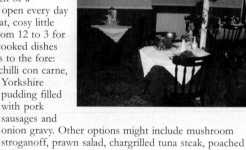

Yorkshire pudding filled with pork sausages and

onion gravy. Other options might include mushroom stroganoff, prawn salad, chargrilled tuna steak, poached halibut and a classic lamb Guard of Honour. Mondays are quiz-and-pizza nights and Thursday is steak night, with fillet, sirloin or rump with mushrooms, chips, peas, onion rings fried in the special house batter and a choice of creamy sauces. The Old Crown has a beer garden and ample off-road parking.

12 THE GOAT INN

Long Road, Skeyton, nr Aylsham,
Norfolk NR10 5DH
☎ 01692 538600
🌐 www.skeytongoatinn.co.uk

Mother and daughter Jo and Judie, along with Jem and Steve, create a particularly friendly, relaxed ambience at the **Goat Inn & Restaurant**. Their smiles and obvious enthusiasm contribute greatly to the enjoyment of a visit to this well-known pub, which is equally popular with the good folk of North Norfolk and with the many tourists who pass this way. The picture-postcard frontage of the 16th century thatched inn promises much, and the Goat's interior does not disappoint, its several rooms decorated and furnished in keeping with the building's age.

Real ales from Adnams and Woodfordes Breweries are on tap to quench thirsts in the bar, and a fine selection of home-cooked food in the restaurant with its big brick hearth from 12 to 2 (to 3 on Saturday) and from 6 o'clock, all day on Sunday. Typical choices run from whitebait to burgers, beer-battered cod, smoked haddock with mustard sauce and a poached egg, poached salmon with a Cajun sauce, lasagne, lamb hot pot, beef or mushroom stroganoff and T-bone steak. Two Sundays a month give visitors the chance to show their versatility: brainpower comes to the fore for the quiz on the first Sunday of the month, while vocal chords get exercised at the karaoke sessions on the last Sunday of the month. The pub's six-acre grounds off the A140 north of Aylsham includes a large garden with a terrace and children's play area, and an approved site for touring caravans and tents. A vast marquee can be hired for functions, parties and receptions, with room for up to 150 seated or 250 buffet-style.

235

13 BON VISTA GUEST HOUSE

12 Alfred Road, Cromer,
Norfolk NR27 9AN
☎ 01263 511818
e-mail: jim@bonvista-cromer.co.uk
🌐 www.bonvista-cromer.co.uk

Bon Vista Guest House is a comfortable Victorian building close to the seafront at the West Cliff end of Cromer. Tastefully renovated to retain many of the best original features, the house has five guest bedrooms – three doubles, a family room and a superior room with one superking or two twin beds; all have en suite facilities, television and beverage tray. Cromer has a wide variety of attractions for the visitor, including golden sands, the delightful pier, golf, cycling, fossil collecting, birdwatching and amazing sea views; within a short drive the area has many more places of interest, among them the National Trust properties of Felbrigg Hall, Blickling Hall and Sheringham Park. Bon Vista, which is open all year round, is a comfortable, quiet and civilised base for discovering all that this lovely part of Norfolk has to offer.

14 THE ROMAN CAMP INN

Holt Road, Aylmerton, nr Cromer,
Norfolk NR11 8QD
☎ 01263 838291

For more than 10 years Vanessa Wright has been welcoming a true mix of regulars to the **Roman Camp Inn** – singles, couples, families, senior citizens – as well as tourists and holidaymakers. The inn has a busy, lively public bar, a comfortable lounge with huge sofas and a feature fireplace, and a smartly appointed restaurant with intimate lighting, panelling and some modern stained glass. Outside are a garden, patio and huge car park. Traditional and contemporary cuisine, with everything freshly prepared on the premises, covers a fine range of appealing dishes on the regular menu and daily specials board: whole grilled codling, smoked salmon & prawn cocktail, chicken skewers with a satay sauce, steaks, beef stroganoff, minted lamb burger, chicken

breast served on a herb risotto with a

sun-dried tomato sauce. For visitors looking for a comfortable base for touring North Norfolk, the inn has 16 letting bedrooms, all with en suite facilities, two with access for wheelchairs. The location, south of Sheringham off the main A148 Cromer-Holt road, puts many of the area's top places of interest in easy reach, including Cromer, East and West Runton, the Norfolk Shire Horse Centre and the National Trust's Felbrigg Hall.

15 FAIRLAWNS GUEST HOUSE

26 Hooks Hill Road, Sheringham,
Norfolk NR26 8NL
☎ 01263 824717
e-mail: info@fairlawns-sheringham.co.uk

Tourists, holidaymakers, walkers, cyclists, birdwatchers, golfers......all are welcome at **Fairlawns Guest House**, where Anne and Phil Race are the most welcoming of hosts.

Attention to detail is evident throughout, from the traditionally appointed sitting room and the bright conservatory restaurant, where an excellent breakfast is served, to the five outstanding en suite bedrooms. Each has its own appeal, and all have television with DVD, internet connection, telephone and beverage tray. The late-Victorian building, only half a mile from the sea, has a large garden where guests can stroll, sit and relax, enjoy a drink or try their hand at croquet or putting.

16 NORTH NORFOLK RAILWAY

Sheringham Station, Sheringham,
Norfolk NR26 8RA
☎ 01263 820800
e-mail: enquiries@nnrailway.com
⊕ www.nnr.co.uk

When the Midland & Great Northern Joint Railway was extended from Holt to Sheringham and Cromer in 1887, it gave birth to the tourist industry in North Norfolk. Over a hundred years later, much remains the same. The views of coast and country are as breathtaking as ever. Poppies still flaunt their scarlet beauty every summer. And the Poppy Line, successor to the M&GN, carries thousands of visitors each year on one of the most scenic steam heritage railways in Britain – a 5.5 mile trip from Sheringham along the coast to Weybourne and up through the heathland to Holt.

17 PRETTY CORNER TEA GARDENS

Upper Sheringham, Norfolk NR26 8TW
☎ 01263 822766
e-mail: lmpadfield@aol.com
⊕ www.prettycorterteagardens.co.uk

What started in 1926 as a modest wooden pavilion has developed down the years into a popular café and tea garden that's a favourite with walkers,

cyclists, motorists, families, children and dogs. The menu at **Pretty Corner**, making use of fresh local ingredients, includes sandwiches, toasties, wraps, jacket potatoes, salads, chilli, daily specials and a choice for vegetarians and children. Home-made cakes, scones and desserts should definitely not be missed, and the excellent food is accompanied by a selection of hot and cold drinks. When the sun shines, patrons can enjoy their food out on the patio or in the garden. In cooler times the scene moves into the tea room, where a wood-fired stove keeps things cosy and works of art by talented local artists are on display and for sale. Walkers

can enjoy the many trails available through the woodland area surrounding the café where children can look at the varied pondlife and wildlife and meet the cute Pekin bantam hens.

18   LETHERINGSETT WATERMILL 🏛

Riverside Road, Letheringsett, Holt,
Norfolk NR25 7YD
☎ 01263 713153

In the attractive village of Letheringsett is a fully functional water powered Flour Mill generally accepted to be the only producing one in Norfolk. You are invited to visit this outstanding part of working Norfolk history.

The Norfolk red brick Mill was built in 1802 on a Doomsday site. Until 1982 when restoration work was started, the Mill was slowly falling into disrepair The miller and his staff would like to welcome you to see their skills of making flour using this traditional method on their demonstration days (see back cover for details) when the miller will give a running commentary. If however you would prefer to visit the mill when standing idle you are more than welcome.

Staff are always on hand and ready to answer any of your Questions - we are proud to share our interest and knowledge. Before you leave perhaps you would like to purchase some of the flour you have seen being made during your visit or browse in our Gift Shop.

The Ducks outside are always hungry!

19   VILLA-ROSE HOTEL

30-31 Princes Road, Great Yarmouth,
Norfolk NR30 2DG
☎ 01493 844748 mob: 07887607624
e-mail: maxrockach@aol.com
🌐 www.villarosehotel.co.uk

Max Rockach offers a delightful home for home for guests at **Villa-Rose**. Situated just moments from the seafront and the shops, this warm, friendly place provides high standards of quality and comfort, and the bedrooms, all en suite, are equipped with remote-control TV, tea/coffee tray and hairdryer.

Guests can take their ease and plan their days in the lounge, and in the spacious dining room a daily changing menu offers plenty of choice of generously served home-cooked food.

21   GREAT YARMOUTH ROW HOUSES 🏛

Great Yarmouth, Norfolk NR30 2RQ
☎ 01493 857900
🌐 www.english-heritage.org.uk

Experience the sights and sounds of yesterday's Great Yarmouth. Visit these unique and vividly-presented houses, one set in c.1870 and the other in 1942, just before incendiary bombing. Find out how Yarmouth's 'Herring Girls' lived, hear an original BBC wartime broadcast and

'Mr Rope's sea shanties'. See the amazing collection of artefacts rescued from Row houses after World War II bombing, and contrast tenement conditions with 'respectable' merchant's interiors.

Open daily April to September

20 THE RUMBOLD ARMS

107 Southtown Road, Great Yarmouth,
Norfolk NR31 0JX
☎ 01493 653887
e-mail: info@therumboldarms.co.uk
🌐 www.therumboldarms.co.uk

Owners Robert & Matt put their many years experience in the catering and hospitality business at the **Rumbold Arms**. Situated by the harbour in Great Yarmouth, this sociable pub has a strong local following and also provides a pleasant place for visitors to the town. In the roomy bar area or outside on the patio or lawn (heated canopy due late 2007), patrons can enjoy a drink or something to eat

from the regularly changing menu. Home-smoked produce are available (cheese, kippers, haddock, salmon, sausages etc – also for takeaway) and Thursday night's curry specials are great favourites with every dish freshly cooked to order using authentic Indian recipes. Other choices run from baguettes, home made dishes and light meals to our Sunday carvery and the hunger busting Rumbold Pigout Combo Meal or of course an excellent steak! Drinks include a wide selection of soft drinks, good selection of lagers, bitters, Guinness, constantly changing Real Ales, malt whiskies and an expertly chosen wine list. The Pub has a self contained function room that's a popular venue for a party or any special occasion. The pub's name commemorates Charles Edward Rumbold, a keen supporter of the 1832 Reform Act that was the basis of modern democracy.

22 THE GARDEN HOUSE

Yarmouth Road, Hales,
Norfolk NR14 6SX
☎ 01508 548468
e-mail: info@halesgardenhouse.co.uk
🌐 www.halesgardenhouse.co.uk

The **Garden House** re-opened its doors in April 2007 after top-to-toe refurbishment. Hosts Michael Thomas and Katie Lawes are attracting plenty of local support, and the pub's position near Beccles, just off the A146 Lowestoft-Norwich road, makes it a popular place for tourists to pause for refreshment. The bar and restaurant are separated by a feature woodburning stove, and when the sun shines the large garden really comes into its own. The lunchtime menu comprises sandwiches, toasties, jacket potatoes and pub classics such as beer-battered cod and haddock, scampi, home-cooked ham & eggs, chilli, lasagne and steak, ale & mushroom pie; on Sunday the

carvery always brings in the crowds. The evening menu offers a good selection of starters and an expanded choice of traditional main courses. The Garden House is open lunchtime and evening Monday to Saturday and all day Sunday. Monday is quiz night.

23 THE KINGS ARMS

High Street, Ludham, Norfolk NR29 5QQ
☎ 01692 678386 Fax: 01692 678188
e-mail: kingsarmsludham@hotmail.com
🌐 www.kingsarmsludham.co.uk

In a sleepy village a short walk from Womack Staith, the **Kings Arms** is a convivial Broads pub serving a fine variety of cooked-to-order dishes in the bar and the new 80-cover restaurant. The choice runs from hot baguettes, burgers and jacket potatoes to fish specials, pasta, pizza, steaks, garlic chicken, the pie of the day, the Sunday carvery and spicy Mexican, Cajun and Indonesian dishes.  Look up and you'll see a model train rushing round the restaurant among the ceiling beams. The pub has wheelchair access to the restaurant and toilets, and baby-changing facilities. Outside is an area where children can romp in safety.

24 THE LION

West Somerton, nr Great Yarmouth,
Norfolk NR29 4DP
☎ 01493 393289

Hosts Tony and Tracy welcome guests to **The Lion**, a friendly village pub situated five minutes' walk from Somerton Staith and just a mile from the coast. At the heart of the local community, it has a traditionally appointed bar (pool and darts teams play in the local leagues) and a lounge/ dining area where classic pub dishes make good use of seasonal  local produce. The Lion has outdoor seating for the summer and ample car parking. The pub is open 7 days a week 12-3pm and 6pm-11pm (closed Monday lunchtime).

25 THE WHITE HORSE

The Street, Neatishead, nr Wroxham,
Norfolk NR12 8AD
☎ 01692 630828
e-mail: matt_nudd@hotmail.com

In a little village off the A1151 on the edge of the Broads, Matt Nudd is the long-time host at the **White Horse**. Very much a locals' favourite, it also provides a perfect opportunity for visitors to the Broads to enjoy the character and atmosphere of a real pub-lover's pub. The little slate-floored bars and dining area  are delightful spots to make friends over a glass of real ale or to settle down to a home-cooked meal based on prime local produce. The pub has its own moorings a short walk away.

26 THE NEW INN

Front Street, Worstead, Norfolk   NR28 9RW
☎ 01692 536296
e-mail: Kevin@worstead.co.uk

The **New Inn** is a particularly friendly, convivial pub with an affable, enthusiastic landlord in Kevin Uglow. It's very much at the social heart of Worstead, a famous little village 12 miles northeast of Norwich off the A149 or B1150. Kevin is a beer devotee who takes great pride in his ales, which usually include brews from Deuchars and Adnams as well as regularly changing guests. The

little bar with its feature fireplace and the small side lounge are the perfect spots for enjoying a chat with the locals over a glass or two, and in the equally appealing dining area home-cooked dishes feature prominently on across-the-board menus. All the familiar favourites appear, from sausages and steaks to salmon, chicken and the ever-popular Sunday roasts. The pub is open from 12 to 3 and from 6.30 Monday to Friday and all day Saturday and Sunday. It hosts quiz nights on Wednesdays – monthly in summer, every two months in winter – and occasional karaoke evenings.

Worstead was once a busy little industrial centre that gave its name to the hardwearing cloth made in the region. Many of the weavers' cottages still stand in the narrow side streets, and

the grand 14th century Church of St Mary is evidence of the town's former prosperity. The still-active Guild of Weavers has placed some old looms in the north aisle of the church and from time to time organises demonstrations of the ancient skill of weaving.

Each July the village stages a weekend of events to raise money for the upkeep of the church. This event brings many thousands of visitors to the village, many of whom also visit the church and the New Inn, where Kevin, his staff and his lovable rescue dog Pumpkin keep out the welcome mat throughout the year.

241

The Street, Dilham, Norfolk NR28 9PS
☎ 01692 536398

The **Cross Keys** occupies a prominent position on the main street of Dilham, a pleasant Norfolk village just off the A149 six miles northeast of North Walsham. Sheila and Trevor Hardingham fell in love with the place and made their dreams come true when they took over the lease early in 2003. Their enthusiasm is clearly infectious, as they have built up a large and loyal following for their pub, as a local meeting place, a pleasant stop for travellers and tourists and as a popular choice for a function or special celebration. Easy to spot with its long white-painted frontage and red-tiled roof, it's a lovely place to visit at any time, but it really comes into its own in the summer, when the scene shifts from the bars to the beer garden or the patio overlooking the pub's four rink bowling greens – the Cross Keys fields

teams in the local leagues and also welcomes other bowlers and bowling teams. Starting life in the 18th century as a coaching inn and much altered and extended down the years, the pub has public and lounge bars, with pool and darts played in the former and a log-burning stove a cosy focal point in the latter. Adnams Bitter, Greene King IPA and Guest Ales are the regular real ales, and the bars also stock a large selection of other draught and bottled beers, lagers and cider.

Food is served every lunchtime and evening from menus that cater for

appetites large and small. Sandwiches, burgers, omelettes and salads provide lighter or quicker snacks, while among the favourite main dishes are scampi, fish specials, lasagne, beef & Guinness pie, steaks, chilli con carne and the traditional Sunday roasts. Sheila and Trevor are the most welcoming of hosts and look forward to welcoming new faces at their cheerful pub, which stands at the top end of the Norfolk Broads and is conveniently placed for the tourists who flock to the Broads in their thousands in the holiday season.

28 THE COCKEREL TEA ROOM

North Street, North Walsham,
Norfolk NR28 9DH
☎ 01692 403743
e-mail: mark@thecockerel.com

Enthusiastic owners Mark and Claire Rushen changed careers – Mark from IT, Claire from clothes retailing – when they took over **The Cockerel** in the spring of 2007. Once a public house (The Cock closed in 1968), it is now a splendid little licensed tea room/restaurant, tucked away on the north side of town opposite one of the main car parks but easily recognised by its striking pink-painted exterior.

Inside, the traditional furnishings and the décor are equally eye-catching, and chairs set at well-spaced tables allow plenty of space to eat and drink in comfort. At the back is a pleasant courtyard patio for sipping and snacking in the sun. The little bar is stocked with a full range of drinks, from ales and lager to Guinness, cider, wines by glass or bottle, spirits and soft drinks.

Food service starts at opening time (9.30) when traditional or vegetarian cooked breakfasts, things on toast, sandwiches, omelettes,

cakes and pastries get the day off to a good start. Lunchtime brings ploughman's platters, baked potatoes, egg & chips and all-time favourites such as scampi, garlic mushrooms, cod, haddock or plaice & chips, cottage pie, steak & kidney pie, steaks and mixed grill. The Cockerel is open from 9.30 to 3.30, Sunday from 12 to 3, and also Friday and Saturday evenings from 7 to 10 with a different English Bistro Menu; closed

Wednesday. North Walsham is a busy country town with a handsome Market Cross. It has plenty to interest the visitor, but anyone leaving without sampling Mark and Claire's hospitality is definitely missing a treat. Horatio Nelson spent some years in North Walsham at the Paston School, and if The Cockerel had been around in his day he'd probably have slipped anchor from time to time and popped in for a snack.

Mundesley, nr Cromer,
Norfolk NR11 8BQ
☎ 01263 720448

The railways first brought visitors to Mundesley to enjoy the bracing sea air and the superb sandy beach. The trains have long gone, so the tourists and holidaymakers now arrive by car or coach at this super place on the B1159 seven miles southeast of Cromer. **The Ship** is a handsome flint-faced building right on the seafront, and its combination of good hospitality, good food, good beer and good fun have made it one of the busiest and most popular of all the pubs in the region. The long hours are another plus, ensuring that nobody arriving with a thirst or appetite will go away disappointed.

Breakfast service starts at 10 o'clock, and visitors can build their own plateful from the many individual items on the menu, together with unlimited tea or coffee, toast and jam. Egg, bacon or sausage rolls and eggs or beans on toast provide for less hearty appetites. Morning coffee with scones, cakes and biscuits takes the field at 10.30, and lunch from noon includes soup, sandwiches with interesting, generous fillings, panini, jacket potatoes, ploughman's platters, fish & chips, salads and daily specials, Afternoon tea takes over at 3.30, and dinner from 6 offers an excellent selection of meat, fish and vegetarian dishes. Finally, late-night snacks – hot dogs, burgers, fish & chips – are served in the bar from 9.30. Smaller portions are available of many dishes for children, or grown-ups with lighter appetites. Friday is pie night, with three home-made pies added to the menu, Saturday is steak night (with live music), and the Sunday carvery offers a choice of traditional roasts, with fish and vegetarian alternatives.

The Ship has a large garden directly

overlooking the beach, which many consider to be the finest in Norfolk. The hospitality, the ambience and the talented hands in the kitchen make this a popular venue for functions, parties and wedding receptions – and they'll even bake a celebration cake for the occasion!

29 THE JOLLY FARMERS

Swanton Abbot, nr North Walsham,
Norfolk NR10 5DW
☎ 01692 538542

Until recently the **Jolly Farmers** was a popular watering hole for the local RAF base. The base has gone, but Mike Smethurst's 300-year-old pub, with a splendid brick-and-flint frontage and steeply-raked roof, remains very much at the heart of village life, with a convivial, down-to-earth ambience, traditional pub games, live music at the weekend, simple pub grub, real ales and a summer beer festival.

31 WHINCLIFF

Cromer Road, Mundesley,
Norfolk NR11 8DU
☎ 01263 721554

Anne and Alan Cutler offer a home from home by the sea in **Whincliff**, their handsome villa situated on the gorse-covered cliffs at the quiet top end of Mundesley. The B&B accommodation comprises a single room, a double room and an en suite family room for two adults and up to two children. The  house has a pleasant garden at the back, and off-road parking is available in the driveway. The Cliff Path is a short walk away, leading down to one of Norfolk's quiet, unspoilt beaches. Open all year; pets welcome.

32 CAFE LILIA

Station Road, Mundesley,
Norfolk NR11 8JH
☎ 01263 722282
e-mail: clair.debenham@btinternet.com

Mother and daughter Jean and Clair Debenham share the cooking at **Cafe Lilia**, their delightful café on a busy shopping street in Mundesley. They prepare a good choice to cater for all appetites, from baguettes and toasties to jacket potatoes, salads, breakfasts, tasty pies and special dishes of the day. Cafe Lilia is open from 9.30 to 4  Tuesday to Saturday; closed Monday; open for Sunday lunch with advance bookings.

33 CASTAWAYS HOLIDAY PARK

Paston Road, Bacton-on-Sea,
Norfolk NR12 0JB
☎ 01692 650436
e-mail: castaways.bacton@hotmail.co.uk
🌐 www.castawaysholidaypark.co.uk

Castaways Holiday Park is a small, family-run business in the peaceful seaside village of Bacton, where the lyrical composer E J Moeran lived for many years. Richard and Anna Hollis offer a choice of self-catering accommodation, comprising three-bedroom lodges sleeping up to eight guests, one- or two-bedroom flats and two- or three-bedroom  caravans. The park has a shop for daily essentials, a clubhouse and a bar serving drinks and meals.

35 THE QUEENS HEAD

High Street, Foulsham, nr Dereham,
Norfolk NR20 5AD
☎ 01362 683339

The **Queens Head** stands on the main street of Foulsham, off the A1067 Norwich-Fakenham road (leave on any of the minor roads between Foxley and Guist). This area of rural Norfolk has much to attract the visitor, whether it's walking or cycling in the quiet, pleasant countryside or exploring the places of interest, including Foxley Wood Nature Reserve, the remains of the Saxon cathedral at North Elmham or the magnificent Church of St Peter & St Paul at Salle. And when the walking and the cycling and the sightseeing have generated a thirst and an appetite, leaseholder Jenny Adams, her staff and Wallis the schnauzer are all waiting to dispense hospitality. The pub has all the expected appeal of a traditional country hostelry, with hanging baskets adding splashes of colour to the black-and-white, tile-roofed frontage and a wealth of old beams and handsome wood inside. Greene King Abbot Ale, Adnams Best and Woodfordes Wherry are on tap to quench thirsts, and fresh-air appetites are satisfied with a good selection of home-cooked food. The menu majors on well-loved pub classics such as cod or haddock

in beer batter; ham, egg & chips; gammon steak with pineapple; fisherman's and steak pies; chilli con carne; lasagne (meat or vegetarian); scampi; steaks and curries. The Queens Head is open lunchtime and evening Monday to Friday and all day Saturday and Sunday.

34 HOLLY FARM COTTAGES

High Common, Cranworth, Norfolk IP25 7SX
☎ 01362 821468
e-mail: jenniemclaren@btinternet.com

In a pleasant village setting off the A1075 between Watton and Dereham, **Holly Farm Cottages** provide a delightful base for tourists or holidaymakers, with many of the county's attractions within easy reach. The two single-storey self-catering cottages, each sleeping up to four, are equipped with everything needed for a carefree stay, including a

double bedroom and double sofa bed, fully-fitted kitchen, sitting room, and bath/shower room. There is a separate utility room with washing machine and tumble-dryer. The garden is fully fenced offering safe off-road parking. Pets are welcome. This is an excellent base for a walking or cycling holiday, and golf and fishing are available nearby.

HIDDEN PLACES GUIDES

Explore Britain and Ireland with *Hidden Places* guides - a fascinating series of national and local travel guides.

Packed with easy to read information on hundreds of places of interest as well as places to stay, eat and drink.

Available from both high street and internet booksellers

For more information on the full range of *Hidden Places* guides and other titles published by Travel Publishing visit our website on

www.travelpublishing.co.uk
or ask for our leaflet by phoning
01752 276660 or emailing
info@travelpublishing.co.uk

36 THE MARSHLAND ARMS

School Road, Marshland St James, nr Wisbech, Cambridgeshire PE14 8EY
☎ 01945 430319
e-mail: marshlandarms@msn.com

Recent refurbishment has transformed the **Marshland Arms**, which stands at the northern end of the fens, on a minor road off the A47, 4 miles east of Wisbech. Host and chef John Wood puts out the welcome mat for all who visit his home cooking is a major magnet for its loyal clientele. He offers an impressive choice of traditional pub fare including fish & chips and steak & kidney pie as well as a comprehensive main menu selection ranging from gammon, steak ribs to the aptly named moo, oink, cluck. The menu is supplemented by daily specials such as salmon kebabs, minted lamb shank and

curries. There is a full range of deserts to follow.

The inn has a lovely beer garden and plenty of off-road parking. The area round the pub has many places of interest to visitors, and for those discovering the attractions the Marshland Arms is ready and waiting with its excellent hospitality and refreshment.

37 THE WINE LODGE

27-29 High Street, Feltwell,
Norfolk IP26 4AF
☎ 01842 828474
⊕ www.feltwellwinelodge.co.uk

When rugby-loving Gerald Williams left the Forces he set about realising his dream of owning a Free House. Along with manager Janet Jackson he has built up a loyal local following at the **Wine Lodge**, but first-time visitors can expect an equally warm and genuine welcome. The owner has ensured that his major renovation programme will not spoil the traditional look of the 17th century premises, and the bars, lounge and restaurant provide a relaxed, civilised ambience for enjoying a drink or a home-cooked meal. Picnic benches at the front and a new covered patio at the rear provide an alfresco option.

The Wine Lodge is open all day for drinks, and classic pub fare is served from 12 to 3 and 5 to 8 (not Sunday evening). Terrestrial rugby matches are shown on a big-screen TV, and weekends bring karaoke sessions, discos or live music. Feltwell is a small farming community with a Post Office, two shops and three churches, two of them with Listed status. For guests wanting a pleasant base for touring the area, the Wine Lodge has three quiet, comfortable letting rooms.

38 CASTLE RISING CASTLE

Castle Rising, Norfolk PE31 6AH
☎ 01553 631330
⊕ www.english-heritage.org.uk

Explore the imposing keep and vast earthworks of this Norman castle. Set amid 12 acres of mighty earthwork defences, this is one of the largest and most ornate Norman buildings in all England. Discover the stronghold's fascinating history - including its links with 'Wicked Queen Isabella' - in our audio tour.

40 THE FEATHERS HOTEL

Manor Road, Dersingham,
Norfolk PE31 6LN
☎ 01485 540207
e-mail: feathershotel@btclick.com
⊕ www.thefeathershotel.co.uk

Maxine and Tony Martin welcome guests from all over the world to the **Feathers**, a handsome 18th century carrstone building less than a mile from Sandringham. Comfort, prompt, personal service and good food are watchwords, and the six excellent bedrooms, all with en suite facilities, guarantee a pleasant, relaxing stay. Real ales from Adnams and Bass are served in the bar,

and in the restaurant an extensive menu of home-cooked dishes caters for all tastes and appetites.

39 SANDRINGHAM HOUSE

Sandringham, Norfolk PE35 6EN
☎ 01553 772675 Fax: 01553 541571
e-mail: enquiries@sandringhamestate.co.uk

Sandringham House is the charming country retreat of Her Majesty The Queen hidden in the heart of sixty acres of beautiful wooded gardens. Still maintained in the style of Edward and

Alexandra, Prince and Princess of Wales (later King Edward VII and Queen Alexandra), all the main ground floor rooms used by The Royal Family, full of their treasured ornaments, portraits and furniture, are open to the public.

More family possessions are displayed in the Museum housed in the old stable and coach houses including vehicles ranging in date from the first car owned by a British monarch, a 1900 Daimler, to a half-scale Aston Martin used by Princes William and Harry. A display tells the mysterious tale of the Sandringham Company who fought and died at Gallipolli in 1915, which was made into a TV film "All the King's Men".

With so much to see and do, and a warm and friendly welcome whenever you visit, Sandringham is the epitome of English country house life – don't miss it!

41 CHENEY HOLLOW COTTAGES

Cheney Hill, Heacham, nr King's Lynn, Norfolk PE31 7BX
☎ 01485 572625
e-mail: cottages@cheneyhollow.co.uk
🌐 www.cheneyhollow.co.uk

Sue and Pete, who previously ran their own pub in Essex, extend a warm welcome to all their guests at **Cheney Hollow Cottages**. They are a 'pet friendly' establishment but Katie the cat remains in charge! Ideally suited for couples, these two spotless, well

equipped, one bedroom detached cottages make an ideal base for year round self catering holidays. For walking, bird watching, cycling, exploring the beautiful Norfolk countryside and unspoilt coastline or for just relaxing in the peaceful one acre gardens of Cheney Hollow. A travel cot is available and each cottage has its own comfortable sofa bed to accommodate extra guests.

Garden Cottage is a pretty carrstone and brick single storey property with its own patio, located in the gardens of Cheney Hollow. It has an open plan kitchen and lounge with French doors leading into a Victorian style conservatory. The bedroom has pine furniture, comfortable King size bed with fluffy pillows and duvet. The bathroom has an air (bubble) bath with power shower over.

Guest Cottage is a delightful, traditional style carrstone and brick cottage built around the 1850's. The entrance hallway leads into the kitchen and lounge which has French doors leading out onto its' own large sunny patio. Upstairs, the bathroom has bath with power shower over. The large bedroom has comfortable twin beds (which can be zipped together if requested) and lovely views over the gardens.

Cheney Hollow cottages are within easy walking distance of all village amenities, bus stops and beaches

Lynn Road, Sculthorpe, nr Fakenham,
Norfolk NR21 9QG
☎ 01328 856161
e-mail: beccy68@hotmail.com

The Barnett family – Steve, Elaine and daughter Beccy – and their chef Kevin Boyden are the talented team at **Sculthorpe Mill**, which stands close to the A148 a mile or

so west of Fakenham (signposted at Sculthorpe). For two centuries a working mill, this superb old brick building has found a new role as a Greene King pub, a splendid restaurant and a comfortable hotel. Kevin and his team prepare a wide selection of dishes to cater for all palates and appetites, with bar and à la carte menus available at lunchtime and in the evening. The menus, based on seasonal local produce, are mainly traditional English, with some European specialities and always a pie of the day. Greene King ales head the list of drinks, and there's a good selection of wines. The accommodation at the Mill comprises six newly refurbished

en suite bedrooms, one with a four-poster bed and all commanding lovely views.

There's plenty to see and do in the area, including walks in beautiful scenery and a number of grand country mansions. The location, on the banks of the River Wensum, is a major asset, and the banks and grounds are home to a wide variety of wildlife. Not surprisingly, the mill is a popular venue for functions, wedding parties and other special occasions. The restaurant can seat 50 in comfort, and for larger numbers a marquee can be erected in the garden.

43 THE WHITE HORSE INN

Fakenham Road, East Barsham,
nr Fakenham, Norfolk NR21 0LH
☎ 01378 820645
e-mail: vince@whitehorseinn.co.uk

The **White Horse Inn** is a Grade II listed building dating from the 17th century, extended down the years and sympathetically refurbished to retain period character in cosy, comfortable and convivial surroundings. Vince and Sue Shearer brought many years' experience when they took over here in 2003, and they have made it a place to seek out for a drink, a meal or a base for touring the region. In the beamed main bar, warmed in winter by a big open fire, visitors can join the locals for a chat and a glass or two of real ale; the selection includes Adnams Bitter and Broadside and Charles Wells Bombardier, and the bar also stocks two dozen malt whiskies. The inn is open for drinks from 12 to 3 and from 6.30 in the evening everyday.

Food is an important side of the business, and there are seats for 90 in the eating areas. Lunchtime sandwiches and snacks are replaced in the evening by a wide ranging menu and daily specials that put the emphasis on classic pub dishes such as scampi, beer-battered haddock, steaks, steak & kidney pudding, steak, Guinness & mushroom pie, lasagne, curries, mingling with the likes of Cajun-spiced or sweet & sour chicken, pork with orange sauce and navarin of lamb.

For Bed & Breakfast guests, the inn has three comfortably appointed en suite rooms – a twin, a double and a family room. A full English breakfast sets guest up for a day's exploring the region, and there's certainly plenty to discover. East Barsham stands on the River Stiffkey a short drive off the A148 north of Fakenham, where the attractions include National Hunt racing, The Museum of Gas & Local History, Pensthorpe Waterfowl Park and walks in the Norfolk Wildlife Trust's ancient woodland in Foxley Wood. Also within an easy drive are Houghton Hall, the Shrine of Our Lady of Walsingham and the Wells & Walsingham Light Railway.

2-4 Greevegate, Hunstanton,
Norfolk PE36 6BJ
☎ 01485 532487

Fish and Chips cooked the traditional way keep the crowds flocking to **Fishers of Huntingdon**. Jane and Mark Wilson and their staff celebrate the great heritage of fish and chips as the nation's favourite fast food. Fish is well known as one of the most nutritious of foods, and one of the most easily digested, while potatoes are an excellent source of minerals, vitamins and carbohydrates.

On a prime site on the main street of Hunstanton, a short walk from the beach, Fishers has the unmistakable buzz of a popular, well-run restaurant that appeals both to the local community and the tourist trade. Jane and Mark are certainly a very busy couple – Mark is usually hard at work cooking and Jane is hard at work everywhere, maintaining, along with their staff, the highest standards of quality, service and hospitality. It is a tribute to their hard work and dedication that Fishers is almost as busy in the winter, when the tourists have mostly gone, as at the height of the summer season.

The fish options include all-time favourites cod, haddock and plaice, with rock eel, scampi, cod roe and fishcakes in support. The chips are prepared from potatoes peeled and cut on the premises, and all the fried food is cooked in vegetable oil. Fishers also caters for other tastes: non-fishy favourites include Pukka pies (beef & onion, steak & kidney, chicken & mushroom), chicken, saveloys, foot-long sausages and spam fritters. And for those who don't want fish or meat there are vegetarian sausages and burgers and vegetable kiev. This is definitely a place to bring a healthy appetite, and the hungriest diners can take the Fishers Challenge – prime giant cod with large chips, traditional mushy peas or garden peas, bread roll,

baked beans and salad garnish, served with a choice of tea, coffee or large soft drink. Those who succeed in clearing their plates are rewarded with a free dessert of their choice – perhaps chocolate lumpy bumpy or lemon meringue float. Opening hours are 12 to 8 seven days a week, with some variations out of season. Next door to the restaurant, Fishers has a very popular takeaway service. A Liverpool poet wrote that 'love is fish and chips on winter nights'. A visit to Fishers suggests that he should have added 'and winter days and summer days and summer nights'!

46 THE WHITE COTTAGE

19 Wodehouse Road, Old Hunstanton,
Norfolk PE36 6JW
☎ 01485 532380

Guests return time after time to enjoy the friendly ambience and home-from-comfort of the **White Cottage** guest house. Mrs Una Burton, whose home this has been for 30 years, is a landlady of the old school, with a loyal clientele hat includes walkers, birdwatchers and golfers as well as tourists exploring the many delights of this part of north Norfolk.

The brick bungalow, built in the 1930s, has a spacious entrance hall and a comfortable television/reading lounge, and when the sun shines the pleasant garden is a nice place for a gentle stroll. The guest bedrooms are attractively furnished and centrally heated, with washbasins – one room has en suite facilities. Breakfast is served in a light, airy dining area furnished in pine and decorated with some interesting pieces collected by Una. Evening meals are available with prior notice. Wodehouse Road is approached from the main A149, a road that runs all the way round Norfolk from Great Yarmouth to King's Lynne, following the coast for most of its route. It's a short walk from the house to the sea, here it's not just the sandy beach that is the draw –

the Discover Lifeboat Station is also here, open for visits on Sunday mornings and at other times by appointment. The golf course, too, is just moments away, and the busy resort of Hunstanton is a mile down the road.

This grand place, the only east coast resort that actually faces west, is well known for its huge stretches of sandy beach, multi-coloured cliffs and the Sea Life Sanctuary. For many visitors, a boat trip to Seal Island to watch the seals basking in the sun at low tide is a must. Other local attractions include RSPB reserves at Holme, Snettisham and Titchwell, Ringstead Down nature reserve, Norfolk Lavender, Sandringham, Holkham Hall and walking on the Peddars Way and the Norfolk Coast Path. And after a day's exploring it's always a pleasure to return to the warm, welcoming surroundings of the White Cottage.

45 THE WASH & TOPE HOTEL

10-12 Le Strange Terrace, Hunstanton,
Norfolk PE36 5AJ
☎ 01485 532250

Locals and tourists are equally well catered for at the **Wash & Tope Hotel**, which Paul Crawford and Louise Pride have made a great place for a drink, a meal or a comfortable stay. Behind its smartly painted facade on one of Hunstanton's main streets, the hotel has a long, roomy bar (Greene king IPA and guests) and a recently restyled restaurant serving an impressive selection of

meat, fish and vegetarian dishes ranging from light snacks to meat and fish pies, lasagne, stone-baked pizzas, super curries, beer-battered cod, chilli con carne and Sunday lunchtime roasts. The ten sea-view bedrooms, six en suite, provide an ideal base for exploring the many attractions of Hunstanton.

47 HOLKHAM HALL & BYGONES MUSEUM

Wells-next-the-Sea, Norfolk NR23 1AB
☎ 01328 710227 Fax: 01328 711707
⊕ www.holkham.co.uk

In a lakeside deer park on the beautiful North Norfolk coast stands **Holkham Hall**, one of Britain's most majestic stately homes, seat of seven generations of the Earls of Leicester. This classic 18th century mansion in Palladian style is a veritable treasure house of artistic and architectural history, and each part has its separate character and appeal, from the stunning grandeur of the Marble Hall and the magnificence of the State Rooms to the old kitchen with its original pots and pans and the elegant formal gardens. In addition to the superb house and gardens there are other attractions at Holkham, including a Bygones Museum crammed with over 4,000 domestic and agricultural artefacts, nursery gardens, a pottery shop, restaurant and tearooms.

48 ARCH HOUSE

Mill Road, Wells-next-the-Sea,
Norfolk NR23 1DB
☎ 01328 710112
e-mail: jon@archhouse.co.uk
⊕ www.archhouse.co.uk

Quality is the keynote in everything owners Jon and Kate Reynolds offer at **Arch House**, a substantial redbrick building dating from 1830. It was originally the home of the local excise man, and its prominent location gave him a good view of the activities of the townsfolk. The ten en suite guest bedrooms provide a comfortable base for walkers,

birdwatchers and tourists discovering the surrounding area, and guests can enjoy a stroll in the garden at the back of the house. A full Norfolk breakfast, including locally produced bacon and sausages, is served in the smartly modernised dining room, where an evening meal is available by arrangement.

50 THE WHITE HORSE

The Street, Badwell Ash,
nr Bury St Edmunds, Suffolk IP31 3DP
☎ 01359 259909

The Simpson family – husband Ashley, wife Tracy and daughter Claire – are the friendly hosts at the **White Horse**, a substantial village inn a few miles east of Bury (reached off the A143, the A1088 or the A14 (J47). Greene King IPA is the regular real ale served in the heavily beamed bar, and in the roomy restaurant diners enjoy Tracy's

traditional pub fare. Darts and pool are the favourite White horse games, and social occasions include live regular music and karaoke sessions and quiz nights on winter Sundays. The pub is open Monday to Thursday evenings, lunchtime and evening on Friday and all day Saturday and Sunday.

49 BRIG SQUARE HOLIDAY COTTAGES

5 Brig Square, Freeman Street,
Wells-next-the Sea, Norfolk NR23 1BH
☎ 01328 710440
e-mail: briggssquare@btconnect.com

For almost 40 years master builder Ray Hewitt has been offering top-quality self-catering accommodation in **Brig Square Holiday Cottages**. Brig Square is a group of well-preserved buildings close to the quay, some of which date back to 1648, superbly maintained by Ray, who is always ready to give a helping hand or friendly advice. Some of the cottages enjoy views over the marshes and out to sea, and during the summer months the Square is adorned with colourful window boxes and hanging baskets.

The largest unit, at the top of the Square, sleeps up to 8 guests; it has a spacious pine-beamed lounge-diner and a kitchen-diner leading to a south-facing garden on the ground floor, two double bedrooms and bathroom on the first floor and an attic room with three single beds on the second floor. Two other cottages, each sleeping up to 5 guests, are also at the top of the Square, and a cosy bungalow

overlooking the garden square is an ideal retreat for a couple. All the cottages have private parking, televisions, DVD's, conventional cookers and microwave ovens, complete with laundry facilities and hairdryers. Cots, highchairs and stairgates can be provided on request. Duvets and pillows are provided, but not bed linen or towels. Brig Square was once owned by the Admiralty and the maritime connections are strong.

One of the most notable sons of Wells was John Fryer, who was born in the village in 1753 and lived for some time in the Square. At

the age of 33 he was appointed sailing master to Captain Bligh on *The Bounty* and remained loyal to his captain (though rendering very little help) at the time of the mutiny. He later rose to the top in the Navy as Post Captain and commanded several ships. He died in 1817 (the same year as Bligh) and was buried in the churchyard of St Nicholas in Wells. His original gravestone is in the church, replaced in the yard with a plaque inscribed 'John Fryer RN 1753-1817 Sailing Master of His Majesty's armed vessel Bounty'.

51 KILN FARM GUEST HOUSE

Kiln Lane, Elmswell, nr Bury St Edmunds,
Suffolk IP30 9QR
☎ 01359 240442
e-mail: davejankilnfarm@btinternet.com

Dave and Jan Copeman welcome visitors to
Kiln Farm Guest House, which enjoys a
secluded setting among country roads off the
A14 (leave at J47). The B&B accommodation
comprises six en suite bedrooms, and the
house has a
licensed bar,
a
conservatory
with TV and
a restaurant
where
breakfasts
(and evening
meals by

prior arrangement with Jan) are served. The
owners also have a small caravan site with
five pitches. Elmswell (to the north) and
Woolpit (to the south) are only a mile away,
and the farm is ideally placed for exploring
some of Suffolk's finest towns and villages.

53 BRICKWALL FARM HOUSE 4 STAR

Wetherden, nr Stowmarket,
Suffolk IP14 3JW
Tel: 01359 244118 Mob: 07730929777
🌐 www.brickwallfarmhouse.co.uk

A superb self-catering accommodation for up
to 12 guests, **Brickwall Farm House** is a
fine Grade II listed Tudor period property
amid beautiful Suffolk countryside walks. It
has a wealth of period features throughout
with two spacious reception rooms, with
piano, 4-5 twin bedded and family bedrooms,
one ensuite. An outdoor
trampoline and games/gym
room. Perfect spot to
explore East Anglia -
racing, Newmarket; sailing,
market shopping, Ipswich;
Cathedral, Bury St
Edmunds; punting, colleges, Cambridge;
Agricultural Museum, Stowmarket; music,
Aldeburgh; seaside, Felixstowe; plus many
wonderful stately homes, excellent restaurants
and village pubs. The farmhouse is an ideal
base for groups of friends, wedding parties,
family groups, courses and small conferences.

52 MUSEUM OF EAST ANGLIAN LIFE

Stowmarket, Suffolk IP14 1DL
☎ 01449 612229 Fax: 01449 672307
🌐 www.eastanglianlife.org.uk

The Museum of East Anglian Life
occupies a 75-acre site in the heart of
Stowmarket. Its rich collections of social,
rural and industrial history include a number
of historic buildings such as a working
watermill, a smithy, a chapel and a 13th
century farmhouse.

There is something for the whole family to
enjoy with a variety of farm animals, adventure
playground, picnic sites, café and gift shop.
Throughout the year the Museum holds special
events as well as demonstrations of crafts and
engines in steam. The Museum is open from
April to October.

54 THE MAGPIE

Norwich Road (A140), Little Stonham,
nr Stowmarket, Suffolk IP14 5JY

☎ 01449 711287

e-mail: info@www.thestonhammagpie.co.uk

🌐 www.thestonhammagpie.co.uk

Mark and Belinda Rudderham and their family attract a loyal, mature clientele to **The Magpie**, which lies on the A140 Norwich road, just north of the junction with the A1120 east of Stowmarket and halfway between Ipswich and Diss. Traditional and contemporary elements combine harmoniously in the 16th century coaching inn, where the public areas include an intimately lit restaurant overlooking the patio and duck pond, and a large games room with darts, pool, dominoes, shove ha'penny….and plenty of

seats for spectators! Bar manager Steve keeps an excellent cellar, with a good selection of real ales and lagers, fine wines and an extensive choice of spirits. Familiar home-cooked dishes are served every day from noon to 9 Monday to Saturday and from noon to 8 on Sunday, prepared from local ingredients that reflect the seasons by head chef son-in-law Sam, ably assisted by Connie. Everything is fresh and full of flavour, and among the favourites are excellent fish specials and super pies; senior citizens 2-course specials are served Monday to Friday lunchtimes. While at the Magpie check-out the Magpie's Pantry where you can purchase home-made preserves and chutneys and delicious cakes and pies are made to order.

Besides their close involvement with all aspects of running this outstanding inn, the Rudderhams' hobbies revolve around their animals – the ducks on the pond, chickens, dogs and a couple of Belinda's horses who visit from time to time. This is very much a place for the family, with the animals to talk to, a large adventure playground and a field that's big enough for ball games. It's also a meeting place for several local clubs and groups, including owners of classic Triumph cars on the first Tuesday of each month. The Magpie is close to a number of visitor attractions, including Stonham Barns, incorporating the Redwings Horse Sanctuary and Owl Sanctuary.

55 THE CASTLE INN

Castle Street, Framlingham,
nr Woodbridge, Suffolk IP13 9BP
☎ 01728 724033

The **Castle Inn** is a delightful pub with a welcome for the whole family. It stands very close to Framlingham Castle and provides an ideal break for families taking a tour of the castle, with a very friendly atmosphere and plenty of room for children to enjoy themselves. Lightwood is used to eyecatching effect in the bar, and picnic benches are set outside under parasols overlooking the duck pond.

The bar serves a good range of drinks, and a large menu of traditional dishes satisfies fresh-air appetites: the choice includes freshly filled baguettes, Cromer crab, cod cooked in local beer batter and prime Suffolk ham. In the courtyard stands Castle Craft and Collectables, selling hand-crafted goods and unique gift ideas. The pub and the craft shop are both open throughout the year.

56 HIGH HOUSE AND WOODLODGE

Cransford, nr Woodbridge,
Suffolk IP13 9PD
☎ 01728 663461 Fax: 01728 663409
e-mail: info@highhousefarm.co.uk
🌐 www.highhousefarm.co.uk

At **High House** and **Woodlodge** Tim and Sarah Kindred provide a choice of accommodation in an idyllic country setting that's a perfect base for exploring the heart of rural Suffolk. The former is a beautifully restored 15th century

farmhouse with two bedrooms (an en suite double and a large family room with adjacent bathroom) for B&B guests. The latter is a comfortable three-bedroom retreat furnished and equipped to a high standard for self-catering guests. Both stand in attractive gardens, and guests have direct access to paths through 18 acres of woodland.

57 THE CRETINGHAM BELL

The Street, Cretingham, Suffolk IP13 7BJ
☎ 01728 685419

The **Cretingham Bell** is a neatly kept village inn, originally four cottages, where Craig Muffett, his brother and his wife have invested time and resources in major refurbishment. Their popular free house, the essence of an English country inn, is open from 11 every day, serving real ales and a fine variety of

dishes, some traditional, others with a European, Spanish or Mediterranean slant. The Cretingham Bell is also a popular holiday and tourist base, with three en suite bedrooms (a double and a twin) for Bed & Breakfast guests.

58 THE SWAN INN

Harleston Road, Fressingfield,
Suffolk IP21 5PE
☎ 01379 586280
e-mail: matthewmsb@aol.com

A warm and friendly welcome awaits visitors
to the **Swan Inn**, where Matt and Sam
(Samantha) combine their talents as chef and
host in fine style. Hanging baskets make a
colourful summer show at the front, while
inside the look is appealingly traditional, with
oak beams, open
fires and pictures
of the inn and
the village in
days gone by.
Cask Marque-
accredited ales
are on tap in the
bar, and Matt
produces a fine

variety of dishes, some pub classics, others
with a Mediterranean twist. Regular events
include theme food nights, barbecues and hog
roasts. The Swan is closed on Mondays
except for Bank Holidays.

59 THE WHITE HORSE INN

Darsham Road, Westleton,
nr Saxmundham, Suffolk IP17 3AH
☎ 01728 648222
e-mail: jennie@westleton-whitehorse.co.uk
🌐 www.westleton-whitehorse.co.uk

Rick and Jennie Powling offer a friendly
greeting, Adnams real ales, home-cooked food
and B&B accommodation at the **White Horse
Inn**. The inn has three lovely guest rooms –
an en suite double, a twin and a single available
all year round. Behind the inn is a large beer
garden with plenty of seating and room for
children to romp in safety. Nestled between
the A12 and the sea, Westleton is well placed
for exploring Suffolk's Heritage Coast:
Minsmere bird sanctuary and the 'lost' town of
Dunwich are just minutes away. Each August a
Barrel Fair takes
place on the village
green, where the
main barrel-pushing
events are
supported by side
shows and morris
dancing.

60 THE BELL INN

The Street, Middleton, nr Saxmundham,
Suffolk IP17 3NN
☎ 01728 648286
🌐 www.middleton-bell.co.uk

The **Bell Inn** is a delightful part-thatched
village pub set in extensive grounds close to
Suffolk's Heritage Coast and Minsmere Bird
Sanctuary. In the convivial surroundings of
the beamed
bar patrons
can enjoy
Adnams
beers
straight
from the
cask,
meanwhile
the

restaurant is a comfortable spot for enjoying a
meal based on local produce and freshly
cooked to order (no food Tuesday).
Traditional music features strongly in the bar,
and the village hosts the famous Ceremony
of the Cutty Wren every Boxing Day night.

61 THE LION INN

Main Road, Theberton, Suffolk IP16 4RU
☎ 01728 830185

Friendly, enthusiastic Michael and Caroline
Jeffery run the **Lion Inn**, which stands on
the main road of Theberton, within easy
reach of
Minsmere
Bird
Reserve,
the 'lost'
town of
Dunwich
and other
coastal
attractions.
In their
Grade II
listed inn

they welcome locals, walkers, holidaymakers
and families (along with their dogs!) with a
good choice of real ales and tasty home-
cooked food. The Lion has a pleasant beer
garden and patio and a capacious car park.
The hosts can provide accommodation and
camping facilities.

62 THE GRIFFIN INN

High Street, Yoxford, Suffolk IP17 3EP
☎ 01728 668229
🌐 www.thegriffin.co.uk

The building that is now the **Griffin Inn** first saw the light of day in 1358, when it was the memorial court for the local lord of the manor. It became an inn some 200 years later, and the long tradition of hospitality is being continued in fine style by Kenny and Maria and their staff. It stands on a corner site in the main street of Yoxford, and behind the black-and-white slate-roofed exterior it has a wealth of old-world charm, with original wall and ceiling beams, a splendid log fire, scrubbed wooden tables, pew seating and a sofa in the corner. Once the haunt of smugglers, it now attracts a wide cross-section of patrons, both from the local community and from further afield. Adnams and guest real ales are on tap to quench thirsts, and a decent selection of wines can be enjoyed on their own or to accompany a meal. Locally sourced produce is the basis of the dishes that are served every lunchtime and evening and all day until 9 o'clock on Saturday and

Sunday. Well-priced, generously served dishes include classics such as beer-battered cod, pasta with various sauces and steak, kidney and mushroom pie cooked in Adnams Ale. Sandwiches and hot and cold snacks are available for lighter/quicker options, and children can choose from their own special menu. The Griffin has another string to its bow in the shape of three guest bedrooms with en suite or private bathroom, television (including satellite channels) radio-alarm clock and hot beverage tray. Yoxford is an attractive village that was once an important stop on the London-Yarmouth coaching route. It's a

pleasant place to explore, with pink-washed cottages, interesting shops and a church that dates mainly from the 14th and 15th centuries. A cast-iron signpost outside the church has hands pointing to London, Yarmouth and Framlingham. Yoxford is also an excellent base from which to explore the delights of the Suffolk countryside and coast. One of the region's main attractions, the RSPB reserve at Minsmere, is a few minutes' drive from the Griffin. Pub hours are 12 to 12 Monday to Saturday, 12 to 11 on Sunday.

63 THE GEORGIAN GUEST HOUSE

6 North Terrace, Saxmundham,
Suffolk IP17 1AY
☎ 01728 603337
e-mail: enquiries@thegeorgian-house.com
🌐 www.thegeorgian-house.com

Ian and Gill Bray welcome guests of all ages to
the **Georgian Guest House**, an ideal base for
exploring Suffolk's coast and countryside. Parts
of the building date back to Tudor times, and
the owners have kept much of its original
character while providing modern comfort and
amenities
(including a
luxurious hot
tub). The seven
guest bedrooms
are all en suite,
with TV, DVD
player,
telephone,

beverage tray and hairdryer. Day rooms
comprise a licensed lounge, a well-stocked
library (books, music, games and puzzles) and
a dining room where a multi-choice breakfast
is served. Packed lunches and evening meals
can be provided on request.

261

64 THE SHIP INN AT BLAXHALL

Blaxhall, nr Snape, Suffolk IP12 2DY
☎ 01728 688316

The **Ship Inn at Blaxhall** is enjoying a new lease of life under licensee David Snell and chef Sharon Curtis. Local residents had to put up a real fight to save this lovely little country pub from being converted by the previous landlord into a country house. They won the fight, restoring it to its rightful place as the heartbeat of the local community. The locals love it, and it is now attracting growing patronage from all over the region. Sharon came here with almost 30 years experience at The Crown in Snape, and she puts that experience to excellent use in creating a wide range of dishes on her interesting blackboard menus. Quality is

firmly to the fore throughout, as Sharon insists on the finest and freshest local ingredients for her classic dishes. Fish and shellfish come straight from the markets at Lowestoft to provide an extensive and constantly changing seafood menu. Steaks are supplied by a top butcher in nearby Wickham Market. To accompany the food or to enjoy on their own are a choice of up to six real ales – Woodfordes Wherry, Fullers London Pride and a guest from Bateman's are the regulars – and a fine wine list that visits the top wine-producing regions of the world. Food and drink are served either in the traditionally furnished, interconnecting dining areas or outside in the newly created beer garden.

Another element in the revival of this outstanding inn is the regular live music evenings featuring top local bands. The Ship is open from 12 to 3 and from 6 to midnight, and food is served every session except Monday evening. Booking is recommended, particularly in the summer season, to be sure of getting a table. The inn is an excellent venue for a party, and it's also a lovely place to spend a night or two: four chalets with en suite facilities provide quiet, comfortable Bed & Breakfast accommodation.

The Ship stands by a country road in the village of Blaxhall, 2 miles from the famous Snape Maltings and just 6 miles from the coast at Aldeburgh. It lies off the B1069 south of Snape and can also be reached from the A12 via Little Glemham.

65 YE OLDE COACH & HORSES INN

Melton Road, Melton, nr Woodbridge,
Suffolk IP12 1PD

☎ 01394 384851

e-mail: info@yeoldecoachandhorses.co.uk

🌐 www.yeoldecoachandhorses.co.uk

Ye Olde Coach & Horses is a traditional inn dating from the 16th century, located in Melton, close to the River Deben and just north of Woodbridge. Easily found a short drive from the main A12, this is definitely a place to return to again and again for its superb hospitality and outstanding food and drink. Owner Chris Martin and his hardworking staff provide an unbeatable choice of dishes that really do cater for all tastes and appetites. The à la carte menu in the beautiful timbered restaurant tempts with the freshest fish and seafood dishes – lemon sole, cod, haddock, lobster, king, jumbo and tiger prawns – chicken and duck, lamb and pork, and wonderful Scottish steaks – fillet, sirloin, T-bone, mighty 21oz chateaubriand. This choice is comprehensive enough, but it's only half the story! The inn also has another, equally appealing outlet, the Cobra Brasserie specialising in Indian dishes headed by curries on all levels of the temperature gauge, from mild kormas and masalas and baltis up to Madras and vindaloos. Visitors to Ye Olde Coach & Horses are equally well served on the drinks front: real ales from Adnams, Greene King, Shepherd Neame, Deuchars and Theakston, John Smiths Smooth, draught Guinness, Scrumpy Jack, the renowned draught Hoegaarden White Beer, 300+ wines from around the world, loads of champagnes, a vast selection of spirits including 40 cognacs. The inn is also a top-class business venue, with seminar and conference rooms, excellent business services and parking for 70 cars.

66 SUTTON HOO

Tranmer House, Sutton Hoo, Woodbridge, Suffolk IP12 3DJ
☎ 01394 389700
🌐 www.suttonhoo.org.uk

In the early 7th century, about 200 years after Roman government was withdrawn from Britain, this place was chosen to make a great monument to a new kind of English power. Over about

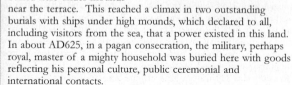

50 years an aristocratic was buried here under mounds near the terrace. This reached a climax in two outstanding burials with ships under high mounds, which declared to all, including visitors from the sea, that a power existed in this land. In about AD625, in a pagan consecration, the military, perhaps royal, master of a mighty household was buried here with goods reflecting his personal culture, public ceremonial and international contacts.

Sutton Hoo kept its secret for more than 1300 years, until, on the very brink of war in 1939, an incomparable buried treasure was discovered here. The sight of a huge buried ship, and the wealth of precious objects found within it, led to decades of further excavation and research, provoking questions that still await answers. The new exhibition which tells these stories has been made possible by a major grant from the Heritage Lottery Fund, and by the generous financial support of many other private and public bodies and individuals.

67 EAST ANGLIA TRANSPORT MUSEUM

Chapelroad, Carlton Colville, Lowestoft, Suffolk NR33 8BL
☎ 01502 518459

Here at Carlton Colville you will find a museum unique to the last detail, for this is the only place in the British Isles where visitors can not only view but also ride on all three principal forms of public transport from the earlier part of the 20th century.

Once inside the museum there is so

much to see and do that you'll want to stay all day. Whether you take a ride on the trolleybus service, there is a new discovery to be made every minute. Or why not soak up the real atmosphere of the past with a walk along our period street – complete with authentic street furniture. There is also ample opportunity to view the many vehicles in the museum collection, and see how these are being restored to their former glory.

Hear the swish of trolleypoles, the purr of the diesel engine or the rhythmic hiss of steam, making this a real trip back in time.

68 COASTERS OF SOUTHWOLD

12 Queen Street, Southwold,
Suffolk IP18 6EQ
☎ 01502 724734
e-mail: oliverwalker@hotmail.co.uk
🌐 www.coastersofsouthwold.co.uk

Business partners Oliver (Olly) Walker and Pete Woodward had for many years had an interest in catering and a passion for good food when they shared their enthusiasm by acquiring **Coasters of Southwold**. Dating from about 1750, the building was once the village Post Office and had been a restaurant for 40 years when the partners took it over.

Great food is served throughout the day, seven days a week: breakfasts, lunches and evening meals (last orders 9pm) make excellent use of local produce, and the weekly changing main menu is supplemented by a tempting selection of daily specials. The stylishly

modernised interior is warm and inviting, and the restaurant opens out on to a courtyard where diners can enjoy their food and drink alfresco when the sun shines. Coasters is a deservedly popular place, so booking is advisable to be sure of a table at peak times.

69 THE KINGS HEAD HOTEL

25 High Street, Southwold,
Suffolk IP18 6AD
☎ 01502 724517
e-mail: info@kingsheadsouthwold.com
🌐 www.kingsheadsouthwold.com

Jack Fountain looks forward to greeting visitors to the **Kings Head Hotel**, a traditional family hostelry with ancient beams, period photographs, prints from a local gallery and golfing memorabilia. Jack had several years' experience in the pub industry, including a spell at the White Hart in Halesworth, before taking over this Adnams hostelry in April 2007 at the tender age of 24. The Kings Head is open all day, every day for

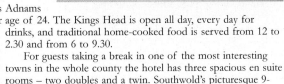

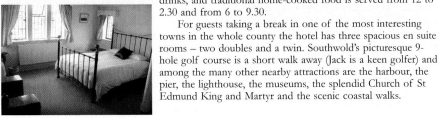

drinks, and traditional home-cooked food is served from 12 to 2.30 and from 6 to 9.30.

For guests taking a break in one of the most interesting towns in the whole county the hotel has three spacious en suite rooms – two doubles and a twin. Southwold's picturesque 9-hole golf course is a short walk away (Jack is a keen golfer) and among the many other nearby attractions are the harbour, the pier, the lighthouse, the museums, the splendid Church of St Edmund King and Martyr and the scenic coastal walks.

70 EARSHAM PARK FARM

Old Railway Road, Earsham, nr Bungay,
Suffolk NR35 2AQ
☎ 01986 892180
e-mail: bobbie@earsham-parkfarm.co.uk
🌐 www.earsham-parkfarm.co.uk

'The only complaint we have is that we didn't find you sooner.' That's a typical comment by guests at **Earsham Park Farm**, where Bobbie Watchorn has been providing outstanding Bed & Breakfast accommodation for nearly 20 years. Her comfortable Victorian farmhouse, combining period charm with modern comforts, stands at the end of a half-mile drive off the A143, 3 miles west of Bungay on the Norfolk/Suffolk border. Overlooking the Waveney Valley, this elegant farmhouse provides an ideal base for exploring the East Anglian countryside, and the three en suite bedrooms, one with a splendid four-poster, feature antique furniture, embroidered linen, thick fluffy towels, hairdryer, television, radio and beverage tray. The house is at the heart of a 600-acre

working farm with arable crops, a herd of breeding pigs, lots of wildlife, lovely walks and beautiful views. Bobbie, a keen gardener, artist, sculptor and upholder of green principles, is also a super cook, and her breakfasts make the perfect start to the day. Highlights are the home-baked bread, the free-range eggs, the locally cured bacon (from the Earsham pigs) and the home-produced sausages; the bacon and the sausages (herby or peppery) can be bought to take home.

71 THE OTTER TRUST

Earsham, Bungay, Suffolk NR35 2AF
☎ 01986 893470

The Otter Trust is the largest and oldest otter conservation organisation in the world. Its collection of otters and its

breeding successes with the British otter are unique. It's highly successful reintroduction programme, using young British otters bred at its centres, has released over 100 young otters which have thrived and bred in the world so that the population has returned to normal. Three lakes are home to a wide selection of European waterfowl. The flock of free-flying Barnacle geese is probably the largest in the country. The resident birds are joined by masses of wild waterfowl, many of which spend the entire summer on the lakes with their numbers swelled in the winter by hordes of visiting migrants.

72 THE SWAN INN

Barnby, nr Beccles, Suffolk NR34 7QE
☎ 01502 476646

Tucked away in a village off the A146 between Beccles and Lowestoft, the **Swan Inn** attracts visitors from all over the region to enjoy the superb seafood dishes that are the speciality of its restaurant. Host and leading Lowestoft fish merchant Donny Cole secures the pick of the catch to offer a truly

impressive choice. Meat-eaters and vegetarians are not forgotten, and real ale fans will also find an excellent selection. The Swan has won many awards, including Britain's Best Seafood Pub of the Year.

73 SIDEGATE GUEST HOUSE

121 Sidegate Lane, Ipswich, Suffolk IP4 4JB
☎ 01473 728714
e-mail: bookings@sidegateguesthouse.co.uk
🌐 www.sidegateguesthouse.co.uk

This award winning guesthouse is on the site of the side gate to Round Wood, Lord Nelson's 'dream cottage' which he bought in 1797. Sally and Richard extend a very warm welcome and an assurance that nothing is too much trouble for their guests.

East Anglia has a wealth of attractions to satisfy all interests. Constable Country is just a stone's throw away, as is the only museum in the UK dedicated to the men and women in the Second World War resistance network. As experienced event managers, your hosts can organise bespoke Blue Badge guided tours, golfing breaks, river cruises and barge trips – in fact anything that makes your stay more memorable.

All bedrooms – two of which are on the ground floor - have en suite shower

rooms, complementary toiletries, tea, coffee and biscuits, television and a hairdryer. Breakfast includes fresh fruit salad, free range eggs and a locally sourced range of bacon and sausages. There is free wireless internet connectivity throughout and daily newspapers, magazines and books available in the guest lounge.

74 THE BRAMFORD COCK

The Street, Bramford, Suffolk IP8 4DT
☎ 01473 747939

The **Bramford Cock** is a much-loved local with traditional décor and furnishings, open every lunchtime and evening and all day Friday, Saturday and Sunday. Host Bill Stoddart is a very popular figure in the locality, and his customers can be sure of the warmest of welcomes, whether they're familiar faces or first-timers. Food is a major part of the business,

and big blackboards list the day's dishes, which include classics like gammon, steaks, lasagne, burgers, curries and scampi, and always a roast. A special attraction on Tuesdays and Fridays is an authentic Indian buffet.

75 THE WHITE HORSE

Tattingstone, Suffolk IP9 2NU
☎ 01473 328060
🌐 www.whitehorsetattingstone.co.uk

Young, enthusiastic tenants Caroline and Andy Hurley have quickly made their mark at the **White Horse**, an attractive old slate-roofed standing off the A137 four miles south of Ipswich. Offering real ales and a good choice of satisfying pub food, it's popular with locals, walkers, cyclists and tourists, and several local clubs and

societies regularly meet here. Behind the pub is a beer garden, and beyond it a field for caravans and tents. The pub is open lunchtime and evening and all day Friday to Sunday.

76 THE QUEENS HEAD

Erwarton, nr Ipswich, Suffolk IP9 ILN
☎ 01473 787550
e-mail: allyson@erwartonqueen.com

In a village signposted off the B1456 Ipswich-Shotley Gate road, the **Queens Head** looks out over fields to the Stour Estuary. Ancient beams combine with modern furnishings in the bar, and when the weather is kind the ionic benches set outside are in demand. Leaseholder Allyson Richardson numbers locals, tourists, walkers and boaters among her clientele, and she keeps them all happy with a fine selection

of home-cooked dishes – fish cooked in the special 'house' batter is a surefire winner.

78 THE KINGS HEAD

90 High Street, Hadleigh, Suffolk IP7 5EF
☎ 01473 828855

Mike Ager runs a traditional pub of wide appeal, a substantial building on a corner site in the delightful little market town of Hadleigh. Equally popular with locals, families, walkers, cyclists and tourists, the **Kings Head** has a large dining area where the menus offer anything from sandwiches and snacks, to seafood specialities, Sunday roasts and a full à la carte choice. Drinks include a good range of ales. The pub is open from 10 o'clock every day.

77 THE BRIARS & MANSARD COTTAGE

c/o High View, Back Lane, Washbrook, Ipswich, Suffolk IP8 3JA
☎ 01473 730494
e-mail: bookings@suffolkholidays.com
ⓦ www.suffolkholidays.com

Owned and run by the Steward family, **The Briars and Mansard Cottage** are beautifully restored timber-framed 18th century cottages, decorated and furnished to a very high standard and retaining many fine period features.

The Briars has three bedrooms (a double, a twin and a single), a bath/shower room, plenty of living space and full kitchen facilities. Mansard Cottage with one double/twin room, is equally well appointed. The cottages are ideally placed for exploring the Suffolk coast and countryside – Ipswich, Lavenham, Sudbury, Long Melford, Hadleigh, Kersey, Cavendish, Bury St Edmunds, Constable Country and the Heritage Coast are all within easy driving distance. There are lots of public footpaths around the village offering pleasant walks through woodland and open countryside.

79 BOX TREE FARM

Kettlebaston, nr Lavenham,
Suffolk IP7 7PZ
☎ 01449 741318
e-mail: junecarpenter@btinternet.com
🌐 www.boxtreefarm.350.com

Country-lovers make tracks for **Box Tree Farm**, where June and Mike Carpenter provide

peace, space and comfort in three en suite bedrooms. Residents have the use of a spacious drawing room, and breakfast is served in an elegant dining room (evening meals by arrangement). The rural theme is strong throughout the farmhouse, which stands in trim gardens surrounded by acres of farmland.

80 THE OLD CONVENT

Kettlebaston, nr Lavenham,
Suffolk IP7 7QA
☎ 01449 741557
e-mail: holidays@kettlebaston.fsnet.co.uk

Resident owners Val and Peter Gutteridge offer guests a choice of accommodation in the pretty village of Kettlebaston, a short drive east of Lavenham. In the **Old Convent**, a 17th

century thatched cottage with ancient beams and doors, stone floors and low ceilings, they have three characterful en suite bedrooms for B&B guests; close by, the newly refurbished, "Rector's Retreat", provides a self-catering option, with easy access for less mobile guests. Both are open all year. Cash and cheque only. Colour brochure available.

81 AMICI CUCINA ITALIANA

47 Gainsborough Street, Sudbury,
Suffolk CO10 2ET
☎ 01787 374298
e-mail: amicisudbury@aol.com

Art-loving visitors to Sudbury make a beeline for Gainsborough House, where the painter Thomas Gainsborough was born in 1727. But art-lovers and anyone else with an interest in good food will time their visit to the town to be able to sample the delights of the next-door restaurant **Amici Cucina Italiana**. Owners Yvon (from Sicily) and Hadleigh Piret are both passionate about food and top-class local produce, and what goes into their kitchen comes out as superb Southern Italian dishes with both traditional and contemporary elements. The décor is smart and modern, with work by local artists exhibited on the walls. Amici is the perfect choice for anything from a cup of coffee and a quick bite to a family get-together or a romantic dinner for two. Opening times are 10.30 to 2.30 and 6 to 10 Tuesday to Saturday.

82 THE ROSE & CROWN

North Street, Hundon, nr Sudbury,
Suffolk CO10 8ED
☎ 01440 786261

Andy and Helen Brame welcome guests of all ages, along with their children and dogs, to the **Rose & Crown**, a quintessential village inn with oak beams and warming winter fires behind its pinkwashed exterior. Outside are two big gardens with plenty of seating and play areas.

The daughter of the house cooks good basic pub dishes typified by sausages with mash

or chips, burgers and warming winter hotpots, along with lunchtime sandwiches and snacks. The pub, which is open all day, every day, stands on the main street of Hundon, a quiet rural village off the B1063, 3 miles north of Clare.

83 THE BROOK INN

Bures Road, Great Cornard, nr Sudbury,
Suffolk CO10 0JQ
☎ 01787 373166

Since arriving at the **Brook Inn** at the end of 2006 host and chef Jay Innone has built a loyal clientele from Sudbury and the surrounding district. Set in a residential area on the southeast edge of Sudbury, the pub, which dates from the 1880s, has a busy bar for

drinks and snacks and a separate restaurant serving high-quality home-cooked dishes – favourites include steak & ale pie, braised lamb shank, Italian-style chicken, steaks and classic desserts like jam roly poly, spotted dick and chocolate brownies. The inn has a pleasant lawned garden with a play area, and a capacious car park.

84 GLADWINS FARM

Harper's Hill, Nayland, Suffolk CO6 4NU
☎ 01206 262261 Fax: 01206 263001
e-mail: gladwinsfarm@aol.com
🌐 www.gladwinsfarm.co.uk

Just off the A134 Colchester-Sudbury road, **Gladwins Farm** enjoys a lovely quiet setting in the Dedham Vale Area of Outstanding Natural Beauty, a landscape immortalised in paintings by Constable and Gainsborough. In 22 acres of rolling countryside, with

glorious views over the Stour Valley, spacious, warm and comfortable cottages provide luxurious self-catering for 2 to 8 guests. In a new building or converted outbuildings, each has its own individual appeal, but all are superbly furnished and equipped for a relaxed, carefee holiday. One room is in an annexe to the farmhouse, where owners Robert and Pauline

Dossor also have two en suite double rooms for Bed & Breakfast, with books, magazines and television in the residents' lounge and fresh local produce for the breakfasts. Guests have the use of a heated indoor pool, treatment room and sauna, a hot tub in its own gazebo, an all-weather tennis court and a well-stocked fishing lake; a play area and friendly farm animals will keep the children happy for hours.

85 THE PRIORS INN

Priors Avenue, Bury St Edmunds,
Suffolk IP33 3CT
☎ 01284 748941

Caroline Wildman and David Heath are the friendly owners at the **Priors Inn**, a lively, popular local standing half a mile from the centre of Bury. The 1930s redbrick pub is a great place to meet for a drink or to enjoy a wide variety of good honest home cooking – fish cakes, liver & bacon, meat or vegetarian lasagne, breaded scampi,  shepherds pie and stuffed peppers are typical choices on the big blackboard menus, as well as the Sunday Carvery. The inn is open from 5 on Monday (no food), and from noon till late every other day. Live music Friday and Saturday evenings.

87 THE METCALFE ARMS

Lawshall Road, Hawstead,
nr Bury St Edmunds, Suffolk IP29 5NR
☎ 01284 386321
e-mail: themetcalfearms@btconnect.com

The **Metcalfe Arms** is a popular village pub where affable hosts Anne and Nigel provide top hospitality, well-kept real ales and a good choice of food freshly prepared using local produce wherever possible. Typical choices  could include rump steak with a pepper or blue cheese sauce, breaded cod, Suffolk sausages, the day's pasta, fresh fish from Lowestoft, the pie of the week and the hearty Metcalfe Hoggie – a baguette loaded with strips of steak, bacon, onions and mushrooms, topped with melted cheese. Room should definitely be kept for one of the scrumptious desserts – perhaps fruit crumble or chocolate junkyard.

86 WEST STOW ANGLO-SAXON VILLAGE

Visitor Centre, Icklingham Road, West Stow,
Bury St Edmunds, Suffolk IP28 6HG
☎ 01284 728718 Fax: 01284 728277
🌐 www.stedmundsbury.gov.uk/weststow.htm

Between 1965 and 1972 the low hill by the River Lark in Suffolk was excavated to reveal several periods of occupation, but in particular, over 70 buildings from an early Anglo Saxon village. There was also information from about 100 graves in the nearby cemetery. It was decided that such extensive evidence about these people should be used to carry out a practical experiment to test ideas about the buildings that formed the elements of the original village.

Part of the Anglo Saxon Village has been reconstructed on the site where the original (inhabited from around AD420 to 650) was excavated. The reconstructions have been built over a period of more than 20 years. Each of the eight buildings is different, to test different ideas, and each has been built using the tools and techniques available to the early Anglo Saxons. Exploring the houses is an excellent way of finding out about the Anglo Saxons who lived at West Stow. Costumed "Anglo Saxons" bring the village to life at certain times, especially at Easter and during August. The new Anglo Saxon Centre is an exciting addition to the site, housing the original objects found there and at other local sites. Many of the objects have never been seen by the public before.

West Stow Anglo Saxon Village lies in the middle of a beautiful 125 acre Country Park, part of which is a Site of Special Scientific Interest. The park has a number of different habitats, including woodland, heathland, a lake and a river. There is a play area, a bird feeding area and bird hides. The Park is open daily all year, from 9am-5pm in winter, 9am-8pm in summer. Entry to the park is free.

88 THE VICTORIA

North Road, Thurston,
nr Bury St Edmunds, Suffolk IP31 3QH
☎ 01359 230951
e-mail: heather.hatch@btinternet.com

IT expert Heather Hatch is also the host at the **Victoria**, which lies east of bury close to J46 of the A14. Greene king IPA, Abbot Ale and Tribute are on tap to quench thirsts in the bar, and home-cooked food is served in the comfortable restaurant every lunchtime and evening. The impressive menu offers outstanding variety, including steak house specialities, bakes

and pies, gourmet sausages, trout with lemon & parsley butter and 'Continental Cuisine' – lasagne, chilli, paella, chicken tikka masala. The Victoria is a popular venue for office parties, family get-togethers and other special occasions, catering for up to 50.

89 WINES BAR & KITCHEN AT THE SIX BELLS

Felsham, nr Bury St Edmunds,
Suffolk IP30 0PJ
☎ 01449 736268
e-mail: Julie.wine@btconnect.com

David and Julie Wine have given their name to **Wines Bar & Kitchen at the Six Bells**, a traditional village inn down country roads between Bury and Stowmarket. And they've made a name for themselves and their pub with a fine range of interesting food drawing its inspiration from near and far. Typical dishes run

from lamb's liver & bacon to spaghetti with pesto, beef bourguignon and seasonal game and seafood specialities. Open from 5 on Monday, lunchtime and evening, Tuesday to Saturday and all day Sunday.

90 KENTWELL HALL

Long Melford, Suffolk CO10 9BA
☎ 01787 310207 Fax: 01787 379318
e-mail: info@kentwell.co.uk
🌐 www.kentwell.co.uk

Kentwell Hall, a romantic, mellow, moated redbrick Tudor mansion in a

tranquil parkland setting, has a great deal to offer the visitor. The house was built by the Clopton family in the first half of the 16th century with wealth accrued from the wool trade, and the exterior has changed little down the centuries. After the Cloptons, the house saw a succession of owners and tenants before being requisitioned by the Army in the Second World War. It was in a poor state of repair when acquired by the present owner Patrick Phillips in 1970, since when he and his wife Judith have been lovingly restoring the house and its gardens.

The owners have created a rare breeds farm in the superb grounds, where other features

include a restored working ice house, a rose garden, a fern stumpery, a coppice walk, a living sundial and the largest carved tree in England, representing the Tower of Babel.

Kentwell is famous for its re-creations of Tudor domestic life and of wartime Britain, when it saw service as a transit camp. These events take place on Bank Holidays and selected weekends throughout the year, and in the summer a series of open-air entertainment, from jazz to Shakespeare, is invariably well attended. The Hall was the setting for the film version of *Toad of Toad Hall*.

91 NATIONAL HORSERACING MUSEUM 🏛

99 High Street, Newmarket, Suffolk CB8 8JH
☎ **01638 667333** Fax: **01638 665600**
🌐 www.nationalstud.co.uk

"The Newmarket Experience" comprises two separate attractions: **The National Horseracing Museum** and **The National Stud**. The story of racing throughout the ages is told through the Museum's permanent collections, featuring the horses, people, events and scandals that make the sport so colourful.

Highlights include the head of Persimmon, a great Royal Derby winner in 1896; a special display about Fred Archer, the Victorian jockey who committed suicide after losing the struggle to keep his weight down; the skeleton of Eclipse, ancestor of 90 per cent of modern thoroughbreds; items associated with Red Rum, Lester Piggott, Frankie Dettori and other heroes of the Turf. In the Practical Gallery, visitors can learn everything there is to know about the horse and jockey, and experience the thrill of riding on the horse simulator.

The Gallery is staffed by retired jockeys and trainers, who make the world of racing come alive. Special exhibitions have included "*Why* did you get that hat?", a display of Gertrude Shilling's outrageous Ascot outfits. Mrs Shilling (1910-1999) was one of the most colourful and eccentric personalities ever to grace the sport.

The National Stud extends a warm welcome to all its visitors. Breeding top-class thoroughbreds, the 500-acre site has 12 yards, 9 miles of roads and tracks, 60 miles of post and rail fencing, 21 houses, a feedmill and storage for 50 tons of hay and straw - all purpose built between 1963 and 1967.

92 BYERLEY HOUSE ⊨

Warrington Street, Newmarket, Suffolk CB8 8BA
☎ **01638 667870** Fax: **01638 668005**
e-mail: bobbie@sportsdays.co.uk

Bobbie Allen, wife of racehorse trainer Conrad Allen, runs one of the very best B&B establishments in the region, and the perfect base for a few day's racing or tours of the stables and studs, the bloodstock sales or the National Horseracing Museum. In the centre of town, **Byerley House** is a stunning modern brick building with four beautifully appointed double rooms with en suite shower

room and TV. The day gets under orders with an excellent full English breakfast.

93 THE AFFLECK ARMS ‖ ⊨

1 Brookside, Dalham, Suffolk CB8 8TG
☎ **01638 500306**

New licensees Paul and Michelle Hunt have quickly made their mark at the **Affleck Arms**, a delightful old thatched pub with abundant charm and character. Locals, tourists and racegoers come here to enjoy the real ales, which feature small local breweries (Affleck IPA, Adnams Bitter) and Paul's excellent home cooking. Sunday night is games night, with a variety of traditional pub games. The inn has an en suite double room for guests staying overnight.

273

94 HILL FARM

Kirtling, nr Newmarket, Suffolk CB8 9QD
☎ 01638 730253 Fax: 01638 731957

Charming landlady Ann Bailey runs a delightful B&B in a 400-year-old farmhouse in a secluded location surrounded by arable farmland. Behind a sympathetically modernised exterior, old-world charm abounds at **Hill Farm**, with beams and log fires in the dining and sitting rooms and décor in keeping with the age of the

house. The three bedrooms are warm, comfortable and well equipped, and the day starts with a full English breakfast served at a large communal table. Open all year. Cash and cheque only.

95 COLCHESTER CASTLE MUSEUM

Castle Park, High Street, Colchester,
Essex CO1 1TJ
☎ 01206 282939
⊕ www.colchestermuseums.org.uk

Colchester Castle is undeniably one of the most important historic buildings in the country. Colchester was the first capital of Roman Britain and beneath the Castle are the remains of the most famous Roman buildings, the Temple of Claudius. Today if you lay your hand on the stonework of the temple it can be said that you are touching the very foundation of Roman Britain.

To Romans the temple was a symbol of their power and success, but to the native Britons it was a symbol of oppression. The temple became a main target of the rebels led by Queen Boudica who attacked the Roman town of Colchester in AD 60. Around 1076 William I ordered a royal fortress to be built at Colchester. The great stone base of the ruined Roman temple was an obvious foundation for the central tower, or keep, of the castle.

The huge size of the temple meant that the keep of Colchester Castle was the largest ever built in Britain and is the largest surviving example in Europe. For most of its life the Castle was used as a prison. One of the most infamous episodes in its history occurred in 1645 when Matthew Hopkins, the self-styled Witchfinder General, used the Castle to imprison and interrogate suspected witches.

96 HOLLYTREES MUSEUM

High Street, Colchester, Essex CO1 1UG
☎ 01206 282940
🌐 www.colchestermuseums.org.uk

Hollytrees is a beautiful Georgian town house in the grounds of the award-winning Castle Park. Built in 1718 it has been owned by some of the wealthiest families in Colchester and is now a fascinating museum for all to enjoy and explore.

History is told at this vibrant museum with humour and fun in mind, making it an ideal venue for families. Visit the childhood gallery with its a large playroom with snakes and ladders incorporated into the floor. There is a crawling tunnel, toy bins, toddler 'time out' area and exciting displays celebrating Colchester's famous nursery rhymes Old King Cole and Twinkle, Twinkle Little Star.

Meet the many different characters from the past and find out what life was like for them living and working in a house like Hollytrees. Experience Colchester's fascinating past through audio, hands-on activities and stories and be transported back to the days before washing machines, to try out a dolly peg, dress up as a servant, make your own Victorian silhouette and experience the miniature world of the Hollytrees dolls house.

Join in with many special events and changing exhibitions throughout the year that bring history to life the fun way, and don't forget to visit the Museum shop to find that perfect gift. The museum is free admission so you can enjoy it and visit time and time again.

97 THE MARLBOROUGH HEAD INN

Mill Lane, Dedham, nr Colchester, Essex CO7 6DH
☎ 01206 323250
e-mail: jen.pearmain@tiscali.co.uk
🌐 www.marlborough-head.co.uk

The **Marlborough Head Inn** is a historic Grade II listed building in the heart of Constable Country. Jenny Pearman and her staff have created a particularly happy and relaxed environment for visitors, whether they've come for a quiet pint, a home-cooked meal with a glass of wine or a night or two in the comfortable, characterful accommodation. The three letting rooms

comprise the Constable Suite with a four-poster bed and en suite bathroom, the Munnings Room – a double with en suite shower – and the Stour Room with twin beds and en suite shower. Open from 10am to 11pm daily, the inn has a sun-trap terrace and a large walled garden.

98 THE ANGEL

36 Bradford Street, Bocking, nr Braintree, Essex CM7 9AT
☎ 01376 321549
e-mail: janicerlynch@aol.com

Janice Lynch and Bob Brinkley make a fine team at **The Angel**, a popular pub that started life as a coaching inn in the 16th century. Broadside Ale is a popular thirst-quencher, and everything on Janice's menu is fresh and tasty – her lasagne always goes

down a treat. This sociable inn, open from 5 Monday to Friday and all day Saturday and Sunday, fields its own football team and no fewer than seven pool teams in the local leagues.

Coggeshall Road, Stisted, nr Braintree,
Essex CM77 8AB
☎ 01376 331409
e-mail: ballaglass@btopenworld.com
http://uk.geocities.com/
ballaglass@btinternet.com

East of Braintree off the A120 or A131, **Ballaglass** provides a luxurious self-catering holiday base, combining stunning décor with every modern comfort, in a purpose-built unit set in two acres of grounds surrounded by open fields.

The accommodation comprises a large double bedroom with adjacent bathroom and separate shower cubicle; a roomy, well-appointed lounge-diner with two sofa beds and French windows opening onto a sunny patio; and a fully equipped kitchen with electric oven and hob, microwave, fridge and washing machine. Guests are welcome to wander through the gardens, which contain three large ponds, an area devoted to growing fruit and vegetables and a summer house with tables and chairs.

Local shopping is available within a mile, and the owners Sally and Tony Dunn, who live in Ballaglass Cottage opposite the unit, can recommend the best local eating places. They can also arrange to provide groceries on arrival from a shopping list sent to guests with confirmation of their reservations.

This is just one of the many thoughtful touches on the part of the owners, whose aim is to make their guests' holidays as enjoyable as possible and to provide the facilities that they themselves would expect when they go away on holiday. Ballaglass, a haven of peace and tranquillity awarded 4 Stars by the East of England Tourist Board, is a perfect choice for taking a well-deserved break and an ideal base for exploring a part of the country that's rich in scenic and historic interest, with pleasant countryside and picturesque villages.

Among the nearby places of interest are Cressing Temple Barns, Marks Hall Country estate and Paycockes House at Coggeshall. There are several excellent golf courses within a few miles, and horse riding is available nearby. Children under 5 and service dogs are welcome at Ballaglass, by prior arrangement. Cash and cheque only.

100 THE KINGS ARMS

Broad Green, nr Coggeshall, Colchester, Essex CO6 1RU
☎ 01376 562006

Situated on the A120 between Marks Tey and Braintree, 6 miles from the historic walled town of Colchester is the **Kings Arms**, where John Murray looks after the beer while his partner Chris takes care of the country appetites. This late 18th century roadside inn is open all day with a good selection of real ales. Patrons can enjoy a variety of home-

cooked pub favourites including steak and ale pie; chicken, bacon and leek pie; steak and kidney pudding; fish pie; rabbit stew and other game dishes. Sunday roasts and home-made desserts are a speciality. Eating out in the large family garden is an option in warmer weather or enjoy the roaring log fire on colder days.

101 THE WHITE HART

The Street, Great Saling, nr Braintree, Essex CM7 5DR
☎ 01371 850341

Kevin Robinson and Clare Green are the affable hosts at the **White Hart**, which stands in a picturesque village north of the A120 between Dunmow and Braintree. Dating from the early 17th century, the pub has a

traditional look and feel enhanced by oak beams and a delightful galleried restaurant. This was the place where the huffer – a big floury bap – was first baked, and today the kitchen produces a good varied choice of high-quality food, typified by cod or skate fried in Abbot Ale batter, lasagne, curries, steaks, meat pies and hunters chicken with bacon and stilton.

Large beer garden at the rear complete with childrens play area.

103 FROYZ HALL BARN

Pennypot Corner, Halstead, Essex CO9 1RS
☎ 01787 476684 mob: 07738 147743
e-mail: judibutler@dsl.pipex.com
🌐 www.froyzhall.co.uk

Judi combines the roles of busy mother and interior designer with running a self-catering business at **Froyz Hall Barn**. Part of a substantial country estate a mile south of Halstead, the 200-year-old barn has been extensively renovated and refurbished,

while retaining many original features, to provide a top-quality holiday home with the emphasis on comfort and style. The accommodation comprises three spacious bedrooms, a luxurious bathroom, two shower rooms, well-equipped lounge and dining areas and a stylish Christians kitchen with a range cooker. Guests have the use of a 40ft swimming pool and a tennis court; fishing is available on a private lake, and the 1,000 acres of grounds include lovely woodland walks. Froyz Hall is the

perfect place for children, with safe off-road cycling, playing on the trampoline and

climbing frame and getting to know the owner's dogs and horses. Many extra services can be arranged, including catering for dinner parties, babysitting, therapies and fitness instruction. Judi also offer self-catering accommodation for up to eight guests in Lee Road, Aldeburgh. **www.melbourne-villa.co.uk**

104 High Garrett, Braintree,
Essex CM7 5NJ
☎ 01376 324430
e-mail: handhpub@hotmail.com
🌐 www.hare-and-hounds.com

Paul Harper and Steve Watling have transformed the **Hare & Hounds** from a rather tired 'local' into a fresh and

contemporary countryside bar and bistro, with the bonus of comfortable Bed & Breakfast accommodation. Located on the A131 Halstead road just north of Braintree, it attracts a large passing trade as well as the many regulars who come here to enjoy all the good things on offer. The handsome 18th century brick building has been tastefully upgraded within, while retaining a traditional pub atmosphere, and outside is a pleasant beer garden for soaking up the summer sun.

Adnams ales are on tap to quench thirsts, and all tastes and appetites are catered for with lunchtime snacks and light meals, a full lunch and dinner restaurant menu and the Sunday carvery; it's also a popular choice for parties and special occasions. All the food is prepared and cooked on the premises, and the menus combine old favourites with some more contemporary or adventurous dishes. With 12 ounces of prime beef, the burgers are as generous as any you'll see, and other popular orders include filo prawn parcels, spicy chicken wings, cod & chips, steaks, lasagne and steak & kidney pudding. Specials such as lemon & pepper breaded scallops extend the choice even further, and the 'plates to share' – one of them a vegetarian version – are a popular choice for two. The Sunday carvery offers chicken, fish and vegetarian alternatives to the two roast joints. Desserts like bread & butter pudding or chocolate lumpy bumpy make a splendid end to an excellent meal. The bar is open from 6 to 12 on Monday, 12 to 12 Tuesday to Thursday, 12 to 1am Friday and Saturday and 12 to 12 on Sunday. Food times are 6 to 9 on Monday, 12 to 2.30 and 6 to 10 Tuesday to Saturday and 12 to 5 on Sunday. The five upstairs rooms at the Hare & Hounds, three of them with en suite facilities, are popular with business people, motorists and tourists. There's a lot to see in the vicinity, including Cressing Temple Barns, Marks Hall, Paycockes house at Coggeshall and the many historic buildings in Halstead.

104 BRIGHTLINGSEA MOTEL

1 High Street, Brightlingsea,
Essex CO7 0AE
☎ 01206 306611   Fax: 01206 306612
info@brightlingseamotel.co.uk
🌐 www.brightlingseamotel.co.uk

Walkers, cyclists, birdwatchers, sailing folk, families on a coastal getaway......all are welcome at the Breeden family's **Brightlingsea Motel**, a new development in the heart of town next to St James' Church. The motel has six versatile rooms, from a single to a family room, all with TV, internet Wi-Fi facilities,

beverage tray and hairdryer. The family room, with a bath as well as a shower, is equipped for guests with mobility difficulties. Breakfast is served in a bright conservatory overlooking the courtyard.

105 THE COAST INN

108 Coast Road, West Mersea, Colchester,
Essex CO5 8NA
☎ 01206 383568   Fax: 01206 383908
e-mail: info@thecoastinn.co.uk
🌐 www.thecoastinn.cok

Belinda Cross, in the licensed trade for more than 20 years, has been the owner of the **Coast Inn** since 2004. Situated between the Blackwater and Colne estuaries, this unique riverside bar and restaurant offers an attractive mix of traditional wooden floors, log fires and contemporary stylish modern chairs and leather settees, providing a smart, relaxed setting in which to enjoy a drink and a meal. Outside, the garden commands splendid views on the move or at their moorings on the Blackwater River. Mersea has plenty to interest the visitor: much of the island is a nature reserve, and the 'seeding' of the oyster beds has become a popular annual event.

Local produce is in plentiful supply, particularly fish and shellfish, much of which finds its way into the Coast's kitchen. There's also a good choice for

meat-eaters and always some vegetarian options. Locals, tourists, day trippers, yachtsmen, anglers and birdwatchers keep the place busy for both drinks and food – home-baked cakes with morning coffee, lunches, cream teas and dinners. The inn has a ramp for wheelchair access to the bars, and the toilets are also accessible to wheelchair users. Opening hours are 11 to 11 (Sunday 12 to 10.30)

106 THE VICTORY AT MERSEA

92 Coast Road, Mersea Island,
Essex CO5 8LS
☎ 01206 382907
e-mail: victoryatmersea@aol.com
🌐 www.victoryatmersea.com

Peter and Gill Tydie offer a warm welcome to the **Victory at Mersea**, a familiar landmark on the most easterly inhabited island in the UK. Their Edwardian redbrick inn stands right on the waterfront, with fantastic views over the Blackwater estuary. The owners have completely refurbished the inn, with Indian-slate floors, leather sofas and lightwood furniture complementing the pastel décor. The customer always comes first, and among the many other improvements are superior en-suite B & B rooms and new toilets. The chefs produce a wide variety of dishes that put a contemporary touch on traditional pub cuisine, ranging from great steaks and fish, all locally sourced, to homemade pies and pasta. Many of the dishes can be ordered in smaller

portions for children or grown-ups with small appetites. Food is served lunchtime and evening seven days a week and booking is advisable at weekends, particularly for the Sunday roast lunches (served from noon to 6). The Victory has a large patio, a garden with separate children's play area, and private car park.

107 HOME BAY B&B

9 Bay Road, Dovercourt, nr Harwich,
Essex CO12 3JZ
☎ 01255 504428

Syd and Jan Johnson welcome visitors from near and far to their neat semi-detached house just off the High Street and a short walk from the railway station. **Home Bay** offers a cosy little home from home with three quiet, comfortable upstairs bedrooms and a residents' lounge where guests can plan their days. The owners provide a good choice for breakfast, and residents can take the sun on the patio or in the pleasant garden at the back of the house. Open all year.

108 THE GATE

74 Thaxted Road, Saffron Walden,
Essex CB11 3AG
☎ 01799 522321

Newly refurbished, with an appealing mix of old and new elements, **The Gate** is a pleasant spot to pause for a drink or a meal. On the quiet southern edge of town, but close enough for a stroll to the centre, the pub is in the safe hands of David and Victoria Robins. David is an experienced and talented chef, and his dishes, served lunchtime and evening Tuesday to Saturday, run from sandwiches and snacks

to burgers (beef, chicken or veggie), home-cooked ham, bangers & mash, beer-battered cod, Cajun chicken breast, steaks, pies and traditional Sunday roasts which are served from noon to 4pm.

109 THE BLUEBELL INN

High Street, Hempstead, nr Saffron Walden,
Essex CB10 2PD
☎ 01799 599199
🌐 www.thebluebellinn.co.uk

Hard to miss with its cheerful blue-painted
frontage, the **Bluebell Inn** stands on the
main street of Hempstead, on the B1054 east
of Saffron Walden. Host Rod Stokes keeps
his customers happy with good ales, decent
food, excellent service – and a bit of history
thrown in.

The food,
all home-
prepared,
runs a
popular
gamut from
snacks and
sandwiches
to fresh
fish, steaks
and tasty pies. The inn has many pictures and
other items associated with Dick Turpin, who
was born here in 1706 in the time when his
parents kept the inn.

110 THE RED LION

Great Sampford, nr Saffron Walden,
Essex CB10 2RL
☎ 01799 586325

Mark and Karen Ives put out the welcome
mat for all the family at the **Red Lion**, a cosy,
traditional inn with a separate restaurant.
They share the cooking, and the menu tempts
with dishes
running
from bar
snacks to
tempura
prawns,
poachers
chicken,
steaks,
steak pies,

Stilton & vegetable crumble and, to finish, a
scrumptious treacle sponge. Pool and darts
are the favourite games played in the bar, and
for guests staying overnight the inn has two
bedrooms with shared facilities. The Red
Lion is open every session except Monday
lunchtime.

111 THE WHITE HART

High Street, Stebbing, nr Great Dunmow,
Essex CM6 3SQ
☎ 01371 856383

Nick Eldred has for many years been owner and
host at the **White Hart**, which lies amidst some
lovely little cottages 2 miles east of Great Dunmow
off the A120 Braintree road. Dating from the 16th
century, it retains great period charm, with a

handsome white-plastered frontage and a steeply
raked tiled roof. A feature log fire keeps things cosy
in the oak-beamed bar, where the drinks choice
includes Greene King IPA, Old Speckled Hen, guest
ales, very good house wines and a selection of malt
whiskies. Traditional pub fare is served lunchtime
and evening in the bar or restaurant. Decorative
features to take the eye include a collection of
framed cigarette cards and a St Christopher charm
left by Buddy Holly. The White Hart is very much at

the heart of
Stebbing's
social life and
has a separate

area where darts, pool and bar billiards are played; quiz nights
are a popular regular feature, as are the occasional live music
nights. The pub is open lunchtime and evening Monday to
Friday, from 11am to midnight on Saturday and from noon to
midnight on Sunday. No food Sunday evening.

112 THE CHAFF HOUSE

Littlebury Green, nr Saffron Walden,
Essex CB11 4XB
☎ 01763 839278

Only the best will do at the **Chaff House**, where owner Diane Duke provides her guests with a true taste of traditional farmhouse living and an excellent base for tourists. On a 900-acre working farm just across the M11 from Saffron

Walden, she has three letting rooms – a beautifully appointed room with exposed beams and an enormous bed in the house and two in a separate building with their own kitchen, allowing the option of self-catering. When the sun shines, it's nice to sit out among the pretty flowers and plants in the courtyard patio.

113 THE ROSE & CROWN

Crown Hill, Ashdon, nr Saffron Walden,
Essex CB10 2HB
☎ 01799 584337

On a minor road 3 miles northeast of Saffron Walden, the **Rose & Crown** is an attractive roadside pub with a convivial public bar, a little lounge bar, a neat beamed restaurant and a pleasant beer garden. Host and chef Paul Lewis seeks out the best produce, including meat and

poultry from a top local butcher, for his dishes, which run from lunchtime snacks to grilled or battered fish, steaks, summer salads, a super steak, mushroom & ale pie and delicious hot fruit pies, crumbles and puddings made to traditional recipes. Real ales (August Bank Holiday beer festival) and fine wines complement the outstanding food.

114 WALTHAM ABBEY CHURCH

Parish Office, 5A Greenyard,
Waltham Abbey, Essex EN9 1RD
☎ 01992 767897
🌐 www.walthamabbeychurch.co.uk

Come and visit Waltham Abbey Church. Enjoy more than one thousand years of history and beautiful setting, following in the footsteps of King Harold, Henry VIII, Thomas Tallis and others. Near to other attractions including: Lee Valley Park, Royal Gunpowder Mills and the Epping Forest District Museum

- Open daily to the public
- Welcoming and friendly services
- Extensive gardens and grounds
- Audio Tour
- Group visits

115 THE CRICKETERS

Mill Green, nr Ingatestone, Essex CM4 0SD
☎ 01277 352400
e-mail: thecricketers@tiscali.co.uk
🌐 www.thecricketersatfryerning.co.uk

Food is an important part of the business at the **Cricketers**, a fine little village pub dating from the early 19th century. Daily specials, including fresh seafood and seasonal game, add to the choice of excellent home-cooked dishes to

enjoy in the comfortable bar and restaurant or out in the front garden. The pub sign shows players in cricketing gear…but they're actually footballers – see if you can recognise them!

117 THE WHITE HART INN

Swan Lane, Margaretting Tye,
Essex CM4 9JX
☎ 01277 840478
⊕ www.thewhitehart.com

Owner Liz Haines and her team of friendly staff have established **The White Hart** as one of the best pubs in the whole region. The pub is a traditional Essex weather-board building, consisting of a large single bar and an extensive family room/conservatory. The rural Setting lends itself to a number of excellent walks which makes it a popular choice with ramblers, cyclists and tourists. The pub is located on Swan Lane a grade II listed street running from Stock to Galleywood & Margaretting. The frontage is always adorned with flower baskets and boxes and the gardens are beautifully maintained all year round. Inside the bar area is heavily beamed with a vaulted ceiling and a wood burning stove, a welcomed source of warmth on cold winter days all of which adds to the cosy traditional ambience. An extensive collection of beer and champagne bottles decorate the shelves around the bar and the walls are festooned with old pictures (some of the pub in days gone by, and others of agricultural scenes) and pub and brewery memorabilia.

There is always a fine selection of excellent real ales. Liz, ably assisted by Barry Mott, the cellar man, keeps an enviable cellar with house beers coming from local champion brewer Mighty Oak (Oscar Wilde Mild and IPA) and regional stalwart Adnams (Best and Broadside). Apart from this selection, which would get the majority of pubs a fair write-up in the pages of GBBG, Liz always has a minimum of 3/4 other guest ales serving. All are poured direct from the barrel in the tap room behind the bar. They have recently been awarded Chelmsford & Mid-Essex CAMRA Pub of the Year 2007 as a result of their achievements in this area.

The White Hart has an excellent reputation as a really good place to eat. The long standing Chef Ting Sayer puts the emphasis on using only quality produce sourced locally when available. Food is available 7 days a week with a wide range of meals and snacks. A selection of 'Daily Specials' are featured on a huge Blackboard that hangs over the fireplace in the main bar.

Two key events during the year are a stunning Summer Beer Festival in June with over 60 beers, ciders and perry in a Marquee that put the Chelsea Flower Show to shame (in size if not in flora and fauna!!); and a smaller Winter Beer Festival over the last weekend of October. Liz is also hoping to bring Bed & Breakfast on line in the near future.

116 THE SPREAD EAGLE

**Margaretting, nr Ingatestone,
Essex CM4 9JB
☎ 01277 352052**

The **Spread Eagle** is a classic roadside inn that first saw the light of day in 1693. Mick

and Nicky day, here since the spring of 2007, keep their patrons happy with a good choice of drinks to enjoy on their own or to accompany tasty dishes typified by spaghetti Bolognese, braised lamb shank, curries and stews, with desserts like ginger & sultana sponge to round things off in style. Food is served from 12 to 4 Tuesday to Thursday and from 12 to 5 Friday (and in the evening – bookings only). But it's not just the traditional offerings of a quintessential English pub that bring the crowds here: it's also a must for music-lovers, with live music for a variety of tastes performed on Friday and Saturday nights.

118 THE HORSE & GROOM

**Warley Road, Great Warley, nr Brentwood,
Essex CM13 3AE
☎ 01277 220280**

A change of ownership has injected new life into the

Horse & Groom, a handsome 18th century inn on a busy corner site in Great Warley. Stewart and Karen Butler have created a comfortable, convivial ambience for enjoying a drink or a meal. Stewart has been a chef for 30 years, including distinguished service in the Forces, and choices on his interesting menu (served every day from noon to 9) span old favourites like fish & chips, sausage & mash, lasagne and the daily roast to Singapore noodles and tomato-sauced mussels. The pub hosts regular quizzes, music nights, functions and charity events.

119 THE ROSE & CROWN

390 Ongar Road, Pilgrim's Hatch,
nr Brentwood, Essex CM15 9JH
☎ 01277 372322
🌐 www.roseandcrownbrentwood.com

Easy to spot from the Ongar Road, **The Rose and Crown** offers traditional bar food with some interesting Continental twists to keeps the patrons happy. Everything is prepared on the premises, wherever possible from locally sourced produce, and the busy folk in the kitchen include a marvellous pastry chef who has been plying his trade for more than 60 years.

The sunday roasts are particularly popular, and the Christmas menu, available throughout December, guarantees a seasonal feast. The bar in the restaurant was built from timbers and artefacts rescued from a Scottish church. Friday is disco night and on Saturday it's karaoke.

The Rose & Crown is a great place to take a break from the bustle of Brentwood and an ideal spot to pause for refreshment on a journey along the A12 or M25. it's also well set up to cater for special occasions, from family get-togethers to office parties, weddings and funerals. Pilgrims Hatch, which lies across the A12 from its big neighbour Brentwood, takes its name from the pilgrims of Geoffrey Chaucer's day; when travelling, they entered the 'hatch' or gateway into the great forest of Essex as they made their way to the shrine of Thomas à Becket at Canterbury.

120 WEALD COUNTRY PARK

Weald Road, South Weald, Brentwood,
Essex CM14 5QS
☎ 01277 216297
🌐 www.essexcc.gov.uk/countryparks

Weald Country Park is steeped in history. It was once a deer park, and used for hunting by the Abbots of Waltham in around 1063. It has been the site of a great hall with formal gardens and there are even the remains of Iron Age settlement which date from the 1st century BC.

Just across from the Visitor Centre you will find the deer paddock, home to our herd of fallow deer. The deer were reintroduced in 1987 as a reminder that the park was once a Royal Hunting Estate. October to February is the time to watch the stags carrying their full set of antlers.

The Park has almost 500 acres of mixed woodland and grassland plus two lakes and a number of ponds. The woodland is managed for wildlife, timber and recreational use. You can discover a variety of wildlife as you wander along the many woodland pathways. Some areas of grassland are left to grow naturally and so produce a multitude of flowers and colours during the summer. Other areas are mown and provide ideal spots for family picnics and games.

Our Grade II listed barn has been converted into an attractive Centre and can be found at the Visitor Centre car park entrance off Weald Road.

121 TILBURY FORT

Tilbury, Essex RM18 7NR
☎ 01375 858489

Ever wanted to fire a real anti-aircraft gun? Come to **Tilbury Fort** and you can. Discover the history of this most

impressive of English artillery forts, from Henry VIII's time right up to World War II. Walk through Charles II's imposing Water Gate, noticing the mighty gun emplacements which protected London against attack by warships. Tour the ramparts and inspect the guns, while enjoying the panoramic views across the Thames, near the place where Queen Elizabeth I made her famous 'Armada Speech'. In the museum and exhibition housed in the East Gunpowder magazine, you can follow the fortunes of Tilbury, from the creation of its first fortifications in the sixteenth century, to the two World Wars.

122 THE ROSE & CROWN

Minnow's End, Chelmsford Road, Great Waltham, nr Chelmsford, Essex CM3 1AG
☎ 01245 360359 Fax: 01245 362710
e-mail: roseandcrown268@aol.com
🌐 www.roseandcrowngreatwaltham.co.uk

Licensees Richard and Laura welcome visitors to the **Rose & Crown** with warm smiles, a fine variety of real ales and a country menu featuring local produce traditionally cooked. This is definitely a place for real ale fans, with familiar brews from Sharps and Shepherd Neame joined by weekly changing guests from local breweries. The bar is open for food and drink every lunchtime and evening and all day Saturday and Sunday. TV racing in the snug is a Saturday treat for racing fans.

123 THE GENERALS ARMS

The Ridge, Little Baddow, Essex CM3 4SX
☎ 01245 222069 Fax: 01245 222282
🌐 www.generalsarms.co.uk

The Generals Arms is the heartbeat of the pleasant village of Little Baddow, a few miles east of Chelmsford, and easily reached from the A12 (J19 or 20) or the A414 Chelmsford-Maldon road (turn off at Danbury). Flower baskets and tubs

make a colourful show outside in the spring and summer, while inside, the lounge and bar areas and the roomy restaurant take the eye with an appealing mix of traditional and contemporary décor. The huge garden with lawns, trees, bushes, picnic benches and a children's play area, is a real bonus in the warmer months.

There are several ways to generate a thirst and appetite hereabouts – perhaps a walk in ancient Blakes Wood (a designated Site of Scientific Interest) or a walk or a boat trip along the Chelmer & Blackwater Canal – and Debbie and Gary Welfare are ready and waiting to provide refreshment all through the day, seven days a week.

They came here in 2006 after running a pub in Kent for many years and have lost no time in building up a new band of regulars with their friendly, hospitable approach to running the pub. Cask ales, including the popular Spitfire, are kept in A1 condition, and the bar and restaurant menus, plus daily specials, provide an impressive variety of dishes to please all palates. The cuisine is mainly classic English, but influences from the Mediterranean and further afield are also evident. Representing the 'home team' are the likes of prawn cocktail, 'proper' fish & chips, lamb shanks braised in red wine and chargrilled steaks, while from overseas come Japanese-style prawns, Maryland crab cakes, risotto of the day, tagliatelle carbonara and chicken breast wrapped in prosciutto served on pasta with a cream and mushroom sauce. Singles, couples, escapers and business people from busy Chelmsford, motorists, tourists….. all are welcome at The Generals Arms, which also caters admirably for wedding parties and other special occasions. COACH PARTY WELCOME BY ARRANGEMENT.

124 THE BREWERS ARMS

Main Road, Bicknacre, nr Danbury,
Essex CM3 4HD
☎ 01245 224061
e-mail: peter.brown1948@btinternet

The warmth of the welcome is evident the moment you step inside Peter and Karen Brown's busy roadside inn.
Behind the cheerful yellow-painted façade the bars at the **Brewers Arms**, with their open

fires, exposed beams and gleaming brass, buzz with a lively mix of long-time regulars and a constant passing trade. Drinks include Priory Ale, specially brewed for the inn, and in the country-style restaurant a menu of home-cooked pub favourites caters for appetites large and small. The bar is open lunchtime and evening and all day Friday, Saturday and Sunday; food is served from 12 to 2 (not Tuesday) and from 6.30 to 9 (not Wednesday or Sunday).

126 THE ROSE & CROWN

High Street, Maldon, Essex CM9 5EP
☎ 01621 856767

On a prominent corner site on Maldon's High Street, the **Rose & Crown** is a traditional, family-friendly pub with a convivial bar, a separate restaurant and a pleasant beer garden. Sheena Lilley has quickly made her mark since taking over here early in 2007, ensuring

a welcoming, relaxed ambience for all her patrons – and that includes the four resident ghosts! Greene king IPA is the resident real ale, and appetites are satisfied with generously served dishes such as penne pasta, moules marinière, steaks and duck breast with honey and soy sauce. The Rose & Crown is open all day, seven days a week.

127 THE ROUND BUSH

Roundbush Road, Mundon, nr Maldon,
Essex CM9 6NN
☎ 01621 828354
e-mail: the-roundbush@virgin.net
🌐 www.theroundbush.co.uk

The Ibbotson family – Martin, Lilija and Paul – welcome customers old and new to the **Round Bush**, a homely country pub standing in pleasant rolling countryside just outside Mundon, 3

miles south of Maldon. They serve a really good choice of food every day, from sandwiches, jacket potatoes and burgers to cod and haddock grilled, poached or deep-fried in real ale batter, steaks, curries, steak & kidney pie and always some excellent vegetarian dishes. To complement the food there are some good, well-priced house wines. Next to the main building the family runs a café open for breakfast seven days a week.

128 THE KINGS HEAD

High Street, Bradwell-on-Sea,
Essex CM0 7QL
☎ 01621 776224
e-mail: mikeclaykingshead@msn.com

Mike at the stoves and Kay at the bar make an ideal team at the **Kings Head**. Their late-18th century pub in the shadow of the church is everything a traditional English pub should be – comfortable, homely, friendly,

with an equally warm welcome for regular patrons and first-timers, well-kept ales and tasty home cooking. Mike's dishes run from jacket potatoes, burgers, Suffolk ham and steaks to crab cakes, ricotta tortellini and chilli-sauced king prawns. To finish, perhaps apple & Blackberry roll or chocolate fudge cake.

125 THE WELCOME

1 Fullbridge, Maldon, Essex CM9 4LE
☎ 01621 852439

On the northern edge of Maldon, on the bridge that spans the River Chelmer, **The Welcome** is a classic English pub with a history going back some 250 years. Long famous as one of the town's most popular watering holes, it was once called the Old Angel. Its present name is very appropriate, as Ruth Hinds and Mike Waller really are the most welcoming of hosts, attracting strong support not just among the local residents but also with the many visitors to this historic town. A six-week top-to-toe refurbishment programme has preserved the period appeal of the pub, which has a delightful public bar, a country-style restaurant and a small function room for private parties. Outside, there's a good-size riverside terrace and ample car parking space.

Greene King IPA, Adnams Best and two guest beers are on tap to quench thirsts, and snack and main menus cater for appetites large and small with a selection of familiar pub fare.

Snacks include sandwiches and baguettes, ploughman's platters, jacket potatoes, nachos and a tasty beef & onion pie that's also on the main menu. The choice here includes burgers, ham or sausage with egg & chips, omelettes, scampi, minted lamb, chicken curry, liver & bacon, lasagne, chicken, lemon & mushroom pasta, Heybridge bangers & mash, turkey stew with herby dumplings and hunters chicken with bacon, cheese and a barbecue sauce. To finish, perhaps home-made cakes or indulgent pancakes with maple syrup and ice cream. The restaurant is often very busy at peak times, but orders can be placed by phone, and takeaway is available on many dishes. Darts and pool are played in the separate games room, and the pub hosts fortnightly live music sessions. The pub is open all day every day for drinks; food times are 12 to 2.30 Monday to Friday, 5.30 to 9 Wednesday, Thursday and Friday, 12 to 8.30 on Saturday and 12 to 6 on Sunday.

289

129 MARSH FARM COUNTRY PARK

Marsh Farm Road, South Woodham Ferrers,
Chelmsford, Essex CM3 5WP
☎ 01245 321552

Marsh Farm Country Park overlooks the River Crouch and is surrounded by its creeks on three sides. The Park is a SSSI (Site of Special Scientific Interest), as it is a good example of Essex grazing marshes, carrying such rare plants as sea barley and grass vetchling. It is also internationally important as an over-wintering site for brent geese. Over 150 species of bird have been seen around the Park. Every winter the marshes are invaded by droves of wildfowl, making Marsh Farm a popular birdwatching spot.

Marsh Farm Country Park has been many things during its history. Iron age settlers were

attracted here by a river rich for fishing, hunting and salt. There is evidence of salt making scattered across the site in the form of saltpans and 'red hills': saltwater was evaporated by the sun or by using very hot stones, which left a red earth deposit. The sea salt left behind was a highly valued commodity. Over 300 years ago the marshes were drained. A sea-wall was built by the Dutch, transforming tidal creeks into the grazing marshes we see at Marsh Farm today.

In dry weather the sea wall offers a wide, level path; however, during the winter months it becomes very muddy. The Open Farm is fully accessible for wheelchairs.

130 THE KINGS ARMS

12 St Mary Street, Ely,
Cambridgeshire CB7 4ES
☎ 01353 668582
e-mail: the_kings_arms@tiscali.co.uk

In a central location in historic Ely, the **Kings Arms** is a two-storey building dating from the 17th century. It's a pleasant, sociable spot to meet for a drink, with a good selection of real ales and other draught and bottle beers, Guinness, cider and lots on optics. Incoming tenants Andy and Tammy King have recently started providing hot and cold snacks and meals. Pub hours are 11 to 11, Friday and Saturday to midnight, Sunday 12 to 10.30.

131 THE CHERRY TREE

Fordham Road, Soham,
Cambridgeshire CB7 5AH
☎ 01353 720405

The grand St Andrew's Church and Downfield Windmill are among the visitor attractions in Soham, but anyone leaving without sampling the hospitality of the **Cherry Tree** is definitely missing a treat. Martin Whithouse is the affable tenant at this family-run, family-friendly 1950s pub on the edge of Soham town centre. In the roomy lounge and bar or at picnic benches in the beer garden two chefs provide a

good choice of well-priced popular pub dishes, accompanied perhaps by a glass or two of real ale from the Greene King brewery. Open all day, every day.

290

132 THE BELL ¶

Kennett, nr Newmarket,
Cambridgeshire CB8 7PP
☎ 01638 750286
e-mail: mffountain@yahoo.co.uk

Keith and Michelle Fountain, a
Cambridgeshire couple, are making their
mark at **The Bell**, a handsome 16th century,
Grade II listed building with many period
features. Beers, including Greene King Abbot
Ale and IPA, head the list of thirst-quenchers
served all day, and anyone with a thirst for
knowledge
can turn up
for the
fortnightly
quiz
(alternate
Tuesdays,
with a large
bowl of
chips per
team). The

Bell serves excellent pub dishes, with lots of
special offers and events (His 'n' Hers steaks
on Thursday, Sunday lunchtime roasts, early
evening weekday bargains).

134 THE BAKERS ARMS ¶

Hinton Road, Fulbourn, nr Cambridge,
Cambridgeshire CB1 5DL
☎ 01223 880606

Home cooking and well-kept Greene King
ales keep the customers happy at the **Bakers
Arms**, a handsome country inn a short drive
east of
Cambridge. The
dishes on chef-
host Mike
Missing's
regularly
changing menus
range from
snacks and light
bites to steaks,
grills, steak &
ale pie, lasagne,
battered cod,
poached salmon
and spicy

choices such as Mexican chilli or Malaysian
chicken curry. The inn has a good-size
garden.

133 CAMBRIDGE UNIVERSITY BOTANIC GARDEN 🏛

Cory Lodge, Bateman Street, Cambridge,
Cambridgeshire CB2 1JF
☎ 01223 336265
🌐 www.botanic.cam.ac.uk

Opened in 1846 by Professor John Henslow,
Charles Darwin's teacher and mentor, this
heritage-listed Botanic Garden displays over
8,000 plant species,
including important

collections of species tulips, geraniums, lavenders and fritillaries, as
well as the finest arboretum in the East of England.

The landscape has been developed with great horticultural vision
in two major phases. The majestic Main Walk of towering evergreens
forms the backbone of the superb 19th century Garden that also
boasts the flamboyant Glasshouses of tropical and desert plants, and
the Rock Garden, which displays the alpine plants of every continent
geographically and affords a wonderful vantage point over the Lake.
The Woodland Garden is a stunning mix of mature trees and rich
herbaceous underplanting whilst the extraordinary, unique Systematic
Beds, designed in 1845, display over 95 families of hardy herbaceous
plants.

The 20th century Garden reflects the horticultural and scientific
developments of the time: the British Wild Plants collection is
unparalleled; the Dry Garden is an on-going experiment to create a
gorgeous garden that can survive the dry Cambridge climate without any watering; the Genetics
Garden tells the story of the sweet pea experiments undertaken here by William Bateson in the
1900's which led to the modern science of genetics; the ancestry of the modern rose is unravelled
in the Rose Garden and the Winter Garden is an inspirational lesson in achieving colour, beauty
and scent in the winter months.

135 THE WHEATSHEAF

Stow Road, Stow-cum-Quay, nr Cambridge,
Cambridgeshire CB25 9AD
☎ 01223 812196

The hard-working mother-and-daughter team of Julie and Jo run the **Wheatsheaf**, a smartly refurbished 1920s family-run pub on the B1102 east of Cambridge, a short drive from J35 of the A14. In the restaurant they regale their customers with a fine selection of home-

cooking. Fresh fish is a speciality and other dishes might include Cromer crab or grilled lamb cutlets - the whole baked camembert is a super dish to share. Desserts are all home-made and roasts are available on Sundays. Bra snacks and lighter lunches are also available. Closed Sunday evening.

136 THE THREE BLACKBIRDS

Ditton Green, Woodditton, nr Newmarket,
Suffolk CB8 9SQ
☎ 01638 730811 Fax: 01638 730162
⊕ www.thethreeblackbirds.com

Paul Lange, tenant and renowned pastry chef, runs the **Three Blackbirds**, a 17th century thatched building off the B1061 a short drive south of Newmarket. Paul has made his pub a great favourite with locals, racegoers and tourists with its super food, real ales and fine wines. His repertoire runs from lunchtime snacks to

salmon fishcakes, confit of duck, curries, steaks and seafood or ham & mushroom crêpes. The pub has a quaint garden and a large car park.

137 THE RED LION

The Street, Kirtling, nr Newmarket,
Suffolk CB8 9PD
☎ 01638 731976
e-mail: jose.elgallego@btinternet.com

There can't be many better ways of starting or ending a day at Newmarket races than a meal at the **Red Lion**. In a pleasant 15th century village inn, host/chef Jose Alvarez (El Gallego) has created a little corner of his native Spain. The walls are adorned with pictures of flamenco dancers and bullfighters, but the number one attraction is the lengthy selection of Spanish dishes,

from tapas to main courses including paella for two and a dozen ways with steak. Drinks include Spanish wines, real ales and Aspalls Suffolk cider on tap.

138 THE REINDEER

62 The Street, Saxon Street,
nr Newmarket, Suffolk CB8 9RS
☎ 01638 730989
🌐 www.thereindeer.com

In the village of **Saxon Street** a few miles south of Newmarket, off the B1061 or B1063, the **Reindeer** is a handsome country hostelry with a fine reputation for the quality of its cooking. Built

in the middle of the 18th century, it reputedly takes its name from the deer that roamed the orchard that once stood here. The Reindeer is both a popular village local and a destination dining pub. Behind the creeper-covered façade the public areas are in fine traditional style, and when the sun shines the lovely leafy garden really comes into its own. It's very much a place for all the family, and children are guaranteed to have a great time in the play area. The choice for diners runs from a full à la carte menu to bar snacks, daily specials, Sunday roasts and children's meals. Sunday lunch brings a choice of traditionally prepared home cooked roasted meats and vegetarian dishes with fresh seasonal vegetables. The

Reindeer is renowned for the quality of its steaks providing a wide range of extra special dishes for steak night on Friday's. The Reindeer caters for all guests and welcomes diners and drinkers with well-kept ales and a well-chosen list of Old and New World wines. Whether you visit the Reindeer to enjoy the excellent food or for a relaxing drink you will receive a warm welcome in the best traditions of fine hospitality. For guests staying overnight the Reindeer has **four** superior en suite bedrooms. The proximity of Newmarket makes the Reindeer an ideal base for race goers and the area around the inn has many country lanes and picturesque villages to explore.

The historic city of Cambridge is within easy reach at just over 16 miles away, placing the Reindeer in an idyllic location for guests travelling through the area seeking refreshment and accommodation or guests looking for a superior dining and social experience in this premier destination venue. The Reindeer is popular among guests with many diverse interests including a vibrant rambling community visiting Devils Dyke, golfers using the local 18 hole golf course, bird watchers and those pursuing country sports.

139 THE CROWN & PUNCHBOWL

High Street, Horningsea, Cambridgeshire
CB25 9JG
☎ 01223 860643 Fax: 01223 441814
e-mail: info@thecrownandpunchbowl.co.uk

Hospitality, food and accommodation all excel at the **Crown & Punchbowl**, which stands on the main street of Horningsea, 4 miles from Cambridge city centre and a short drive north of the A14 (J34). Owners Roger Hornett and Jeremy Masters, 15 years a restaurateur, acquired the premises in May 2007 and immediately set about a complete programme of redecoration inside and out. Both are classic car fanatics, and Roger is the proud owner of two thoroughbred Bentleys, a 1952 Mk VI and a 1953 Mallalieu

'Big Bore'. The building dates back some 400 years, and the original fabric has remained largely intact while being transformed into a top-class restaurant with comfortable, characterful country accommodation. Friendly, well-trained staff have a warm welcome for all their patrons, who range from employees from the nearby Milton Science Park enjoying a quick lunch to locals, families, tourists and Cambridge University students and dons.

The main dining area (with full disabled access) is a 65-cover

restaurant with traditional wooden flooring, original beams, well-spaced tables and nooks and crannies to provide privacy. There are 12 more covers in a tiled conservatory, beyond which is a 24-cover area for private dining. A varied English and Mediterranean à la carte menu is supplemented by an extensive fish board offering the pick of the daily markets and a lunchtime sausage board with 4 home-made varieties accompanied with 5 types of mash and a similar choice of gravies. Lunch is served from 12 to 2.30 every day and dinner from 6.30 every evening except Sunday. Outside the Crown & Punchbowl evergreen shrubs and deciduous trees enclose a huge car park, and a paved area in front of the conservatory is a pleasant spot

for alfresco dining in the summer months. For guests staying overnight this fine hostelry has 5 recently refurbished double bedrooms with en suite bathrooms, TV, beverage tray and free wi-fi throughout the building.
info@thecrownandpunchbowl.co.uk

140 THE KING WILLIAM

Church Street, Histon, nr Cambridge,
Cambridgeshire CB24 9EP
☎ 01223 233930
e-mail: susieatthekingbill@tiscali.co.uk

The **King William** is a 16th century coaching inn at the top of the village of Histon. The exterior has a very distinctive appearance, with smart white paint, a vast buttress chimney at one end and a steep tiled roof. Inside, exposed brick or plastered walls, original beams and log fires contribute to a very appealing, traditional ambience, and there's a pleasant area for enjoying an alfresco drink outside in the courtyard. This is Susan Eichhorn's second pub; she is passionate about the classic appeal of an English country pub and has made this a popular meeting place for the local community. It's also a delightful escape from the bustle of Cambridge and a good spot to take a break on a journey along the busy A14 (leave at J32). The drinks list is headed by Greene King IPA and Abbot Ale, and there's a happy hour between 5 and 7 on selected drinks. All the food is prepared and cooked on the premises, and the daily changing

blackboard menus make appetising reading: pie of the day (perhaps steak & kidney or chicken & mushroom), warm smoked mackerel salad; gammon with egg or pineapple; chicken with black bean sauce; tandoori chicken; cheese, mushroom & onion pasta; spicy potato wedges; and some scrumptious desserts to finish with a flourish. Senior Citizens' lunchtime specials are served Monday to Saturday. Opening times are 11.30 to 3 and 5 to 11 (Friday to 12, Saturday and Sunday all day).

141 THE WHEATSHEAF

St Peter Street, Duxford,
Cambridgeshire CB22 4RP
☎ 01223 836650
e-mail: colinpearseone@btinternet.com

Colin has lost no time in winning friends at
the **Wheatsheaf**, a sociable pub close to
Europe's premier aviation museum. Open all
day, every day, the smartly refurbished inn
offers a
choice of
cask ales and
popular
'comfort'
dishes
served in a
basket. It
now aslo
offers a full
chinese
menu to either eat in or take away. On the
social side, the Wheatsheaf has a pool table
and Sky Sports TV and hosts monthly disco/
karaoke evenings. Bonuses are beer gardens
front and rear, a children's play area and
ample car parking space.

142 THE ICKLETON LION

9 Abbey Street, Ickleton, nr Saffron Walden,
Essex CB10 1SS
☎ 01799 530269
🌐 www.theickletonlion.co.uk

Old beams, leather sofas, an inglenook
fireplace and pictures of local places of
interest in the cosy bar contribute to the
appealing, traditional atmosphere at the
Ickleton Lion. In their 18th century inn
hosts Chris and Mirela offer a good choice of
real ales and wines, and an interesting variety
of dishes on bar and restaurant menus.
Among the favourites are beer-battered giant
cod, fish cakes, steaks and the ever-popular
Ickleton burger topped with bacon, Stilton
and red
onion
marmalade.
The inn
has a super
lawned
garden
with a play
area.

143 THE COCK INN

High Street, Castle Camps, nr Linton,
Cambridgeshire CB21 4SN
☎ 01799 584207
e-mail: thecockcamps@msn.com

Tucked away down country roads between
Saffron Walden and Haverhill, the **Cock Inn**
is well worth seeking out for the excellent
hospitality dispensed
by hosts Philip and
Lesley Clark. The
18th century
coaching inn has a
delightfully
traditional interior
with beams, an open
fire and an eyecatching collection of Delft
tiles. Abbot Ale, Old Speckled Hen and
Woodfordes Wherry are among the regular
real ales, and home cooking provides a wide
variety of dishes, from classics like beer-
battered cod, steaks and lasagne to five-bean
chilli, prawn-topped salmon steak and super
fruit crumbles. For guests staying overnight
the Cock Inn has three en suite bedrooms in
an adjacent single-storey building.

HIDDEN PLACES GUIDES

Explore Britain and Ireland with
Hidden Places guides - a fascinating
series of national and local travel
guides.

Packed with easy to read information
on hundreds of places of interest as
well as places to stay, eat and drink.

Available from both high street and
internet booksellers

For more information on the full range
of *Hidden Places* guides and other
titles published by Travel Publishing
visit our website on

www.travelpublishing.co.uk
or ask for our leaflet by phoning
01752 276660 or emailing
info@travelpublishing.co.uk

144 THE MANOR HOUSE

Alconbury, nr Huntingdon,
Cambridgeshire PE28 4DY
☎ 01489 890423
e-mail: annjones2@btconnect.com
🌐 www.manorhousealconbury.com

The **Manor House** is a substantial and attractive 16th century hostelry in the village of Alconbury, 5 miles northwest of Huntingdon and close to the junction of the A1 and A14. It's run in fine style by Ann Jones and Brian Kitson and family, and the promise of its long white-painted frontage – flower-decked in summer, steeply-raked tiled roof, windows with tiny criss-cross panes – is amply fulfilled inside. Upright and ceiling beams and open fires paint a traditional picture in the bar, which is open from noon until late in the evening every night of the week.

The Manor House has a fine reputation for its home cooking, and daily menus cater for a wide variety of tastes and appetites. Snackier items include baguettes, jacket potatoes and scrumptious melts with bacon, sausage, steak, tuna or cheese. Typical choices from the main menu run from calamari strips with a sweet chilli dip to cod & chips, ham salad, lasagne, spaghetti carbonara and curries, while daily specials might include liver & bacon with onion gravy or cauliflower cheese (an all-too-rare treat!) and many more including ethnic food evenings.

Smart modern picnic benches are set out under sunshades in the beer garden, and the inn has a large off-road car park that sports an ancient Californian oak tree. Alconbury is a pleasant place for a stroll, with a large village green and an ancient village pump, and the Church of St Peter and St Paul is well worth a visit. There's plenty more to discover nearby, and the Manor House offers a very pleasant civilised base for tourists, as well as an excellent overnight stop for motorists. The six bedrooms all have en suite facilities, television, telephone, tea/coffee tray and there is internet access in the main bar. Very much at the social heart of the village, the Manor House hosts a weekly quiz and monthly live music/karaoke evenings.

145 THE MERMAID INN

High Street, Ellington, nr Huntingdon,
Cambridgeshire
☎ 01480 891450

Young, enthusiastic host Gary Barton continues a 200-year tradition of hospitality at the **Mermaid Inn**, which stands in a picturesque village 4 miles west of Huntingdon and close to Junction 20 of the A14. Greene King ales are served in the cosy little bar, while in the restaurant the chef produces excellent dishes, some classics – fish pie, steaks, roast chicken – others combining traditional and contemporary elements, such as black pudding tower with bacon and a mushroom

sauce. And desserts like chocolate fudge cake should definitely not be missed! For visitors looking for a break in this interesting part of the country the inn has two spacious en suite rooms – a triple and a family room.

146 THE NAGS HEAD

2 Berkley Street, Eynesbury, nr St Neots,
Cambridgeshire PE19 2NA
☎ 01480 476812
e-mail: nags.stneots@btconnect.com
🌐 www.st-neots.co.uk/nagshead

Starting life as a coaching inn, the **Nags Head** is now a cosy little hotel offering comfortable, well-priced B&B accommodation. The eight guest rooms, ranging from a single to family rooms, all have en suite facilities, TV, beverage tray,

hairdryer and wi-fi broadband access. The hotel has a big breakfast room and a residents' lounge with Sky TV and a DVD player with a collection of discs. Open all year. Private car park.

147 THE ANCHOR

High Street, Little Paxton, nr St Neots,
Cambridgeshire
☎ 01480 473199
e-mail: sue@theanchorlittlepaxton.co.uk
🌐 www.theanchorlittlepaxton.co.uk

On a corner site close to the church in Little Paxton, **The Anchor** is thriving under licensees Sue and Tom Merritt. A major element in its success is Sue's super cooking, which offers classic snacks, dishes based on old regional recipes and fish specials (Thursday to Saturday) based on Tom's visits to London's Billingsgate market. The interior of

the 18th century inn has been superbly updated (lots of wood and brass) and outside is a large garden with a play area and a pétanque pitch. Live music Saturday, quiz Sunday.

148 PAXTON PITS NATURE RESERVE

High Street, Little Paxton, Huntingdon,
Cambridgeshire PE10 6ET
☎ 01480 406795

At **Paxton Pits Nature Reserve** you can enjoy gentle strolls as well as longer walks through 75 hectares of lakes, meadow, grassland, scrub and woodland. As well as the Heron and Meadow Trails, the River Trail, and some of the Permissive paths surrounding Paxton Pits are also waymarded. The permissive paths are not part of the reserve but the landowners have given permission for them to be used.

149 THE WHITE HART

2 Cambridge Road, Godmanchester, nr
Huntingdon, Cambridgeshire PE29 2BW
☎ 01480 414050 fax: 01480 458182
⊕ whitehart-godmanchester.co.uk

Susan Cooper and her son Stephen, who run the **White
Hart**, aim to provide a friendly, relaxed atmosphere,
excellent service and food that tastes as good as it
looks. Behind its black-and-white exterior, the 15th
century building has been tastefully refurbished and
renovated while retaining a period feel with oak
flooring and open fireplaces, providing a delightful
ambience
for enjoying
fine dining at its best. Locally sourced produce gets
skilful treatment to produce a mouthwatering selection
of dishes; some are much-loved classics (fishcakes,
Sunday roasts), while others take familiar ingredients
and turn them into deliciously different dishes such as
water melon, feta cheese and pine nut salad, or salmon
with broad beans and a dill and horseradish risotto. The
main menu is supplemented at lunchtime by a choice of
sandwiches, snacks and light meals.

150 THE EXHIBITION

2 King Street, Over, Cambridgeshire
CB24 5PS
☎ 01954 230790

Hands-on tenant Tracy Warkcup worked at **The Exhibition** for two years before taking over the reins with her accountant husband John in the summer of 2007. The pub's name refers to the Great Exhibition of 1851, and the pub sign depicts the Crystal Palace built for the occasion.

Behind the sturdy brick frontage the interior is decorated and furnished in traditional style, with exposed brick, handsome wood panelling, some solid old leather-backed chairs and a big open fire for cooler days. The locals love the place, and the new tenants are always happy to welcome visitors from further afield, who could well become regulars after sampling the excellent hospitality. Adnams and Greene King ales are on tap to quench thirsts, either in the bar or outside at picnic benches under sunshades in the lawned garden. Food is an important part of the business, and two full-time chefs are kept busy

producing a particularly good variety of dishes. All the well-loved pub favourites are there – fresh fish specials, whitebait, meat or vegetable lasagne, curries, steak & ale pie, steaks and a specials board. Lunchtime brings an additional selection of baguettes and sandwiches with interesting fillings (tuna cheese melt, sausage & onion), jacket potatoes and salads.

There are many reasons for visiting this part of the country, including the bird haven of the Ouse Washes, the lovely old town of St Ives and the splendid churches at Swavesey, Fen Drayton and Cottenham; and after a morning or afternoon's sightseeing the staff at The Exhibition are ready with a friendly greeting, a drink and a meal. It stands about 5 miles north of the A14 between Cambridge and Huntingdon (leave at J28 or J29). The Exhibition is open lunchtime and evening seven days a week.

300

151 SLEPE HALL

Ramsey Road, St Ives,
Cambridgeshire PE27 5RB
☎ 01480 463122 Fax: 01480 300706
e-mail: mail@slepehall.co.uk
🌐 www.slepehall.co.uk

Starting life as a Victorian girls' boarding school, **Slepe Hall** is a Grade II listed building offering high standards of service, comfort and cuisine. The best Victorian features have been preserved, sitting happily with the up-to-date comfort and amenities.

The 16 bedrooms, from singles to family rooms, are individual in style and character: some traditional, some modern, several with very splendid four-poster beds. All have en suite facilities, satellite TV, telephone with modem point, radio-alarm clock, tea/coffee tray and hairdryer. The larger Superior rooms are also equipped with CD players. Relaxation is the name of the game throughout this friendly hotel, in the bar, in the lounge or in the pleasant south-facing patio and garden. Slepe Hall provides a good choice for diners, with light meals served in the lounge and bar and more formal eating options in the restaurant. Some dishes are

time-and-trusted favourites such as steaks, sausages & creamed potatoes, liver & bacon, roasts from the carvery and lasagne (meat or vegetarian). Other dishes are more modern or more exotic in style, like chicken, pork & herb terrine, tagliatelle with mint & basil pesto and Thai fish cakes. As well as very comfortable guest accommodation for both leisure and business guests,

Slepe Hall caters admirably for meetings and conferences, with facilities for any number from 2 to 20, and for special occasions. Three rooms are licensed for civil ceremonies, with room for up to 60, and the Brunel Suite, tailor-made for functions, has a private entrance, its own bar, cloakrooms and space for up to 200 guests. The hotel has secure parking for 70 cars. St Ives has plenty to attract the visitor, including the Portland stone statue of Oliver Cromwell, the beautiful parish church and the fascinating Norris Museum. Close by are Wilthorn Meadow, a Site of Natural History Interest, and the Holt Island Nature Reserve. And the Great Ouse provides some wonderful riverside walks. St Ives is very well connected to the main road network, with the A1, A10 and A14 all just a few minutes' drive away.

301

152 FLOODS TAVERN

27 The Broadway, St Ives,
Cambridgeshire PE27 5BX
☎ 01480 467773
e-mail: Michael.buckingham7@ntlworld.com
🌐 www.floodstavern.co.uk

Floods Tavern is a traditional public house offering a warm welcome for all the family, three real ales, decent wines and super food. In the bar or out in the beer garden

by the river, patrons can enjoy a drink and a meal throughout the day. The busy kitchen produces a wide variety of bar food most lunchtimes and evenings. The menu majors on all-time favourites like battered cod, scampi, steaks, lasagne and ham, egg & chips, pasta with spicy meatballs and crab cakes with a sweet chilli sauce are other options, and classics such as spotted dick and chocolate sponge pudding round off a meal in fine style. Children's portions are available, along with a takeaway service. Hosts Mike and Emily create a great ambience in their pub. It's a popular, sociable place at any time, and it really buzzes during the Thursday karaoke sessions and Friday's music nights. It also has a big TV screen for Setanta and Sky Sports.

153 THE WHITE SWAN

Main Street, Woodnewton, nr Oundle,
Northamptonshire PE8 5EB
☎ 01780 470381

The **White Swan** proudly takes its place among the many fine old buildings in the conservation area of Main Street in the village of Woodnewton. Tracy and Steven Anker welcome all who visit their immaculate 18th century inn, whether it's for a drink in the bar or a meal in the bar or restaurant. The food choice is extensive, from baguettes, jacket potatoes and

omelettes to pan-fried duck, all-day breakfast, classic fish & chips, Sunday roasts and cream teas. Picnic benches are set outside, where there is a play area for the kids and a pétanque pitch.

154 ARCHIES

2-4 Crown Court, Oundle,
Northamptonshire PE8 4BQ
☎ 01832 273366

Oundle has much to offer the visitor, including the famous school and specialist shops, and food-lovers can be sure of a real treat if they take time out for a meal at **Archies**, a top-notch café, wine bar and restaurant in the old part of town.

Fresh home-cooked food of the highest quality is the order of the day, and the interesting and varied menus provide plenty of choice for all tastes and appetites. Typical dishes on the globe-trotting main menu run from Caesar salad (starter or main course) and grilled sardines with a spicy tomato salsa to scallops with Thai spices, grilled tuna with an Asian vegetable stew, braise pork belly with apples, and sirloin and fillet steaks. Other options include all-day tapas and home-baked 14" pizzas, and the lunchtime choice also includes sandwiches.

The fine food is complemented by a good choice of wines available by the glass (two sizes) or bottle. the bar and restaurant are comfortable and inviting, and the grill and pizza area in the courtyard provides a pleasant alfresco alternative during the summer months.

155 THE KINGS HEAD

Apethorpe, nr Peterborough,
Northamptonshire PE8 5DG
☎ 01780 470627

Superb home cooking brings visitors from near and far to the **Kings Head**, a fine 19th century sandstone building with a porticoed entrance and small-paned leaded windows. The bar is stocked with a good choice of real ales, while in the comfortable, upmarket restaurant Julia Wells and her team regale diners with an exceptional choice of beautifully prepared dishes, from evergreen favourites such as cod, scampi, chilli and steaks to moules marinière, lemon sole with parsley butter, beef madras and tomato & aubergine bake. The restaurant is open for lunch every day except Monday and Saturday and for dinner every day except Sunday.

158 PECKOVER HOUSE & GARDEN

North Brink, Wisbech,
Cambridgeshire PE13 1JR
☎ 01945 583463
🌐 www.peckoverhouse.co.uk

This lovely Georgian brick townhouse, built c. 1722, is renowned for its very fine plaster and wood rococo decoration and includes displays on the Quaker banking family who owned it and the Peckover Bank. The outstanding 2 acre Victorian garden includes an orangery, summer houses, roses, herbaceous borders, fernery, croquet lawn and 17th –century thatched barn, which is available for weddings and functions.

303

32 High Street, Eye, nr Peterborough,
Northamptonshire PE6 7UP
☎ 01733 222254

The **Spade & Shovel** is being totally transformed and restored to its pristine state by enthusiastic tenants Dave Oakley and Jenny Biggington. They arrived here early in 2007 and spent four weeks tidying up the old place and embarking on a major programme to return it to its status as a friendly village pub appealing both to residents from the neighbourhood and to visitors from further afield.

Real ales are on tap to quench thirsts in the convivial public bar, and the hosts have begun providing a simple (and expanding) choice of popular pub dishes in the little lounge/dining area.

Once again very much at the heart of village life, the Spade & Shovel has a pool table and a dartboard, and all are welcome to join in the quiz held on the third Sunday of each month. The pub has a pleasant beer garden, and off-road parking to the rear. It stands on the main street of Eye, close to the A47 and a short drive east from Peterborough on the road to Thorney. Increasingly popular as an 'escape' from the bustle of Peterborough, it also appeals to tourists, with pleasant walks and attractive views all around. There are also many places of interest for the visitor, including Thorney Abbey and the Heritage Museum, and the market town of Whittlesey with its churches and museum.

And when the walking and the sightseeing are done, it's good to know that Dave and Jenny are ready to provide a warm welcome and generous refreshment at the Spade & Shovel. Opening hours are noon to 1am (till midnight on Sunday).

157 THE ACRE

9 Acre Road, March,
Cambridgeshire PE15 9JD
☎ 01354 657116

Starting life in the 1740s as a grain store for the town mill, **The Acre** is an attractive and substantial building by the River Nene in the centre of March, close to the park and the library. Trish Smith has been at the helm of this delightful inn since 1999, and she and her hardworking staff ensure that nobody leaves thirsty or hungry...or anything less than determined to come back soon. There's plenty of space in the comfortable L-shaped bar, and for the warmer months benches and patio heaters are set out on the front and rear patios and in the side garden.

A riverside stroll or a walk round March is a good prelude to enjoying a drink and a meal at The Acre. Greene King IPA, 2 regularly changing guest ales and home cooking provides plenty of choice for hungry visitors from noon to 10 o'clock at night every day of the week. Pub classics include ploughman's lunches, jacket potatoes with particularly interesting fillings, burgers, battered haddock, scampi, lasagne (vegetarian or meat), chilli (ditto), bangers & mash, steaks and some super pies – steak & ale, chicken, ham & leek. And the chef offers further temptations with some less familiar choices such as mussels provençale or a speciality hot cheeseboard: beer-battered mozzarella, breaded camembert and brie with a cranberry dip. To finish in style, perhaps treacle sponge, deep apple pie or strawberry waffle cheesecake.

The Acre is open long hours every day – from 11am Monday, Tuesday, Thursday, Friday and Sunday, and from 10am Wednesday and Saturday. Closing time is Midnight (1.30am Friday and Saturday). Thursday is quiz night, and the inn hosts a live music evening once a month.

Tourist Information Centres

CAMBRIDGESHIRE

CAMBRIDGE
Wheeler Street, Cambridge, Cambridgeshire CB2 3QB
Public enquiries: 0906 586 2526
Fax: 01223 457549
e-mail: tourism@cambridge.gov.uk

ELY
Oliver Cromwell's House, 29 St Mary's Street, Ely,
Cambridgeshire CB7 4HF
Public enquiries: 01353 662062
Fax: 01353 668518
e-mail: tic@eastcambs.gov.uk

HUNTINGDON
Customer Services Centre, St Marys Street, Huntingdon,
Cambridgeshire PE29 3TN
Public enquiries: 01480 388588
Fax: 01480 388591
e-mail: Hunts.TIC@huntsdc.gov.uk

PETERBOROUGH
3-5 Minster Precincts, Peterborough,
Cambridgeshire PE1 1XS
Public enquiries: 01733 452336
Fax: 01733 452353
e-mail: tic@peterborough.gov.uk

ST NEOTS
The Old Court, 8 New Street, St Neots,
Cambridgeshire PE19 1AE
Public enquiries: 01480 388788
Fax: 01480 388791
e-mail: stneots.tic@huntsdc.gov.uk

WISBECH
2-3 Bridge Street, Wisbech, Cambridgeshire PE13 1AF
Public enquiries: 01945 583263
Fax: 01945 427199
e-mail: tourism@fenland.gov.uk

WITHERNSEA
131 Queen Street, Withernsea,
Cambridgeshire HU19 2DJ
Public enquiries: 01964 615683
Fax: 01964 615683
e-mail: withernsea.tic@eastriding.gov.uk

ESSEX

BRAINTREE
Town Hall Centre, Market Place, Braintree,
Essex CM7 3YG
Public enquiries: 01376 550066
Fax: 01376 344345
e-mail: tic@braintree.gov.uk

BRENTWOOD
Pepperell House, 44 High Street, Brentwood,
Essex CM14 4AJ
Public enquiries: 01277 200300
Fax: 01277 202375
e-mail: tic@brentwood.gov.uk

CHELMSFORD
Visitor Information Centre, Unit 3 Dukes Walk,
Duke Street, Chelmsford, Essex CM1 1GZ
Public enquiries: 0870 225 4801
Fax: 01245 430 705
e-mail: chelmtic@essexcc.gov.uk
website: www.welcometoessex.co.uk

CLACTON-ON-SEA
Town Hall, Station Road, Clacton-on-Sea,
Essex CO15 1SE
Public enquiries: 01255 686633
Fax: 01255 253842
01255 253200
e-mail: emorgan@tendringdc.gov.uk

COLCHESTER
1 Queen Street, Colchester, Essex CO1 2PG
Public enquiries: 01206 282920
Fax: 01206 282924
e-mail: vic@colchester.gov.uk

FLATFORD
Flatford Lane, Flatford, East Bergholt, Suffolk CO7 6UL
Public enquiries: 01206 299460
Fax: 01206 299973
e-mail: flatfordvic@babergh.gov.uk

HARWICH
Iconfield Park, Parkeston, Harwich, Essex CO12 4EN
Public enquiries: 01255 506139
Fax: 01255 240570
e-mail: harwichtic@btconnect.com

MALDON

Coach Lane, Maldon, Essex CM9 4UH
Public enquiries: 01621 856503
Fax: 01621 875873
e-mail: tic@maldon.gov.uk

SAFFRON WALDEN

1 Market Place, Saffron Walden, Essex CB10 1HR
Public enquiries: 01799 510444
Fax: 01799 510445
e-mail: tourism@uttlesford.gov.uk

SOUTHEND-ON-SEA

Pier Entrance, Western Esplanade, Southend-on-Sea,
Essex SS1 1EE
Public enquiries: 01702 215620
Fax: 01702 611889
e-mail: vic@southend.gov.uk

WALTHAM ABBEY

Unit B, 2-4 Highbridge Street, Waltham Abbey,
Essex EN9 1DG
Public enquiries: 01992 652295
Fax: 01992 652295
e-mail: tic@walthamabbey.org.uk

NORFOLK

AYLSHAM

Bure Valley Railway Station, Norwich Road, Aylsham,
Norfolk NR11 6BW
Public enquiries: 01263 733903
Fax: 01263 733922
e-mail: aylsham.tic@broadland.gov.uk

BURNHAM DEEPDALE

Deepdale Farm, Burnham Deepdale, Norfolk PE31 8DD
Public enquiries: 01485 210256
Fax: 01485 210158
e-mail: info@deepdalefarm.co.uk

CROMER

Prince of Wales Road, Cromer, Norfolk NR27 9HS
Public enquiries: 0871 200 3071
Fax: 01263 513613
e-mail: cromertic@north-norfolk.gov.uk

DISS

Meres Mouth, Mere Street, Diss, Norfolk IP22 4AG
Public enquiries: 01379 650523
Fax: 01379 650838
e-mail: dtic@s-norfolk.gov.uk

DOWNHAM MARKET

The Priory Centre, 78 Priory Road, Downham Market,
Norfolk PE38 9JS
Public enquiries: 01366 383287
Fax: 01366 385 042
e-mail: downham-market.tic@west-norfolk.gov.uk

GREAT YARMOUTH

25 Marine Parade, Great Yarmouth, Norfolk NR30 2EN
Public enquiries: 01493 846345
e-mail: tourism@great-yarmouth.gov.uk

HOLT

3 Pound House, Market Place, Holt, Norfolk NR25 6BW
Public enquiries: 0871 200 3071
Fax: 01263 713100
e-mail: holttic@north-norfolk.gov.uk

HOVETON

Station Road, Hoveton, Norfolk NR12 8UR
Public enquiries: 01603 782281
Fax: 01603 782281
e-mail: hovetoninfo@broads-authority.gov.uk

HUNSTANTON

Town Hall, The Green, Hunstanton, Norfolk PE36 6BQ
Public enquiries: 01485 532610
Fax: 01485 533972
e-mail: hunstanton.tic@west-norfolk.gov.uk

KING'S LYNN

The Custom House, Purfleet Quay, King's Lynn,
Norfolk PE30 1HP
Public enquiries: 01553 763044
Fax: 01553 819441
e-mail: kings-lynn.tic@west-norfolk.gov.uk

MUNDESLEY

2 Station Road, Mundesley, Norfolk NR11 8JH
Public enquiries: 01263 721070
Fax: 01263 722796

NORWICH

The Forum, Millennium Plain, Norwich,
Norfolk NR2 1TF
Public enquiries: 01603 727927
Fax: 01603 765389
e-mail: tourism@norwich.gov.uk

SHERINGHAM

Station Approach, Sheringham, Norfolk NR26 8RA
Public enquiries: 0871 200 3071
e-mail: sheringhamtic@north-norfolk.gov.uk

SWAFFHAM
The Shambles, Market Place, Swaffham,
Norfolk PE37 7AB
Public enquiries: 01760 722255
Fax: 01760 723410
e-mail: swaffham@eetb.info

THETFORD
4 White Hart Street, Thetford, Norfolk IP24 1AD
Public enquiries: 01842 820689
Fax: 01842 820986
e-mail: info@thetfordtourism.co.uk

WELLS-NEXT-THE-SEA
Staithe Street, Wells-next-the-Sea, Norfolk NR23 1AN
Public enquiries: 0871 200 3071
Fax: 01328 711405
e-mail: wellstic@north-norfolk.gov.uk

WYMONDHAM
Market Cross, Market Place, Wymondham,
Norfolk NR18 0AX
Public enquiries: 01953 604721
Fax: 01953 604721
e-mail: wymondhamtic@btconnect.com

SUFFOLK

ALDEBURGH
152 High Street, Aldeburgh, Suffolk IP15 5AQ
Public enquiries: 01728 453637
Fax: 01728 453637
e-mail: atic@suffolkcoastal.gov.uk

BECCLES
The Quay, Fen Lane, Beccles, Suffolk NR34 9BH
Public enquiries: 01502 713196
Fax: 01502 713196
e-mail: becclesinfo@broads-authority.gov.uk

BURY ST EDMUNDS
6 Angel Hill, Bury St Edmunds, Suffolk IP33 1UZ
Public enquiries: 01284 764667
Fax: 01284 757084
e-mail: tic@stedsbc.gov.uk

FELIXSTOWE
91 Undercliff Road West, Felixstowe, Suffolk IP11 2AF
Public enquiries: 01394 276770
Fax: 01394 276984
e-mail: ftic@suffolkcoastal.gov.uk

IPSWICH
St Stephens Church, St Stephens Lane, Ipswich,
Suffolk IP1 1DP
Public enquiries: 01473 258070
Fax: 01473 432017
e-mail: tourist@ipswich.gov.uk

LAVENHAM
Lady Street, Lavenham, Sudbury, Suffolk CO10 9RA
Public enquiries: 01787 248207
Fax: 01787 249459
e-mail: lavenhamtic@babergh.gov.uk

LOWESTOFT
East Point Pavilion, Royal Plain, Lowestoft,
Suffolk NR33 0AP
Public enquiries: 01502 533600
Fax: 01502 539023
e-mail: touristinfo@waveney.gov.uk

NEWMARKET
Palace House, Palace Street, Newmarket,
Suffolk CB8 8EP
Public enquiries: 01638 667200
Fax: 01638 667415
e-mail: tic.newmarket@forest-heath.gov.uk

SOUTHWOLD
69 High Street, Southwold, Suffolk IP18 6DS
Public enquiries: 01502 724729
Fax: 01502 722978
e-mail: southwold.tic@waveney.gov.uk

STOWMARKET
Museum of East Anglian Life, Stowmarket,
Suffolk IP14 1DLT
Public enquiries: 01449 676800
Fax: 01449 614691
e-mail: tic@midsuffolk.gov.uk

SUDBURY
Town Hall, Market Hill, Sudbury, Suffolk CO10 1TL
Public enquiries: 01787 881320
Fax: 01787 242129
e-mail: sudburytic@babergh.gov.uk

WOODBRIDGE
Station Buildings, Woodbridge, Suffolk IP12 4AJ
Public enquiries: 01394 382240
Fax: 01394 386337
e-mail: wtic@suffolkcoastal.gov.uk

Towns, Villages and Places of Interest

311

TRAVEL PUBLISHING ORDER FORM

To order any of our publications just fill in the payment details below and complete the order form. For orders of less than 4 copies please add £1.00 per book for postage and packing. Orders over 4 copies are P & P free.

Name:

Address:

Tel no:

Please Complete Either:

I enclose a cheque for £ _____ made payable to Travel Publishing Ltd

Or:

Card No: Expiry Date:

Signature:

Please either send, telephone, fax or e-mail your order to:

Travel Publishing Ltd, 64-66 Ebrington Street, Plymouth, Devon PL4 9AQ

Tel: 01752 276660   Fax: 01752 276699   e-mail: info@travelpublishing.co.uk

	Price	Quantity		Price	Quantity
HIDDEN PLACES REGIONAL TITLES			**COUNTRY PUBS AND INNS**		
Cornwall	£8.99	....	Cornwall	£5.99	....
Devon	£8.99	....	Devon	£7.99	....
Dorset, Hants & Isle of Wight	£8.99	....	Sussex	£5.99	....
East Anglia	£8.99	....	Wales	£8.99	....
Lake District & Cumbria	£8.99	....	Yorkshire	£7.99	....
Northumberland & Durham	£8.99	....	**COUNTRY LIVING RURAL GUIDES**		
Peak District and Derbyshire	£8.99	....			
Yorkshire	£8.99	....	East Anglia	£10.99	....
HIDDEN PLACES NATIONAL TITLES			Heart of England	£10.99	....
			Ireland	£11.99	....
England	£11.99	....	North East	£10.99	....
Ireland	£11.99	....	North West	£10.99	....
Scotland	£11.99	....	Scotland	£11.99	....
Wales	£11.99	....	South of England	£10.99	....
HIDDEN INNS TITLES			South East of England	£10.99	....
			Wales	£11.99	....
East Anglia	£7.99	....	West Country	£10.99	....
Heart of England	£7.99	....			
South	£7.99	....			
South East	£7.99	....			
West Country	£7.99	....	TOTAL QUANTITY:		
OTHER TITLES			POST & PACKING:		
Off the Motorway	£11.99	....	TOTAL VALUE:		
Garden Centres & Nurseries	£11.99	....			

HIDDEN PLACES GUIDES

Explore Britain and Ireland with *Hidden Places* guides - a fascinating series of national and local travel guides.

Packed with easy to read information on hundreds of places of interest as well as places to stay, eat and drink.

Available from both high street and internet booksellers

For more information on the full range of *Hidden Places* guides and other titles published by Travel Publishing visit our website on

www.travelpublishing.co.uk
or ask for our leaflet by phoning **01752 276660** or
emailing **info@travelpublishing.co.uk**

READER REACTION FORM

The *Travel Publishing* research team would like to receive reader's comments on any visitor attractions or places reviewed in the book and also recommendations for suitable entries to be included in the next edition. This will help ensure that the *Country Living series of Guides* continues to provide its readers with useful information on the more interesting, unusual or unique features of each attraction or place ensuring that their visit to the local area is an enjoyable and stimulating experience. To provide your comments or recommendations would you please complete the forms below and overleaf as indicated and send to:

**The Research Department, Travel Publishing Ltd,
64-66 Ebrington Street, Plymouth, Devon PL4 9AQ**

Your Name:

Your Address:

Your Telephone Number:

Please tick as appropriate:

Comments ☐   Recommendation ☐

Name of Establishment:

Address:

Telephone Number:

Name of Contact:

READER REACTION FORM

COMMENT OR REASON FOR RECOMMENDATION:

....
....
....
....
....
....
....
....
....
....
....
....
....
....
....
....
....
....
....

INDEX OF ADVERTISERS

Index of Advertisers

ACCOMMODATION

The Affleck Arms, Brookside, nr Dalham — p 134, 273
Arch House, Wells-next-the-Sea — p 62, 254
Ballaglass, Stisted, nr Braintree — p 145, 276
Becklands Guest House, Horsford, nr Norwich — p 9, 227
Bon Vista Guest House, Cromer — p 17, 236
Box Tree Farm, Kettlebaston, nr Lavenham — p 112, 269
The Briars & Mansard Cottages, Washbrook, nr Ipswich — p 109, 268
Brickwall Farm House, Wetherden, nr Stowmarket — p 72, 256
Brig Square Holiday Cottages, Wells-next-the-Sea — p 62, 255
Brightlingsea Motel, Brightlingsea — p 154, 279
Byerley House, Newmarket — p 132, 273
Castaways Holiday Park, Bacton-on-Sea — p 36, 245
The Chaff House, Littlebury Green, nr Saffron Walden — p 165, 282
Cheney Hollow Cottages, Heacham, nr King's Lynn — p 53, 249
The Cock Inn, Castle Camps, nr Linton — p 206, 296
The Cretingham Bell, Cretingham — p 75, 258
The Crown & Punchbowl, Horningsea — p 204, 294
Earsham Park Farm, Earsham, nr Bungay — p 101, 266
Fairlawns Guest House, Sheringham — p 19, 237
Froyz Hall Barn, Halstead — p 149, 277
The Georgian Guest House, Saxmundham — p 81, 261
Gladwins Farm, Nayland — p 116, 270
The Goat Inn, Skeyton, nr Aylsahm — p 17, 235
The Griffin Inn, Yoxford — p 81, 260
The Hare & Hounds, Braintree — p 148, 278
High House Farm & Woodlodge, Cransford, nr Woodbridge — p 74, 258
Hill Farm, Kirtling, nr Newmarket — p 134, 274
Holly Farm Cottages, Cranworth — p 39, 247
Home Bay B&B, Dovercourt, nr Harwich — p 157, 280
Kiln Farm Guest House, Elmswell, nr Bury St Edmunds — p 71, 256
The Kings Head Hotel, Southwold — p 97, 265
The Manor House, Alconbury, nr Huntingdon — p 209, 297

The Marlborough Head Inn, Dedham, nr Colchester — p 143, 275
The Mermaid Inn, Ellington, nr Huntingdon — p 211, 298
The Nags Head, Eynesbury, nr St Neots — p 212, 298
The Old Convent, Kettlebaston, nr Lavenham — p 112, 269
The Old Pump House, Aylsham — p 15, 232
The Park Hotel, Diss — p 12, 231
The Red Lion, Great Sampford, nr Saffron Walden — p 161, 281
The Reindeer, Saxon Street, nr Newmarket — p 203, 293
The Roman Camp Inn, Aylmerton — p 18, 236
Sculthorpe Mill, Sculthorpe, nr Fakenham — p 53, 250
The Ship Inn at Blaxhall, Blaxhall, nr Snape — p 87, 262
Sidegate Guest House, Ipswich — p 103, 267
Slepe Hall, St Ives — p 216, 301
The Victory At Mersea, Mersea Island — p 155, 280
Villa-Rose Hotel, Great Yarmouth — p 25, 238
The Wash & Tope Hotel, Hunstanton — p 58, 254
Whincliff, Mundesley — p 35, 245
The White Cottage, Old Huntstanton — p 58, 253
The White Horse Inn, East Barsham, nr Fakenham — p 55, 251
The White Horse Inn, Westleton, nr Saxmundham — p 80, 259
The Wine Lodge, Feltwell — p 48, 248
Wymondham Consort Hotel, Wymondham — p 10, 230

FOOD AND DRINK

The Acre, March — p 221, 305
The Affleck Arms, Brookside, nr Dalham — p 134, 273
Amici Cucina Italiana, Sudbury — p 113, 269
The Anchor, Little Paxton, nr St Neots — p 213, 298
The Angel, Bocking, nr Braintree — p 145, 275
Archies, Oundle — p 218, 303
The Bakers Arms, Fulbourn, nr Cambridge — p 202, 291
The Bell Inn, Middleton, nr Saxmundham — p 80, 259
The Bell, Kennett, nr Newmarket — p 199, 291
The Bluebell Inn, Hempstead, nr Saffron Walden — p 161, 281

321

322

PLACES OF INTEREST